It was my dream to become an astronaut, but it seems like it wasn't meant to be. Instead, I'm thinking about traveling to space inside my head. If you're not busy, please join me.

—Katsura Hoshino

Shiga Prefecture native Katsura Hoshino's hit manga series *D.Gray-man* has been serialized in Weekly Shonen Jump since 2004. Katsura's first series "Continue" first appeared in Weekly Shonen Jump in 2003.

Katsura adores cats.

D.GRAY-MAN
VOL. 1
SHONEN JUMP ADVANCED
Manga Edition

STORY AND ART BY
KATSURA HOSHINO

Translation and English Adaptation/Mayumi Kobayashi
Touch-up Art & Lettering/Elizabeth Watasin
Design/Yukiko Whitley
Editor/Michelle Pangilinan

VP, Production/Alvin Lu
VP, Sales & Product Marketing/Gonzalo Ferreyra
VP, Creative/Linda Espinosa
Publisher/Hyoe Narita

D.GRAY-MAN © 2004 by Katsura Hoshino. All rights reserved.
First published in Japan in 2004 by SHUEISHA Inc., Tokyo.
English translation rights arranged by SHUEISHA Inc.

The rights of the author(s) of the work(s) in this publication to be so identified have
been asserted in accordance with the Copyright, Designs and Patents Act 1988. A CIP
catalogue record for this book is available from the British Library.

Printed in the U.S.A.

Published by VIZ Media, LLC
P.O. Box 77010
San Francisco, CA 94107

10 9 8
First printing, May 2006
Eighth printing, January 2010

THE WORLD'S MOST
CUTTING-EDGE MANGA

www.viz.com

www.shonenjump.com

SHONEN JUMP ADVANCED MANGA EDITION

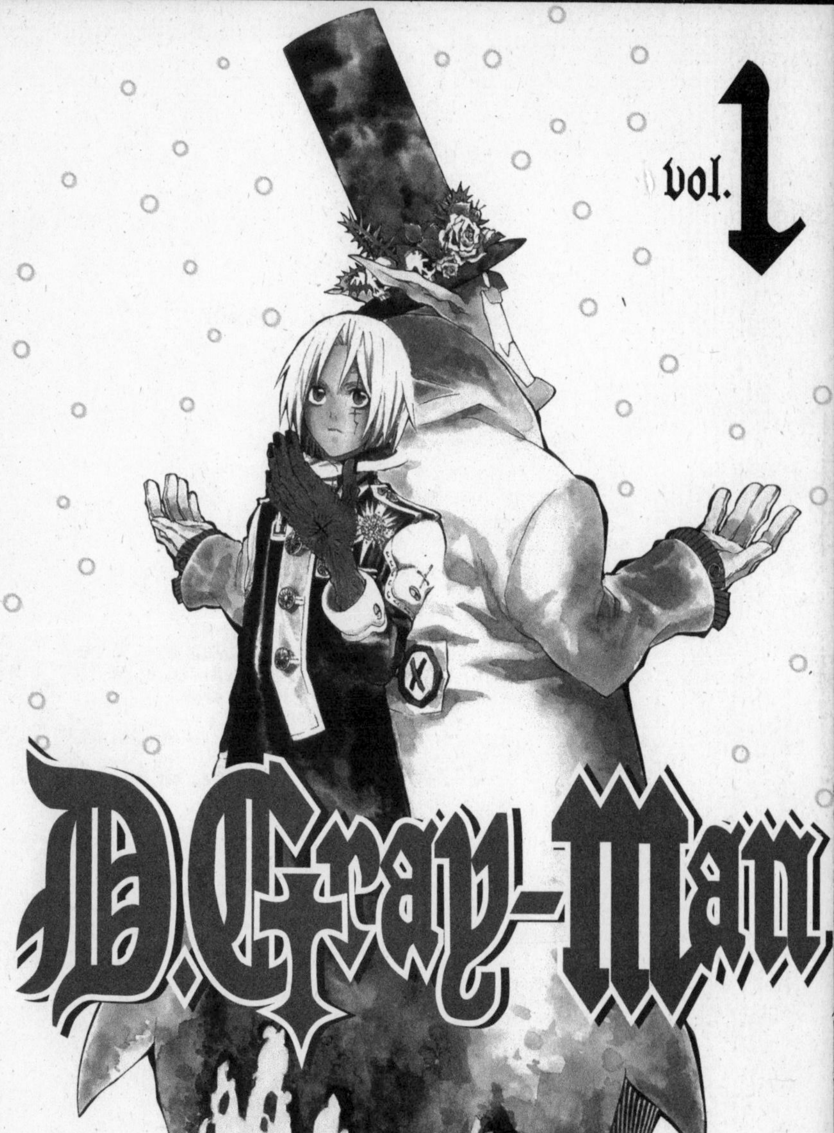
vol. 1
D.Gray-man

STORY & ART BY
Katsura Hoshino

D.GRAY-MAN
Vol. 1

CONTENTS

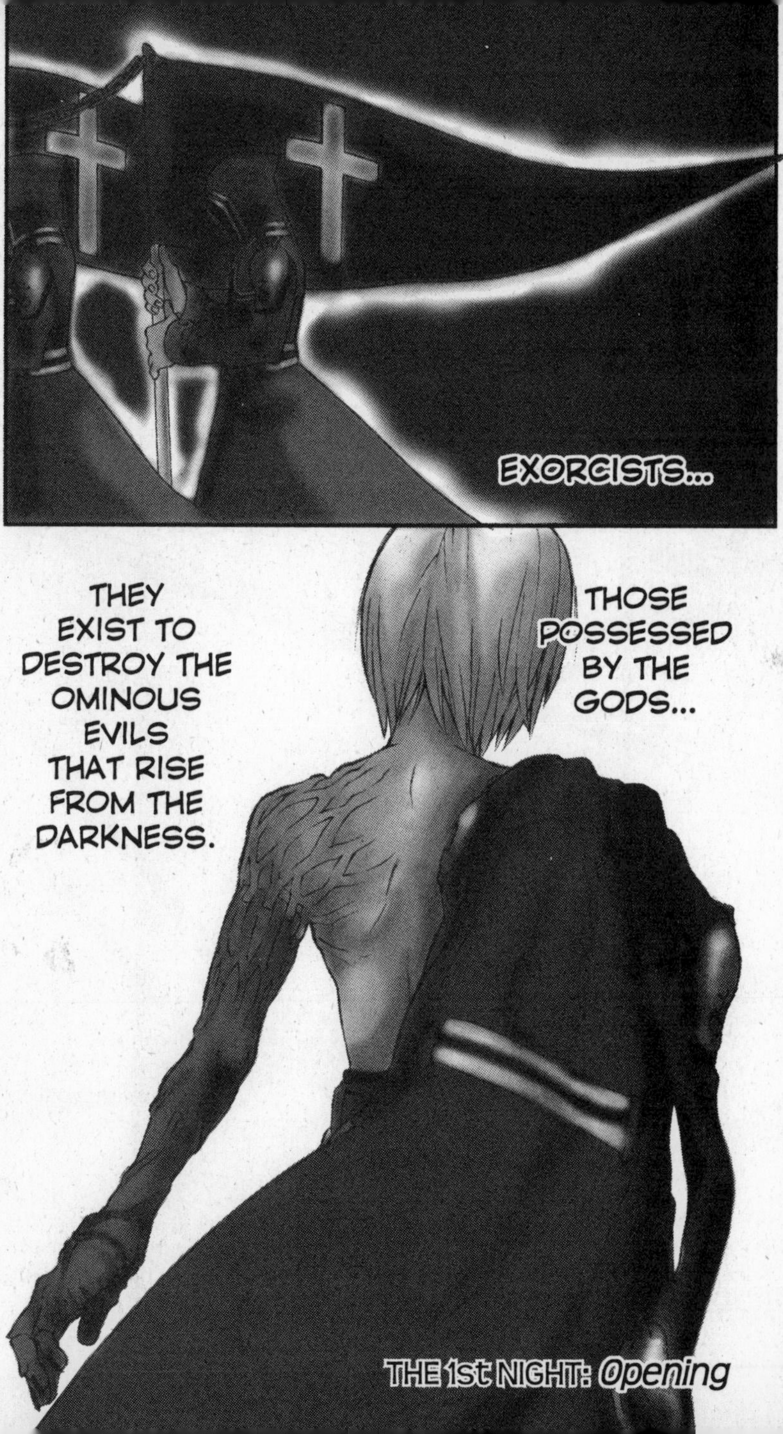
EXORCISTS...
THOSE POSSESSED BY THE GODS...
THEY EXIST TO DESTROY THE OMINOUS EVILS THAT RISE FROM THE DARKNESS.
THE 1st NIGHT: Opening

THE 1st NIGHT: *Opening*

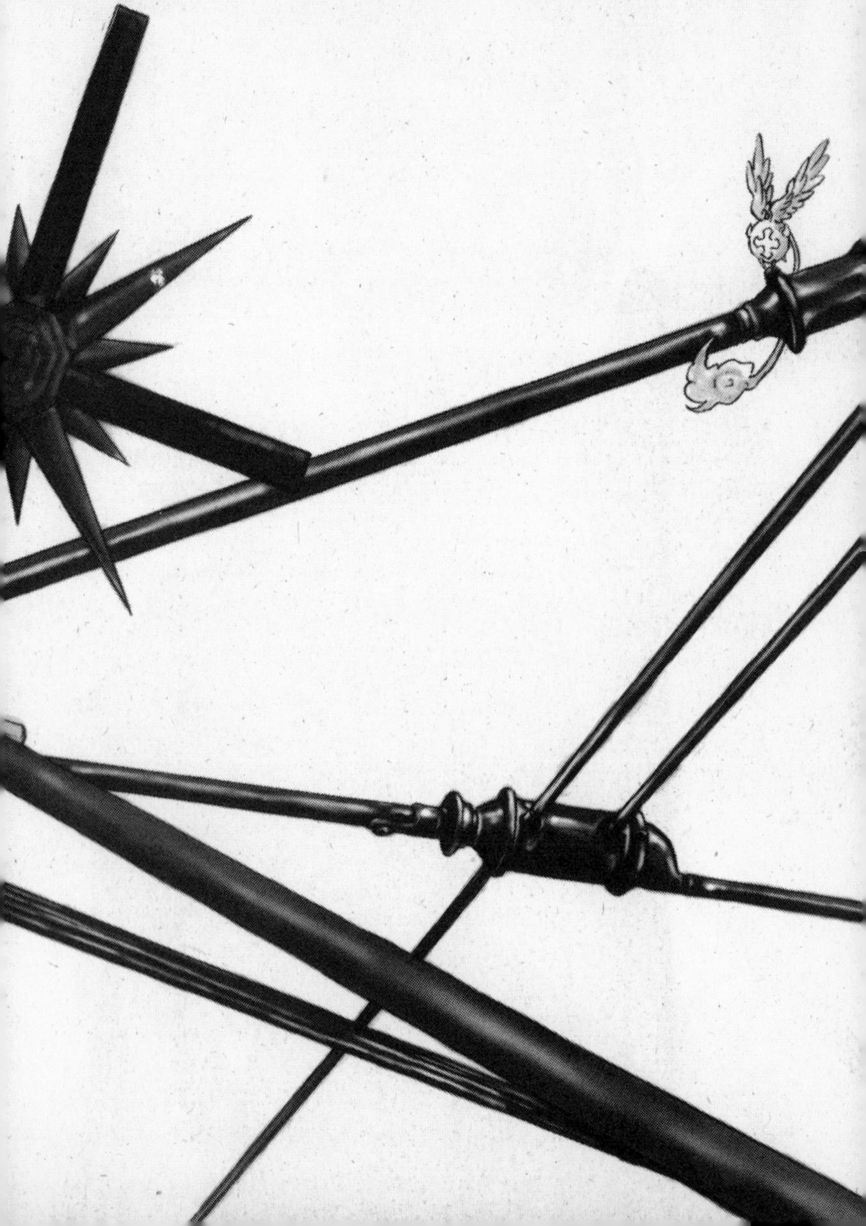

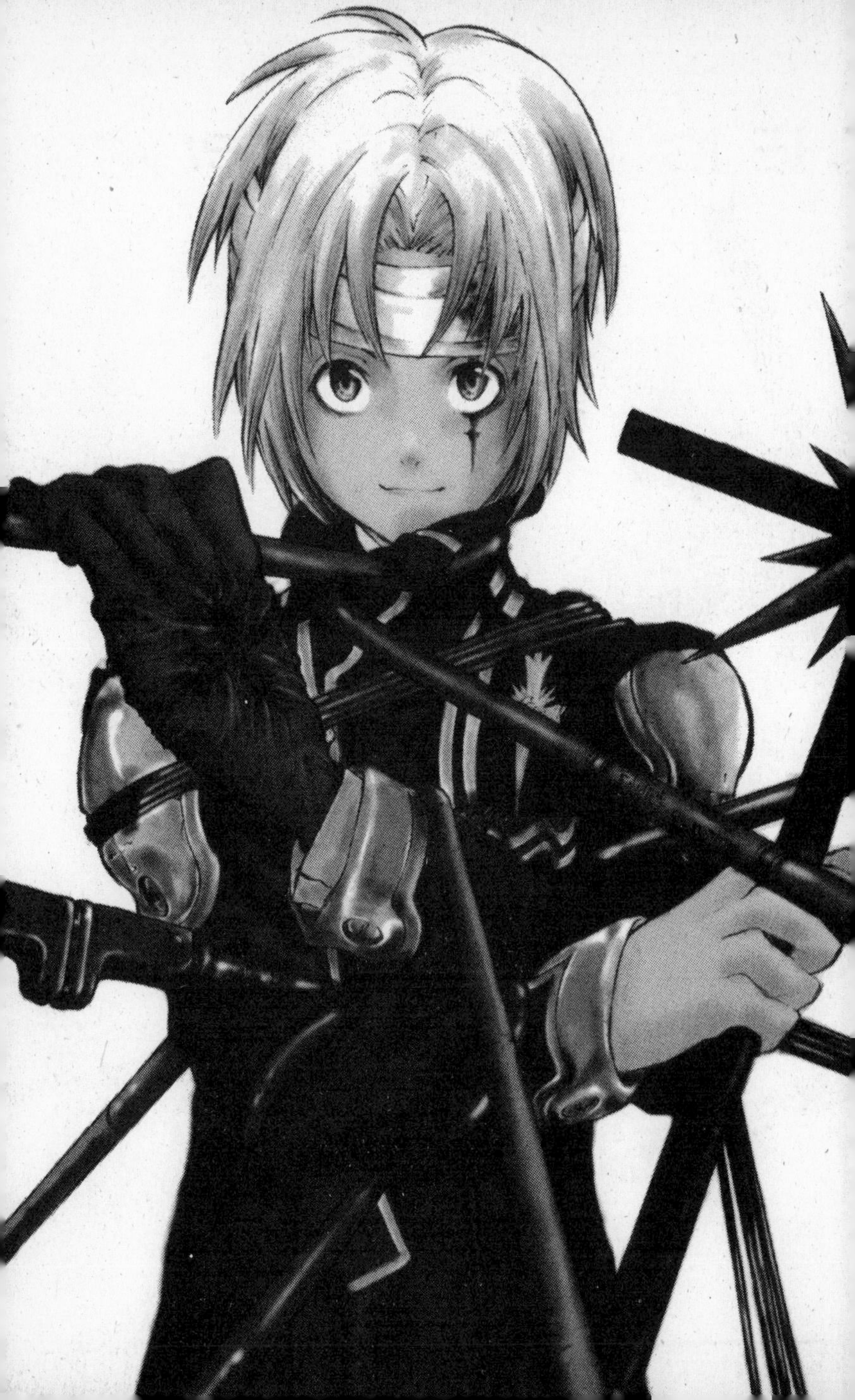

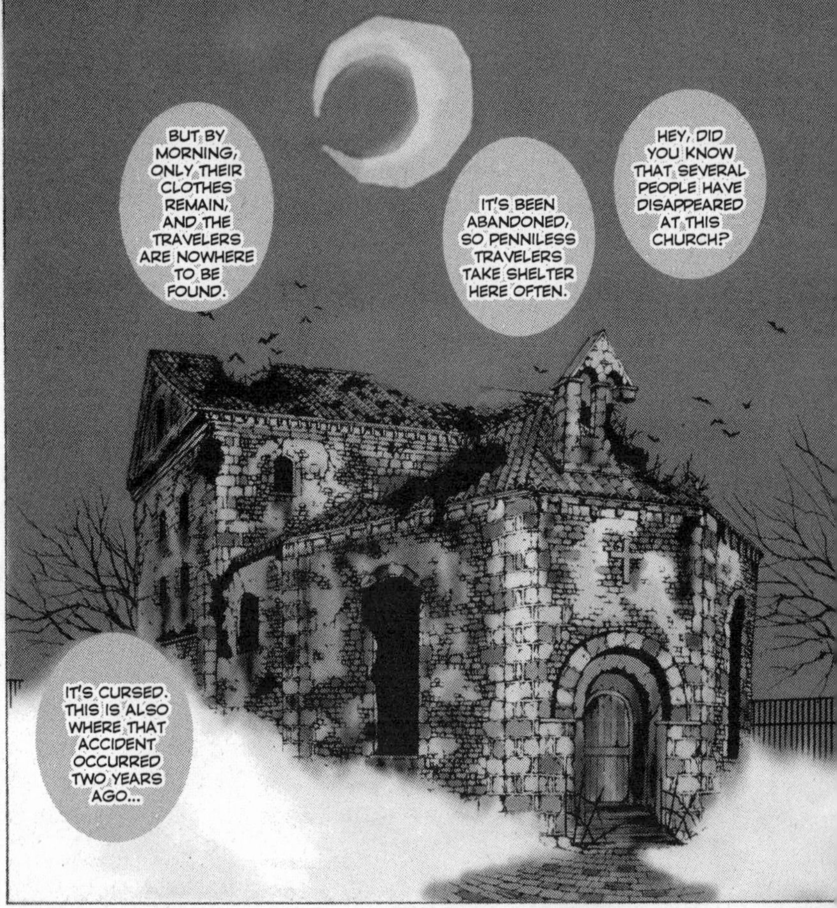
HEY, DID YOU KNOW THAT SEVERAL PEOPLE HAVE DISAPPEARED AT THIS CHURCH?
IT'S BEEN ABANDONED, SO PENNILESS TRAVELERS TAKE SHELTER HERE OFTEN.
BUT BY MORNING, ONLY THEIR CLOTHES REMAIN, AND THE TRAVELERS ARE NOWHERE TO BE FOUND.
IT'S CURSED. THIS IS ALSO WHERE THAT ACCIDENT OCCURRED TWO YEARS AGO...
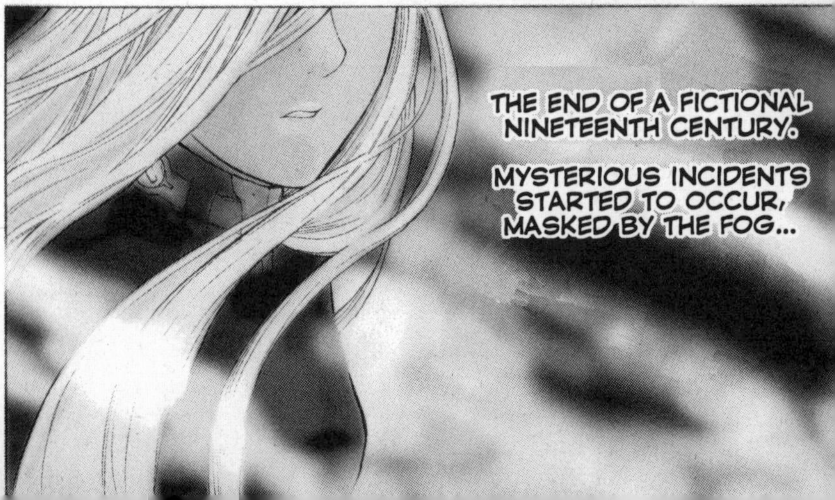
THE END OF A FICTIONAL NINETEENTH CENTURY.
MYSTERIOUS INCIDENTS STARTED TO OCCUR, MASKED BY THE FOG...

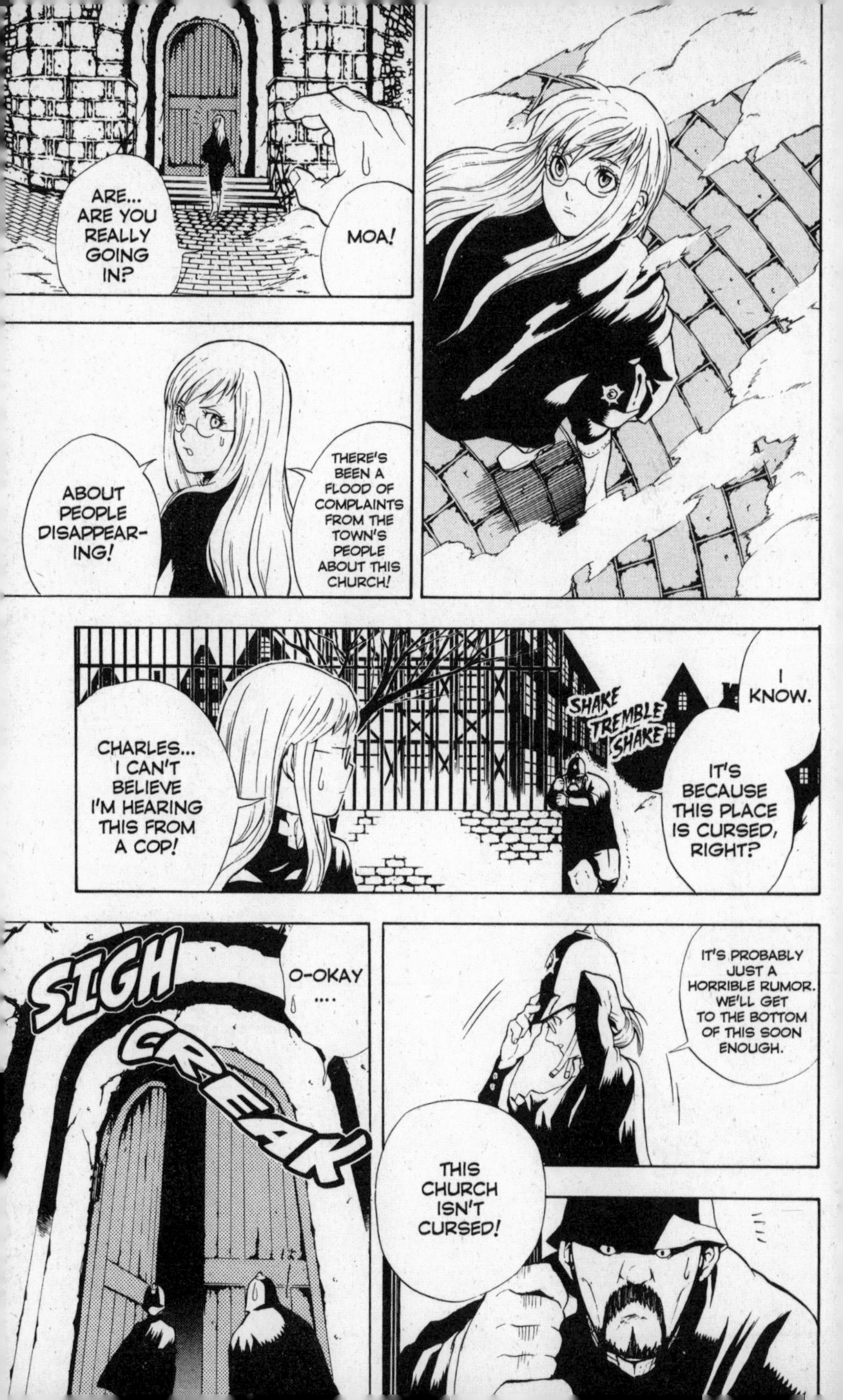

MOA!
ARE... ARE YOU REALLY GOING IN?
THERE'S BEEN A FLOOD OF COMPLAINTS FROM THE TOWN'S PEOPLE ABOUT THIS CHURCH!
ABOUT PEOPLE DISAPPEARING!
I KNOW.
IT'S BECAUSE THIS PLACE IS CURSED, RIGHT?
SHAKE TREMBLE SHAKE
CHARLES... I CAN'T BELIEVE I'M HEARING THIS FROM A COP!
IT'S PROBABLY JUST A HORRIBLE RUMOR. WE'LL GET TO THE BOTTOM OF THIS SOON ENOUGH.
THIS CHURCH ISN'T CURSED!
O-OKAY ....
SIGH
CREAK

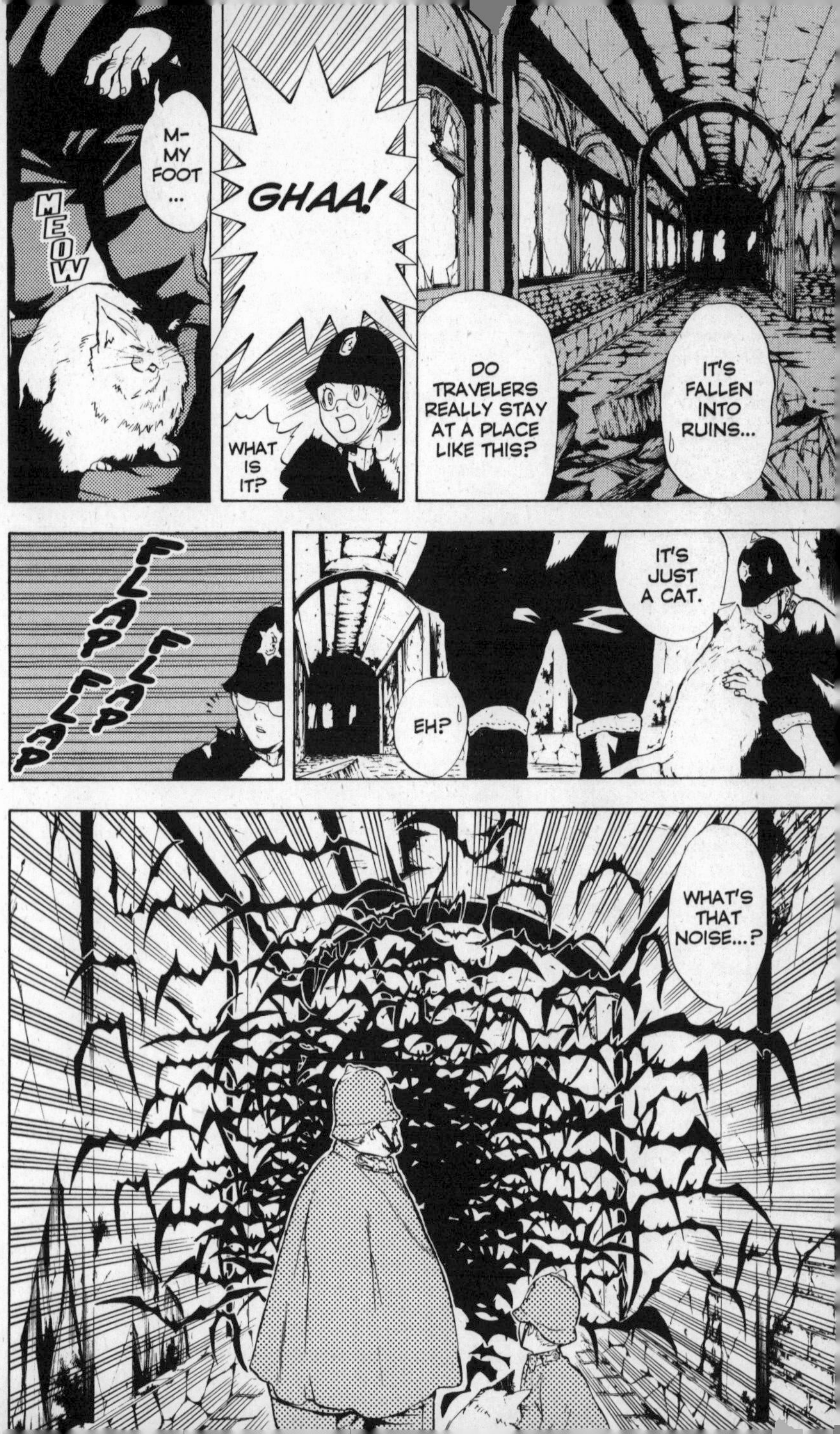
IT'S FALLEN INTO RUINS...
DO TRAVELERS REALLY STAY AT A PLACE LIKE THIS?
GHAA!
WHAT IS IT?
M-MY FOOT...
MEOW
IT'S JUST A CAT.
EH?
FLAP FLAP
FLAP FLAP
WHAT'S THAT NOISE...?

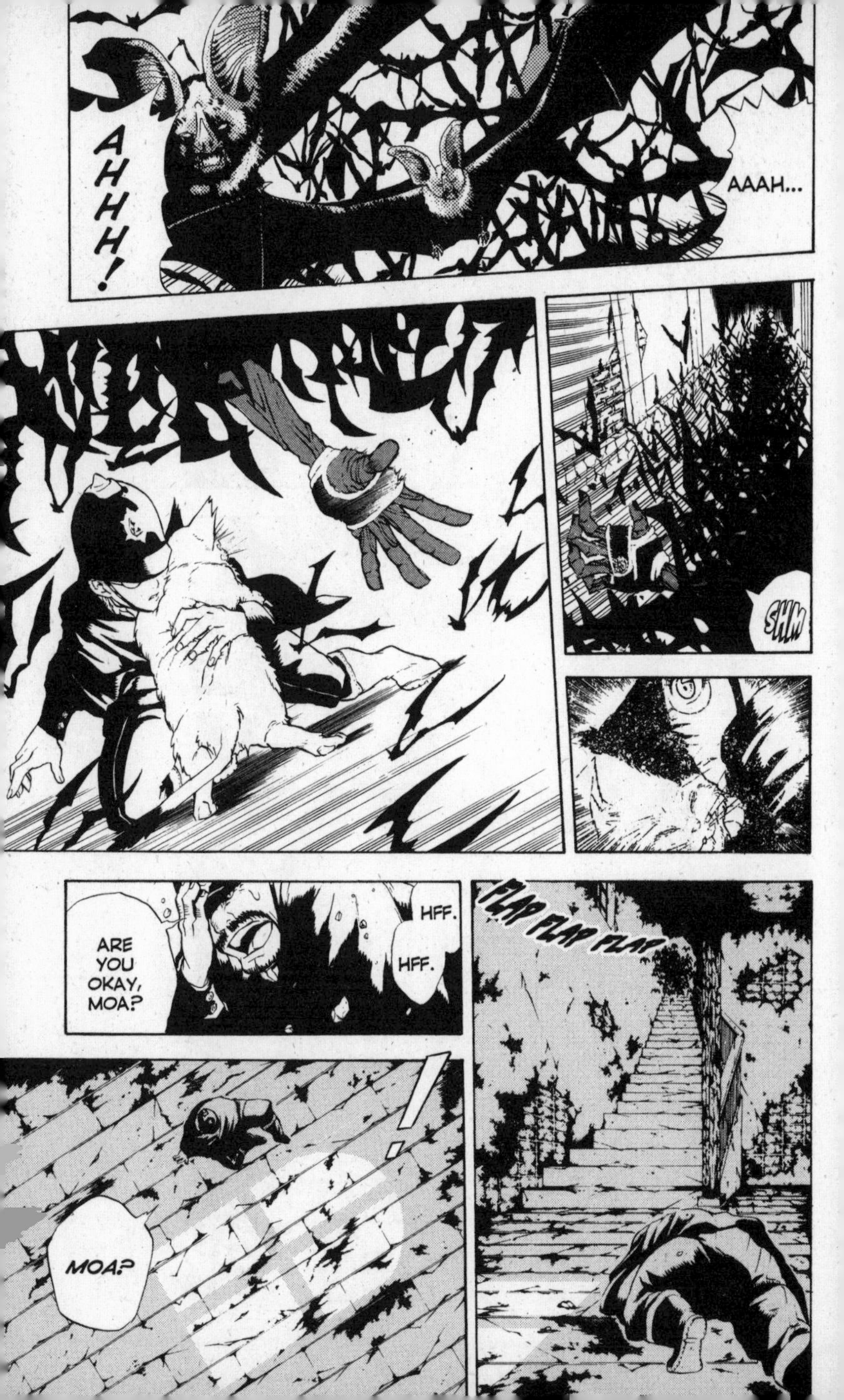
AAAH...
AHHH!
SHM
FLAP FLAP FLAP
HFF.
HFF.
ARE YOU OKAY, MOA?
!
MOA?

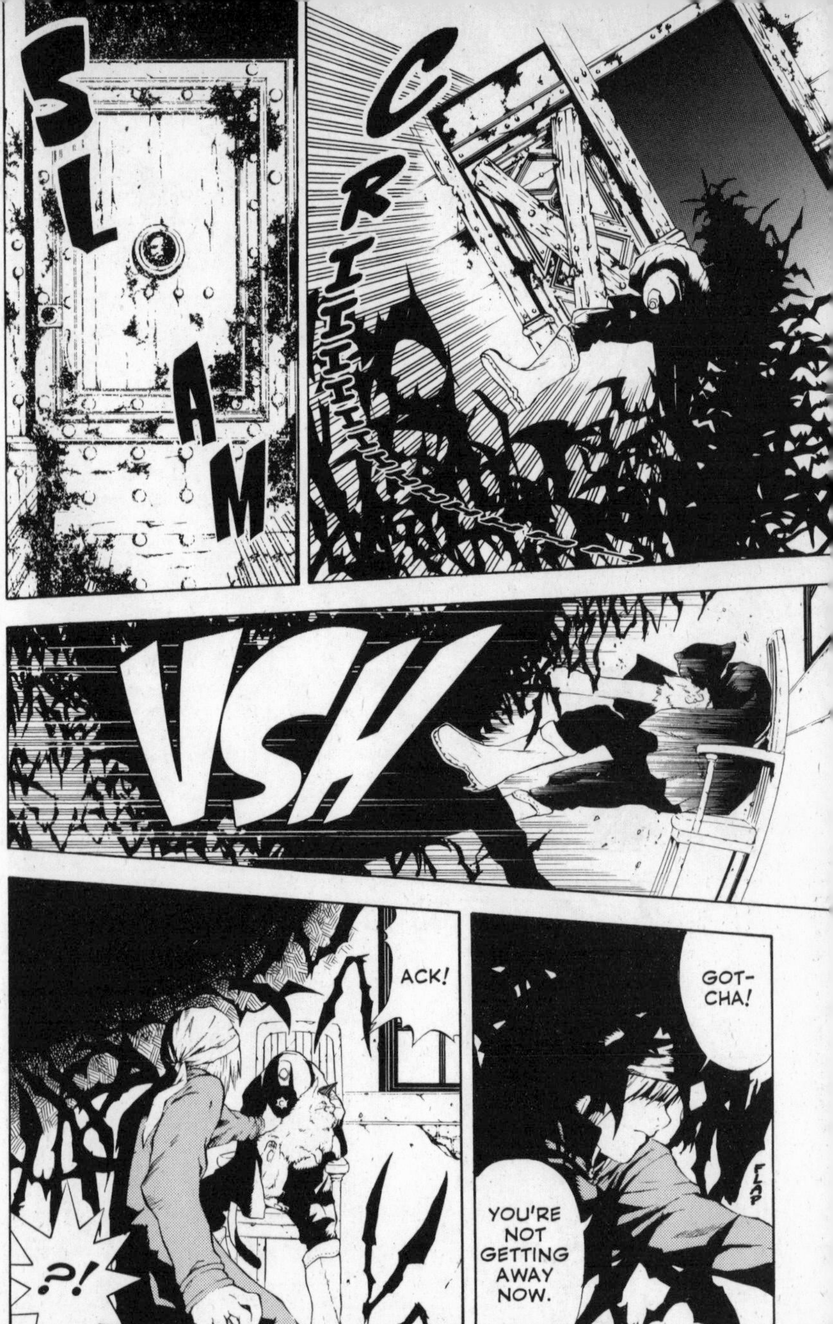
CRIIIIIII
SLAM
VSH
GOT-CHA!
FLAP
YOU'RE NOT GETTING AWAY NOW.
ACK!
?!

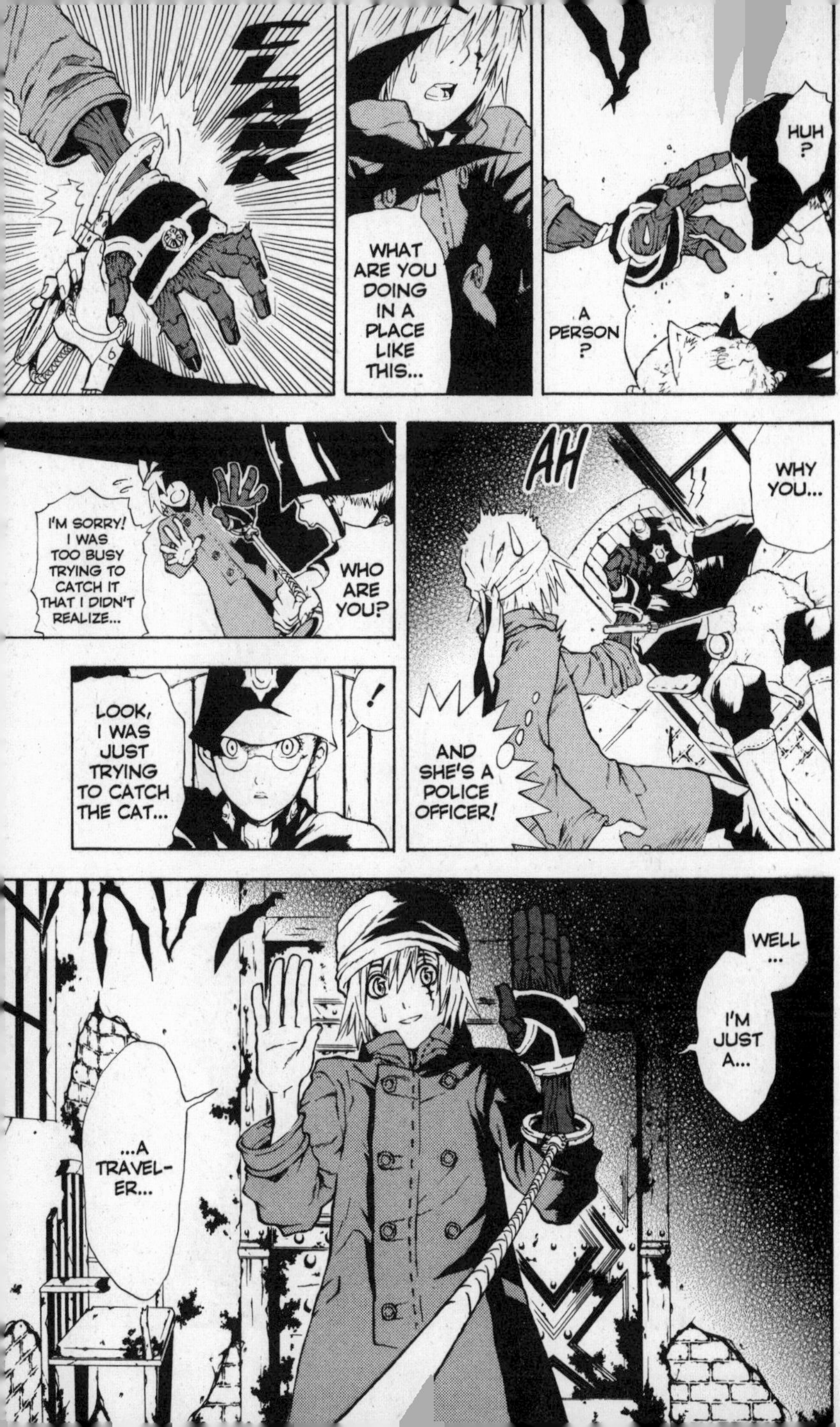
HUH ?
A PERSON ?
WHAT ARE YOU DOING IN A PLACE LIKE THIS...
AH
WHY YOU...
AND SHE'S A POLICE OFFICER!
I'M SORRY! I WAS TOO BUSY TRYING TO CATCH IT THAT I DIDN'T REALIZE...
WHO ARE YOU?
!
LOOK, I WAS JUST TRYING TO CATCH THE CAT...
WELL ...
I'M JUST A...
...A TRAVEL-ER...

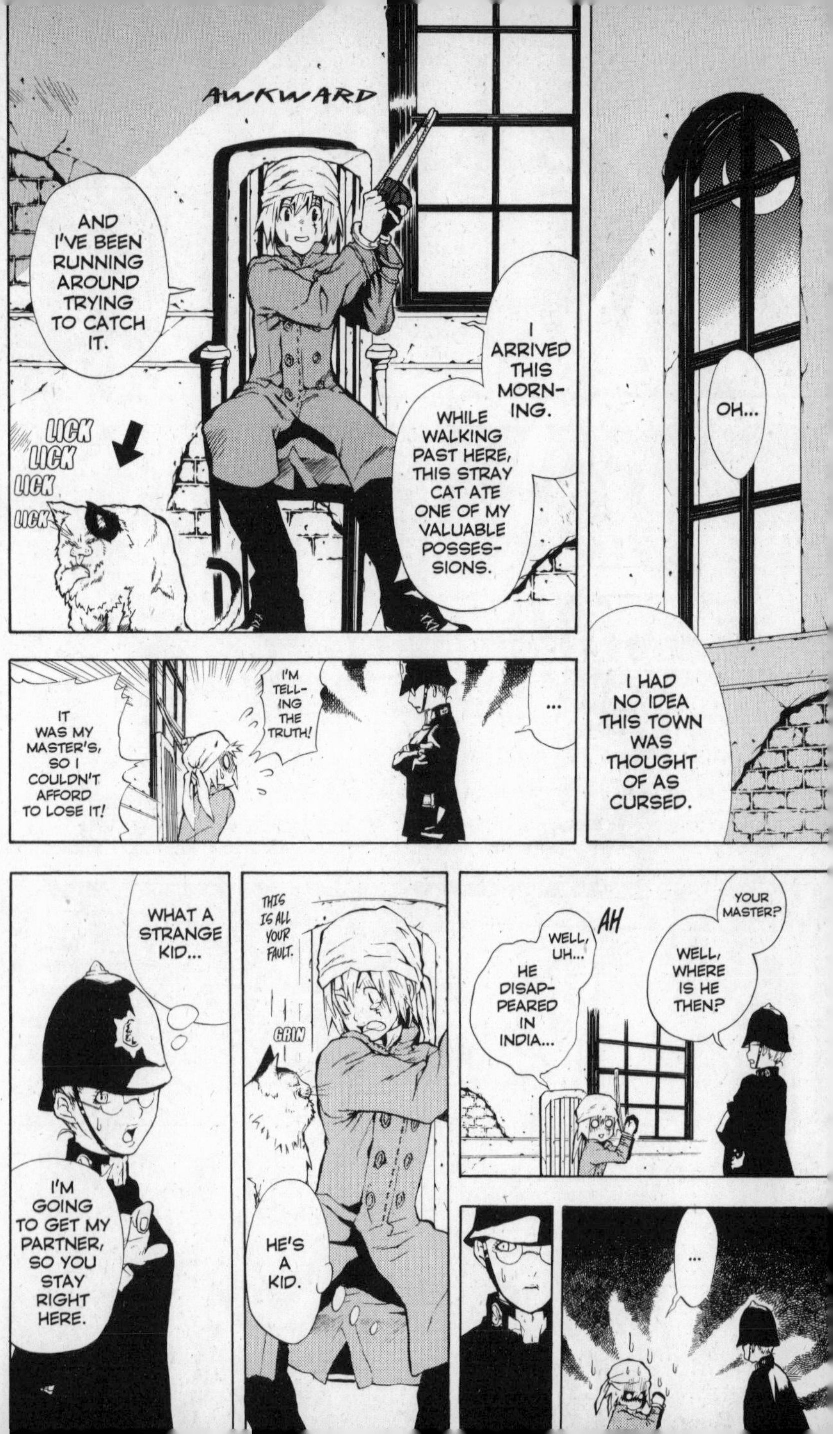
OH...
I HAD NO IDEA THIS TOWN WAS THOUGHT OF AS CURSED.
AWKWARD
I ARRIVED THIS MORNING.
WHILE WALKING PAST HERE, THIS STRAY CAT ATE ONE OF MY VALUABLE POSSESSIONS.
AND I'VE BEEN RUNNING AROUND TRYING TO CATCH IT.
LICK LICK LICK LICK
...
I'M TELLING THE TRUTH!
IT WAS MY MASTER'S, SO I COULDN'T AFFORD TO LOSE IT!
YOUR MASTER?
WELL, WHERE IS HE THEN?
AH
WELL, UH...
HE DISAPPEARED IN INDIA...
...
THIS IS ALL YOUR FAULT.
GRIN
HE'S A KID.
WHAT A STRANGE KID...
I'M GOING TO GET MY PARTNER, SO YOU STAY RIGHT HERE.

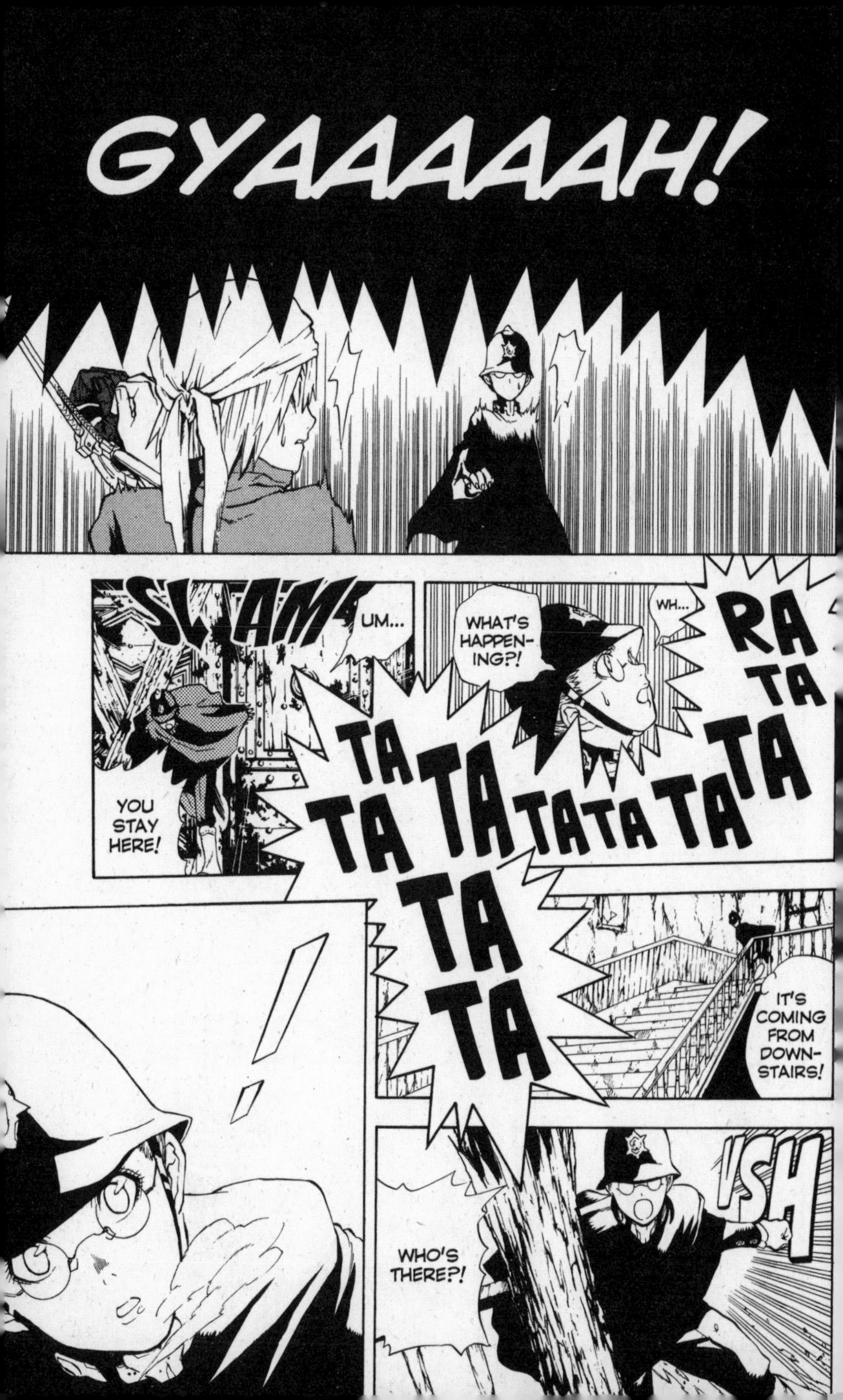
GYAAAAAH!
WH...
WHAT'S HAPPENING?!
RA TA TA TA TATA TA TA TA TA TA TA
SLAM
UM...
YOU STAY HERE!
IT'S COMING FROM DOWNSTAIRS!
ISH
WHO'S THERE?!
!

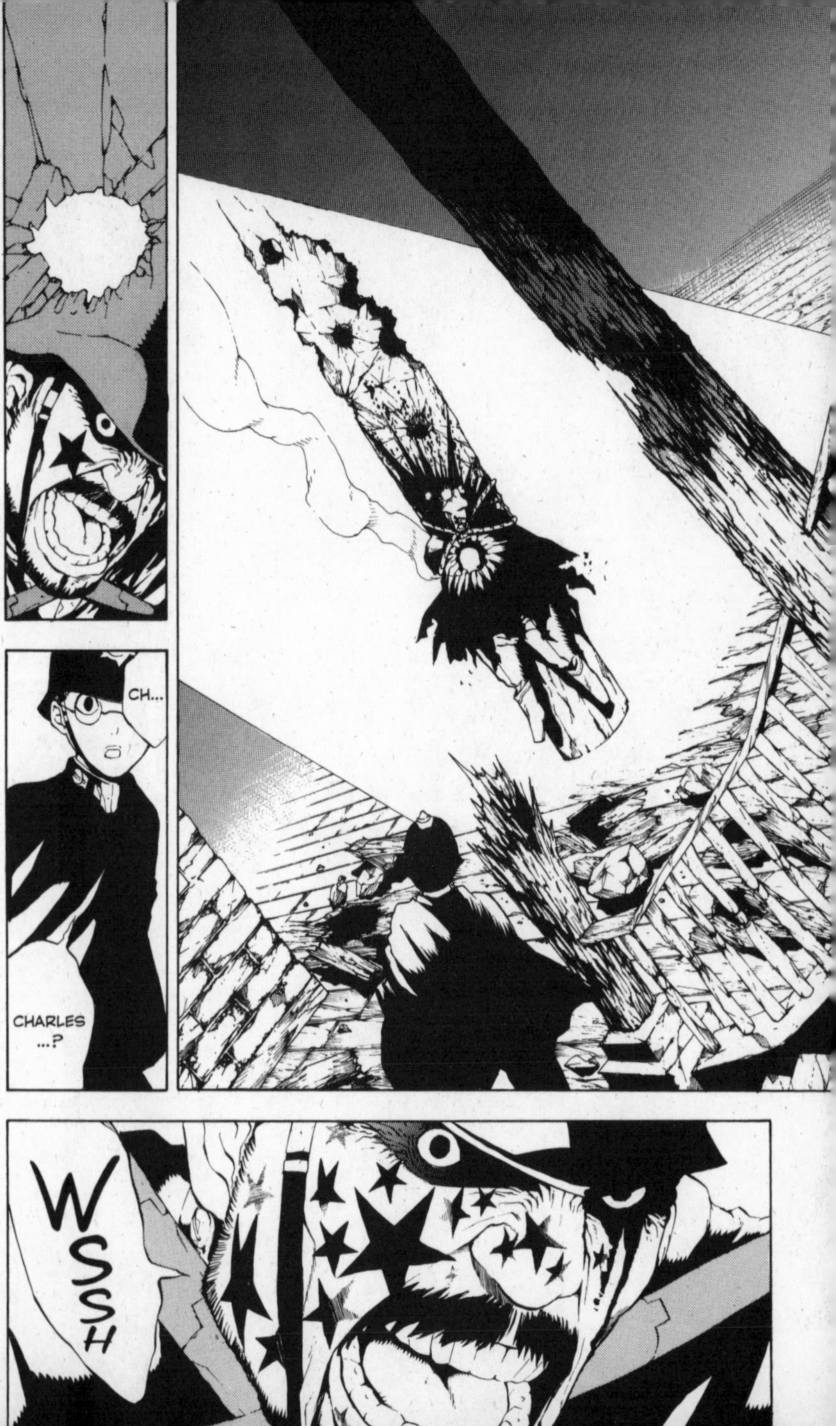
CH...
CHARLES ...?
WSSH

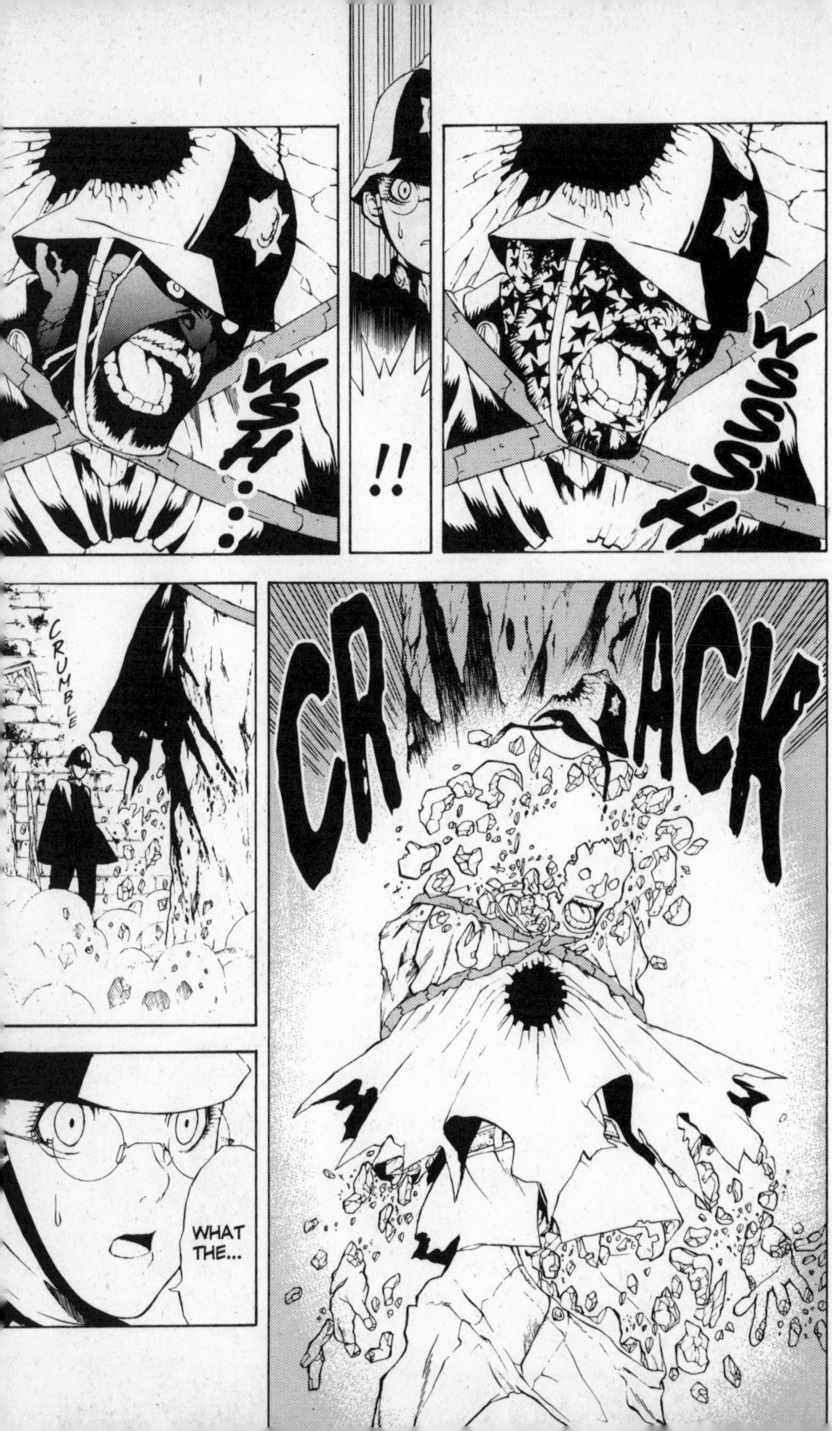
WSSSH
!!
WSH...
CRACK
CRUMBLE
WHAT THE...

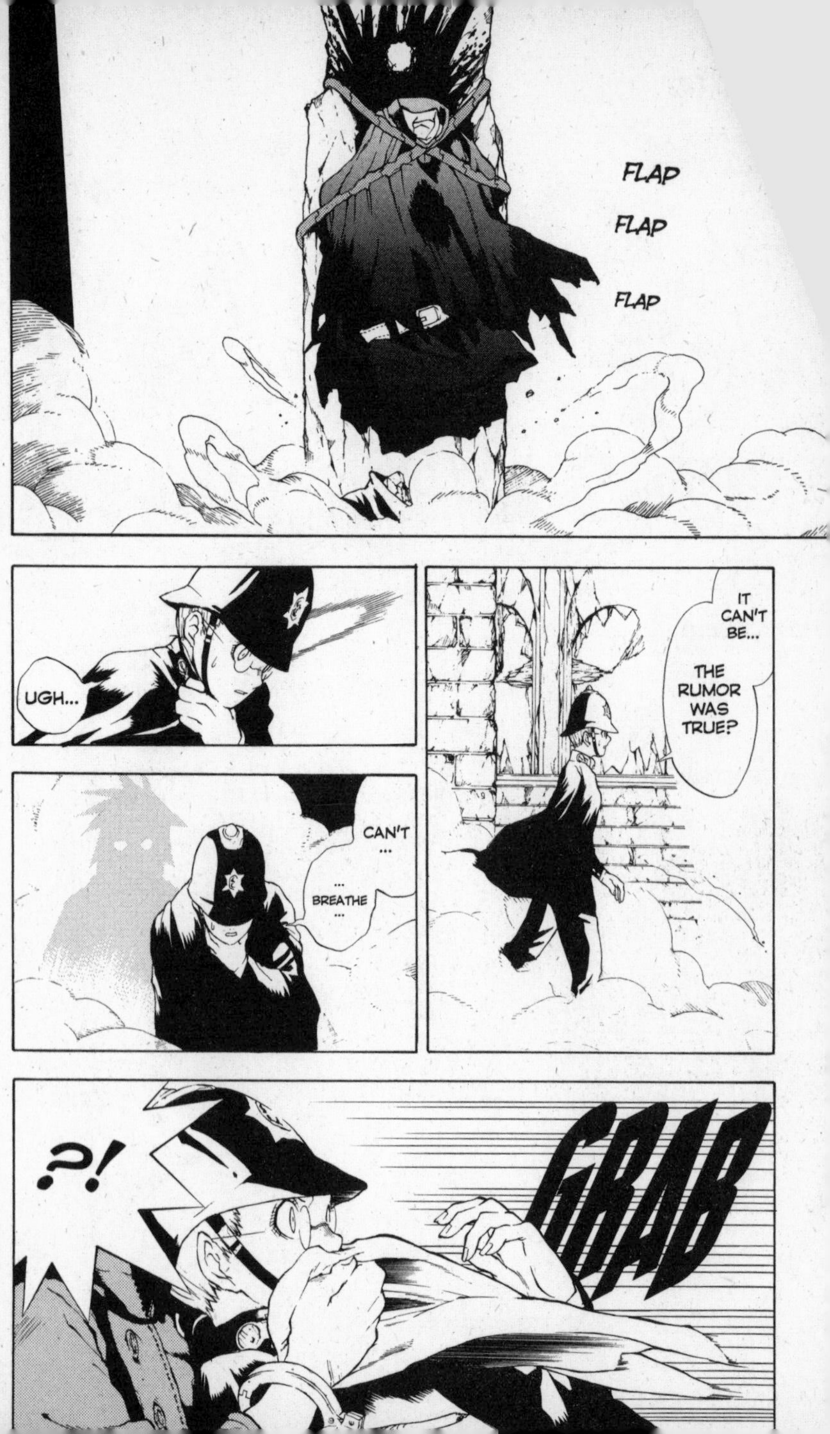
FLAP
FLAP
FLAP
IT CAN'T BE...
THE RUMOR WAS TRUE?
UGH...
CAN'T ...
... BREATHE ...
GRAB
?!

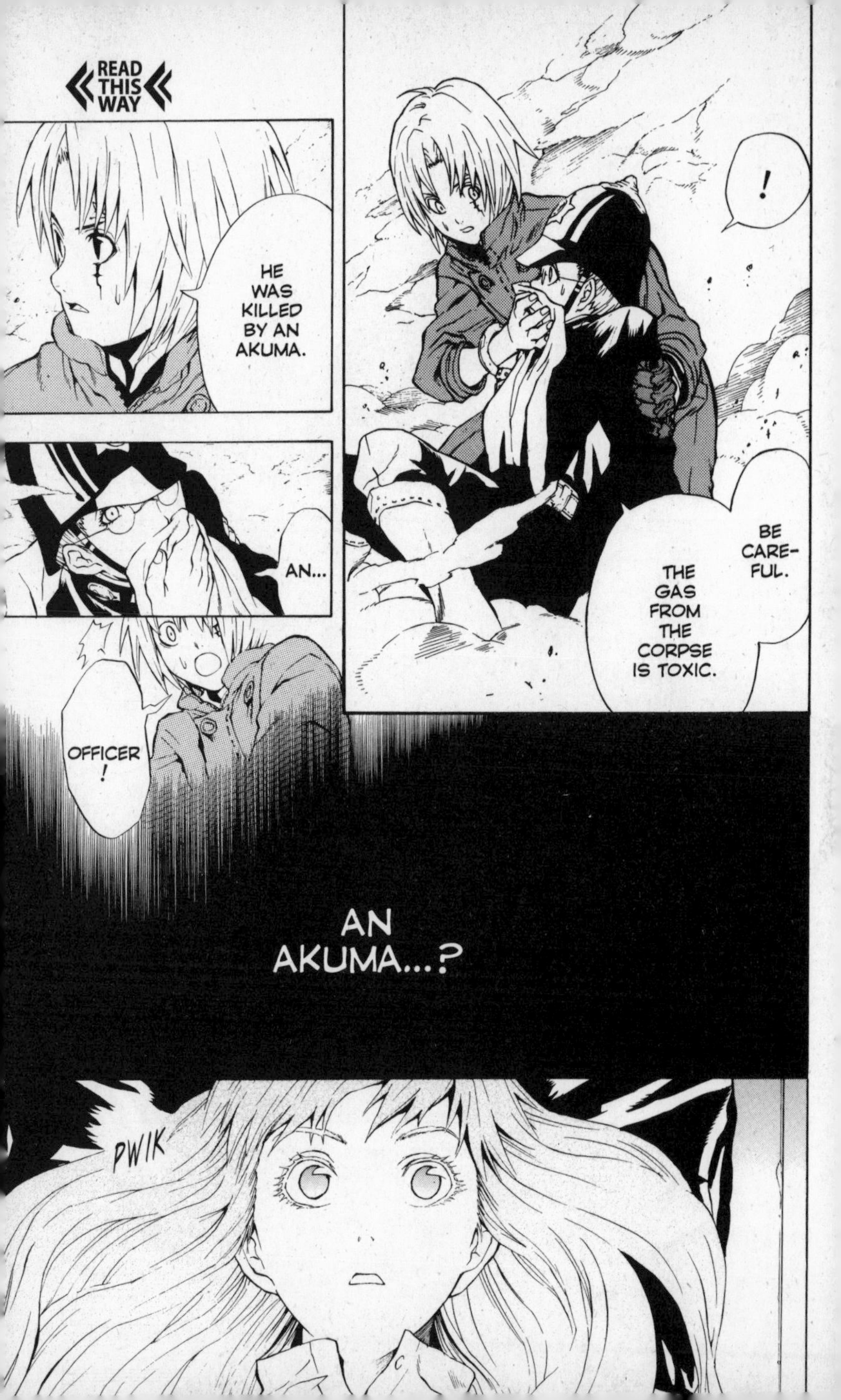
READ THIS WAY
!
BE CARE-FUL.
THE GAS FROM THE CORPSE IS TOXIC.
HE WAS KILLED BY AN AKUMA.
AN...
OFFICER!
AN AKUMA...?
PWIK

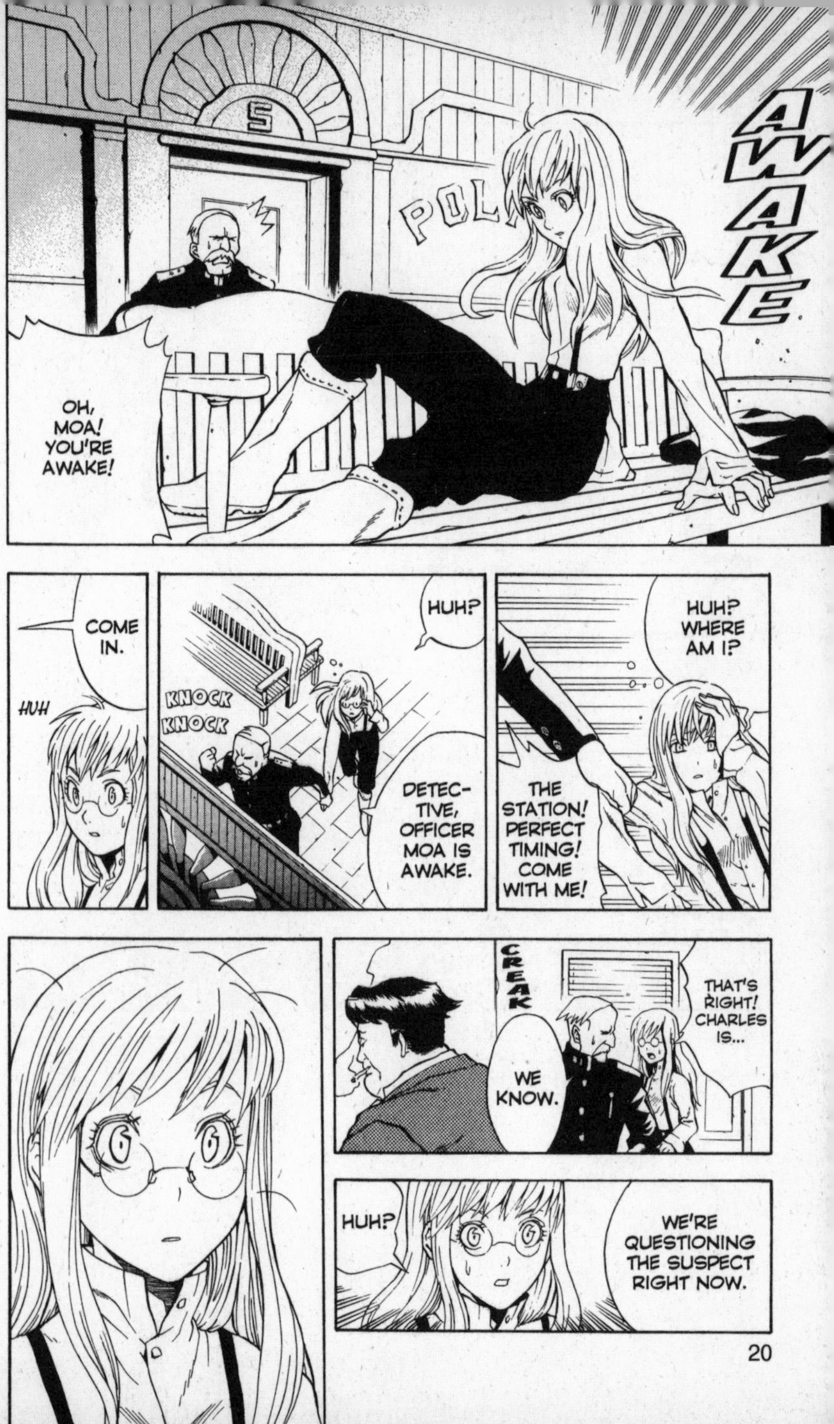
AWAKE
POL
OH, MOA! YOU'RE AWAKE!
HUH? WHERE AM I?
THE STATION! PERFECT TIMING! COME WITH ME!
HUH?
KNOCK KNOCK
DETECTIVE, OFFICER MOA IS AWAKE.
COME IN.
HUH
THAT'S RIGHT! CHARLES IS...
CREAK
WE KNOW.
WE'RE QUESTIONING THE SUSPECT RIGHT NOW.
HUH?

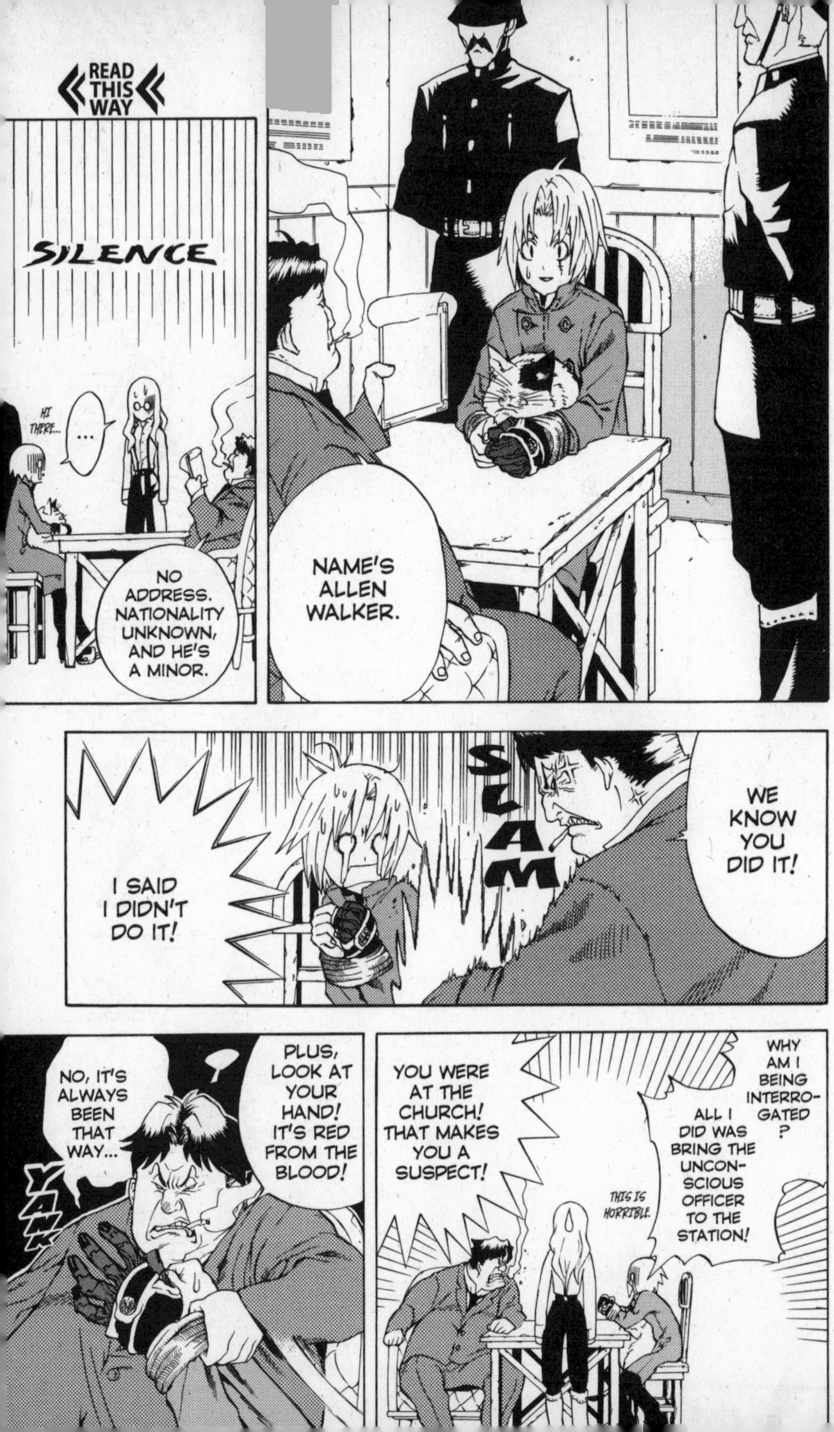
READ THIS WAY
NAME'S ALLEN WALKER.
SILENCE
HI THERE...
...
NO ADDRESS. NATIONALITY UNKNOWN, AND HE'S A MINOR.
WE KNOW YOU DID IT!
SLAM
I SAID I DIDN'T DO IT!
WHY AM I BEING INTERROGATED?
ALL I DID WAS BRING THE UNCONSCIOUS OFFICER TO THE STATION!
THIS IS HORRIBLE.
YOU WERE AT THE CHURCH! THAT MAKES YOU A SUSPECT!
PLUS, LOOK AT YOUR HAND! IT'S RED FROM THE BLOOD!
NO, IT'S ALWAYS BEEN THAT WAY...
YANK

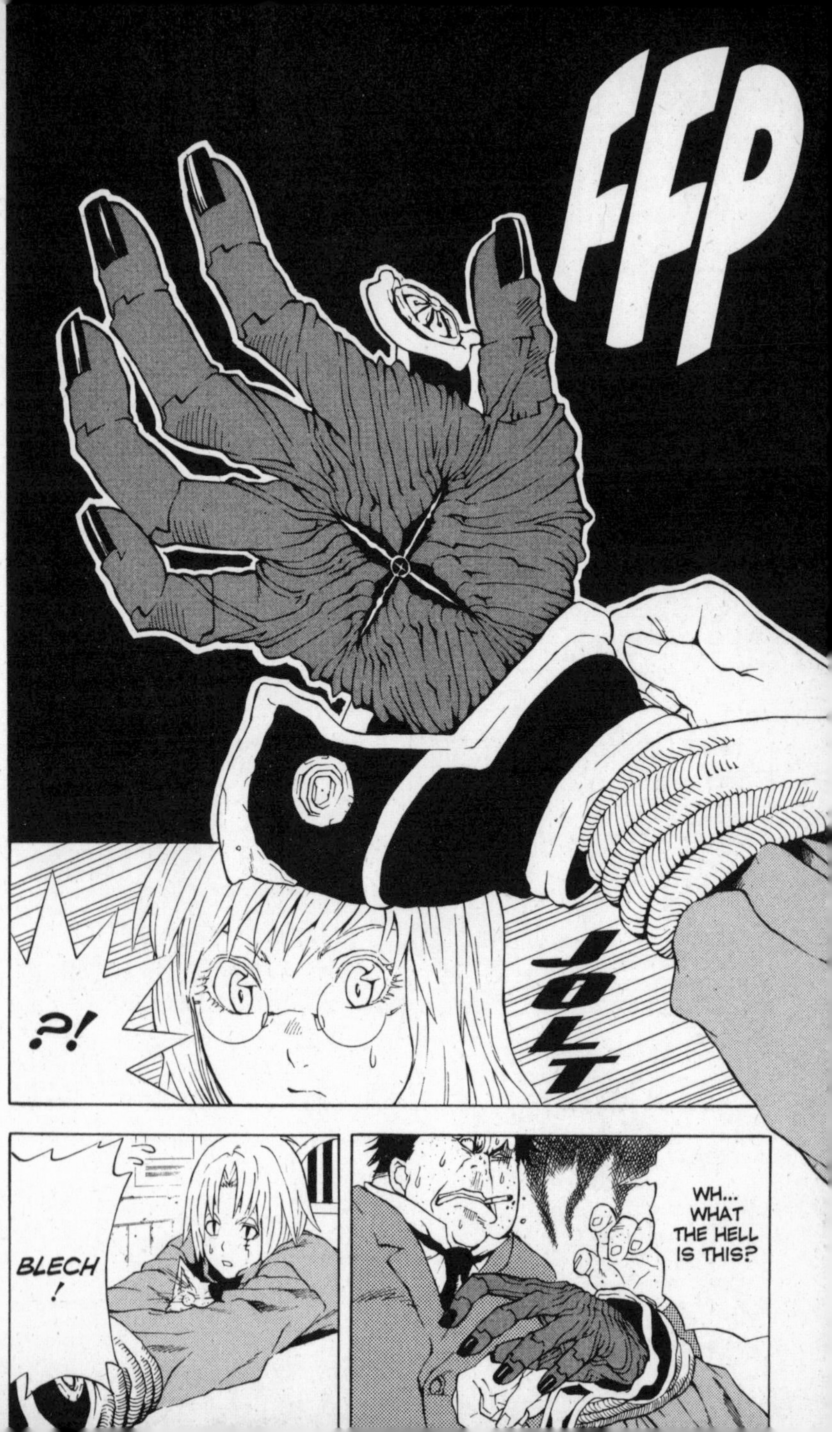
FFP
JOLT
?!
WH... WHAT THE HELL IS THIS?
BLECH!

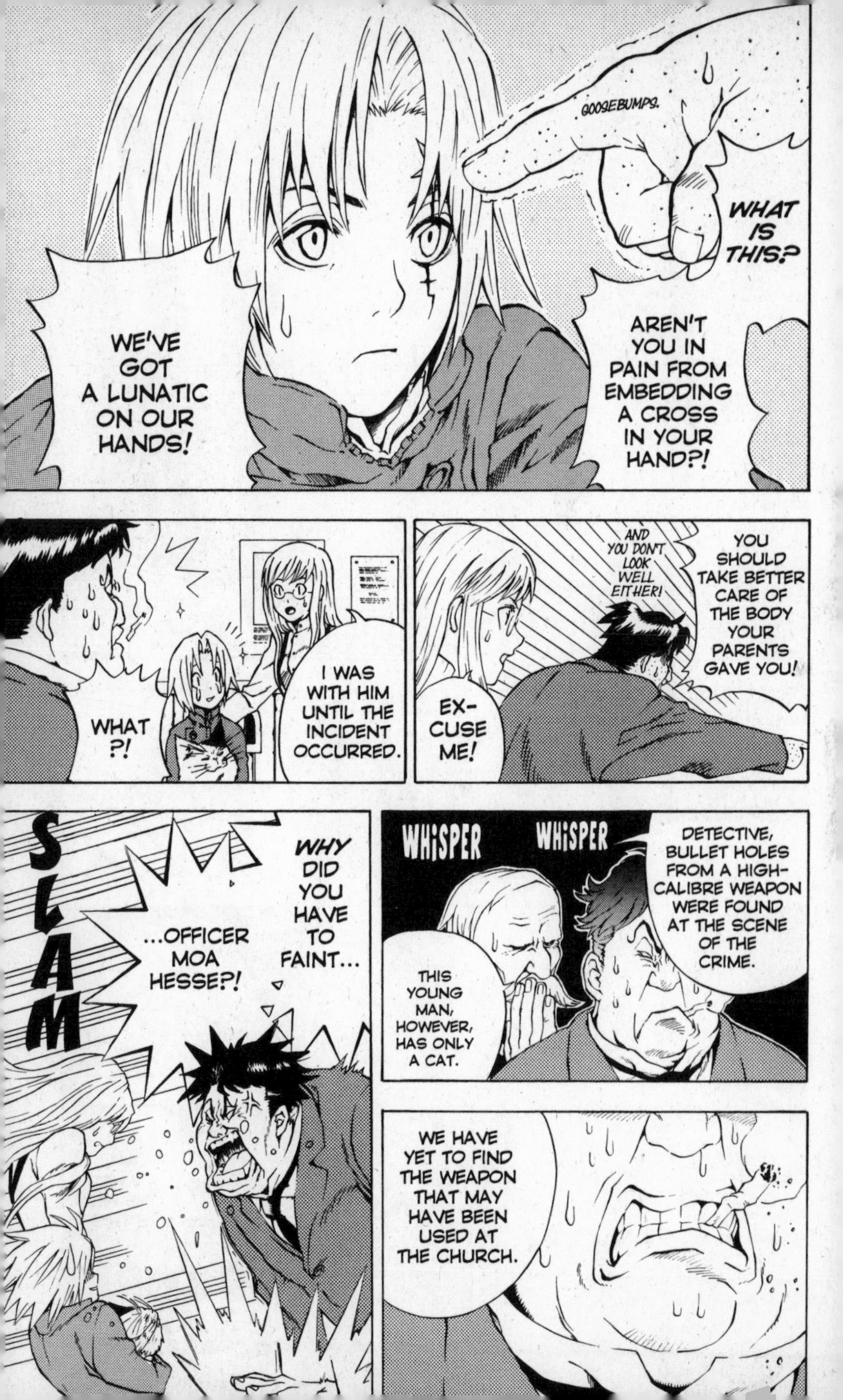
WHAT IS THIS?
GOOSEBUMPS.
AREN'T YOU IN PAIN FROM EMBEDDING A CROSS IN YOUR HAND?!
WE'VE GOT A LUNATIC ON OUR HANDS!
YOU SHOULD TAKE BETTER CARE OF THE BODY YOUR PARENTS GAVE YOU!
AND YOU DON'T LOOK WELL EITHER!
EX-CUSE ME!
I WAS WITH HIM UNTIL THE INCIDENT OCCURRED.
WHAT ?!
DETECTIVE, BULLET HOLES FROM A HIGH-CALIBRE WEAPON WERE FOUND AT THE SCENE OF THE CRIME.
WHISPER
WHISPER
THIS YOUNG MAN, HOWEVER, HAS ONLY A CAT.
WE HAVE YET TO FIND THE WEAPON THAT MAY HAVE BEEN USED AT THE CHURCH.
WHY DID YOU HAVE TO FAINT...
...OFFICER MOA HESSE?!
SLAM

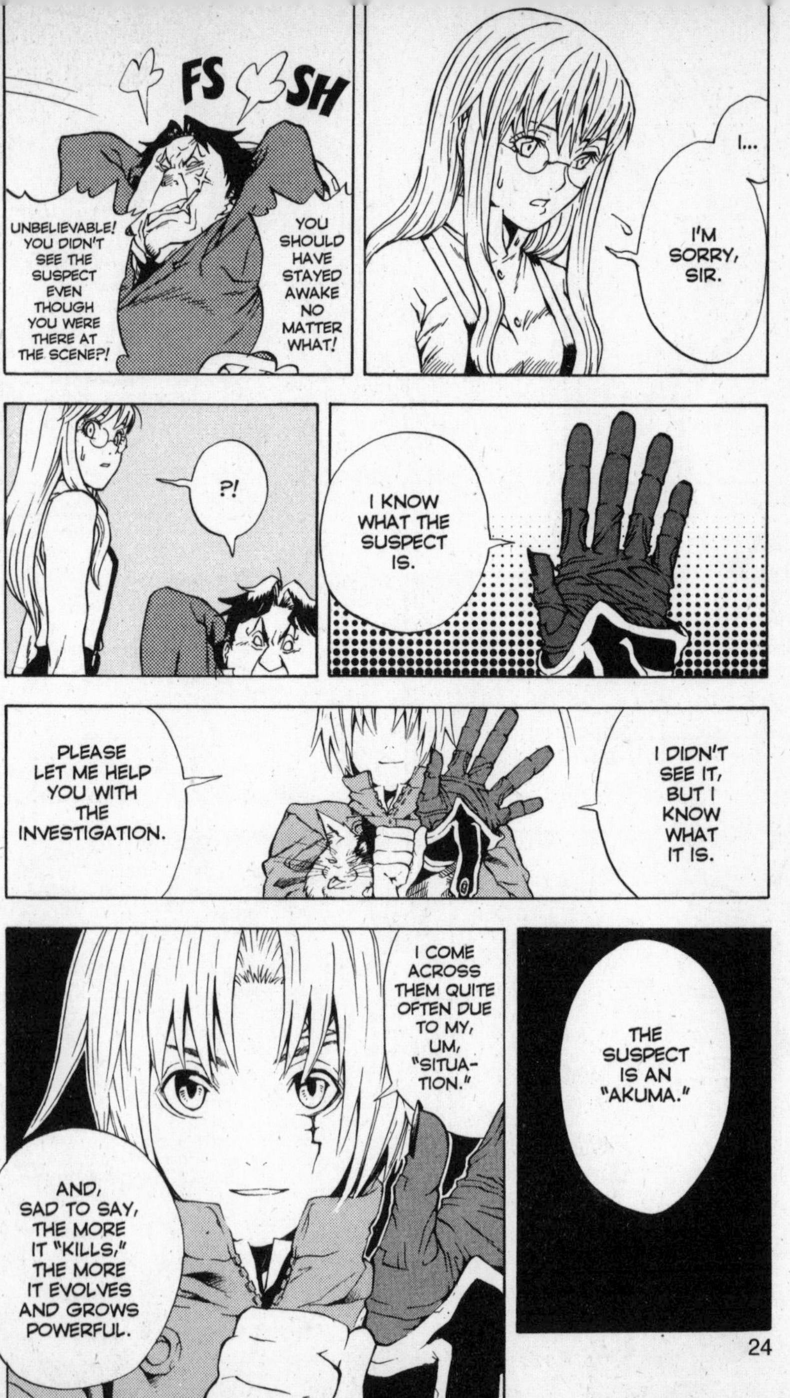

I...
I'M SORRY, SIR.
FS SH
YOU SHOULD HAVE STAYED AWAKE NO MATTER WHAT!
UNBELIEVABLE! YOU DIDN'T SEE THE SUSPECT EVEN THOUGH YOU WERE THERE AT THE SCENE?!
I KNOW WHAT THE SUSPECT IS.
?!
I DIDN'T SEE IT, BUT I KNOW WHAT IT IS.
PLEASE LET ME HELP YOU WITH THE INVESTIGATION.
THE SUSPECT IS AN "AKUMA."
I COME ACROSS THEM QUITE OFTEN DUE TO MY, UM, "SITUA-TION."
AND, SAD TO SAY, THE MORE IT "KILLS," THE MORE IT EVOLVES AND GROWS POWERFUL.

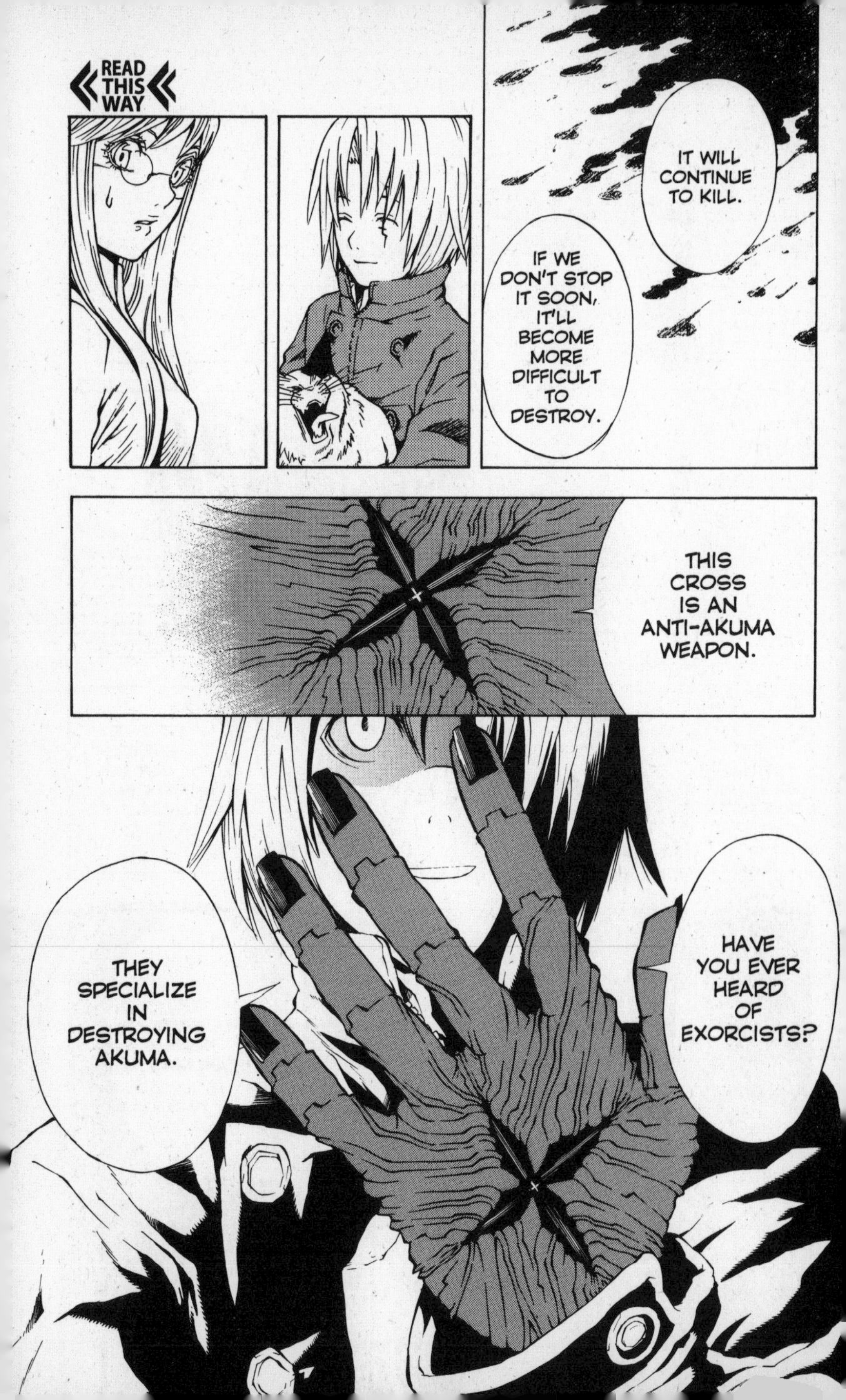
READ THIS WAY
IT WILL CONTINUE TO KILL.
IF WE DON'T STOP IT SOON, IT'LL BECOME MORE DIFFICULT TO DESTROY.
THIS CROSS IS AN ANTI-AKUMA WEAPON.
HAVE YOU EVER HEARD OF EXORCISTS?
THEY SPECIALIZE IN DESTROYING AKUMA.

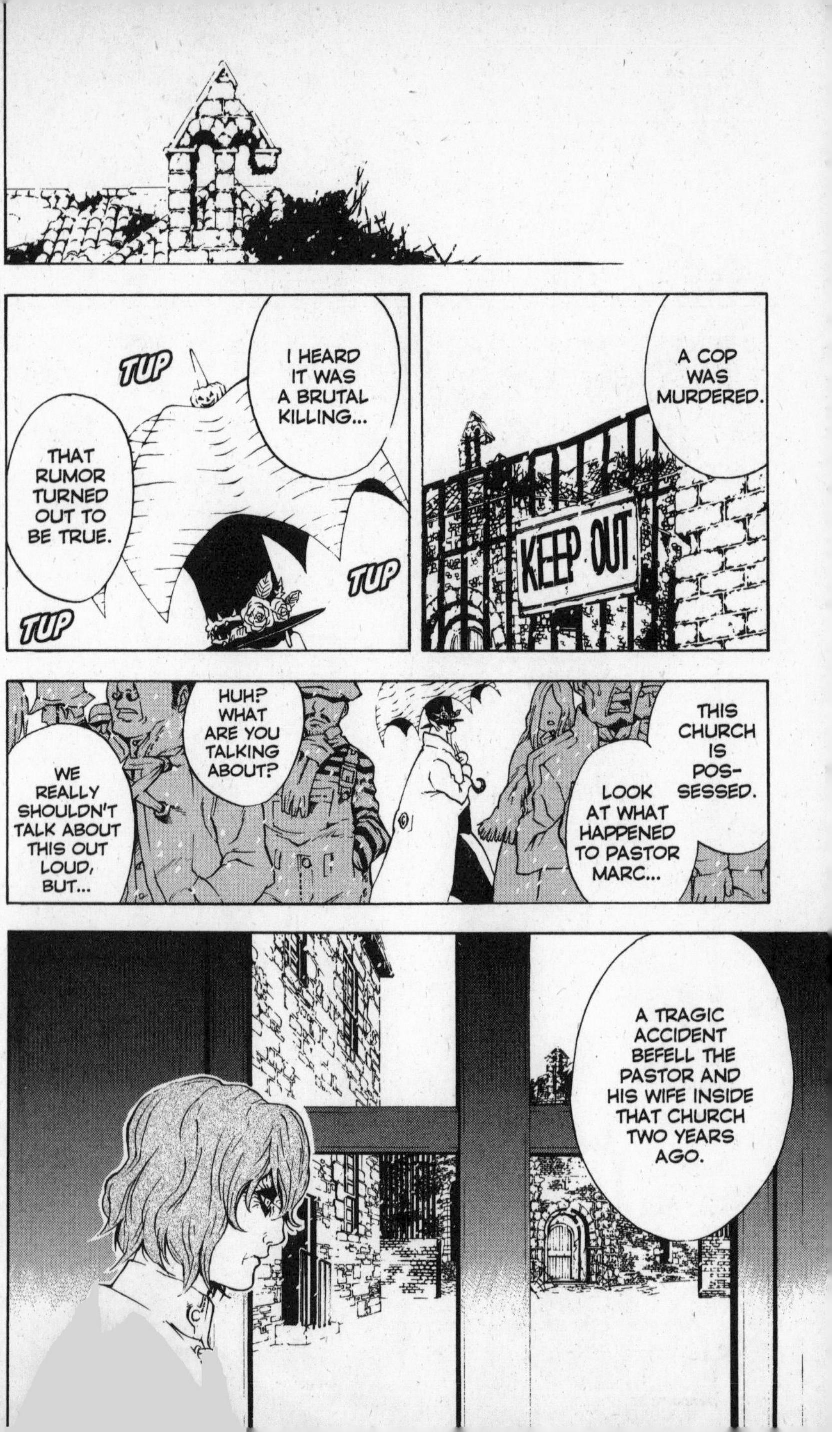
A COP WAS MURDERED.
I HEARD IT WAS A BRUTAL KILLING...
TUP
THAT RUMOR TURNED OUT TO BE TRUE.
TUP
TUP
KEEP OUT
THIS CHURCH IS POS-SESSED.
LOOK AT WHAT HAPPENED TO PASTOR MARC...
HUH? WHAT ARE YOU TALKING ABOUT?
WE REALLY SHOULDN'T TALK ABOUT THIS OUT LOUD, BUT...
A TRAGIC ACCIDENT BEFELL THE PASTOR AND HIS WIFE INSIDE THAT CHURCH TWO YEARS AGO.

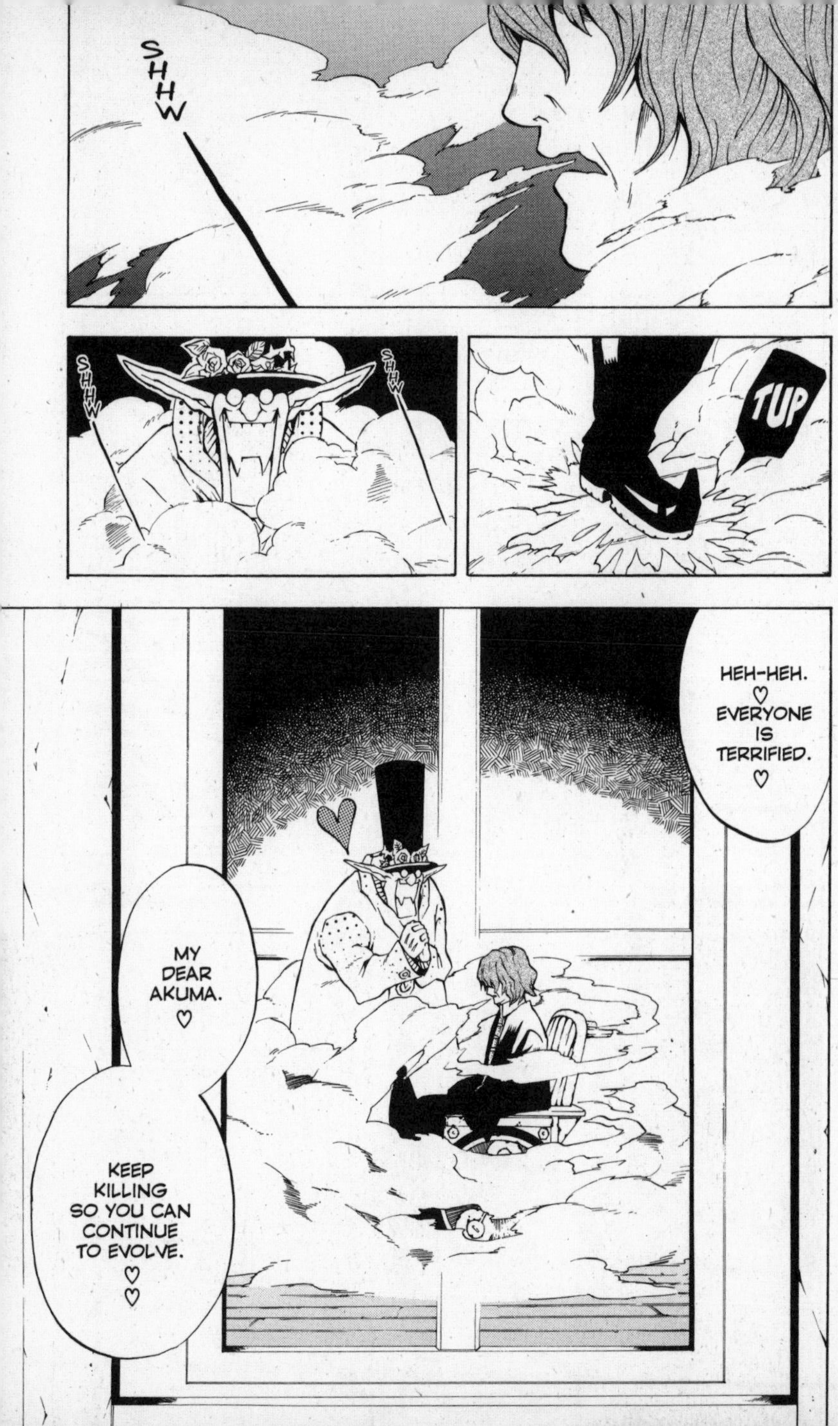
SHHW
TUP
SHHW
SHHW
HEH-HEH. ♡ EVERYONE IS TERRIFIED. ♡
MY DEAR AKUMA. ♡
KEEP KILLING SO YOU CAN CONTINUE TO EVOLVE. ♡ ♡

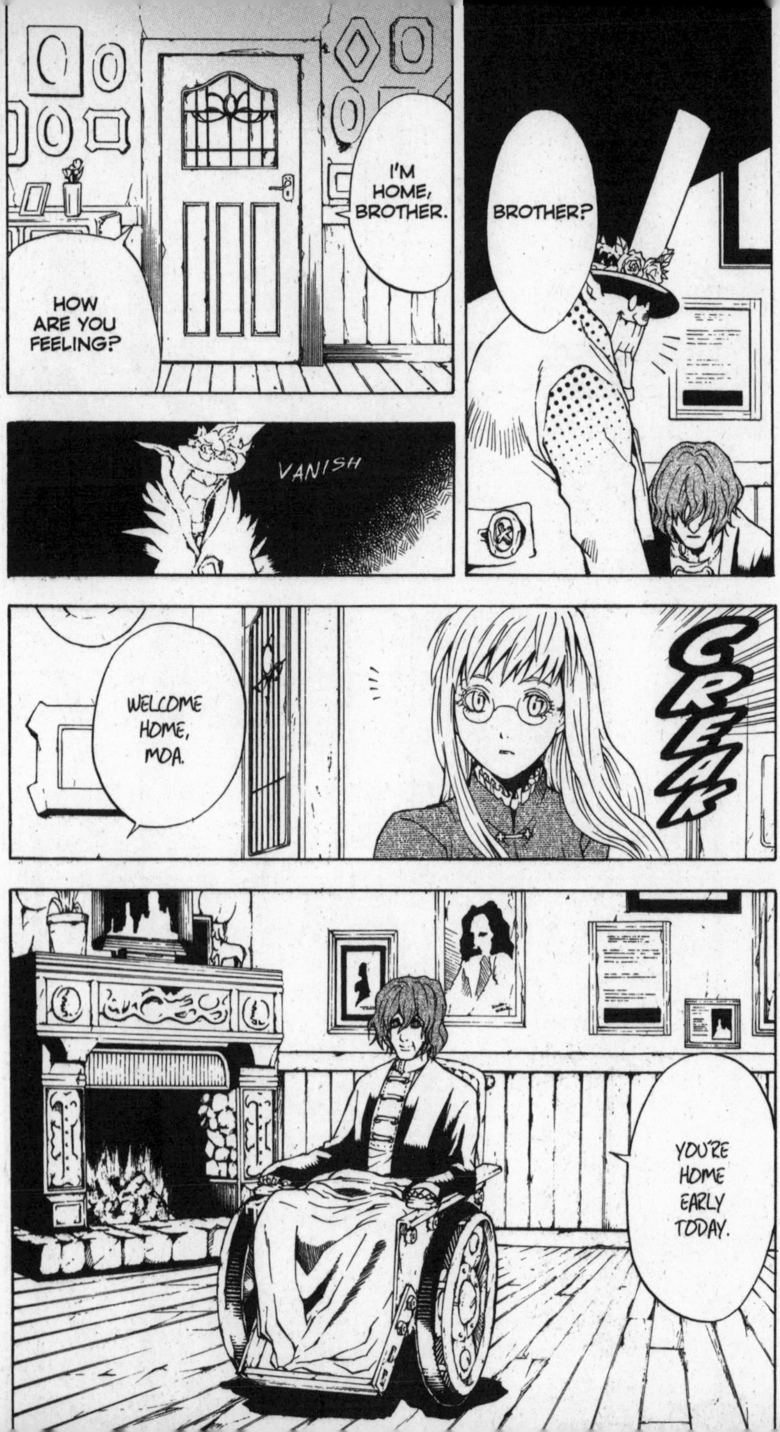
BROTHER?
I'M HOME, BROTHER.
HOW ARE YOU FEELING?
VANISH
CREAK
WELCOME HOME, MOA.
YOU'RE HOME EARLY TODAY.

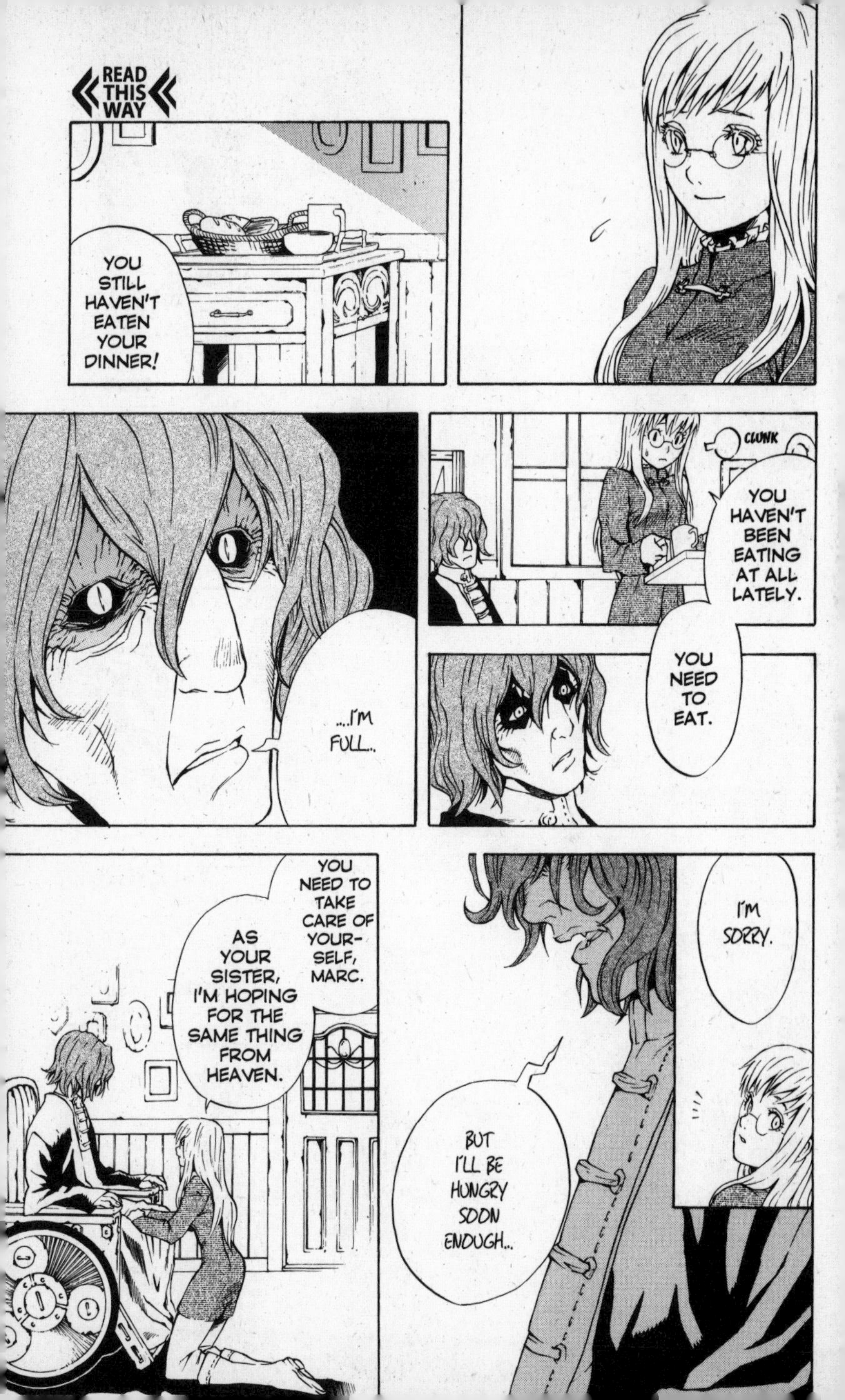
READ THIS WAY
YOU STILL HAVEN'T EATEN YOUR DINNER!
CLUNK
YOU HAVEN'T BEEN EATING AT ALL LATELY.
YOU NEED TO EAT.
...I'M FULL..
I'M SORRY.
BUT I'LL BE HUNGRY SOON ENOUGH...
YOU NEED TO TAKE CARE OF YOUR-SELF, MARC.
AS YOUR SISTER, I'M HOPING FOR THE SAME THING FROM HEAVEN.

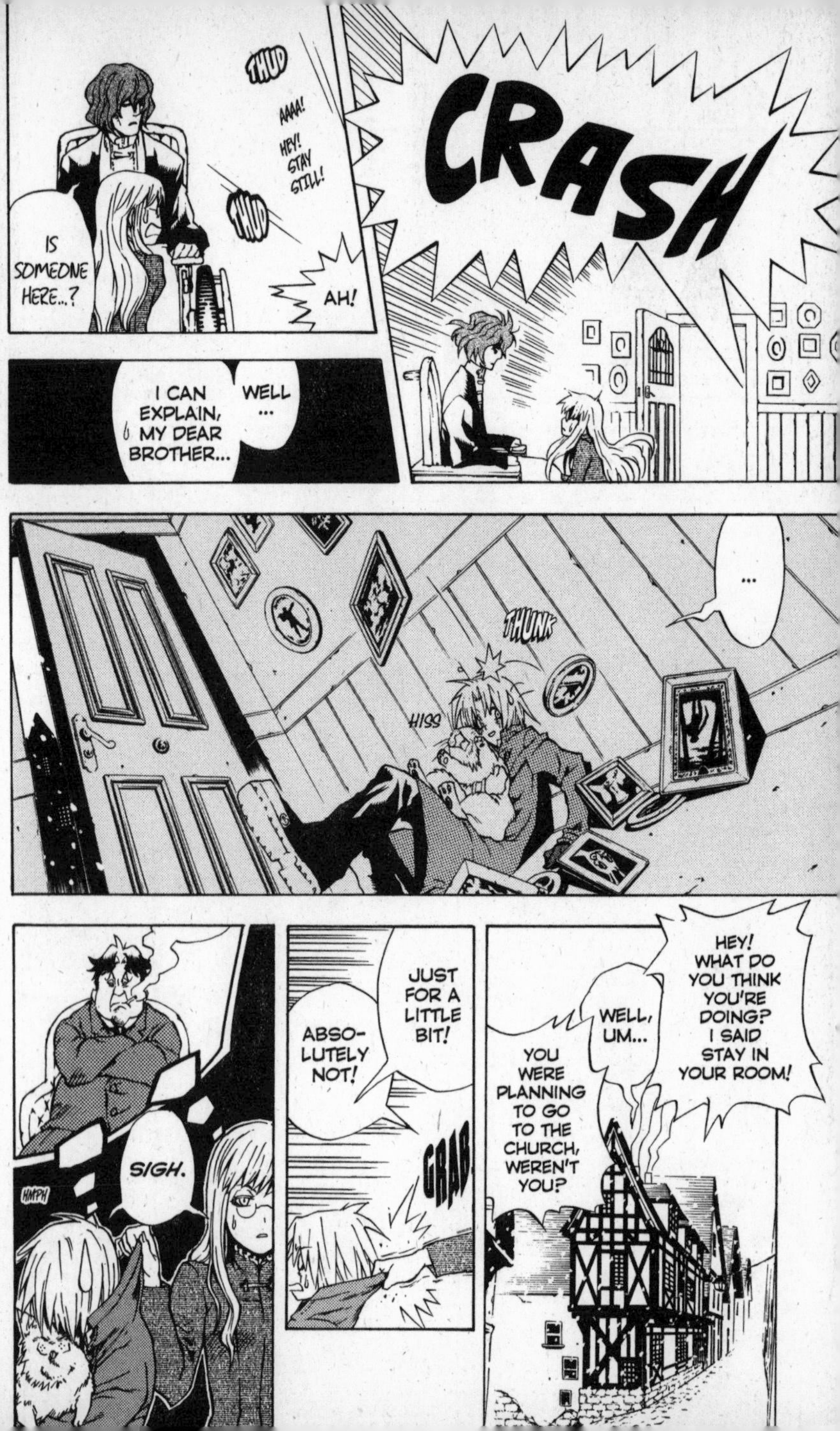
CRASH
THUD
AAAA!
HEY! STAY STILL!
THUD
AH!
IS SOMEONE HERE..?
WELL ...
I CAN EXPLAIN, MY DEAR BROTHER...
...
THUNK
HISS
HEY! WHAT DO YOU THINK YOU'RE DOING? I SAID STAY IN YOUR ROOM!
WELL, UM...
YOU WERE PLANNING TO GO TO THE CHURCH, WEREN'T YOU?
JUST FOR A LITTLE BIT!
ABSO-LUTELY NOT!
GRAB
SIGH.
HMPH

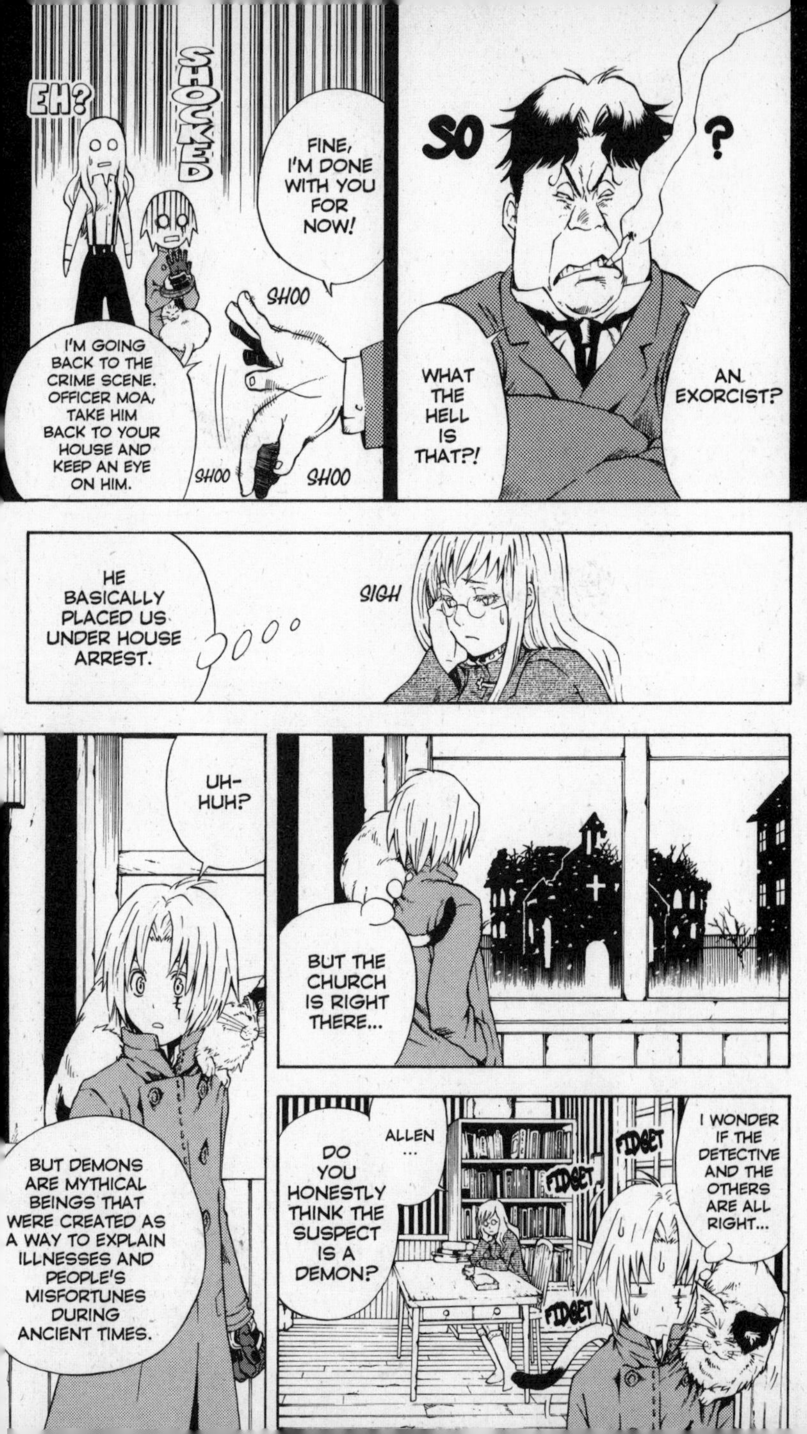
SO
?
AN EXORCIST?
WHAT THE HELL IS THAT?!
FINE, I'M DONE WITH YOU FOR NOW!
SHOCKED
EH?
SHOO
I'M GOING BACK TO THE CRIME SCENE. OFFICER MOA, TAKE HIM BACK TO YOUR HOUSE AND KEEP AN EYE ON HIM.
SHOO
SHOO
SIGH
HE BASICALLY PLACED US UNDER HOUSE ARREST.
BUT THE CHURCH IS RIGHT THERE...
I WONDER IF THE DETECTIVE AND THE OTHERS ARE ALL RIGHT...
FIDGET
FIDGET
FIDGET
ALLEN ...
DO YOU HONESTLY THINK THE SUSPECT IS A DEMON?
UH-HUH?
BUT DEMONS ARE MYTHICAL BEINGS THAT WERE CREATED AS A WAY TO EXPLAIN ILLNESSES AND PEOPLE'S MISFORTUNES DURING ANCIENT TIMES.

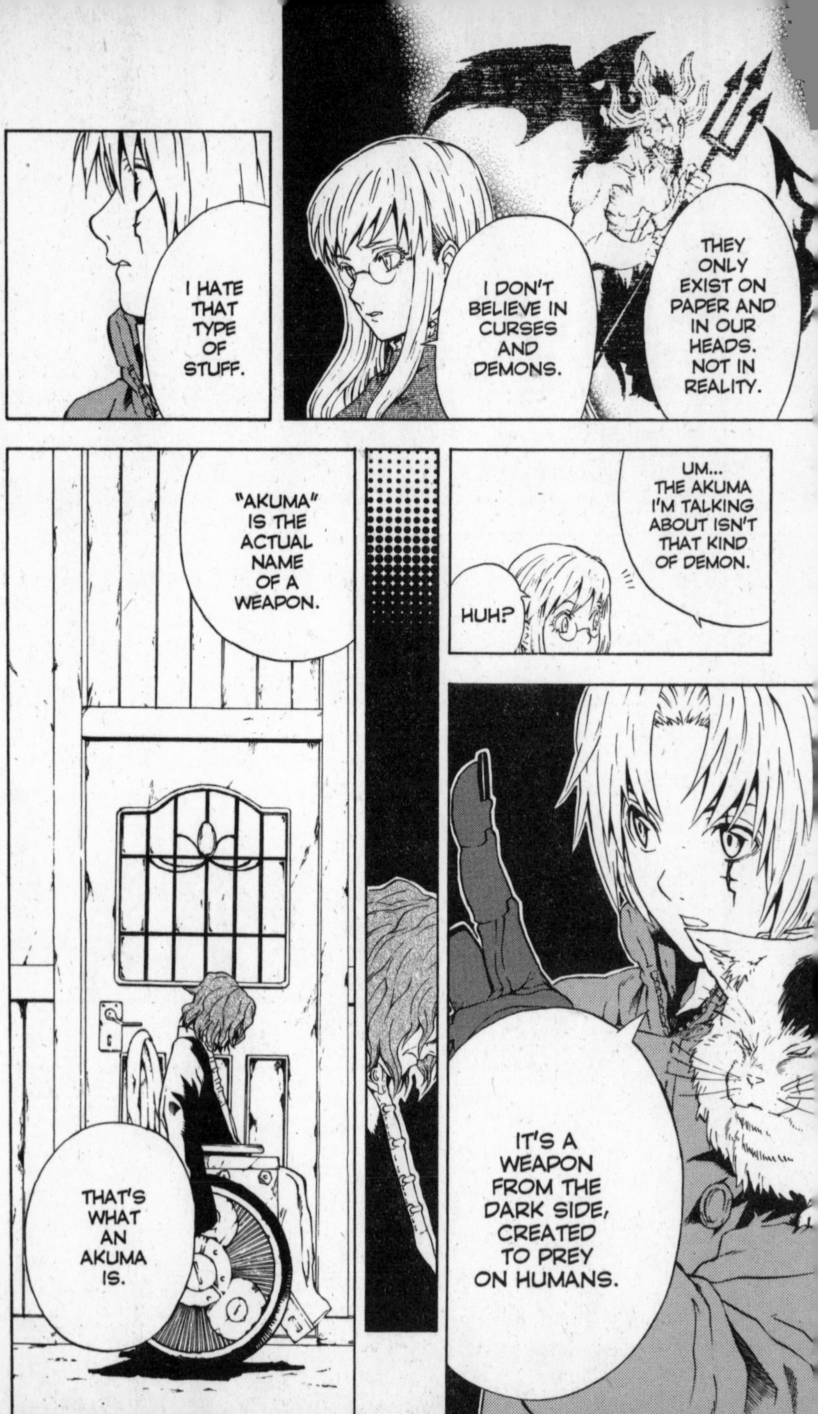
I DON'T BELIEVE IN CURSES AND DEMONS.
THEY ONLY EXIST ON PAPER AND IN OUR HEADS. NOT IN REALITY.
I HATE THAT TYPE OF STUFF.
UM... THE AKUMA I'M TALKING ABOUT ISN'T THAT KIND OF DEMON.
HUH?
IT'S A WEAPON FROM THE DARK SIDE, CREATED TO PREY ON HUMANS.
"AKUMA" IS THE ACTUAL NAME OF A WEAPON.
THAT'S WHAT AN AKUMA IS.

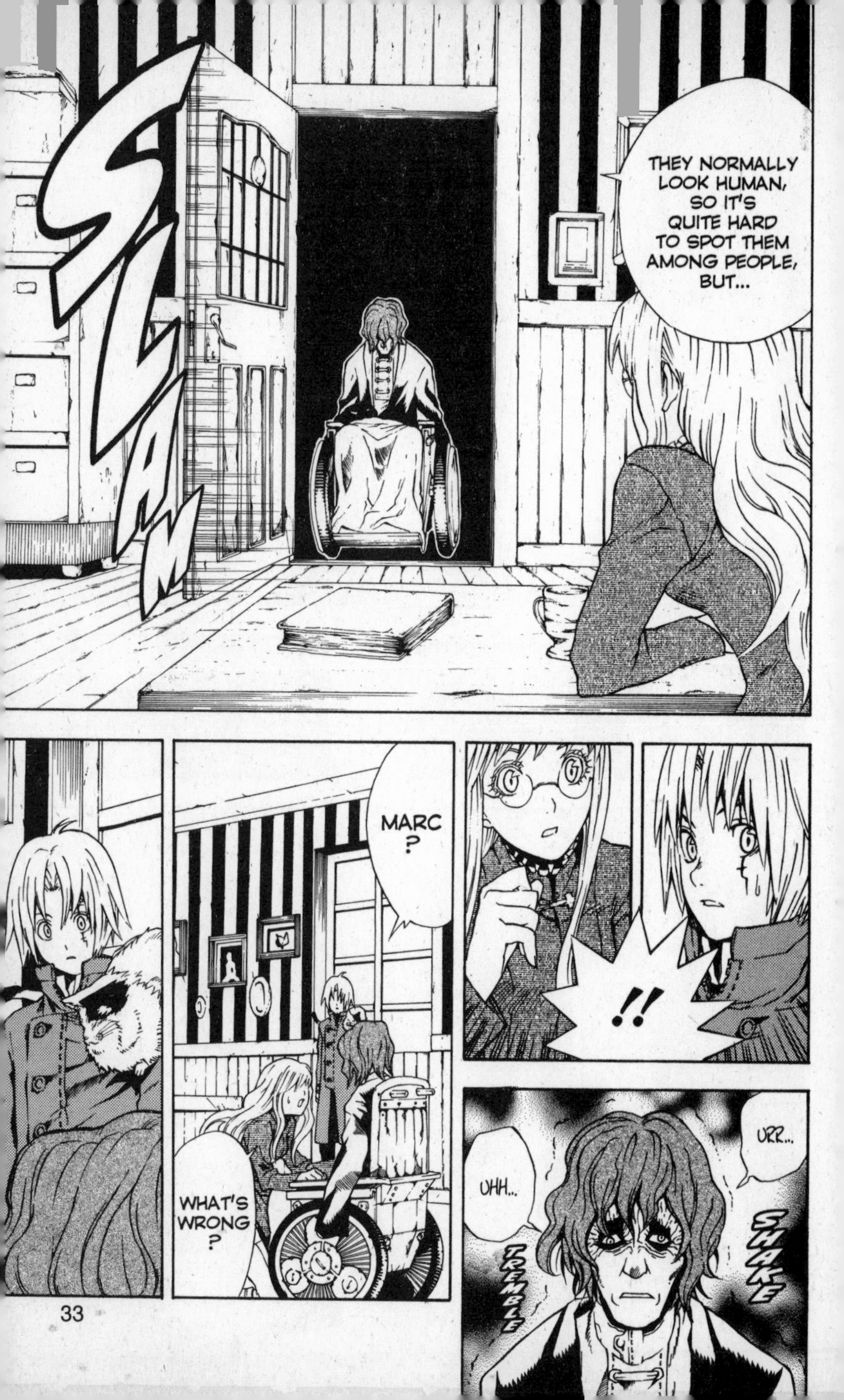
THEY NORMALLY LOOK HUMAN, SO IT'S QUITE HARD TO SPOT THEM AMONG PEOPLE, BUT...
SLAM
!!
URR...
UHH...
SHAKE
TREMBLE
MARC ?
WHAT'S WRONG ?

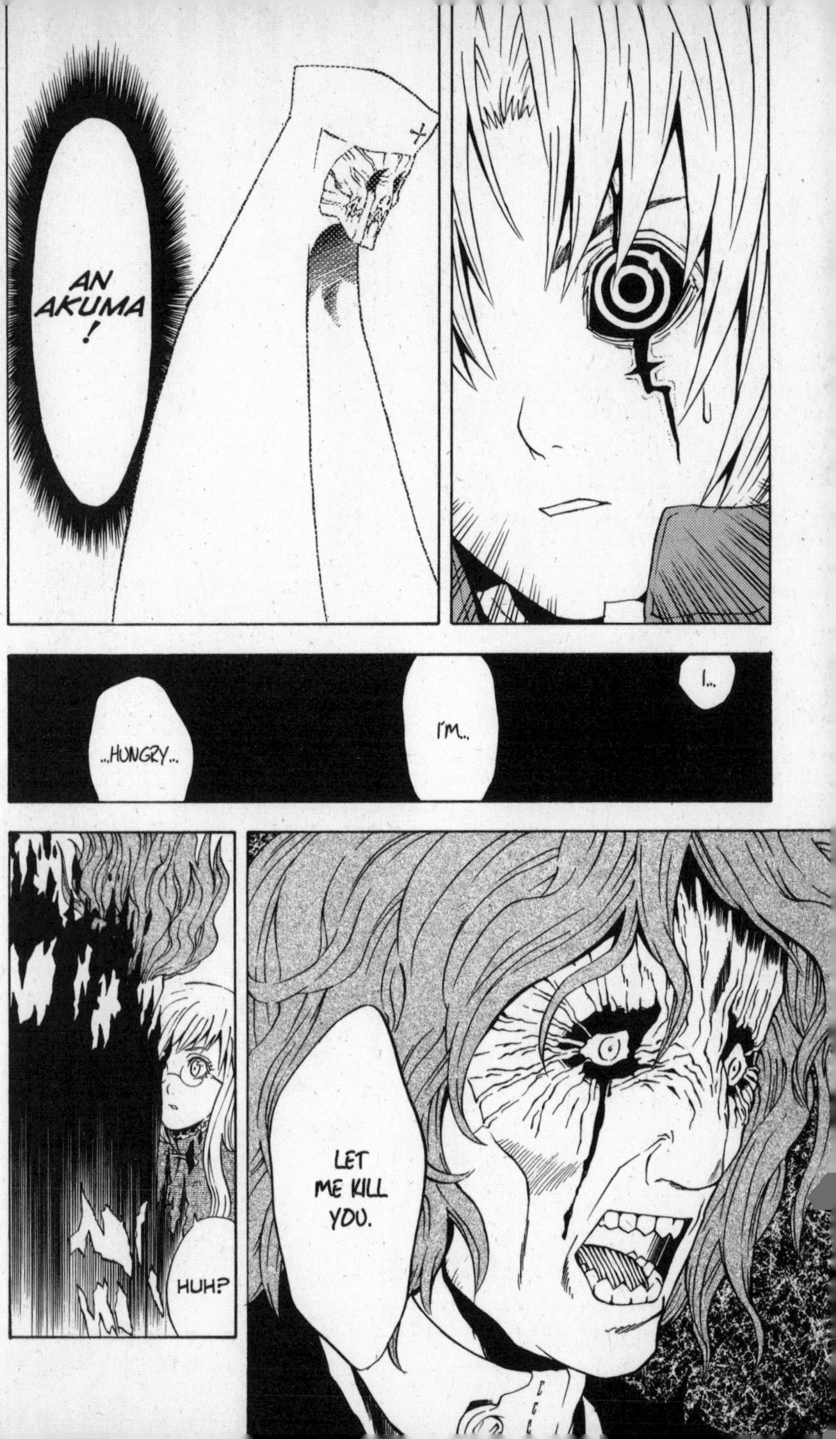
AN AKUMA!
I...
I'M...
...HUNGRY...
LET ME KILL YOU.
HUH?

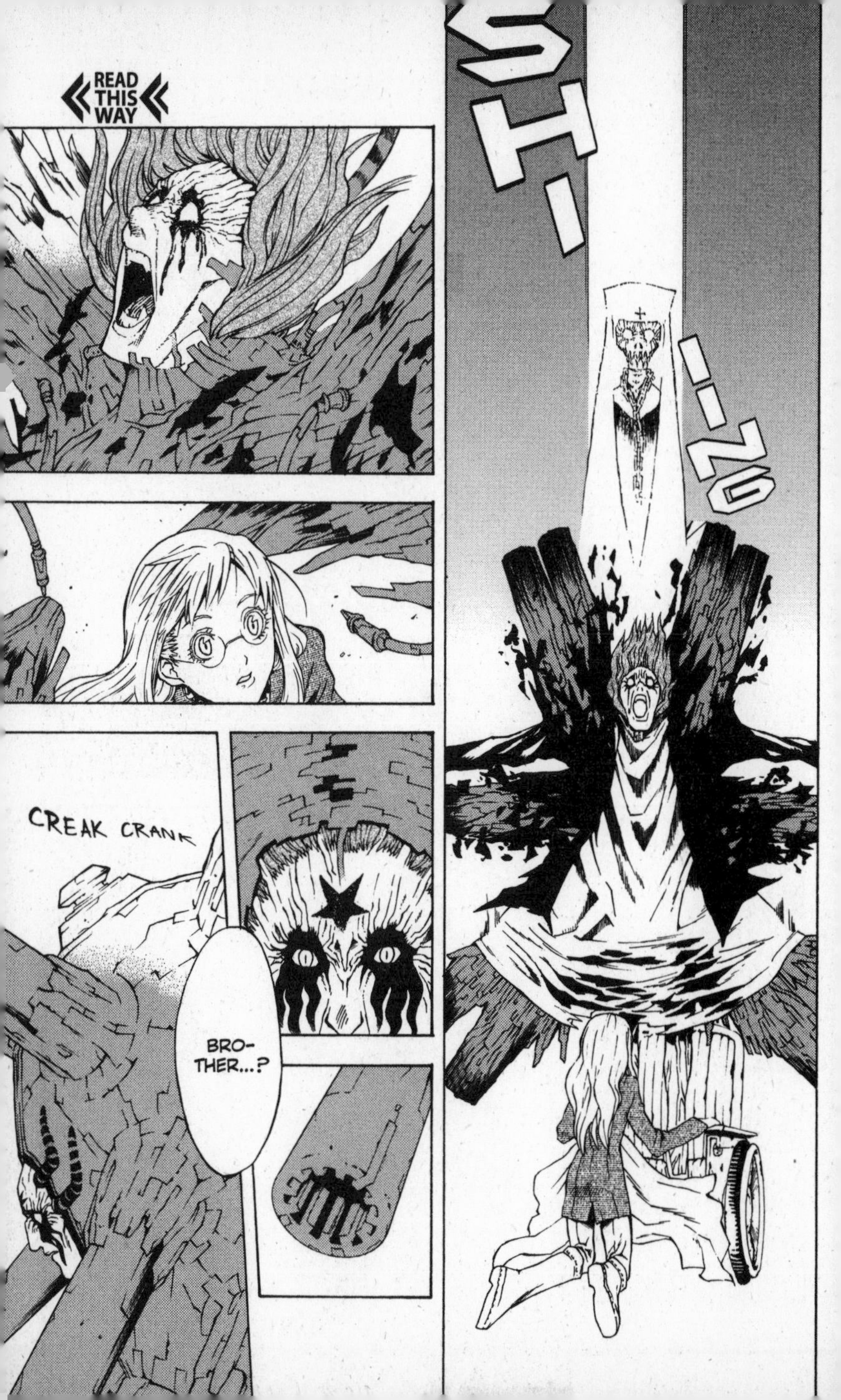
READ THIS WAY
SHI-I-NG
CREAK CRANK
BRO-THER...?

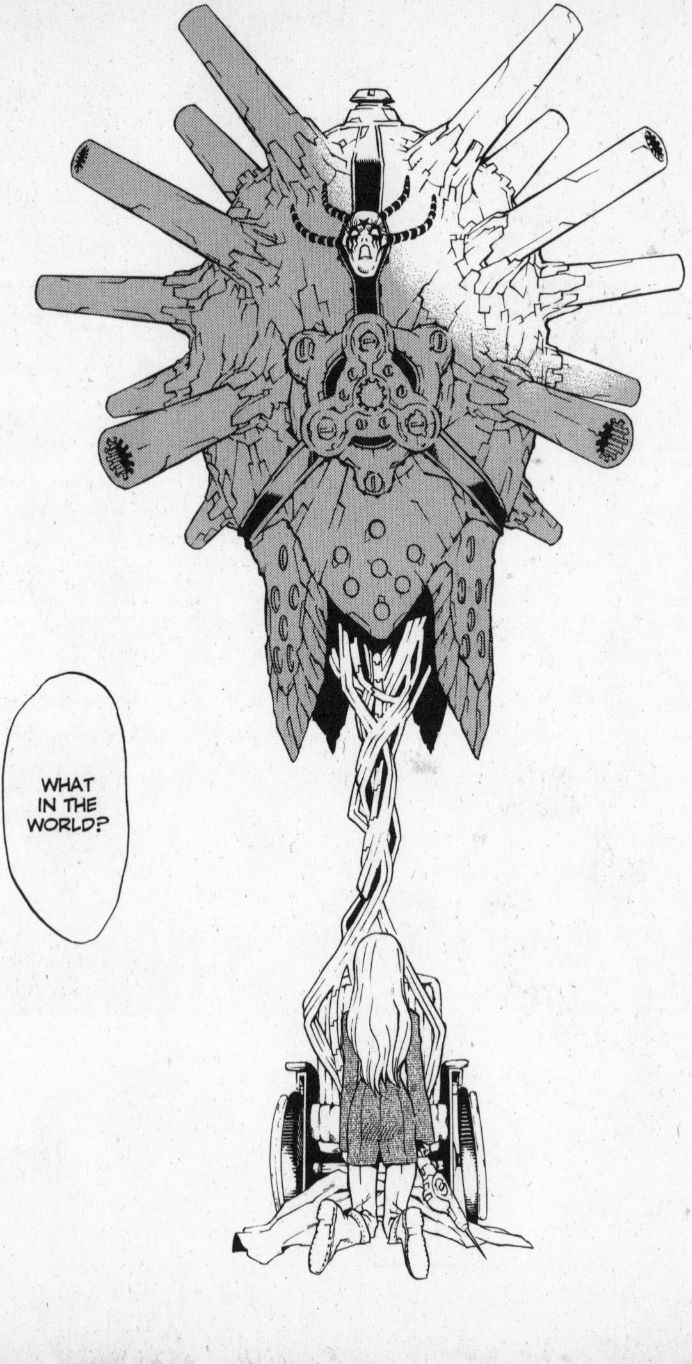
WHAT IN THE WORLD?

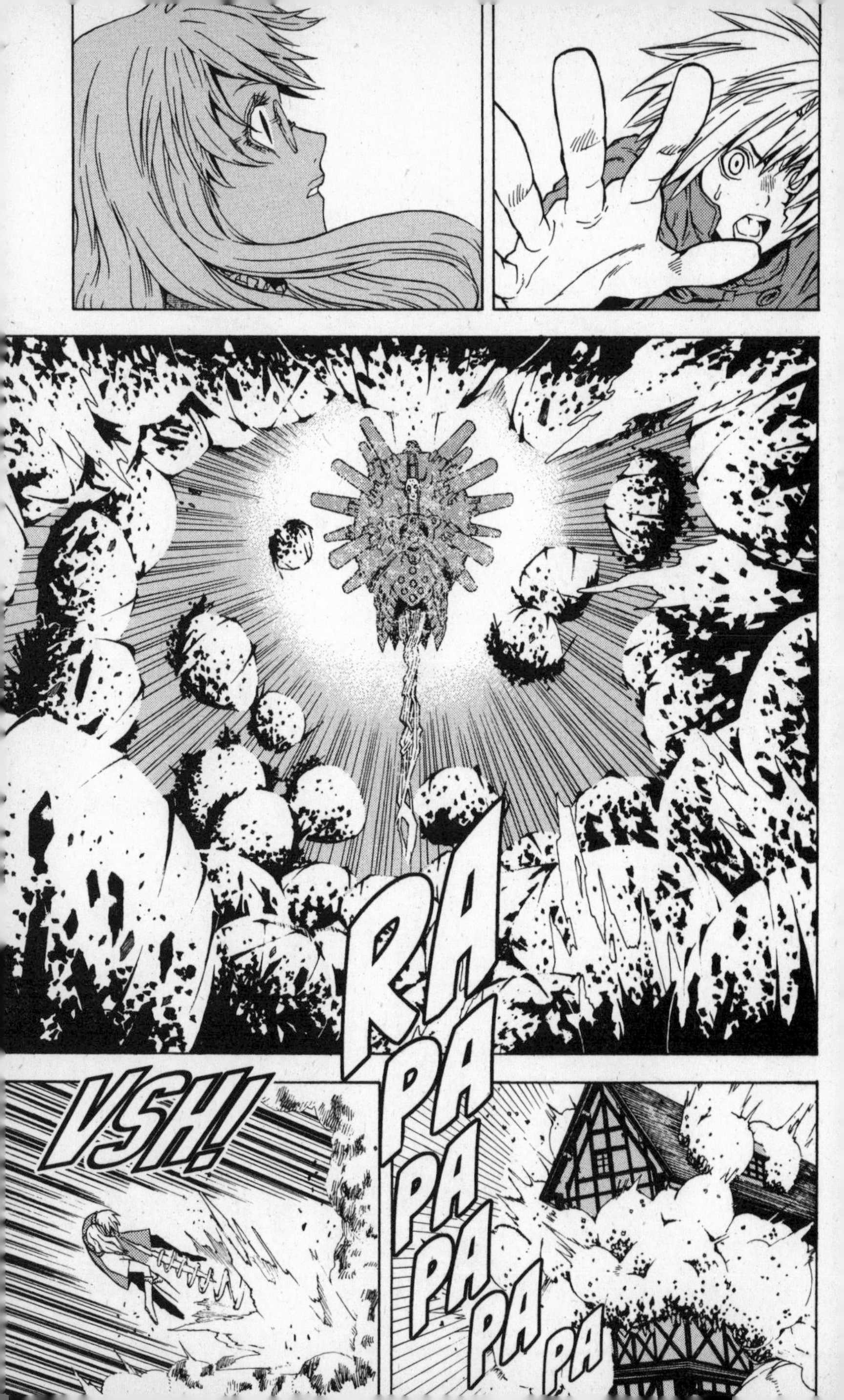
RA PA PA PA PA PA PA PA
VSH!

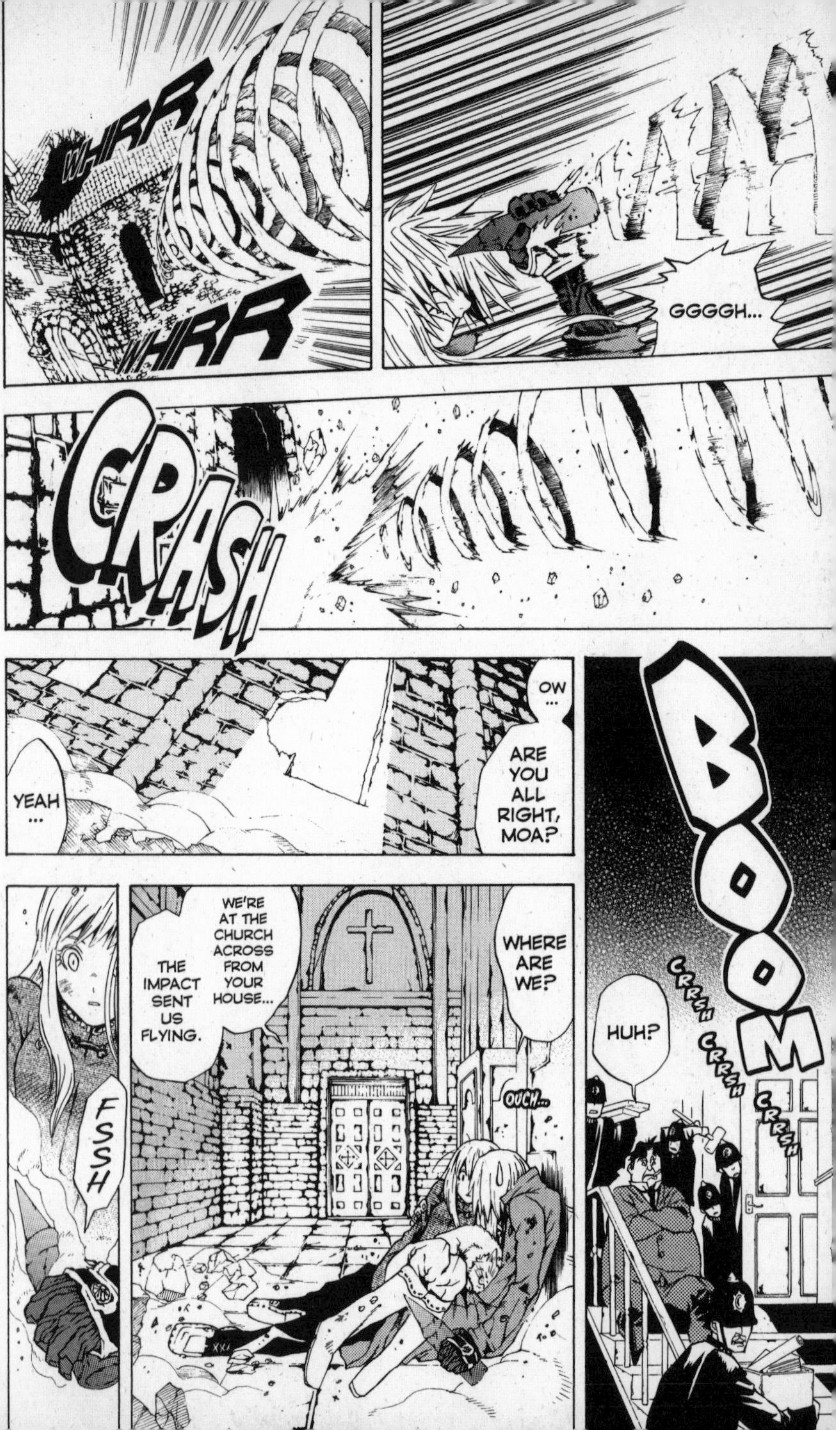
GGGGH...
WHIRR
WHIRR
CRASH
BOOM
CRRSH
CRRSH
CRRSH
HUH?
OW...
ARE YOU ALL RIGHT, MOA?
YEAH...
WHERE ARE WE?
WE'RE AT THE CHURCH ACROSS FROM YOUR HOUSE...
THE IMPACT SENT US FLYING.
OUCH...
FSSH

READ THIS WAY

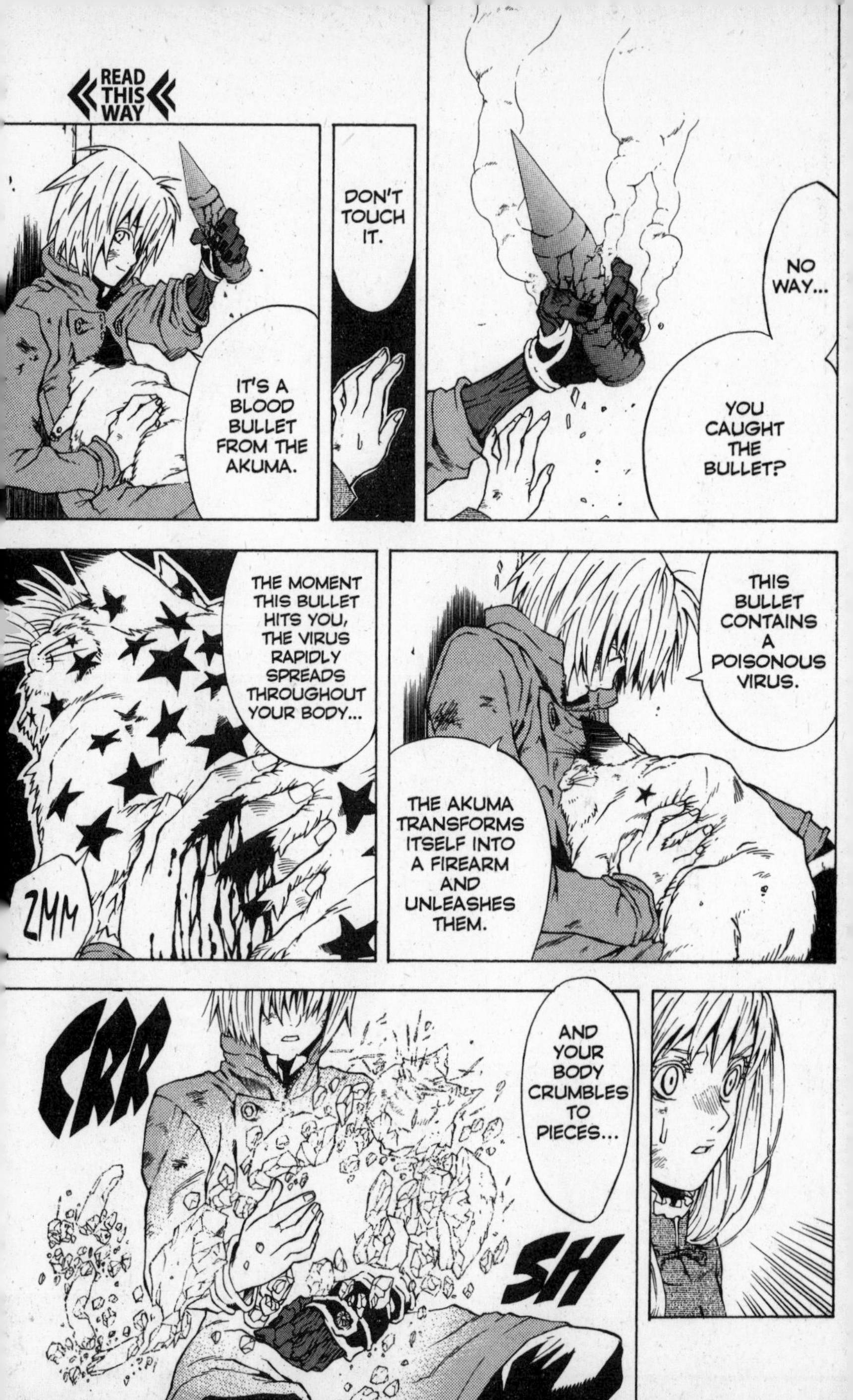
NO WAY...
YOU CAUGHT THE BULLET?
DON'T TOUCH IT.
IT'S A BLOOD BULLET FROM THE AKUMA.
THIS BULLET CONTAINS A POISONOUS VIRUS.
THE AKUMA TRANSFORMS ITSELF INTO A FIREARM AND UNLEASHES THEM.
THE MOMENT THIS BULLET HITS YOU, THE VIRUS RAPIDLY SPREADS THROUGHOUT YOUR BODY...
ZMM
AND YOUR BODY CRUMBLES TO PIECES...
CRR
SH

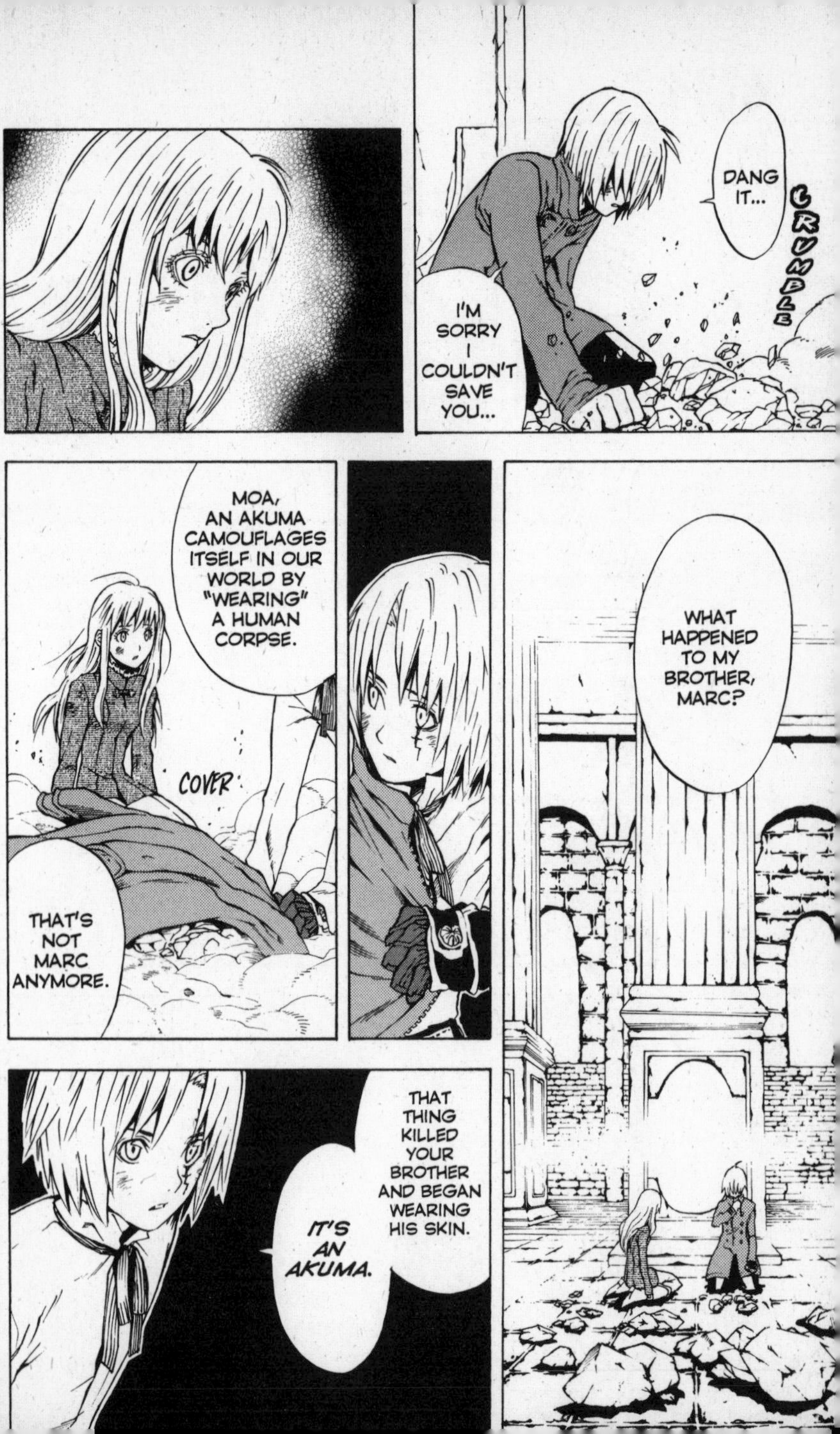

DANG IT...
CRUMBLE
I'M SORRY I COULDN'T SAVE YOU...
WHAT HAPPENED TO MY BROTHER, MARC?
MOA, AN AKUMA CAMOUFLAGES ITSELF IN OUR WORLD BY "WEARING" A HUMAN CORPSE.
COVER
THAT'S NOT MARC ANYMORE.
THAT THING KILLED YOUR BROTHER AND BEGAN WEARING HIS SKIN.
IT'S AN AKUMA.

YANK

MY BROTHER... WAS MURDERED?

IT'S HERE.

?!

HEY! WHAT ARE YOU TWO DOING HERE?!

WHAT THE HELL IS THAT?

DETECTIVE?

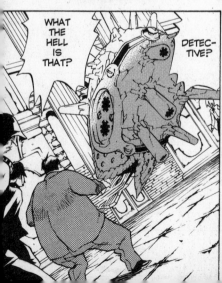

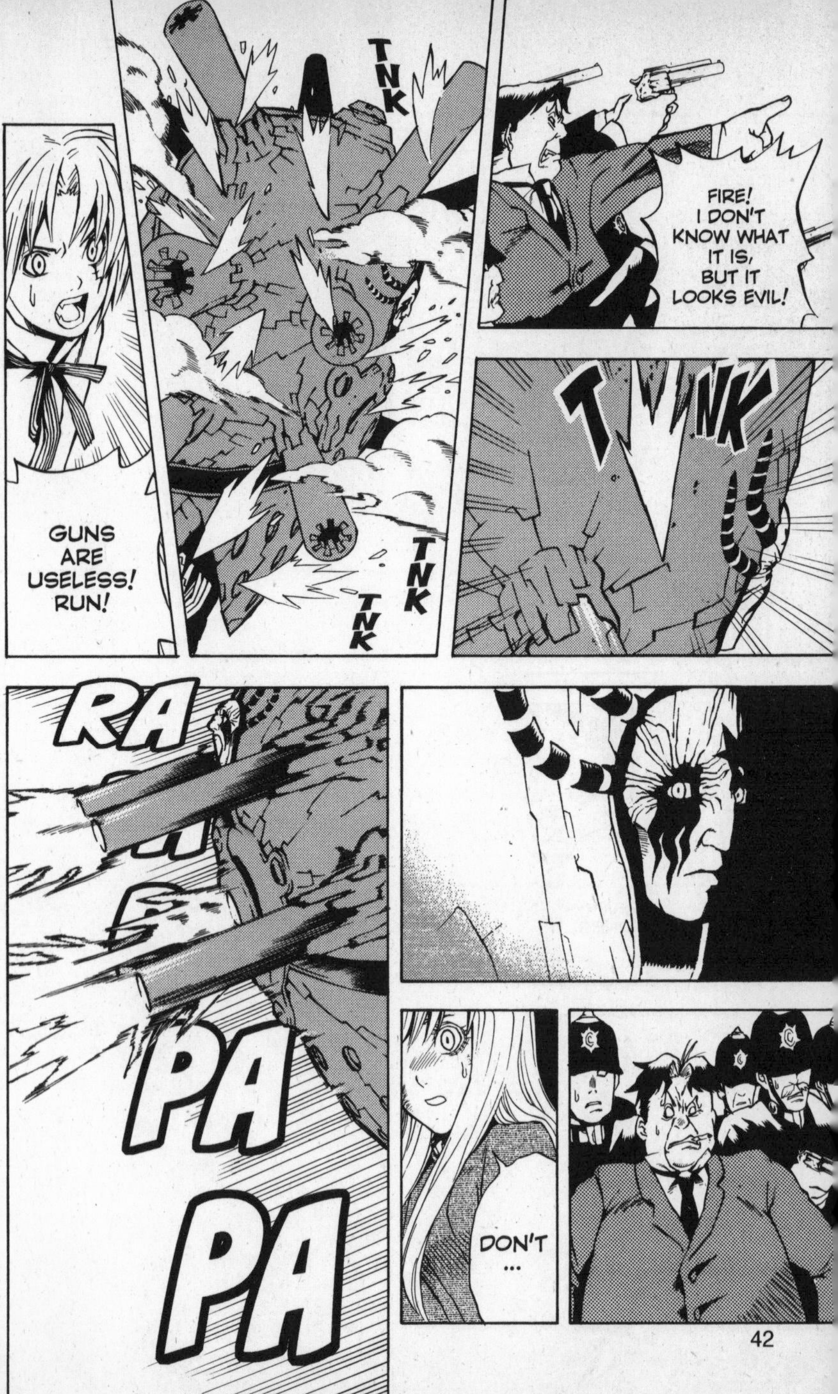
FIRE! I DON'T KNOW WHAT IT IS, BUT IT LOOKS EVIL!
TNK
TNK
TNK
TNK
GUNS ARE USELESS! RUN!
DON'T ...
RA
PA
PA

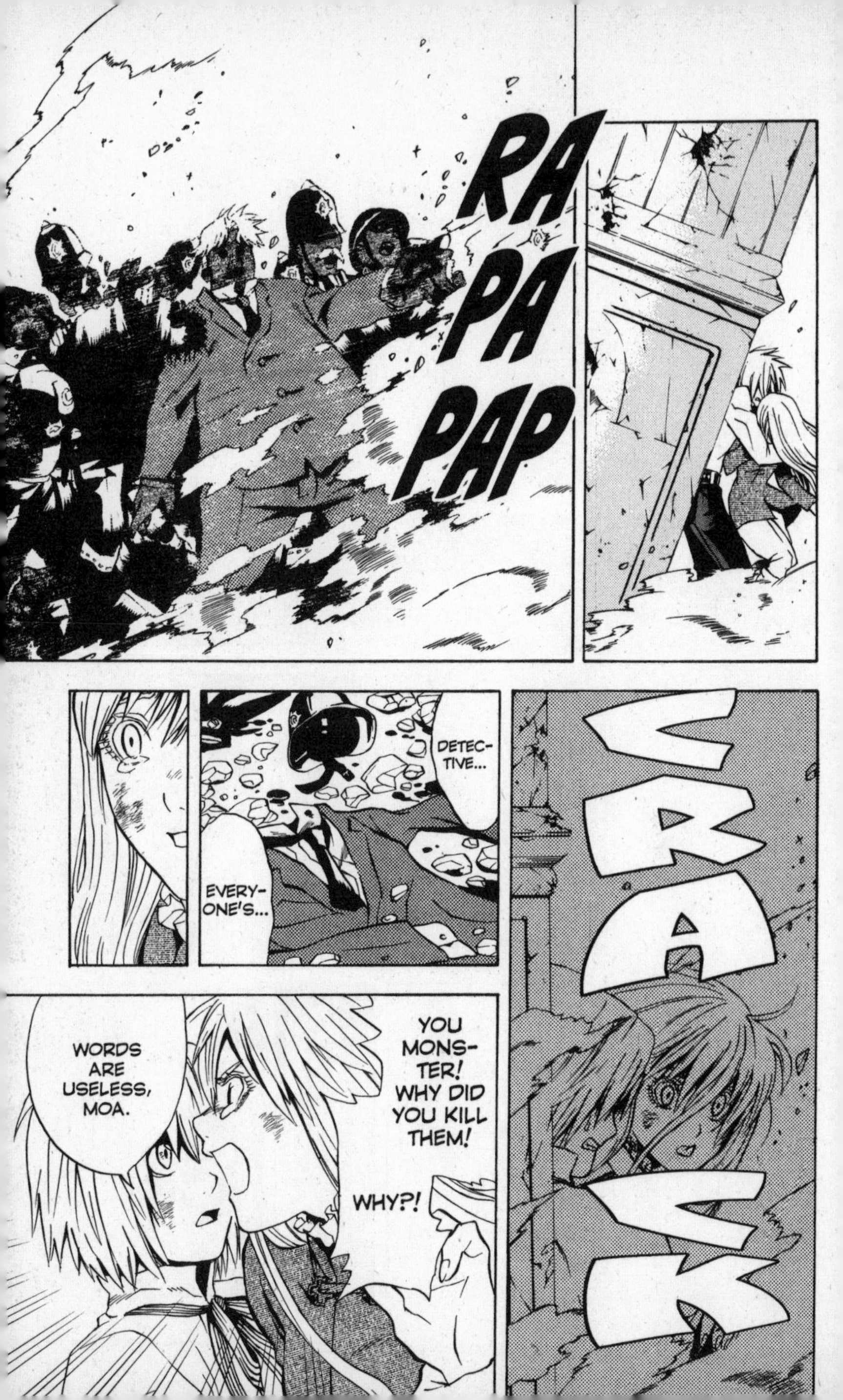
RA PA PAP
VRAKK
DETECTIVE...
EVERYONE'S...
YOU MONSTER! WHY DID YOU KILL THEM!
WHY?!
WORDS ARE USELESS, MOA.

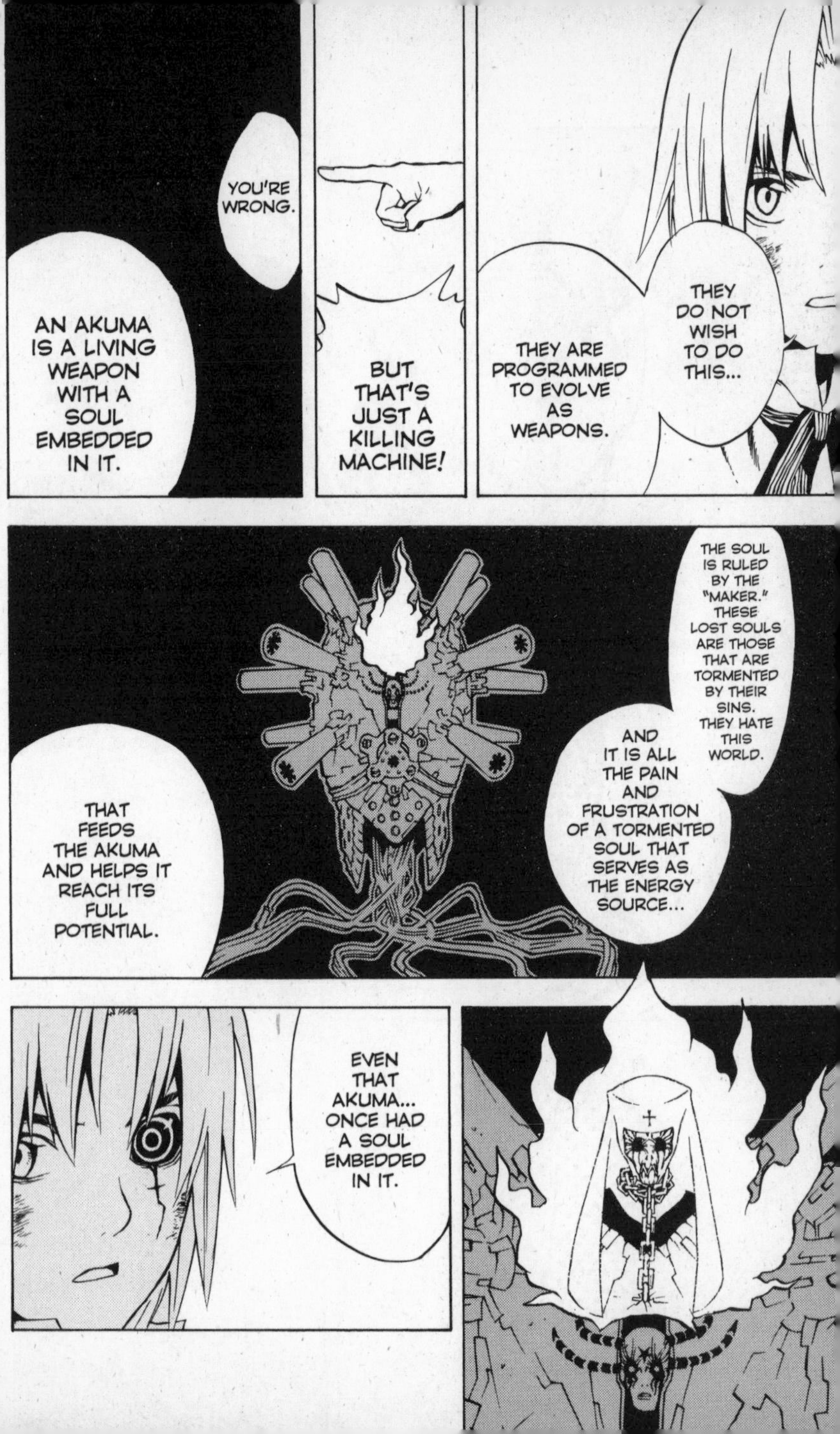
THEY DO NOT WISH TO DO THIS...
THEY ARE PROGRAMMED TO EVOLVE AS WEAPONS.
BUT THAT'S JUST A KILLING MACHINE!
YOU'RE WRONG.
AN AKUMA IS A LIVING WEAPON WITH A SOUL EMBEDDED IN IT.
THE SOUL IS RULED BY THE "MAKER." THESE LOST SOULS ARE THOSE THAT ARE TORMENTED BY THEIR SINS. THEY HATE THIS WORLD.
AND IT IS ALL THE PAIN AND FRUSTRATION OF A TORMENTED SOUL THAT SERVES AS THE ENERGY SOURCE...
THAT FEEDS THE AKUMA AND HELPS IT REACH ITS FULL POTENTIAL.
EVEN THAT AKUMA... ONCE HAD A SOUL EMBEDDED IN IT.

READ THIS WAY

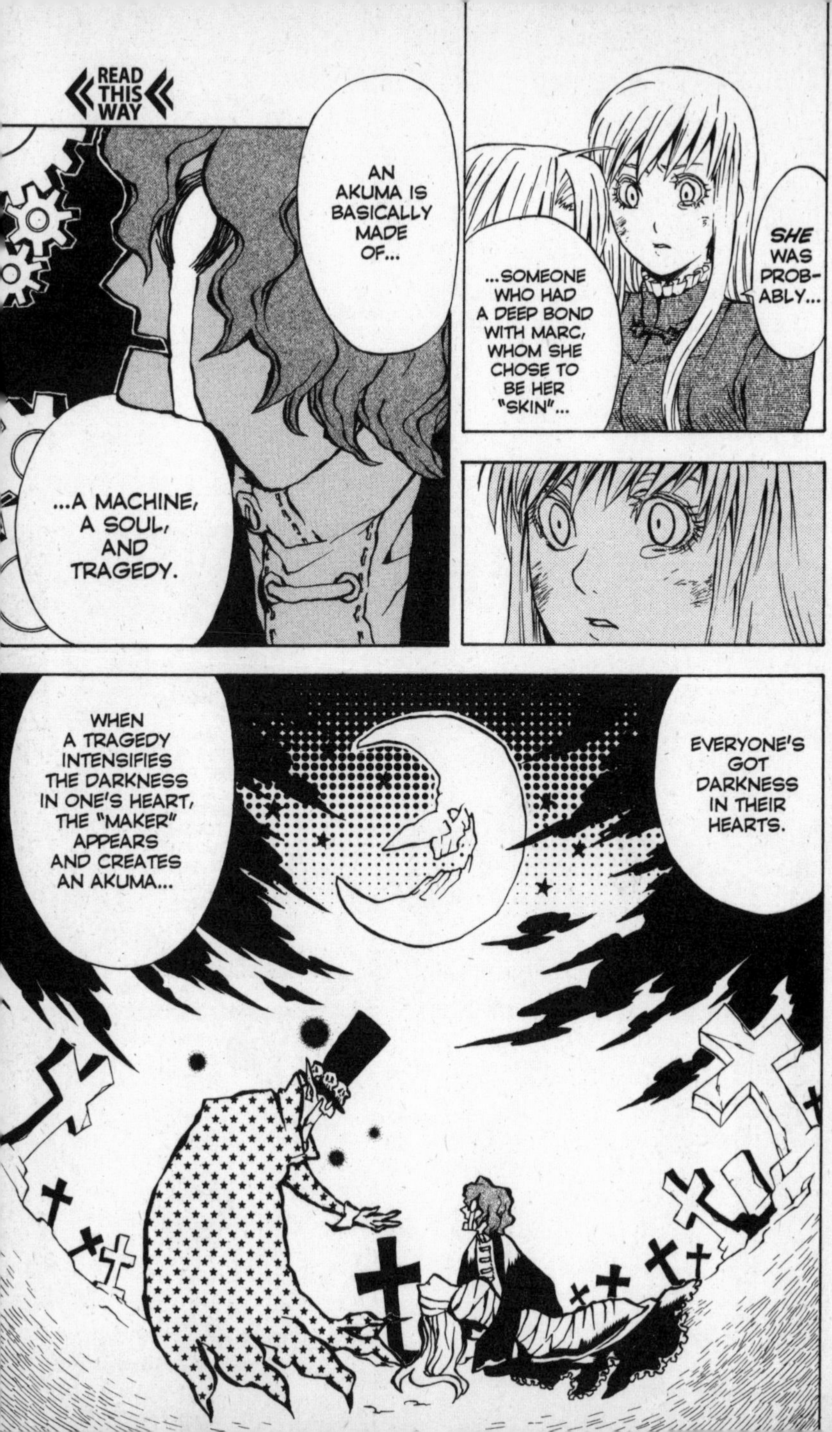
SHE WAS PROBABLY...
...SOMEONE WHO HAD A DEEP BOND WITH MARC, WHOM SHE CHOSE TO BE HER "SKIN"...
AN AKUMA IS BASICALLY MADE OF...
...A MACHINE, A SOUL, AND TRAGEDY.
EVERYONE'S GOT DARKNESS IN THEIR HEARTS.
WHEN A TRAGEDY INTENSIFIES THE DARKNESS IN ONE'S HEART, THE "MAKER" APPEARS AND CREATES AN AKUMA...

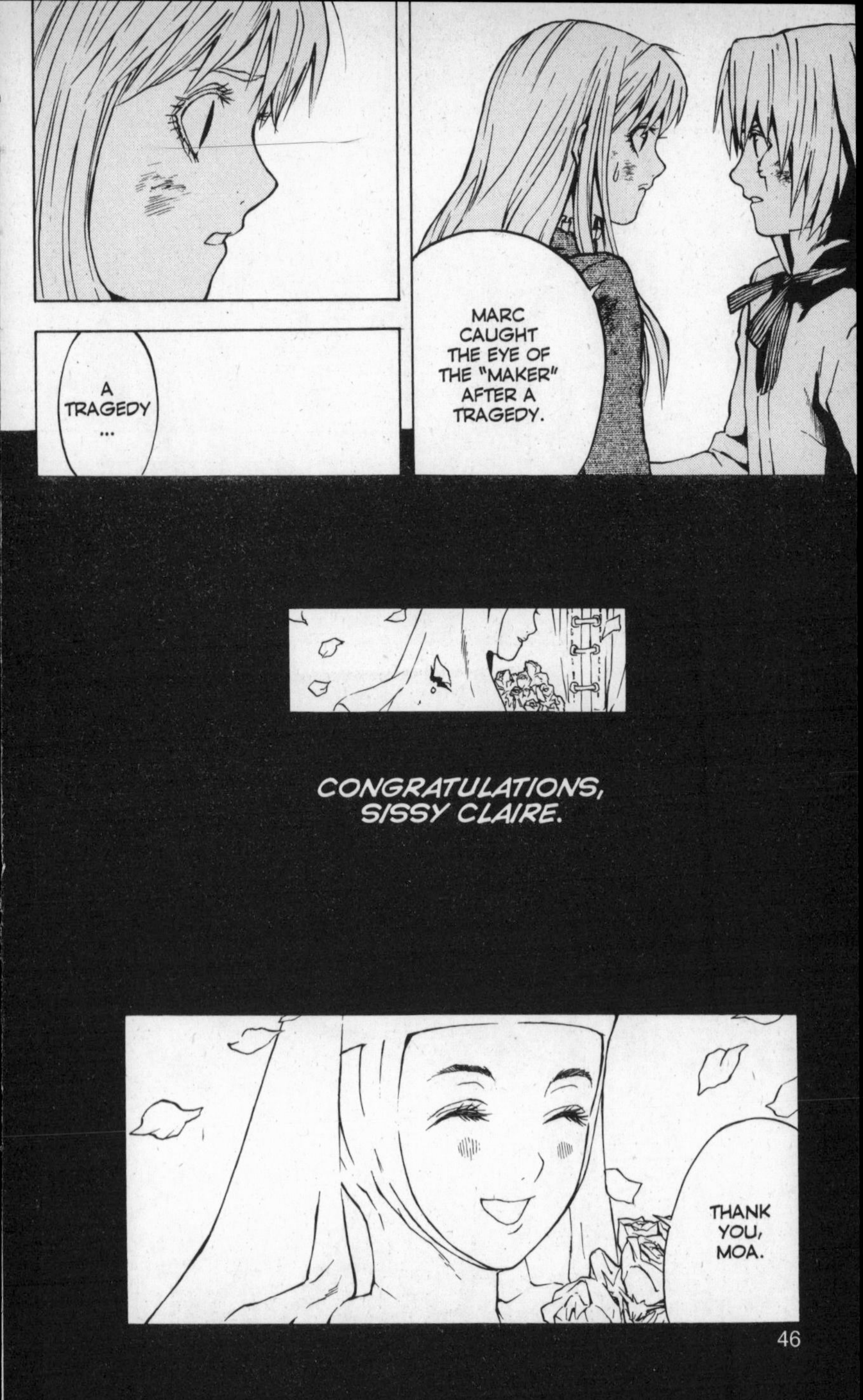
MARC CAUGHT THE EYE OF THE "MAKER" AFTER A TRAGEDY.
A TRAGEDY ...
CONGRATULATIONS, SISSY CLAIRE.
THANK YOU, MOA.

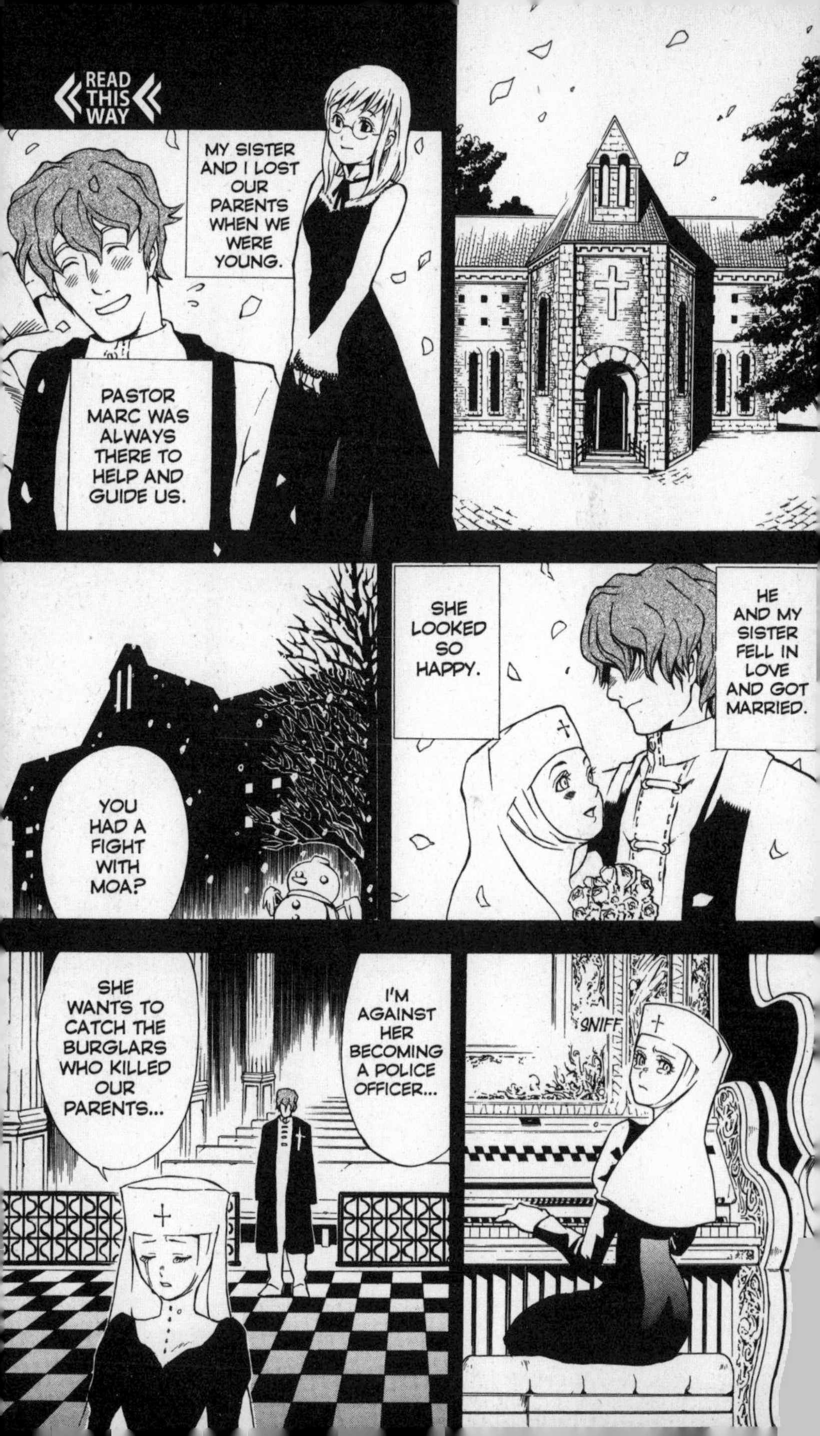
READ THIS WAY
MY SISTER AND I LOST OUR PARENTS WHEN WE WERE YOUNG.
PASTOR MARC WAS ALWAYS THERE TO HELP AND GUIDE US.
HE AND MY SISTER FELL IN LOVE AND GOT MARRIED.
SHE LOOKED SO HAPPY.
YOU HAD A FIGHT WITH MOA?
SNIFF
I'M AGAINST HER BECOMING A POLICE OFFICER...
SHE WANTS TO CATCH THE BURGLARS WHO KILLED OUR PARENTS...

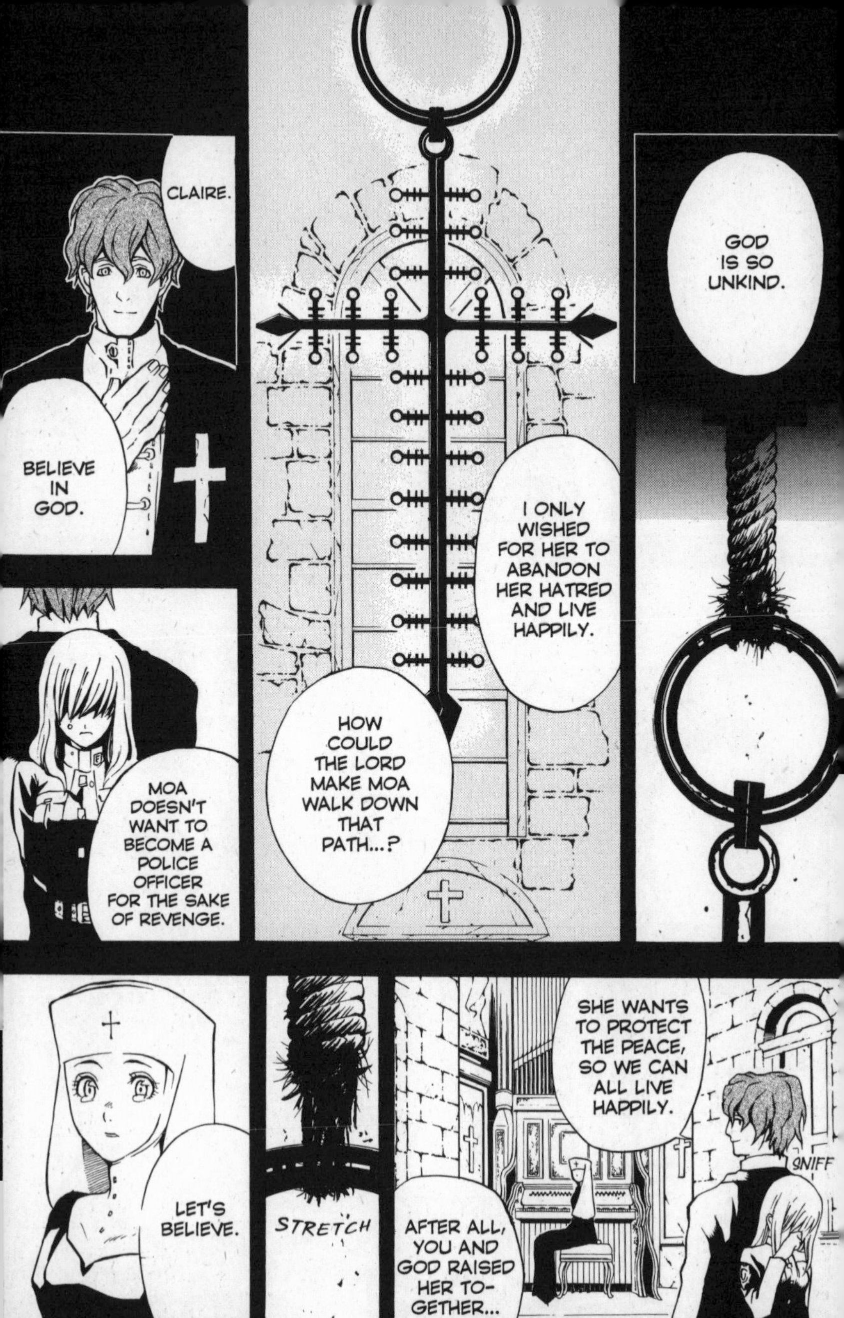
GOD IS SO UNKIND.
I ONLY WISHED FOR HER TO ABANDON HER HATRED AND LIVE HAPPILY.
HOW COULD THE LORD MAKE MOA WALK DOWN THAT PATH...?
CLAIRE.
BELIEVE IN GOD.
MOA DOESN'T WANT TO BECOME A POLICE OFFICER FOR THE SAKE OF REVENGE.
SNIFF
SHE WANTS TO PROTECT THE PEACE, SO WE CAN ALL LIVE HAPPILY.
AFTER ALL, YOU AND GOD RAISED HER TO-GETHER...
STRETCH
LET'S BELIEVE.

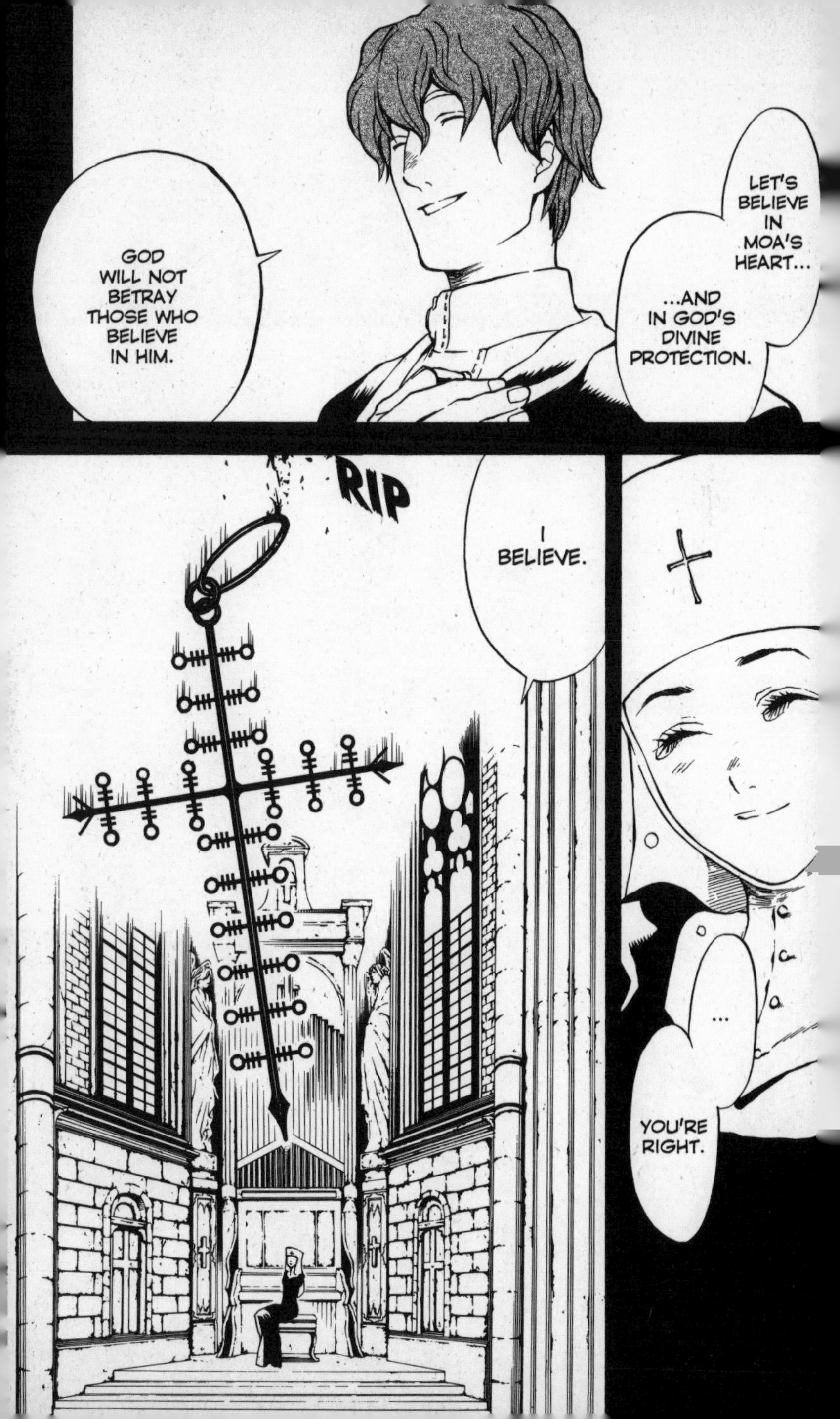
LET'S BELIEVE IN MOA'S HEART...
...AND IN GOD'S DIVINE PROTECTION.
GOD WILL NOT BETRAY THOSE WHO BELIEVE IN HIM.
...
YOU'RE RIGHT.
I BELIEVE.
RIP

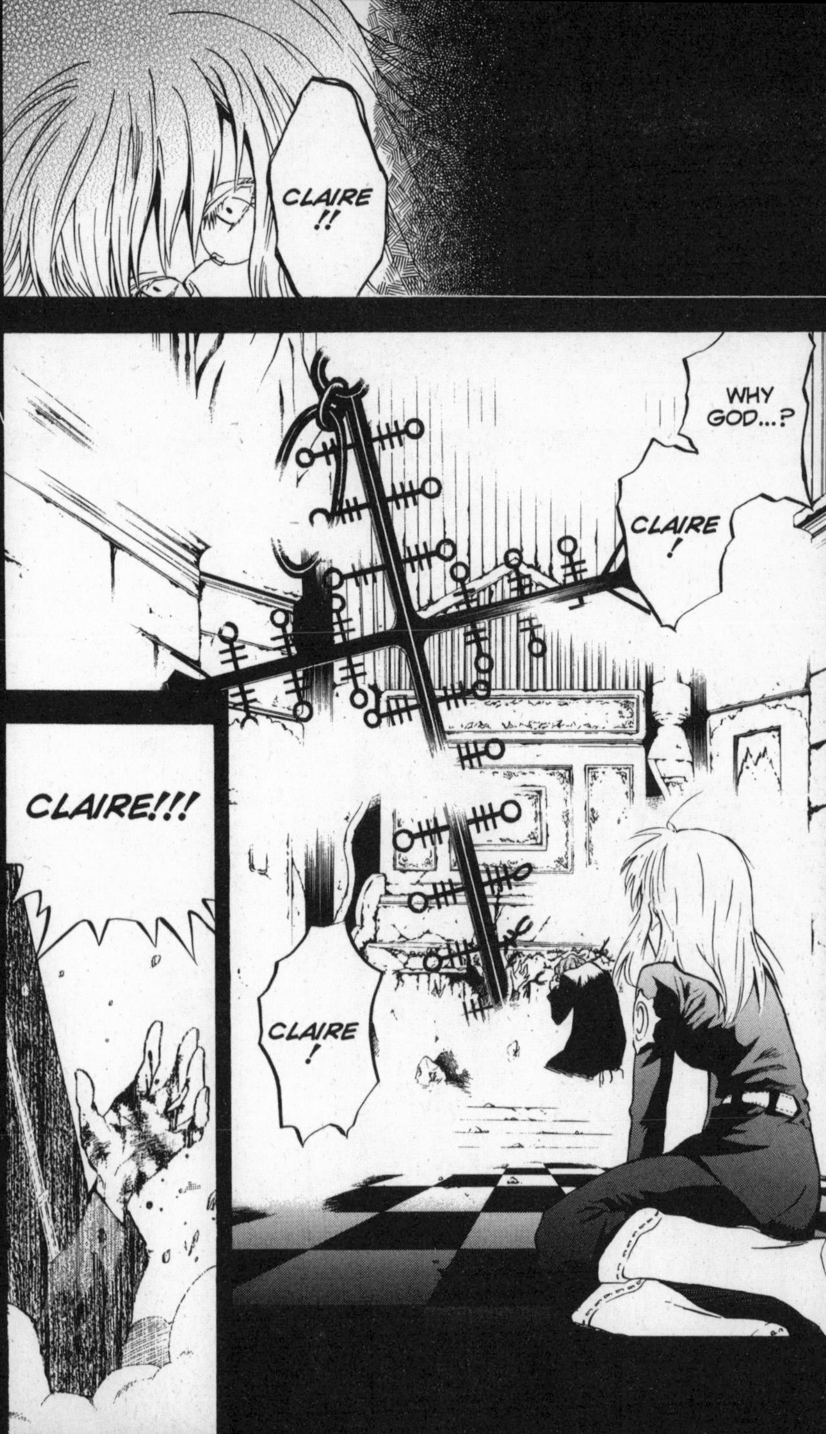
CLAIRE !!
WHY GOD...?
CLAIRE !
CLAIRE !
CLAIRE!!!

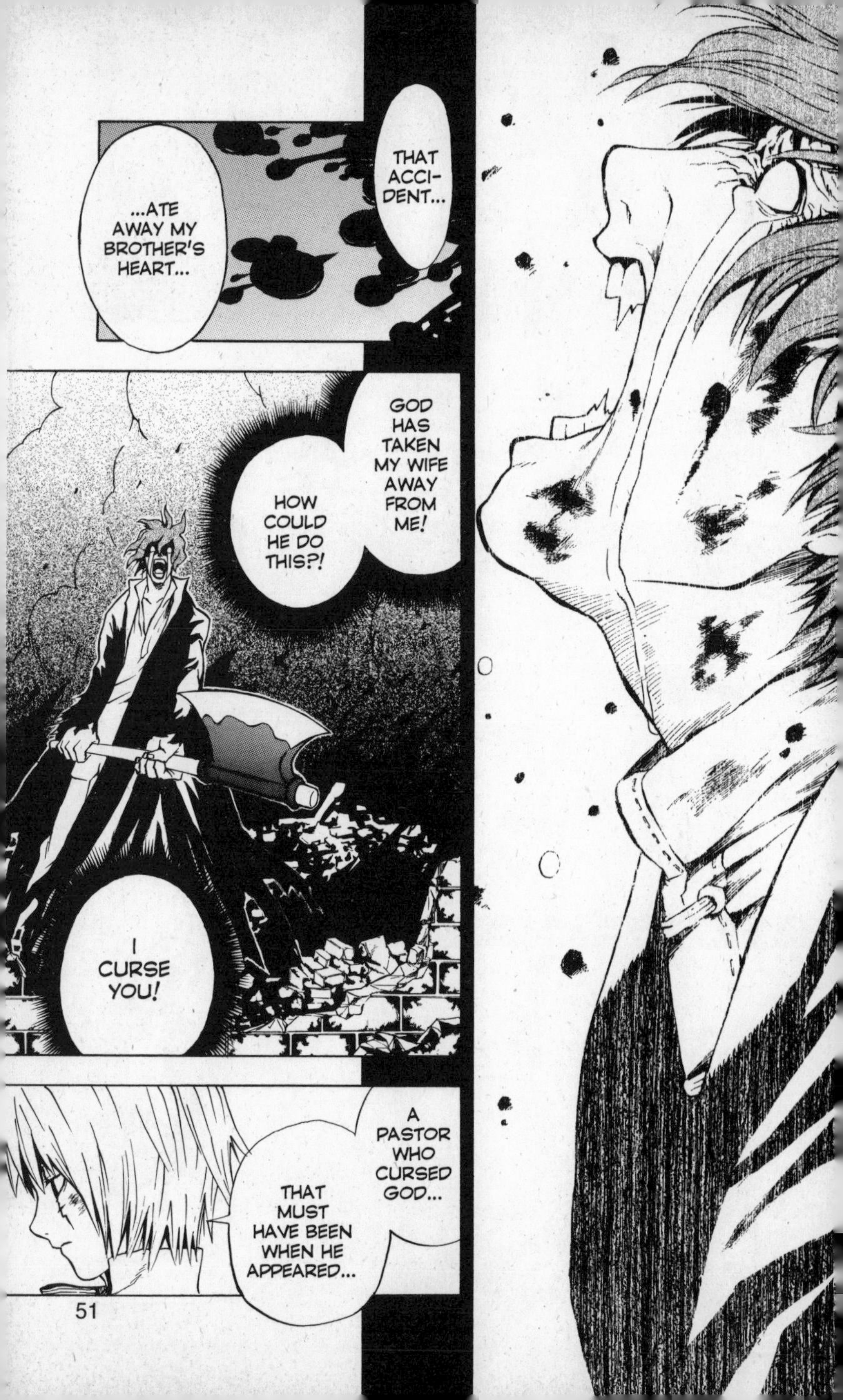
THAT ACCI-DENT...
...ATE AWAY MY BROTHER'S HEART...
GOD HAS TAKEN MY WIFE AWAY FROM ME!
HOW COULD HE DO THIS?!
I CURSE YOU!
A PASTOR WHO CURSED GOD...
THAT MUST HAVE BEEN WHEN HE APPEARED...

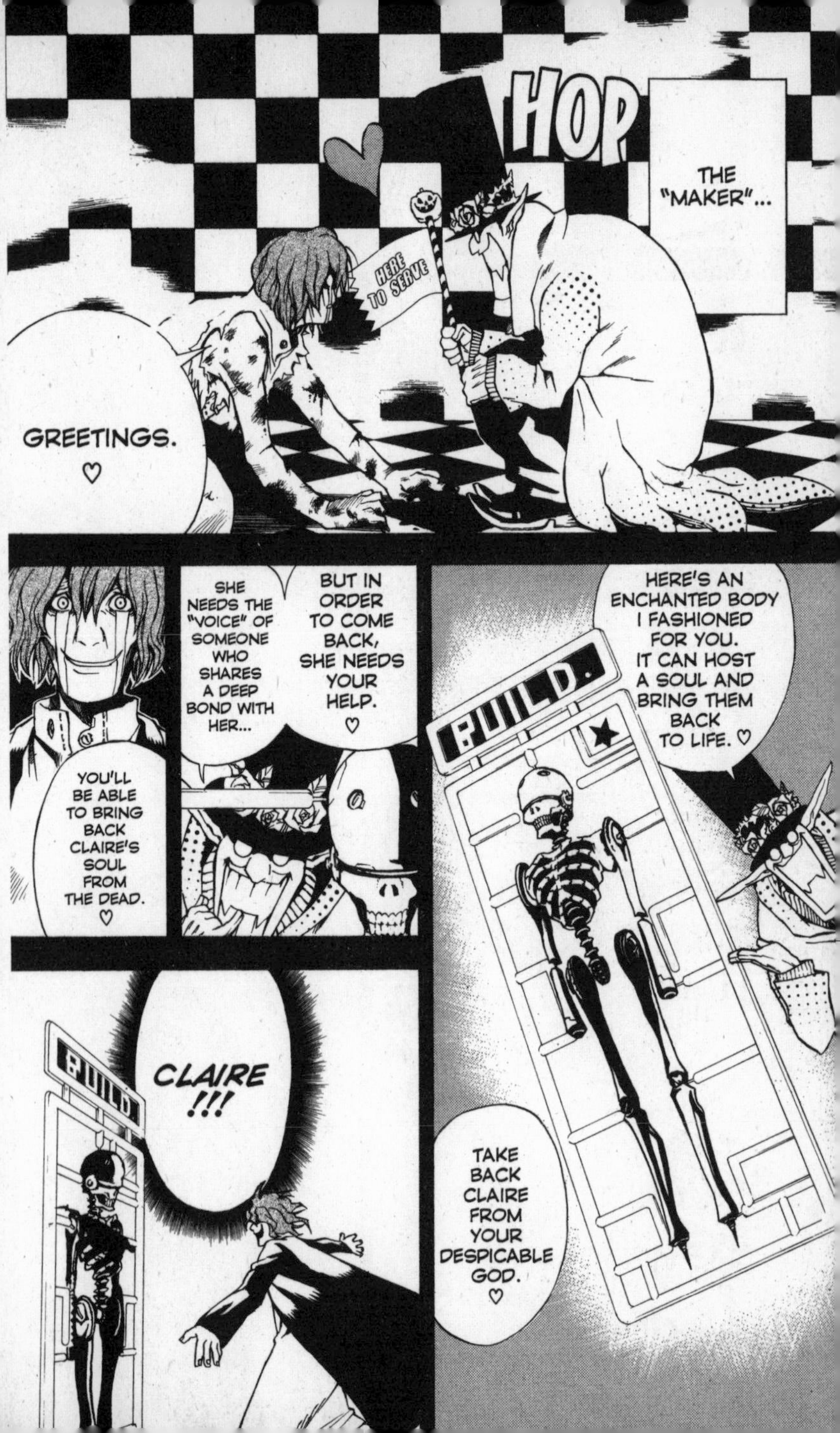
HOP
THE "MAKER"...
HERE TO SERVE
GREETINGS. ♡
HERE'S AN ENCHANTED BODY I FASHIONED FOR YOU. IT CAN HOST A SOUL AND BRING THEM BACK TO LIFE. ♡
BUILD.
TAKE BACK CLAIRE FROM YOUR DESPICABLE GOD. ♡
BUT IN ORDER TO COME BACK, SHE NEEDS YOUR HELP. ♡
SHE NEEDS THE "VOICE" OF SOMEONE WHO SHARES A DEEP BOND WITH HER...
YOU'LL BE ABLE TO BRING BACK CLAIRE'S SOUL FROM THE DEAD. ♡
BUILD.
CLAIRE !!!

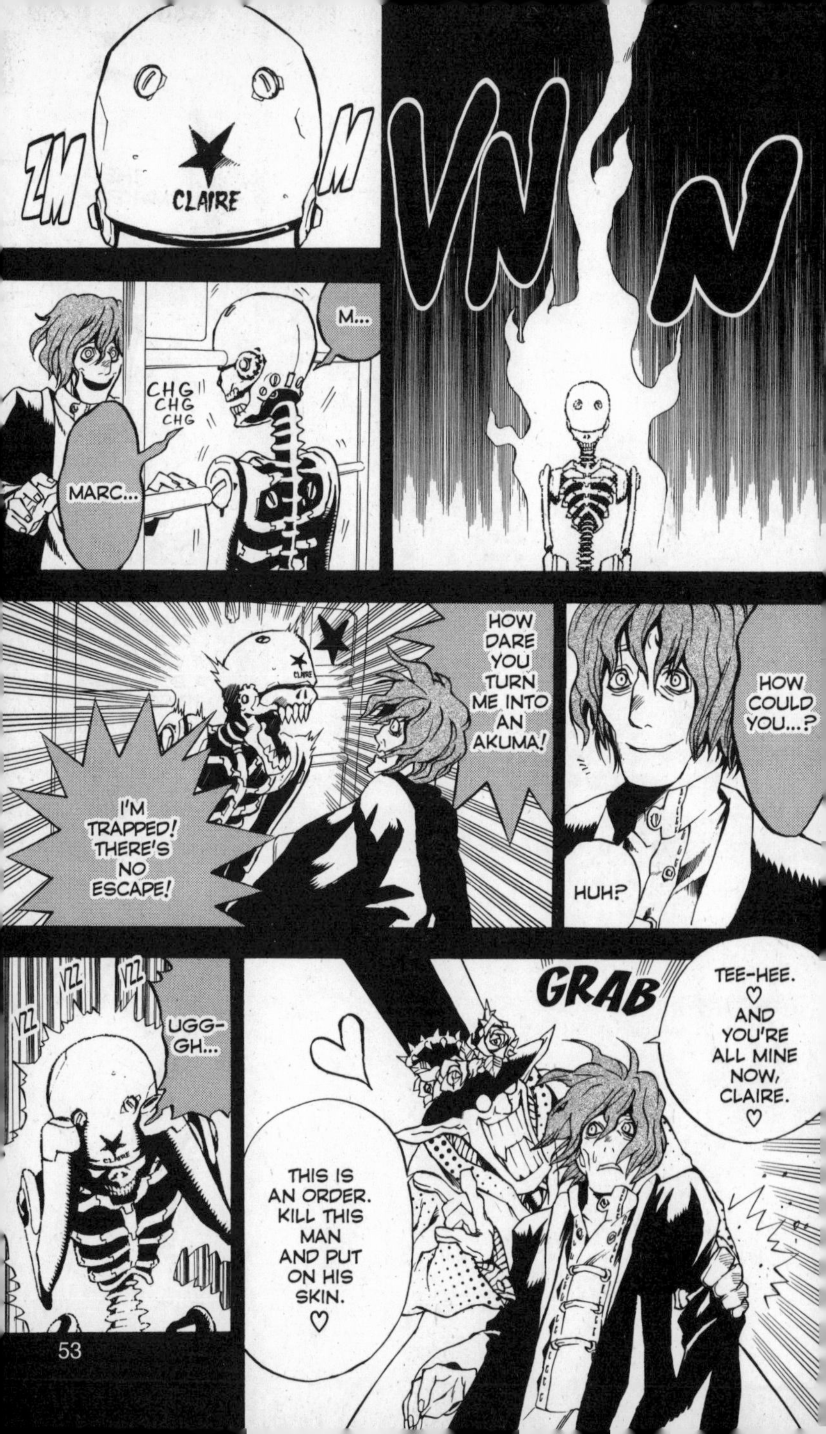
VNN
ZMM
CLAIRE
M...
CHG CHG CHG
MARC...
HOW COULD YOU...?
HUH?
HOW DARE YOU TURN ME INTO AN AKUMA!
I'M TRAPPED! THERE'S NO ESCAPE!
GRAB
TEE-HEE. ♡ AND YOU'RE ALL MINE NOW, CLAIRE. ♡
THIS IS AN ORDER. KILL THIS MAN AND PUT ON HIS SKIN. ♡
VZZ VZZ VZZ
UGGH...

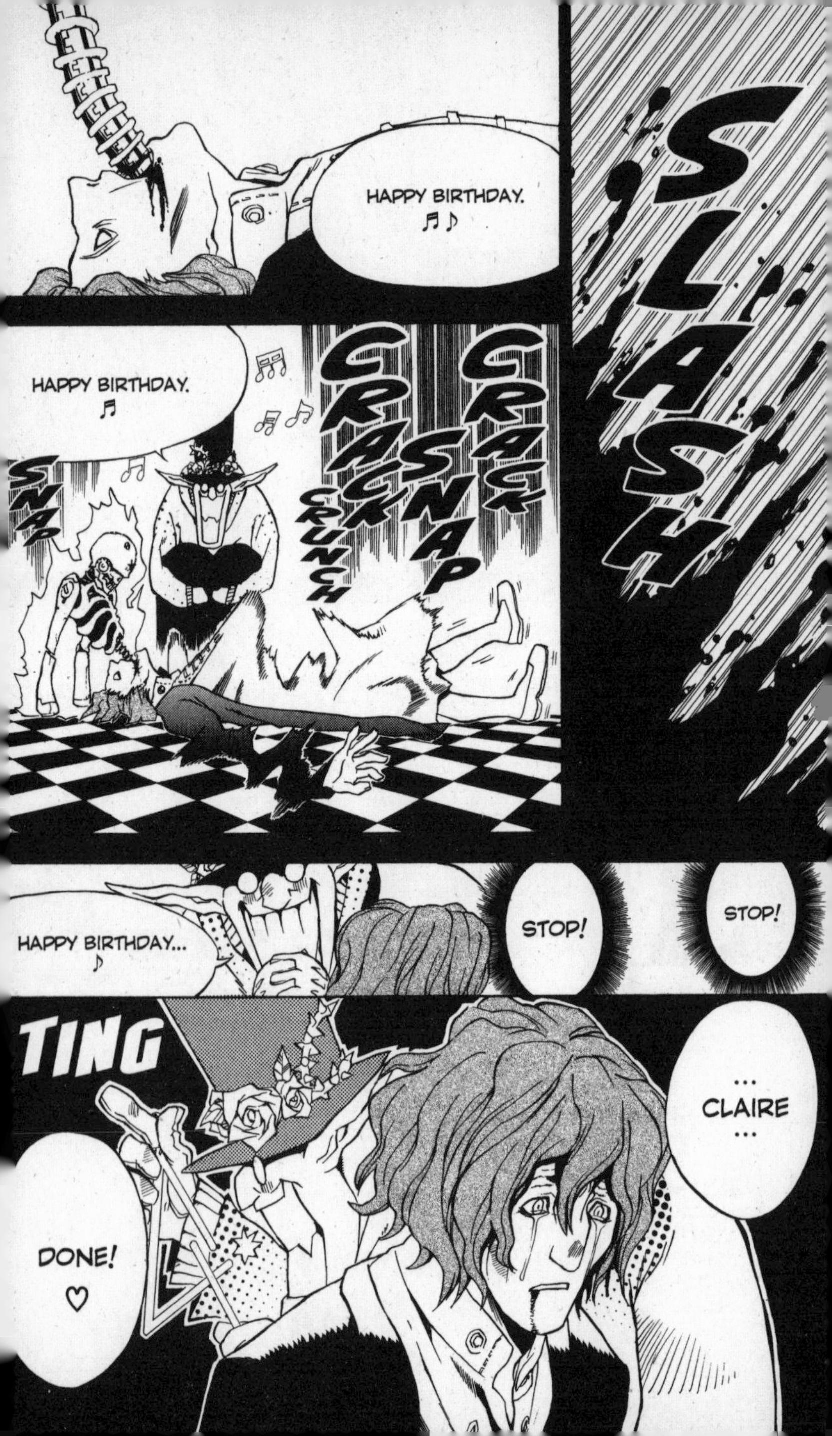
SLASH
HAPPY BIRTHDAY. ♬♪
CRACK
SNAP
CRACK
CRUNCH
HAPPY BIRTHDAY. ♬
SNAP
STOP!
STOP!
HAPPY BIRTHDAY... ♪
...CLAIRE...
TING
DONE! ♡

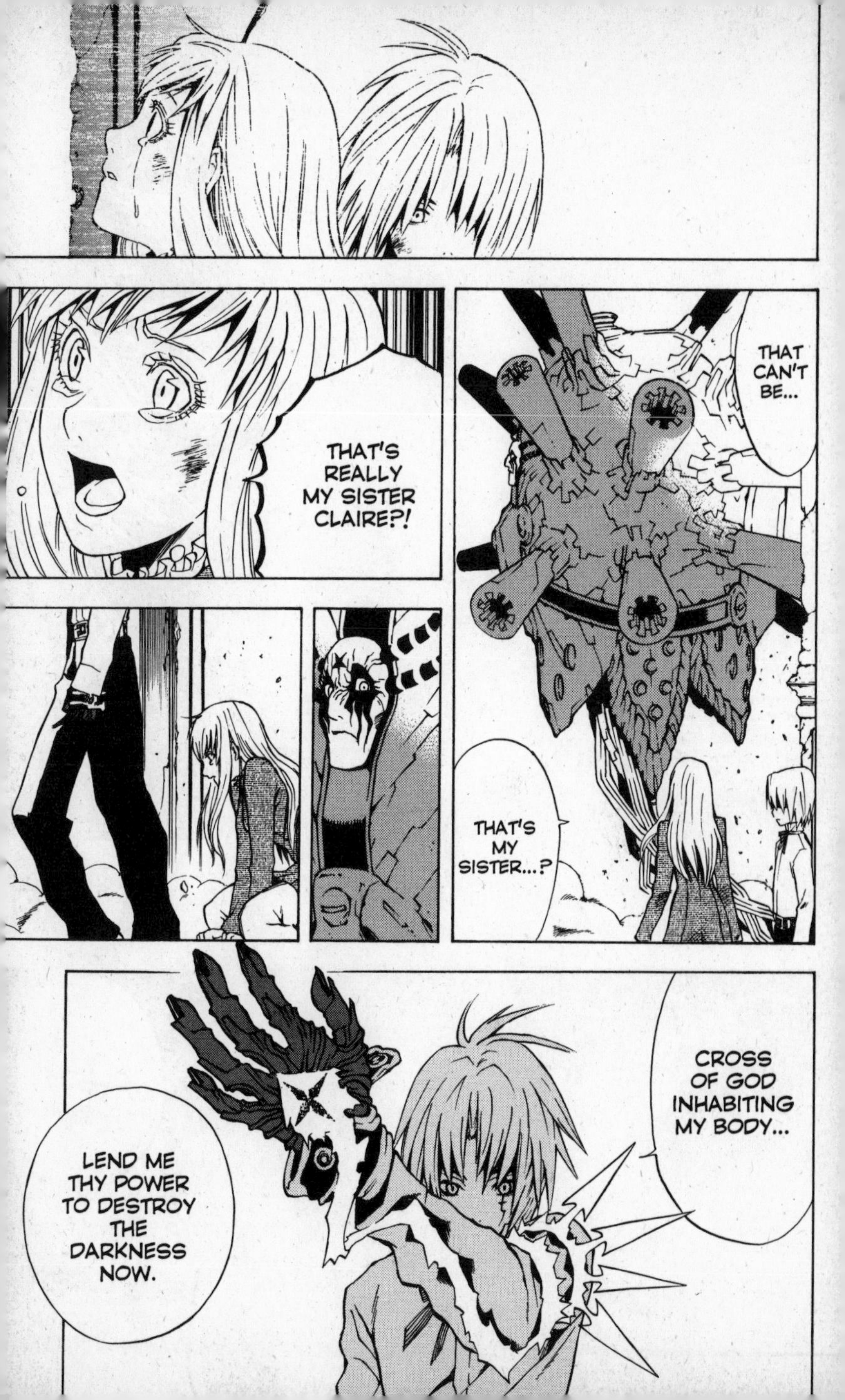
THAT CAN'T BE...
THAT'S MY SISTER...?
THAT'S REALLY MY SISTER CLAIRE?!
CROSS OF GOD INHABITING MY BODY...
LEND ME THY POWER TO DESTROY THE DARKNESS NOW.

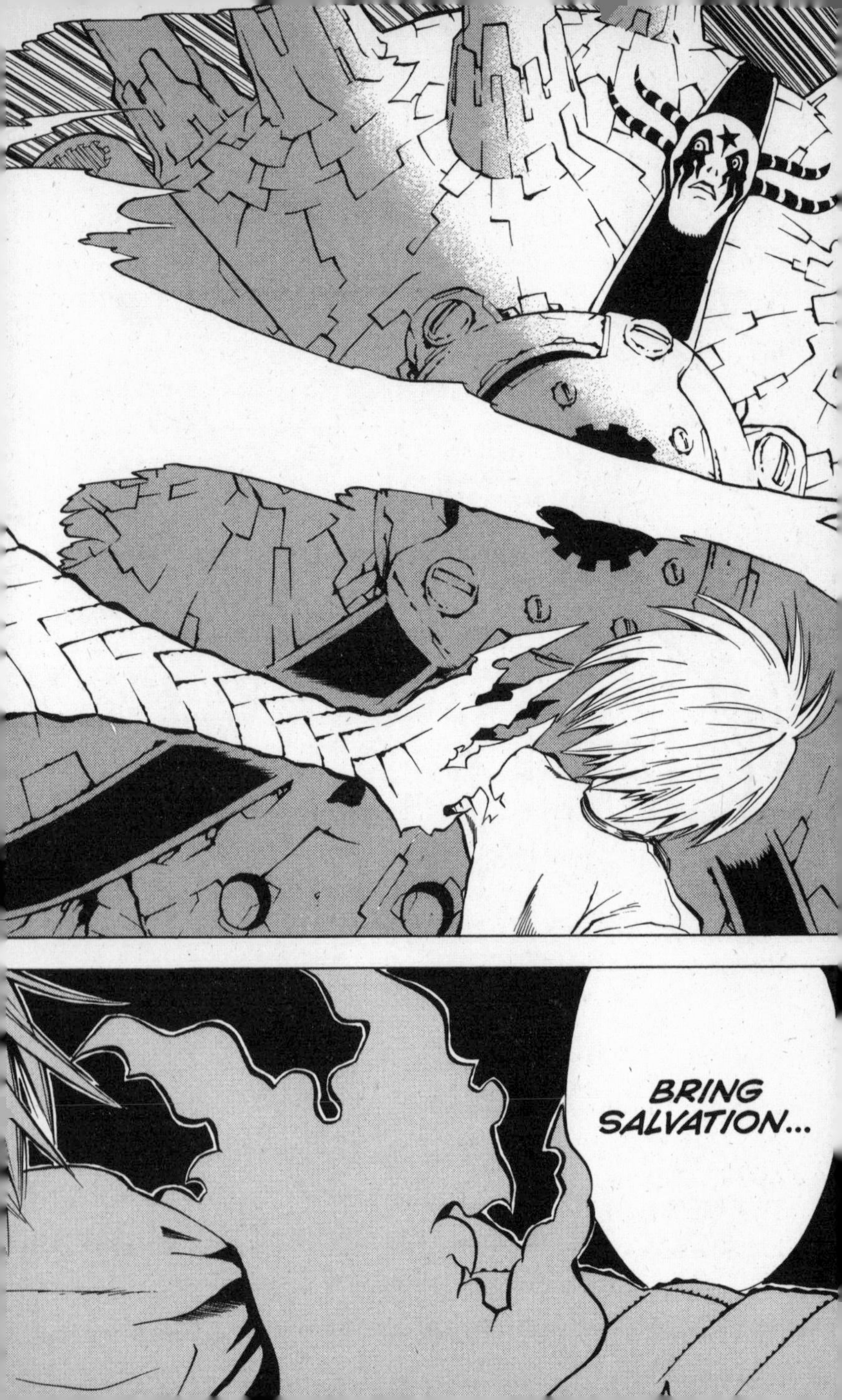
BRING
SALVATION...

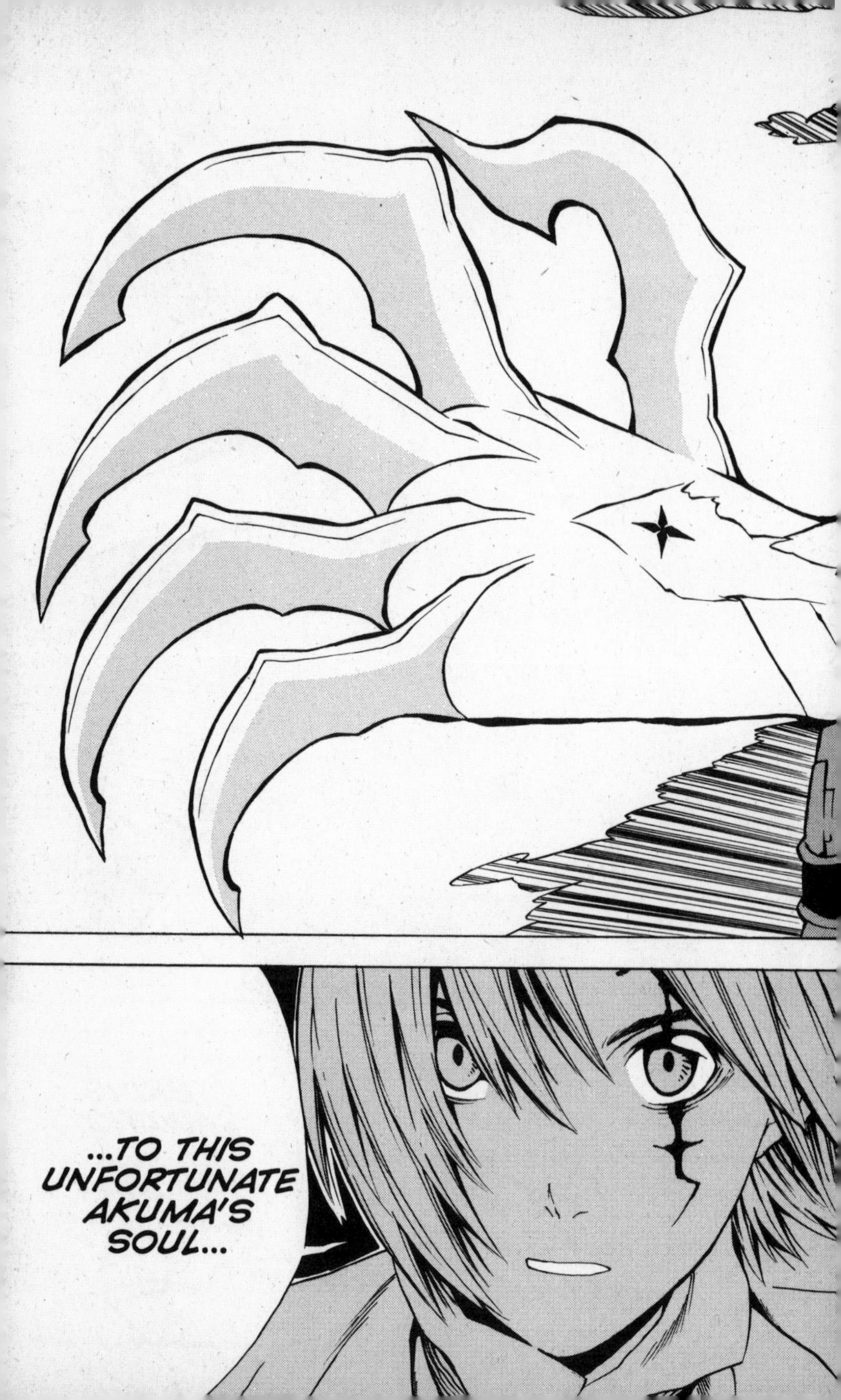
...TO THIS UNFORTUNATE AKUMA'S SOUL...

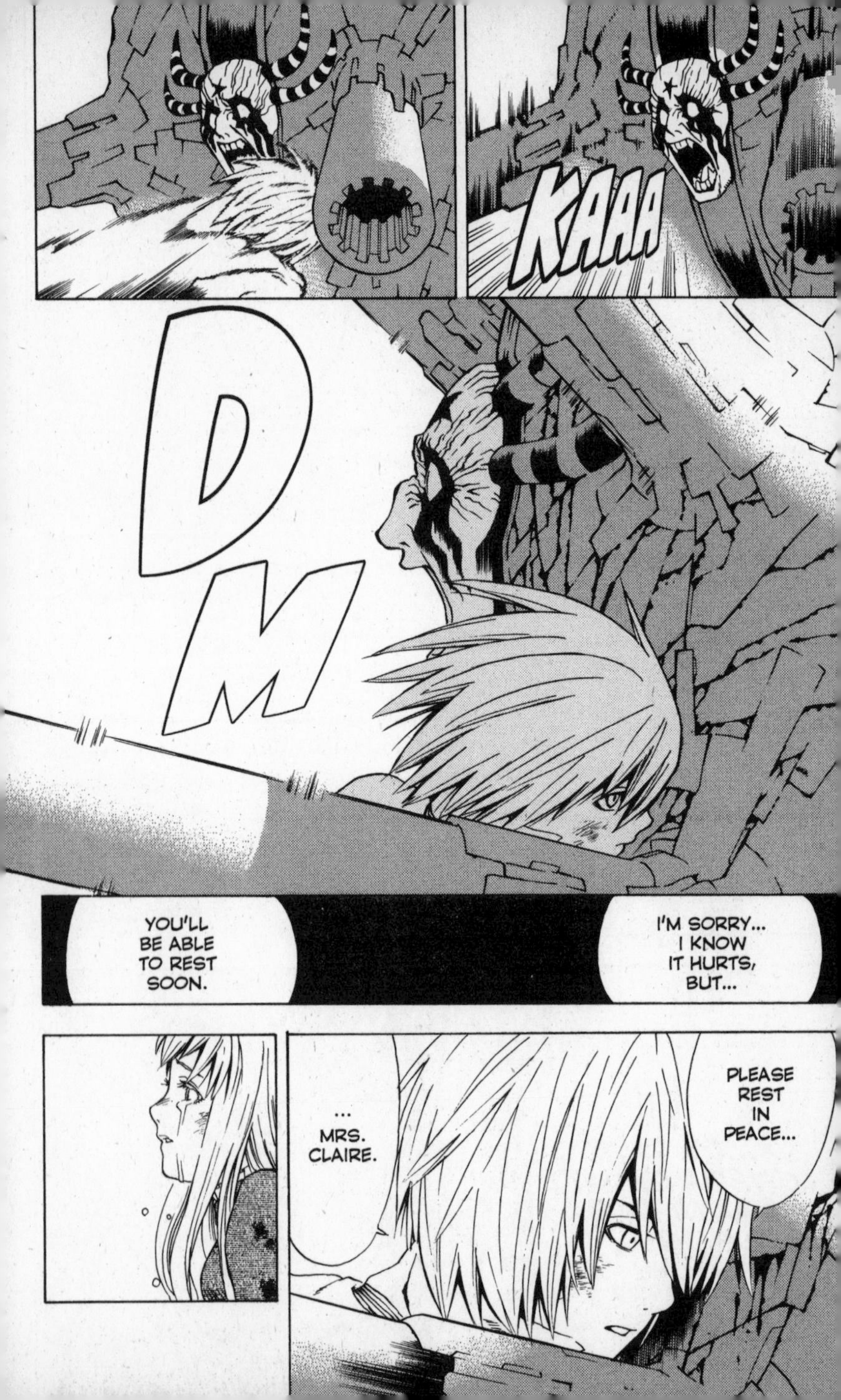
KAAA
DM
I'M SORRY... I KNOW IT HURTS, BUT...
YOU'LL BE ABLE TO REST SOON.
PLEASE REST IN PEACE...
... MRS. CLAIRE.

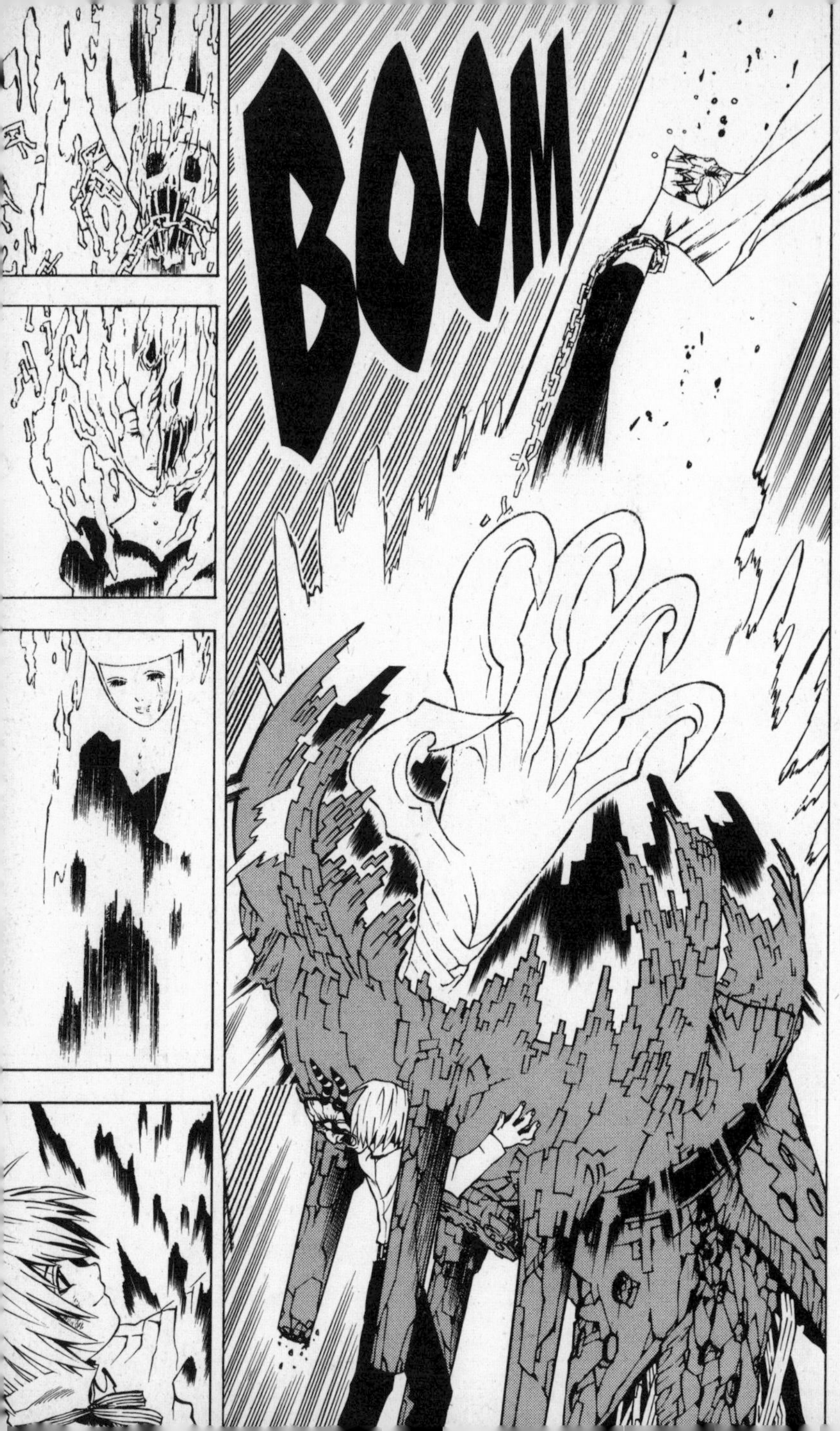
BOOM

FSS

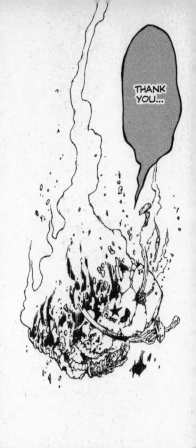

THANK YOU...

I WONDER... IF THEY WERE BOTH ABLE TO GO TO HEAVEN?

SIS...

AND MY BROTHER MARC...

SNIFF

I'M SURE THEY DID...

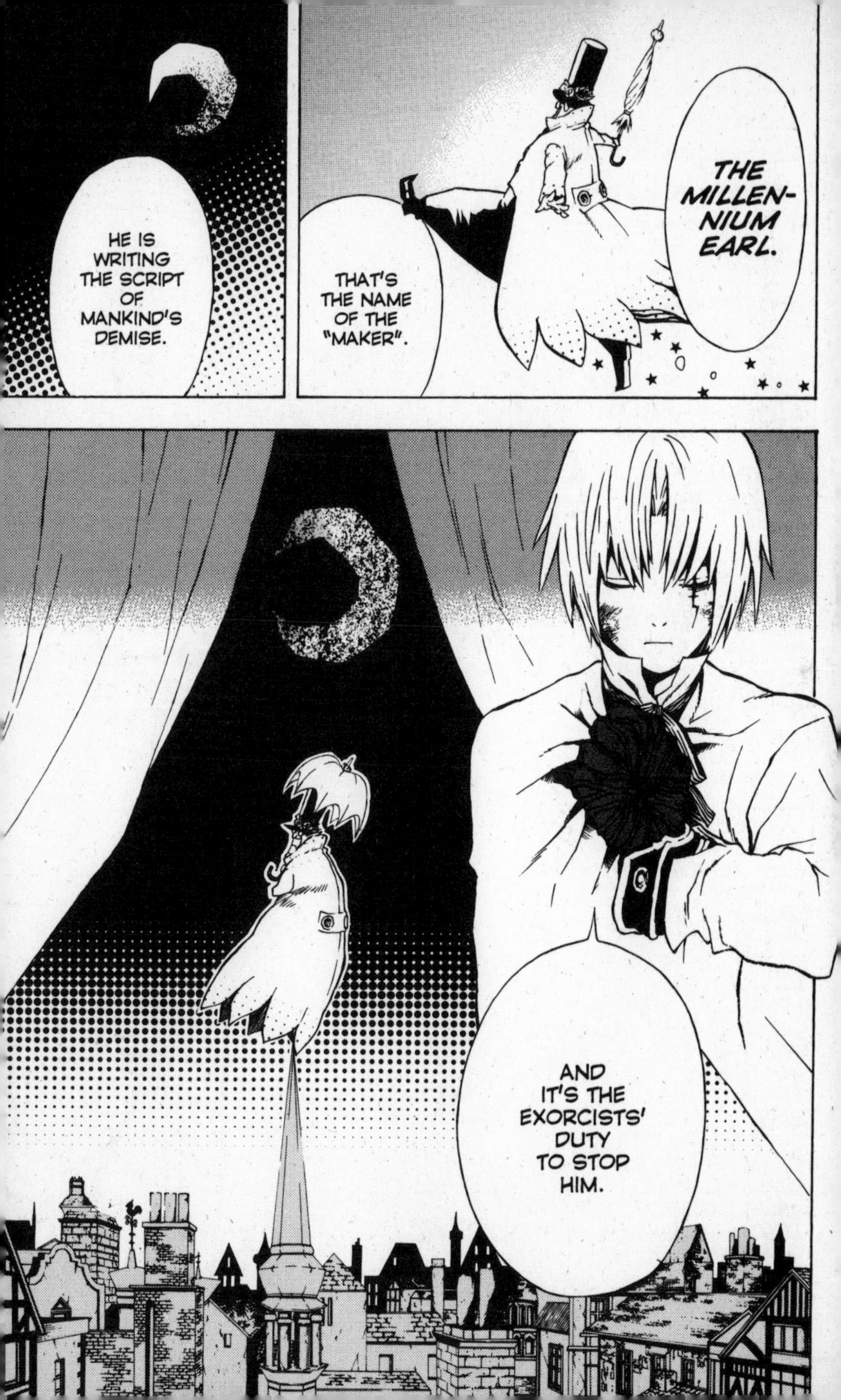
THE MILLEN-NIUM EARL.
THAT'S THE NAME OF THE "MAKER".
HE IS WRITING THE SCRIPT OF MANKIND'S DEMISE.
AND IT'S THE EXORCISTS' DUTY TO STOP HIM.

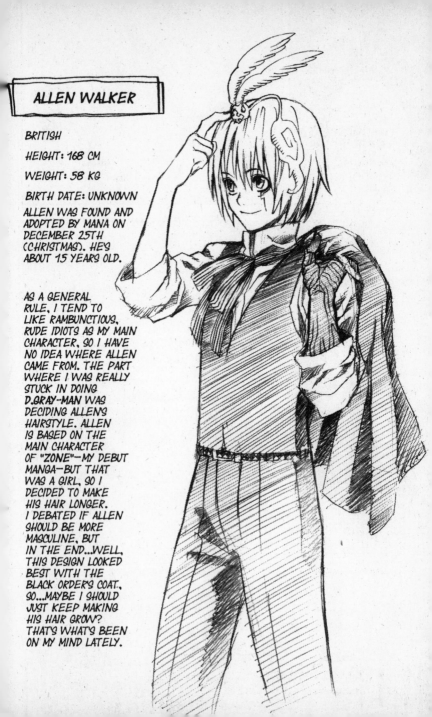

ALLEN WALKER

BRITISH

HEIGHT: 168 CM

WEIGHT: 58 KG

BIRTH DATE: UNKNOWN

ALLEN WAS FOUND AND ADOPTED BY MANA ON DECEMBER 25TH (CHRISTMAS). HE'S ABOUT 15 YEARS OLD.

AS A GENERAL RULE, I TEND TO LIKE RAMBUNCTIOUS, RUDE IDIOTS AS MY MAIN CHARACTER, SO I HAVE NO IDEA WHERE ALLEN CAME FROM. THE PART WHERE I WAS REALLY STUCK IN DOING D.GRAY-MAN WAS DECIDING ALLEN'S HAIRSTYLE. ALLEN IS BASED ON THE MAIN CHARACTER OF "ZONE"—MY DEBUT MANGA—BUT THAT WAS A GIRL, SO I DECIDED TO MAKE HIS HAIR LONGER. I DEBATED IF ALLEN SHOULD BE MORE MASCULINE, BUT IN THE END...WELL, THIS DESIGN LOOKED BEST WITH THE BLACK ORDER'S COAT. SO...MAYBE I SHOULD JUST KEEP MAKING HIS HAIR GROW? THAT'S WHAT'S BEEN ON MY MIND LATELY.

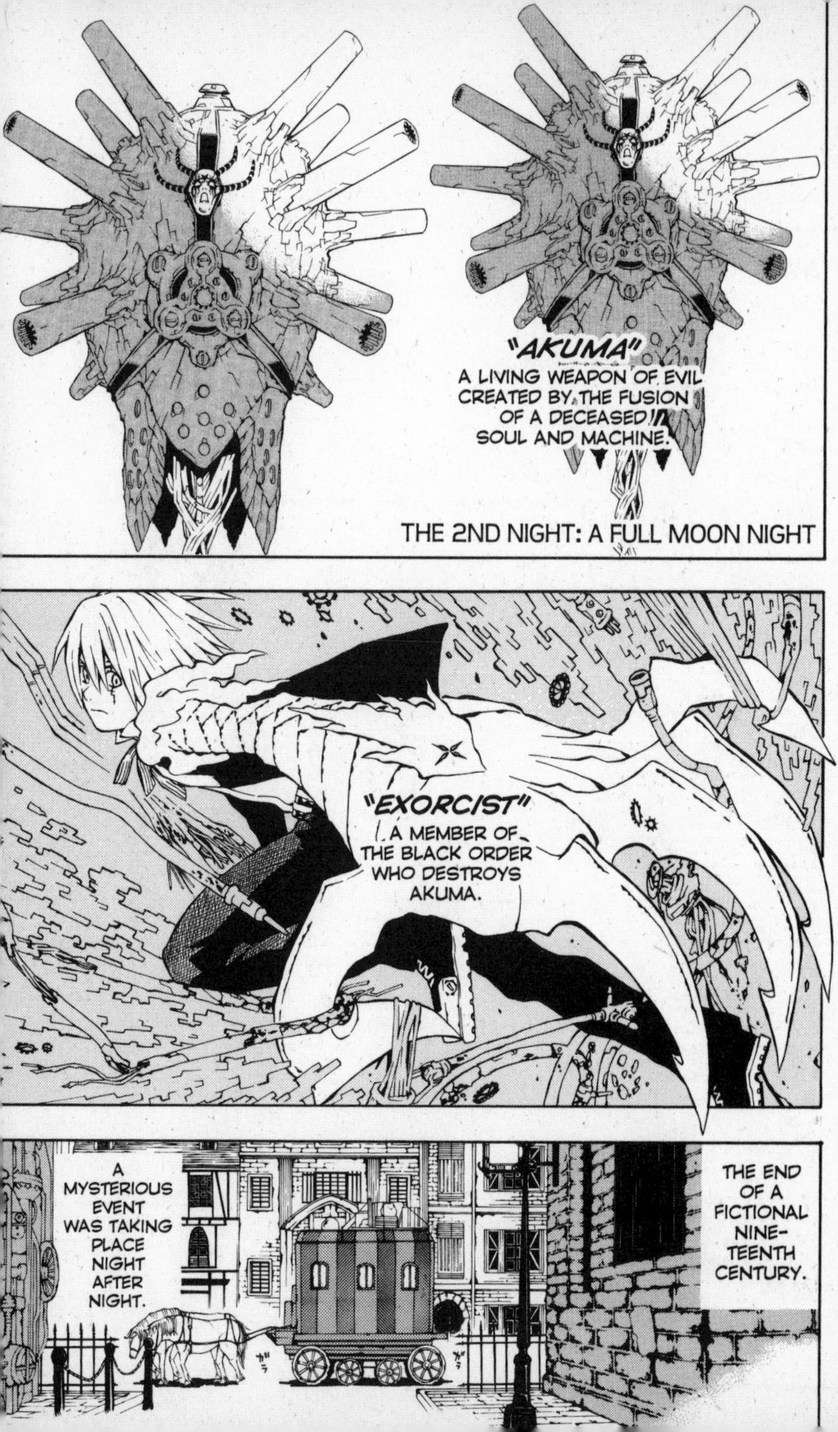
"AKUMA"
A LIVING WEAPON OF EVIL CREATED BY THE FUSION OF A DECEASED SOUL AND MACHINE.
THE 2ND NIGHT: A FULL MOON NIGHT
"EXORCIST"
A MEMBER OF THE BLACK ORDER WHO DESTROYS AKUMA.
THE END OF A FICTIONAL NINE-TEENTH CENTURY.
ガラ
ガラ
A MYSTERIOUS EVENT WAS TAKING PLACE NIGHT AFTER NIGHT.

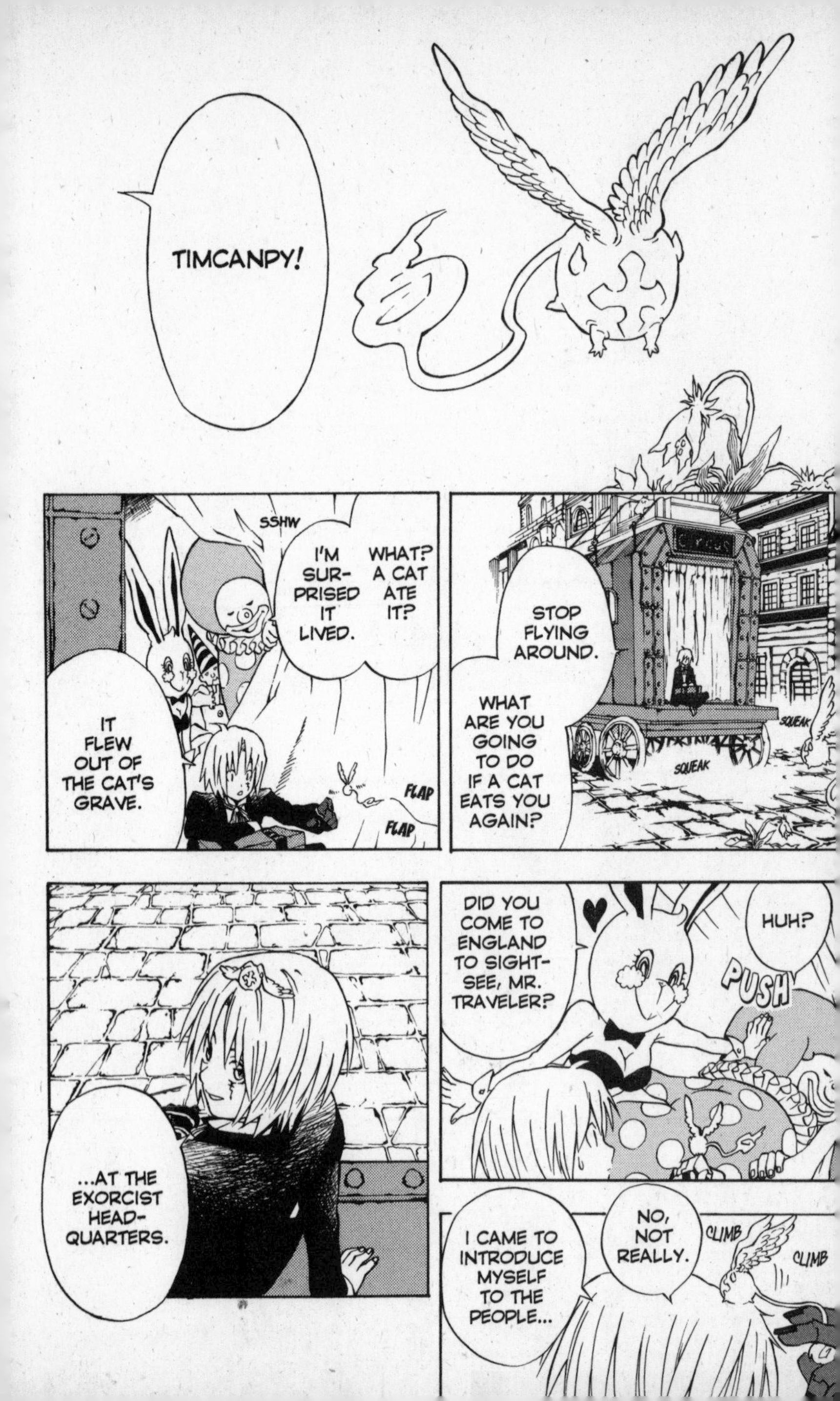
TIMCANPY!
STOP FLYING AROUND.
WHAT ARE YOU GOING TO DO IF A CAT EATS YOU AGAIN?
SQUEAK
SQUEAK
SSHW
WHAT? A CAT ATE IT?
I'M SURPRISED IT LIVED.
IT FLEW OUT OF THE CAT'S GRAVE.
FLAP
FLAP
HUH?
PUSH
DID YOU COME TO ENGLAND TO SIGHTSEE, MR. TRAVELER?
CLIMB
CLIMB
NO, NOT REALLY.
I CAME TO INTRODUCE MYSELF TO THE PEOPLE...
...AT THE EXORCIST HEADQUARTERS.

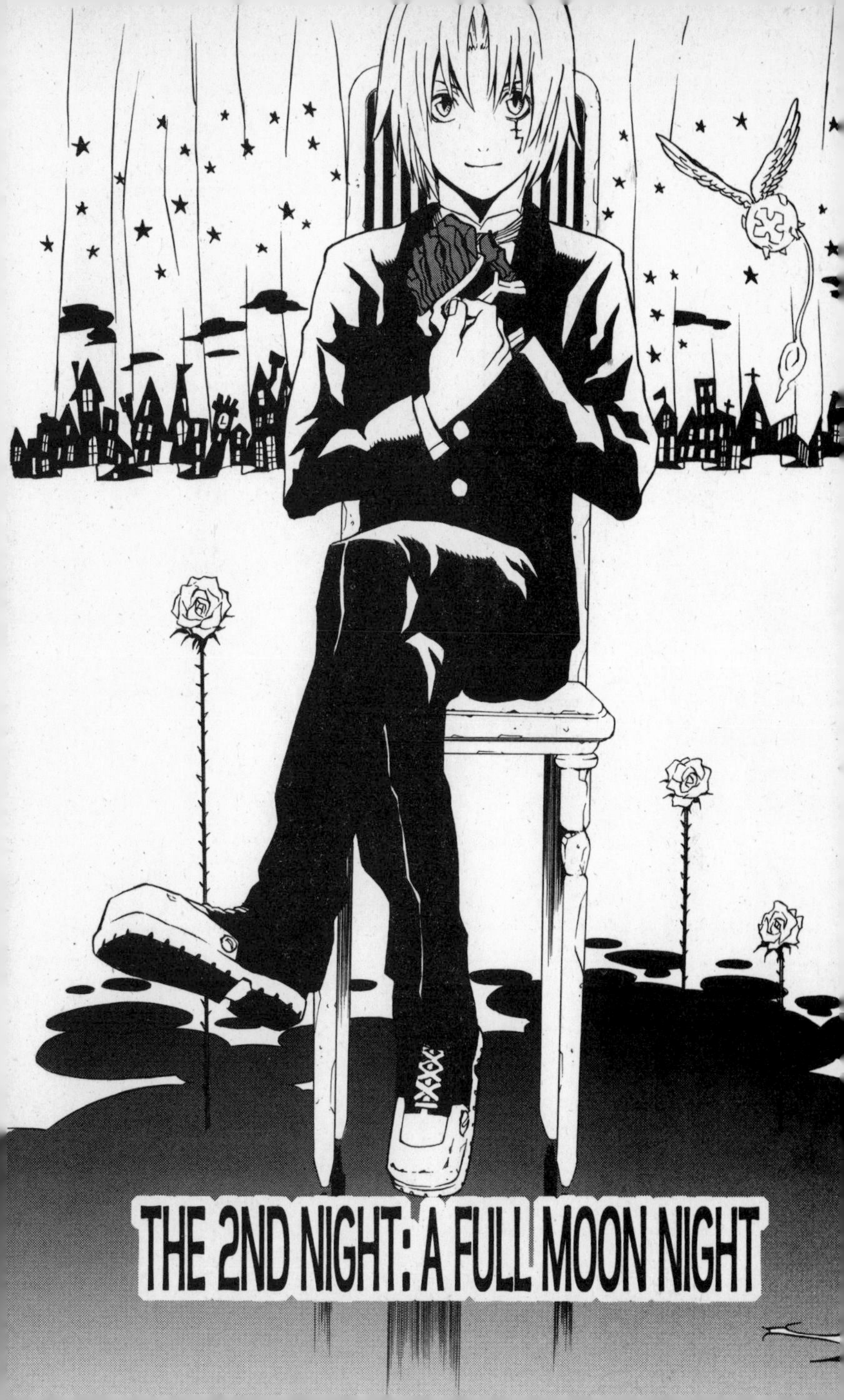

THE 2ND NIGHT: A FULL MOON NIGHT

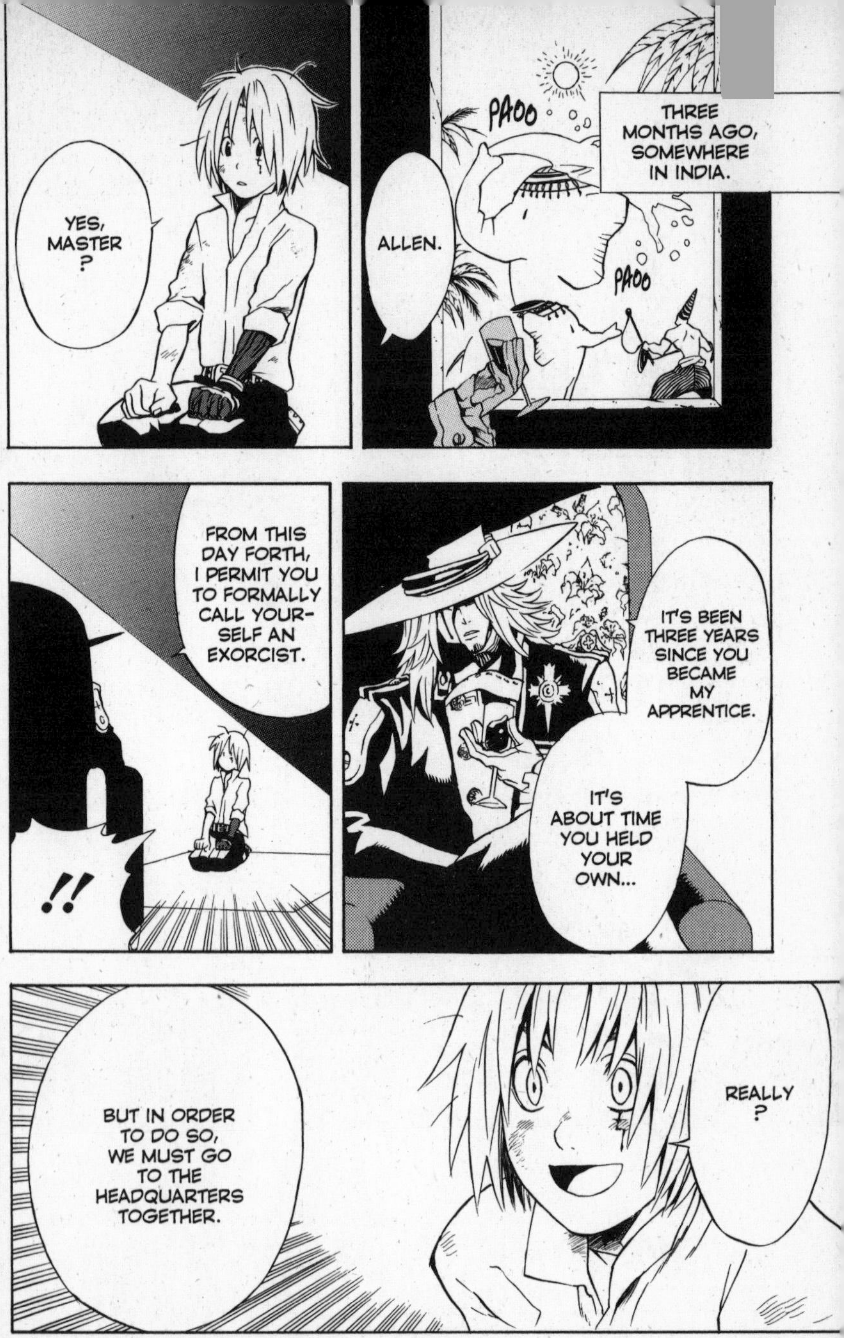
THREE MONTHS AGO, SOMEWHERE IN INDIA.
PAOO
PAOO
ALLEN.
YES, MASTER?
IT'S BEEN THREE YEARS SINCE YOU BECAME MY APPRENTICE.
IT'S ABOUT TIME YOU HELD YOUR OWN...
FROM THIS DAY FORTH, I PERMIT YOU TO FORMALLY CALL YOURSELF AN EXORCIST.
!!
REALLY?
BUT IN ORDER TO DO SO, WE MUST GO TO THE HEADQUARTERS TOGETHER.

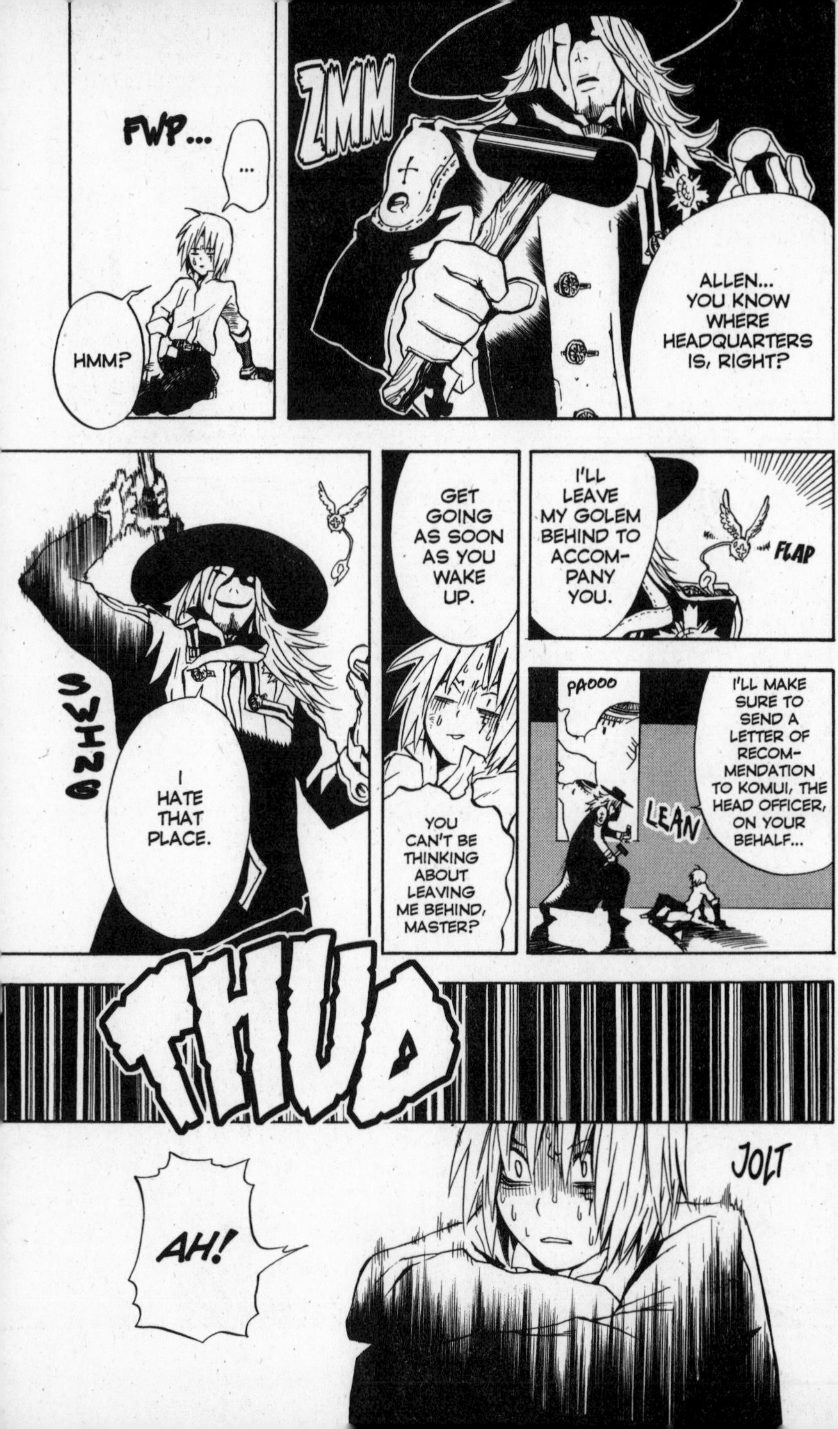
ZMM
ALLEN... YOU KNOW WHERE HEADQUARTERS IS, RIGHT?
FWP...
...
HMM?
I'LL LEAVE MY GOLEM BEHIND TO ACCOM-PANY YOU.
FLAP
I'LL MAKE SURE TO SEND A LETTER OF RECOM-MENDATION TO KOMUI, THE HEAD OFFICER, ON YOUR BEHALF...
LEAN
PAOOO
GET GOING AS SOON AS YOU WAKE UP.
YOU CAN'T BE THINKING ABOUT LEAVING ME BEHIND, MASTER?
SWING
I HATE THAT PLACE.
THUD
JOLT
AH!

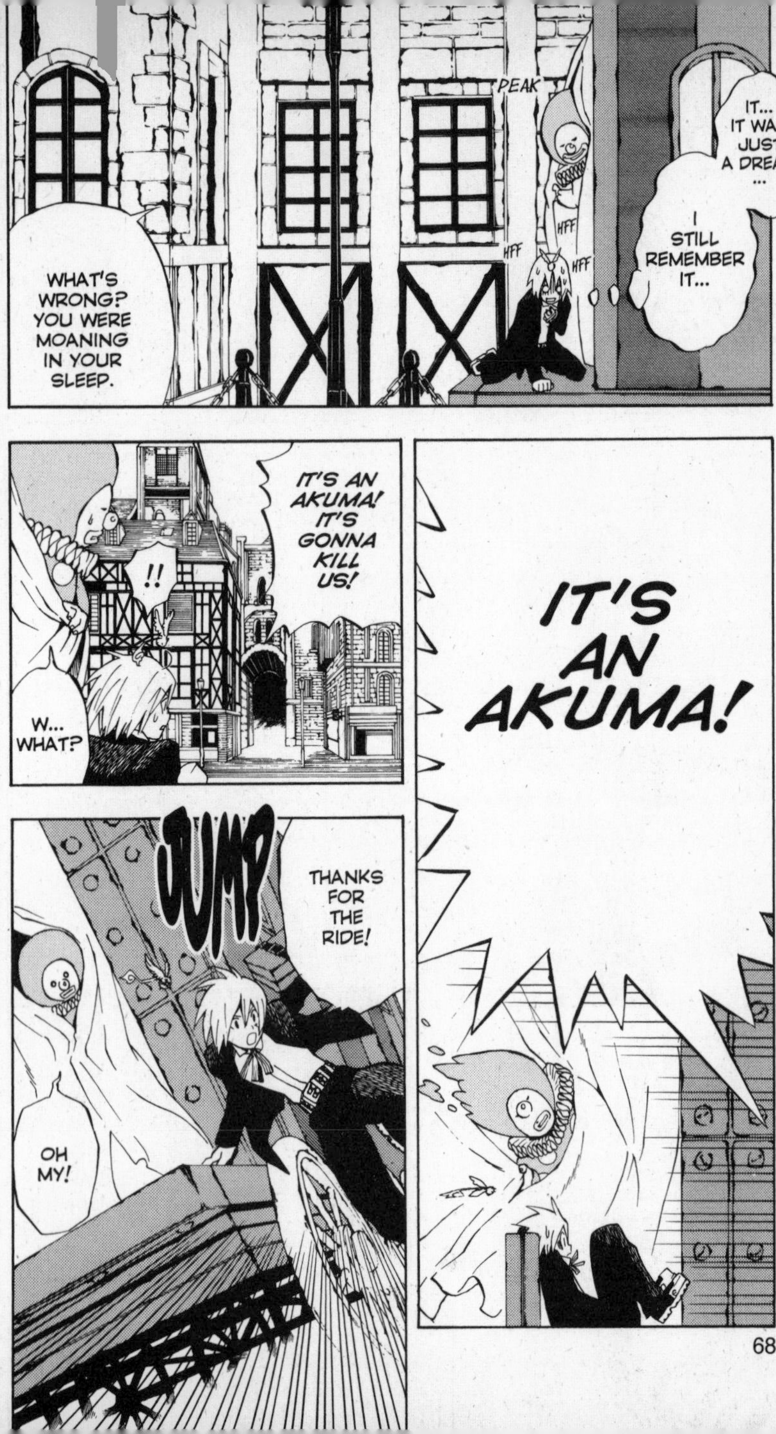
IT... IT WAS JUST A DREAM ...
I STILL REMEMBER IT...
PEAK
HFF
HFF
HFF
WHAT'S WRONG? YOU WERE MOANING IN YOUR SLEEP.
IT'S AN AKUMA!
IT'S AN AKUMA! IT'S GONNA KILL US!
!!
W... WHAT?
JUMP
THANKS FOR THE RIDE!
OH MY!

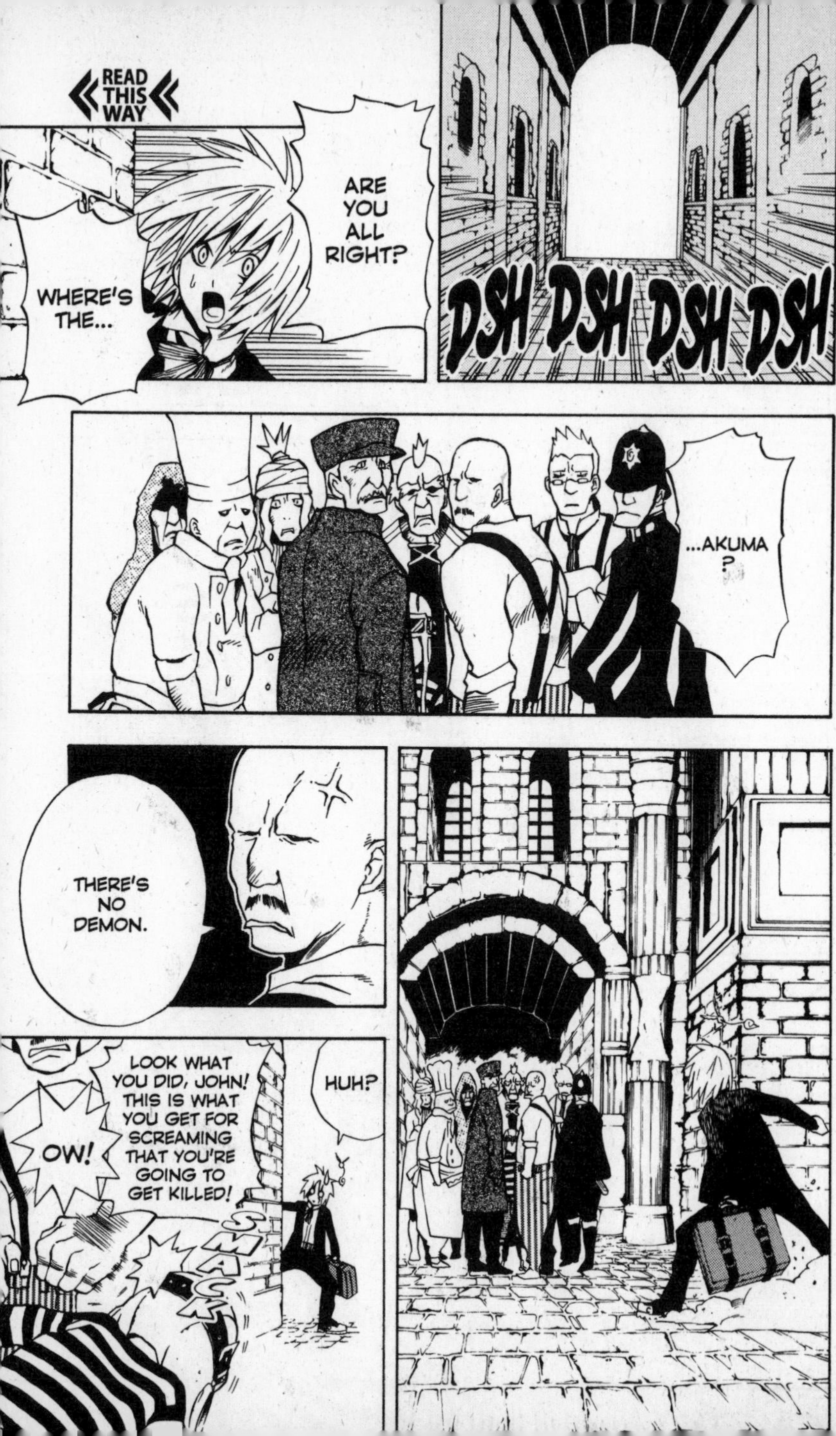

READ THIS WAY
DSH DSH DSH DSH
ARE YOU ALL RIGHT?
WHERE'S THE...
...AKUMA?
THERE'S NO DEMON.
HUH?
LOOK WHAT YOU DID, JOHN! THIS IS WHAT YOU GET FOR SCREAMING THAT YOU'RE GOING TO GET KILLED!
OW!
SMACK

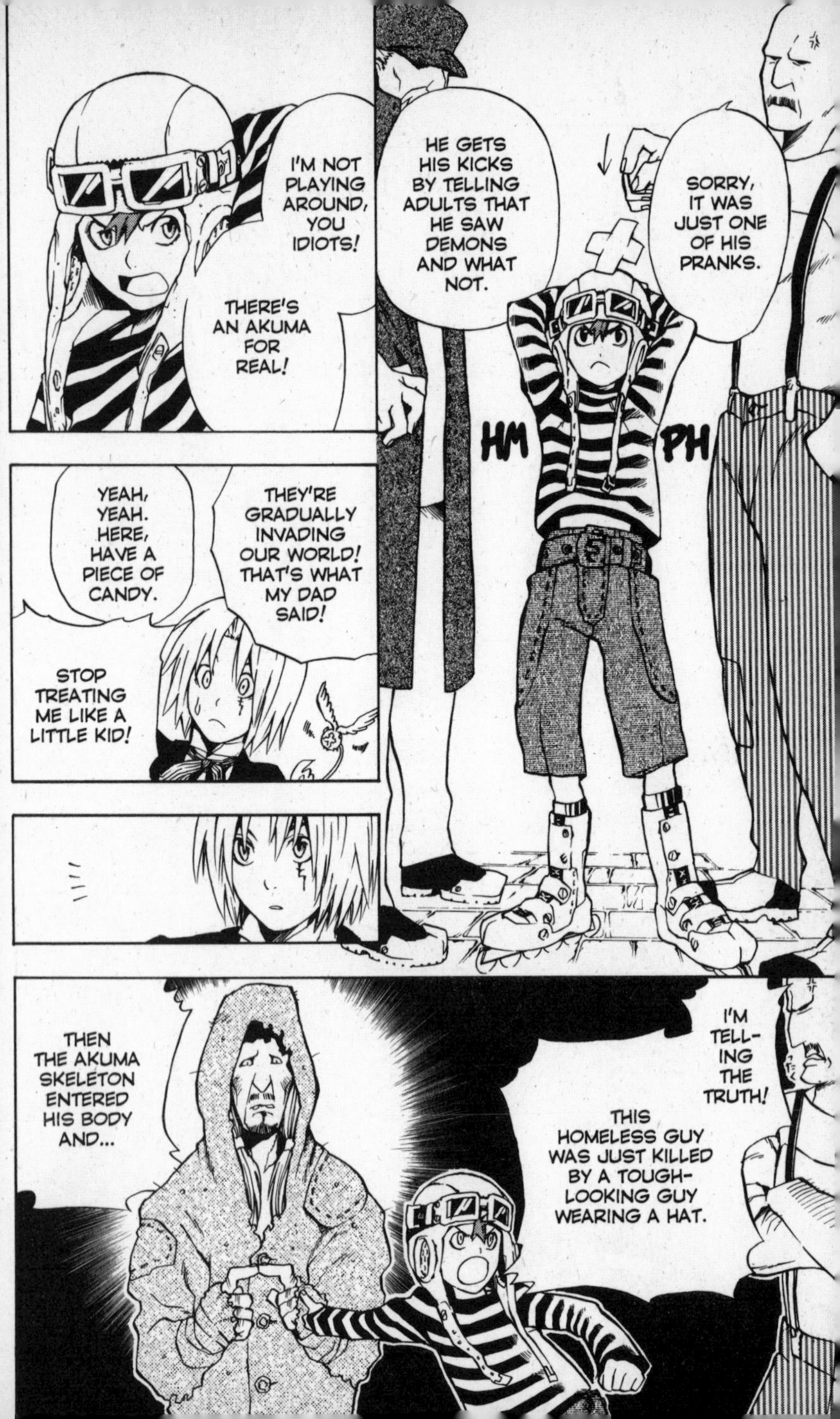

SORRY, IT WAS JUST ONE OF HIS PRANKS.
HE GETS HIS KICKS BY TELLING ADULTS THAT HE SAW DEMONS AND WHAT NOT.
HMPH
I'M NOT PLAYING AROUND, YOU IDIOTS!
THERE'S AN AKUMA FOR REAL!
THEY'RE GRADUALLY INVADING OUR WORLD! THAT'S WHAT MY DAD SAID!
YEAH, YEAH. HERE, HAVE A PIECE OF CANDY.
STOP TREATING ME LIKE A LITTLE KID!
I'M TELL-ING THE TRUTH!
THIS HOMELESS GUY WAS JUST KILLED BY A TOUGH-LOOKING GUY WEARING A HAT.
THEN THE AKUMA SKELETON ENTERED HIS BODY AND...

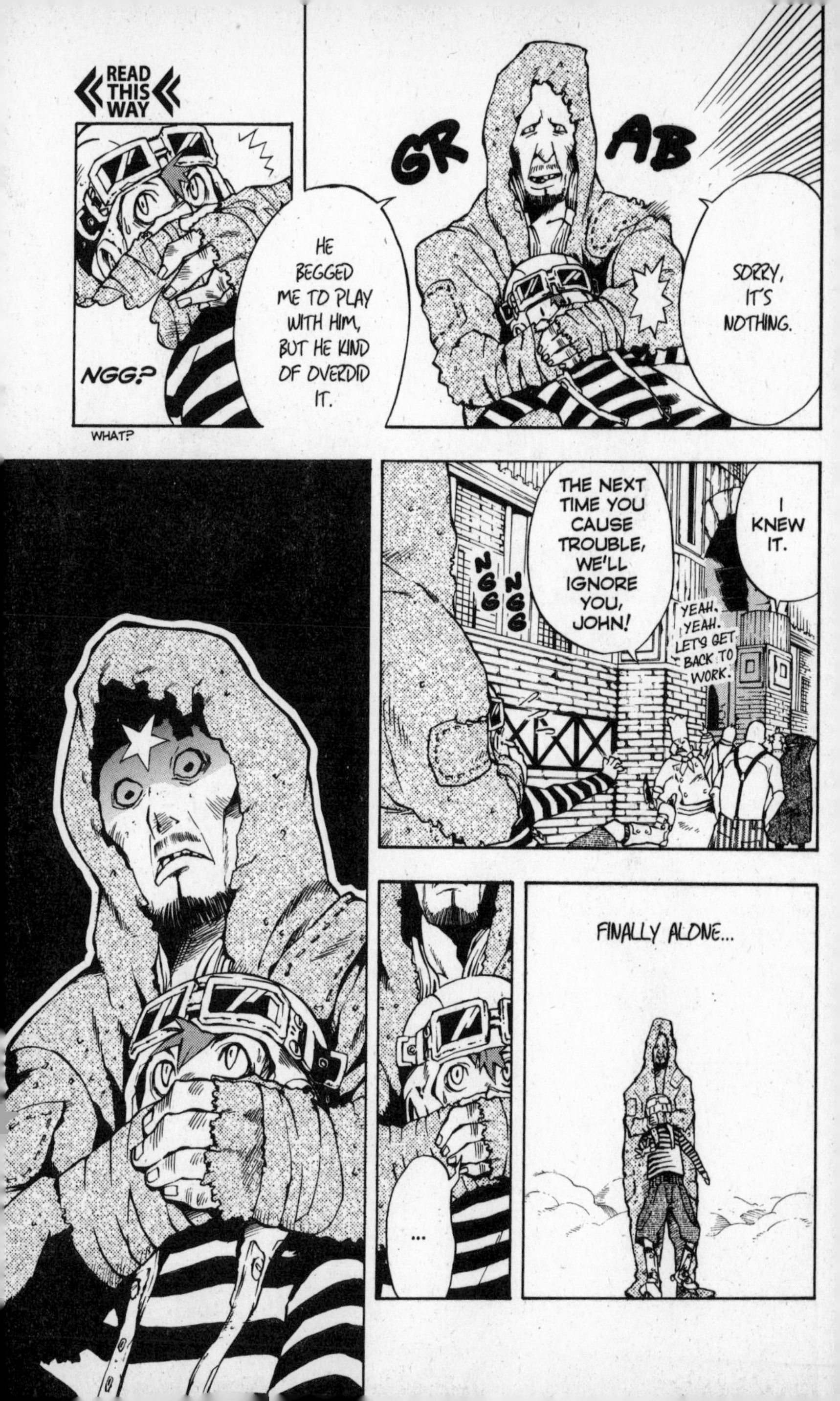
READ THIS WAY
GRAB
SORRY, IT'S NOTHING.
HE BEGGED ME TO PLAY WITH HIM, BUT HE KIND OF OVERDID IT.
NGG?
WHAT?
I KNEW IT.
THE NEXT TIME YOU CAUSE TROUBLE, WE'LL IGNORE YOU, JOHN!
YEAH, YEAH. LET'S GET BACK TO WORK.
NGG NGG
FINALLY ALONE...
...

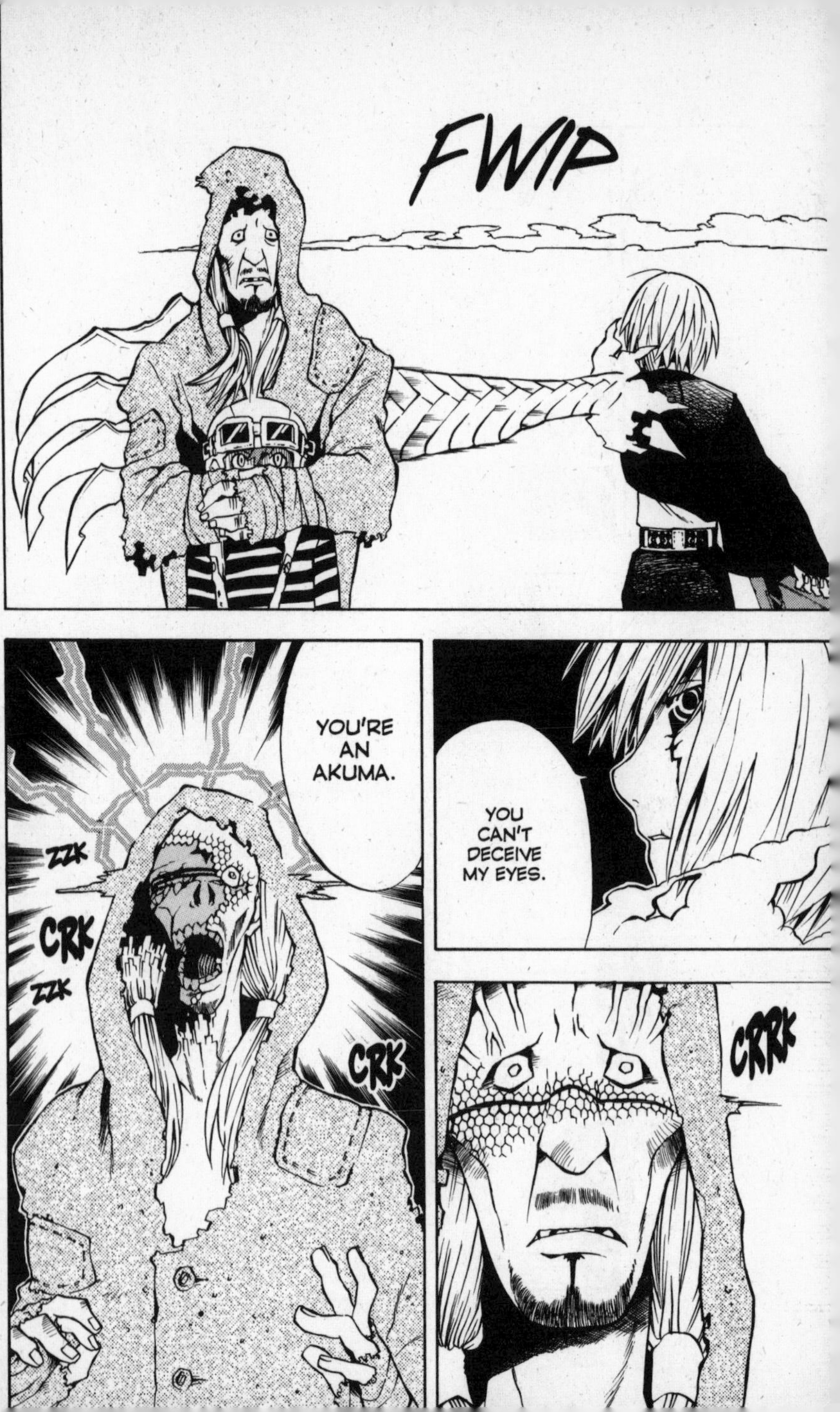
FWIP
YOU CAN'T DECEIVE MY EYES.
CRRK
YOU'RE AN AKUMA.
ZZK
CRK
ZZK
CRK

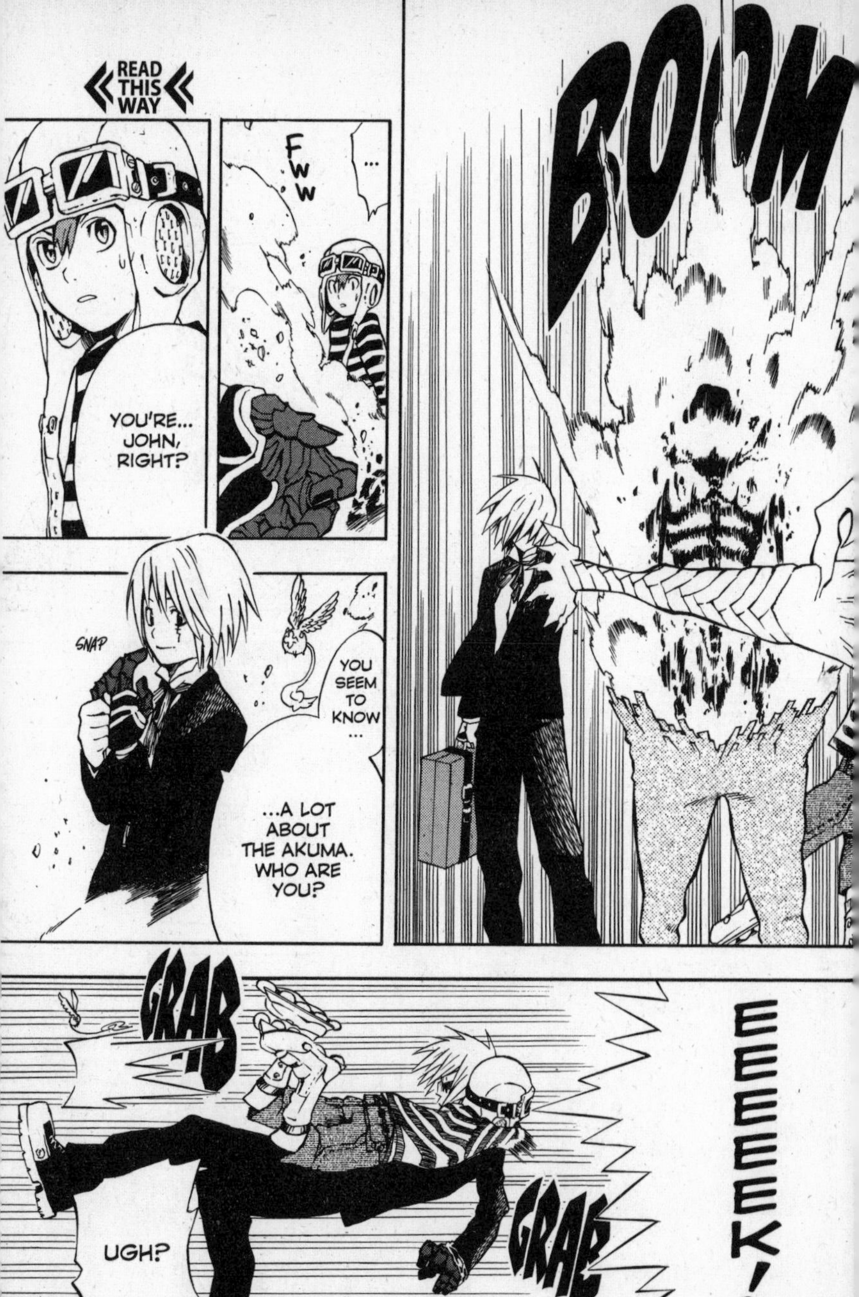
READ THIS WAY
BOOM
FWW
...
YOU'RE... JOHN, RIGHT?
SNAP
YOU SEEM TO KNOW...
...A LOT ABOUT THE AKUMA. WHO ARE YOU?
EEEEEK!
GRAB
GRAB-AB
UGH?

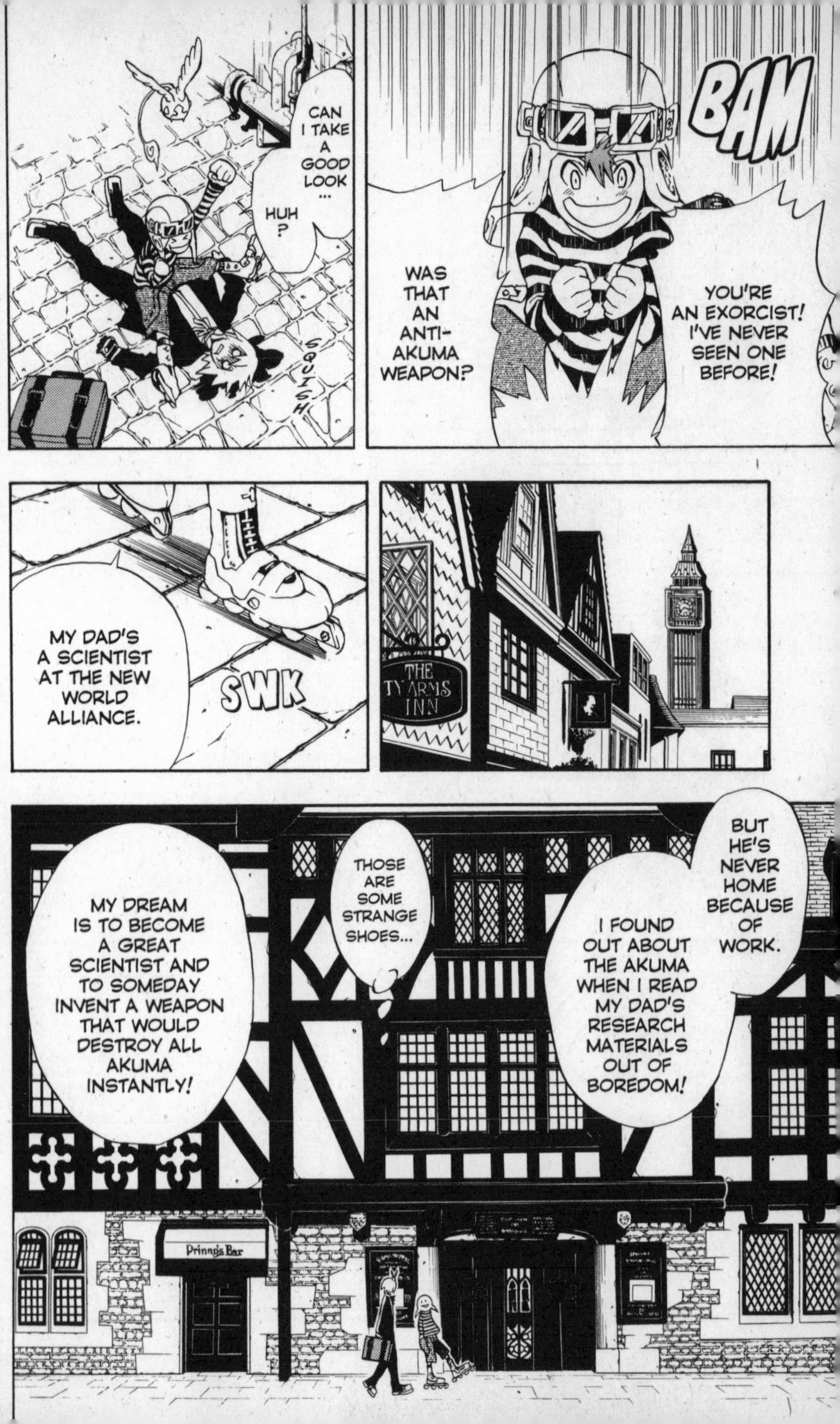
BAM
YOU'RE AN EXORCIST! I'VE NEVER SEEN ONE BEFORE!
WAS THAT AN ANTI-AKUMA WEAPON?
CAN I TAKE A GOOD LOOK...
HUH?
SQUISH
MY DAD'S A SCIENTIST AT THE NEW WORLD ALLIANCE.
SWK
BUT HE'S NEVER HOME BECAUSE OF WORK.
I FOUND OUT ABOUT THE AKUMA WHEN I READ MY DAD'S RESEARCH MATERIALS OUT OF BOREDOM!
THOSE ARE SOME STRANGE SHOES...
MY DREAM IS TO BECOME A GREAT SCIENTIST AND TO SOMEDAY INVENT A WEAPON THAT WOULD DESTROY ALL AKUMA INSTANTLY!

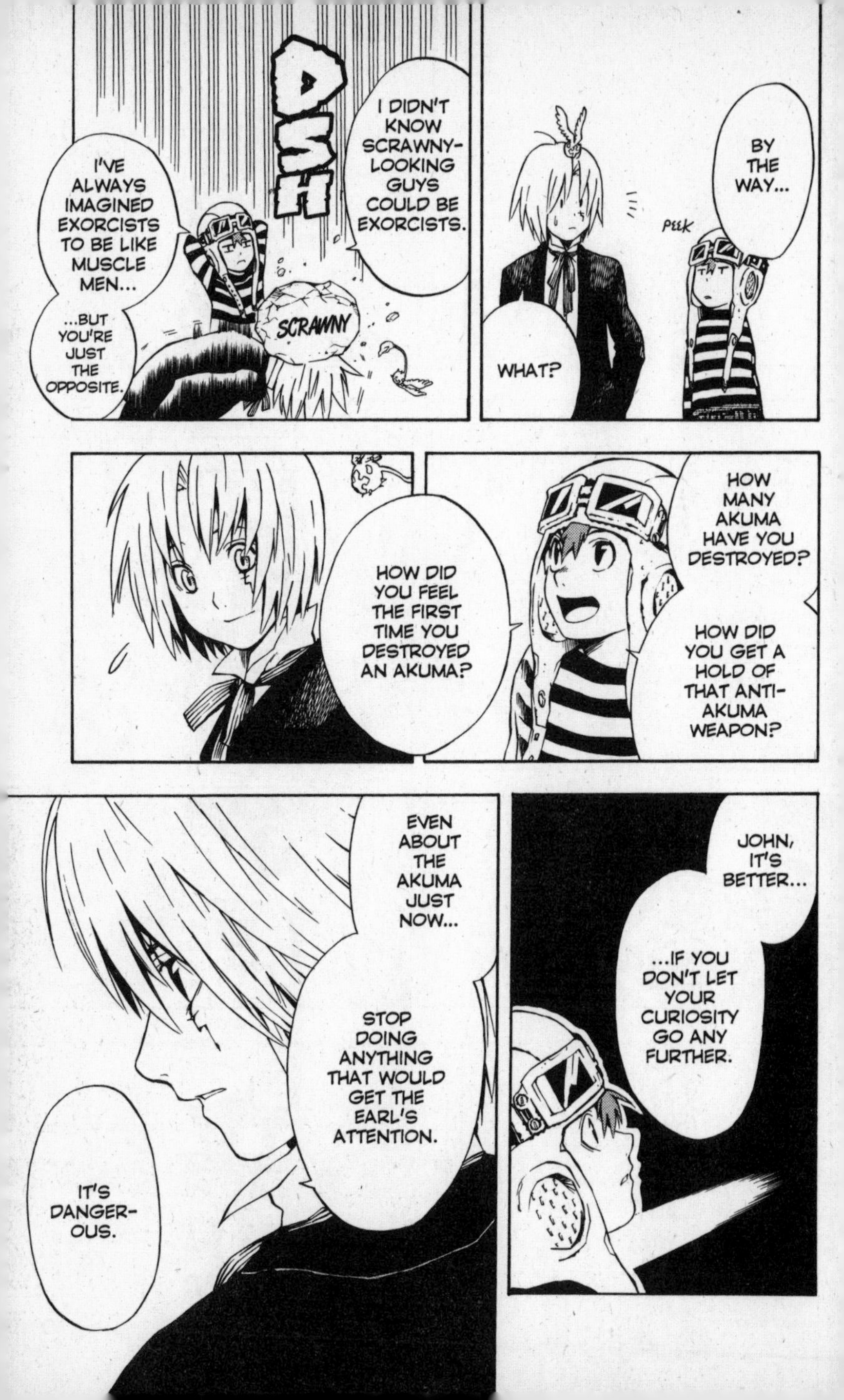
BY THE WAY...
PEEK
WHAT?
I DIDN'T KNOW SCRAWNY-LOOKING GUYS COULD BE EXORCISTS.
DSH
SCRAWNY
I'VE ALWAYS IMAGINED EXORCISTS TO BE LIKE MUSCLE MEN...
...BUT YOU'RE JUST THE OPPOSITE.
HOW MANY AKUMA HAVE YOU DESTROYED?
HOW DID YOU GET A HOLD OF THAT ANTI-AKUMA WEAPON?
HOW DID YOU FEEL THE FIRST TIME YOU DESTROYED AN AKUMA?
JOHN, IT'S BETTER...
...IF YOU DON'T LET YOUR CURIOSITY GO ANY FURTHER.
EVEN ABOUT THE AKUMA JUST NOW...
STOP DOING ANYTHING THAT WOULD GET THE EARL'S ATTENTION.
IT'S DANGER-OUS.

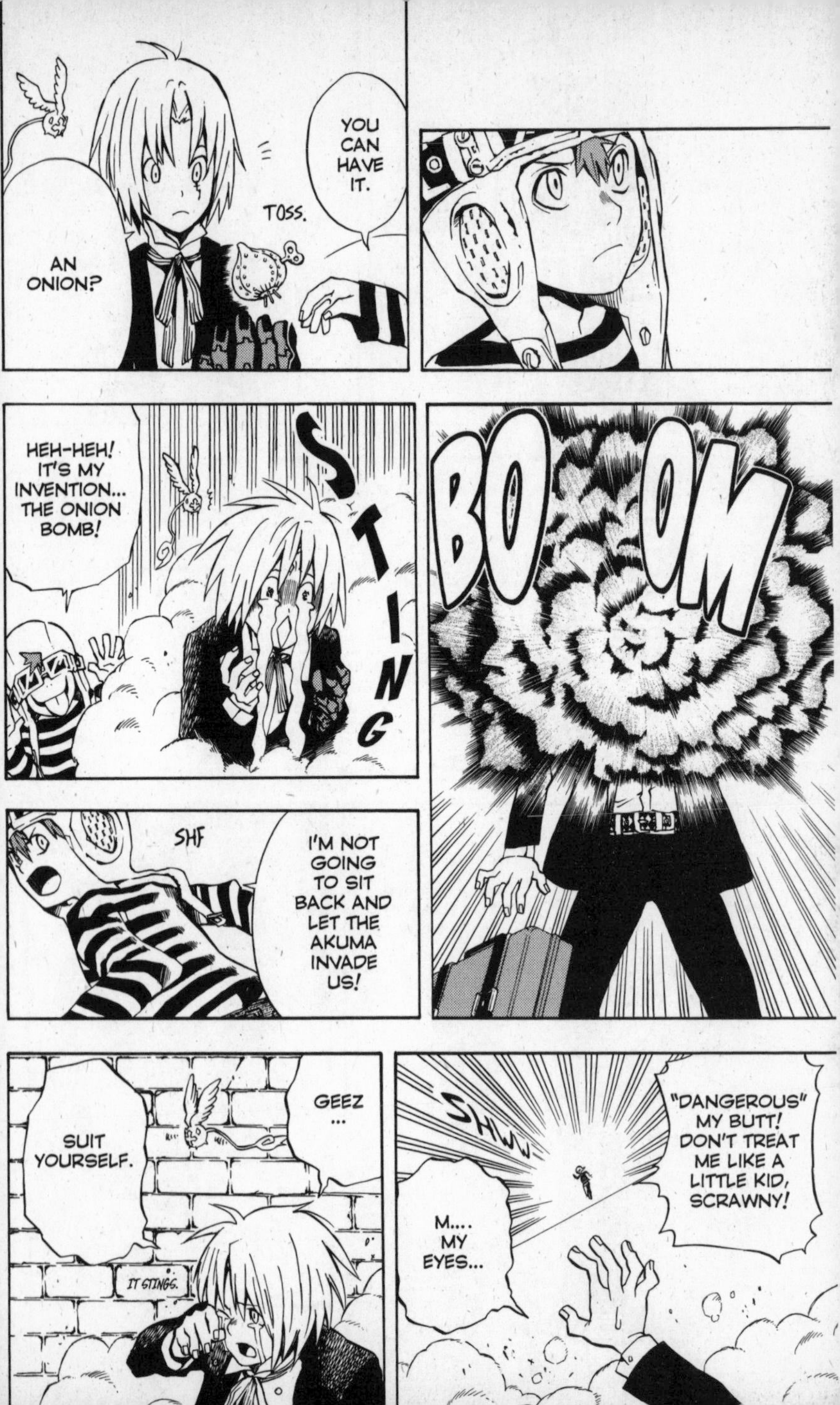
YOU CAN HAVE IT.
TOSS.
AN ONION?
BOOM
STING
HEH-HEH! IT'S MY INVENTION... THE ONION BOMB!
I'M NOT GOING TO SIT BACK AND LET THE AKUMA INVADE US!
SHF
SHWW
"DANGEROUS" MY BUTT! DON'T TREAT ME LIKE A LITTLE KID, SCRAWNY!
M.... MY EYES...
GEEZ ...
SUIT YOURSELF.
IT STINGS.

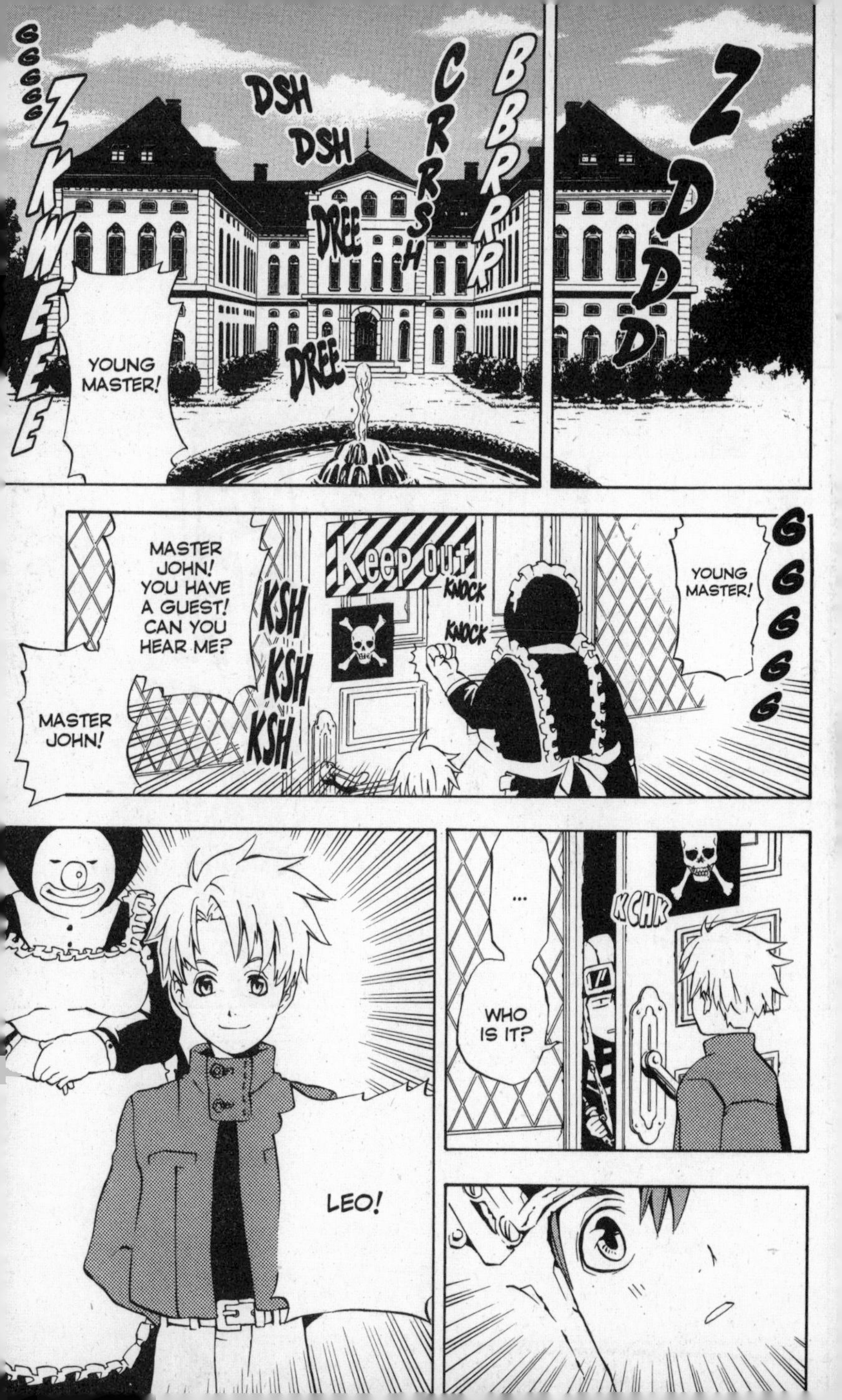

ZDDDD
BBRRRP
CRRSH
DSH
DSH
DREE
DREE
YOUNG MASTER!
GGGG
ZKWEEEE
GGGGGG
YOUNG MASTER!
KNOCK
KNOCK
Keep out
KSH
KSH
KSH
MASTER JOHN! YOU HAVE A GUEST! CAN YOU HEAR ME?
MASTER JOHN!
KCHK
...
WHO IS IT?
LEO!

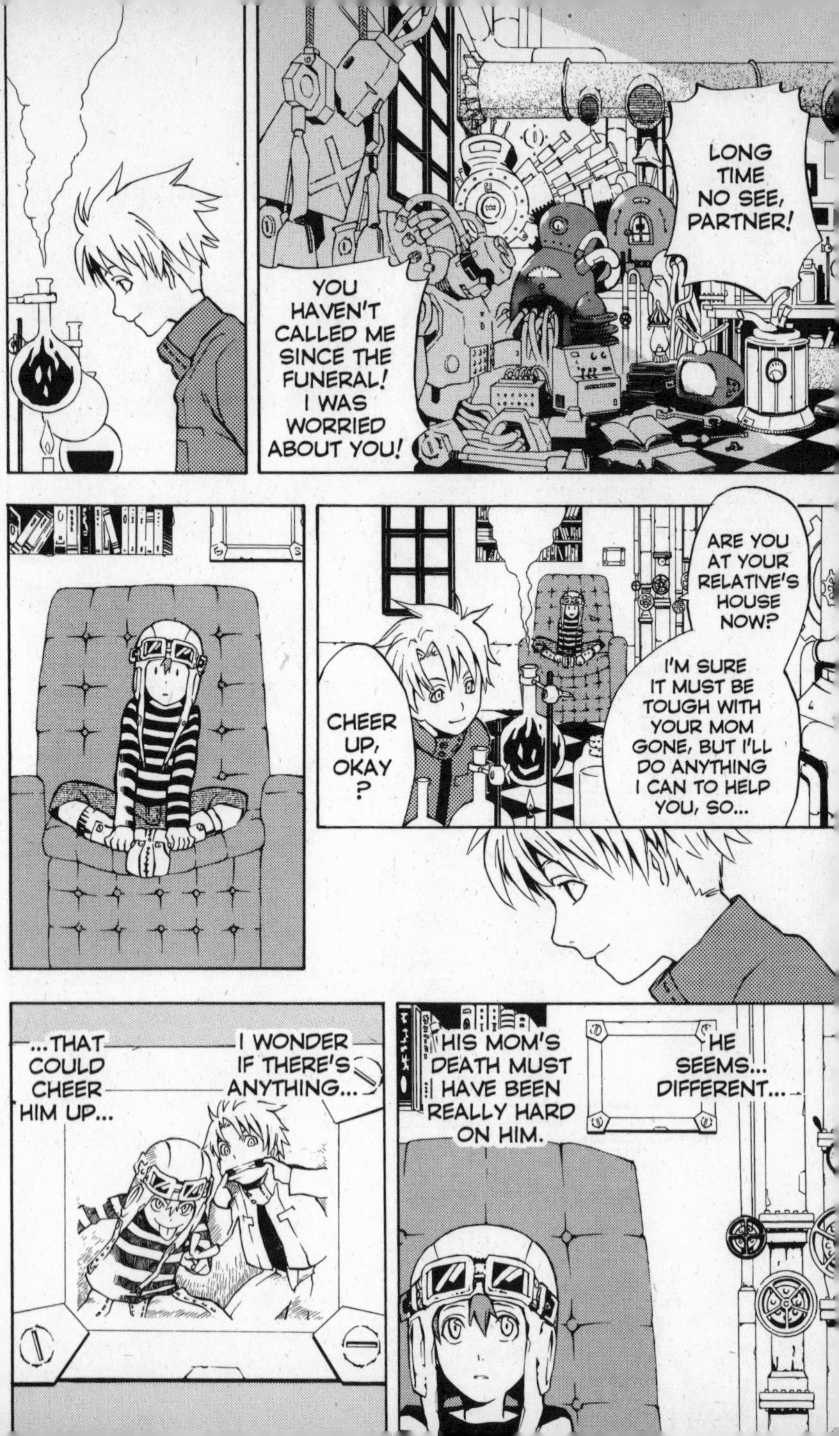
LONG TIME NO SEE, PARTNER!
YOU HAVEN'T CALLED ME SINCE THE FUNERAL! I WAS WORRIED ABOUT YOU!
ARE YOU AT YOUR RELATIVE'S HOUSE NOW?
I'M SURE IT MUST BE TOUGH WITH YOUR MOM GONE, BUT I'LL DO ANYTHING I CAN TO HELP YOU, SO...
CHEER UP, OKAY?
HE SEEMS... DIFFERENT...
HIS MOM'S DEATH MUST HAVE BEEN REALLY HARD ON HIM.
I WONDER IF THERE'S ANYTHING...
...THAT COULD CHEER HIM UP...

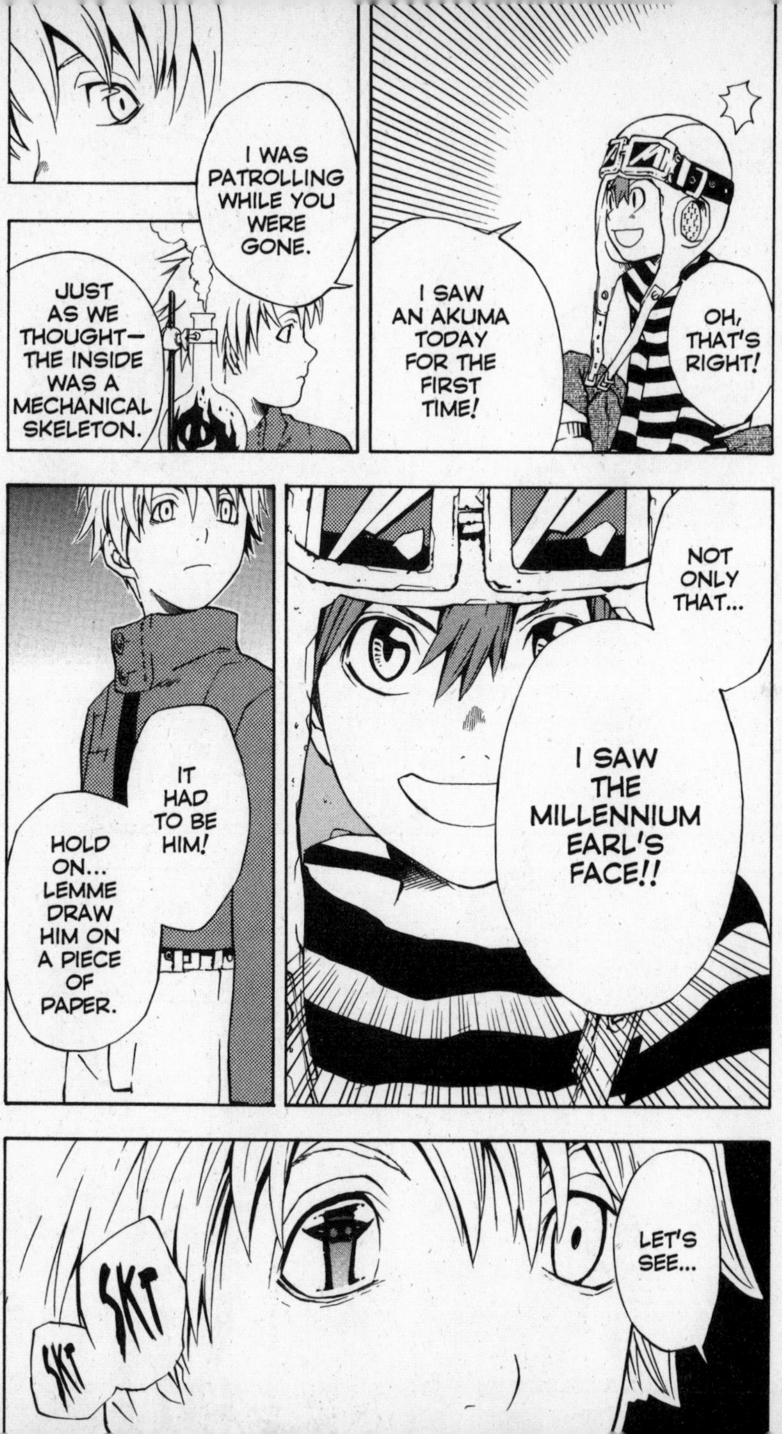
OH, THAT'S RIGHT!
I SAW AN AKUMA TODAY FOR THE FIRST TIME!
I WAS PATROLLING WHILE YOU WERE GONE.
JUST AS WE THOUGHT—THE INSIDE WAS A MECHANICAL SKELETON.
NOT ONLY THAT...
I SAW THE MILLENNIUM EARL'S FACE!!
IT HAD TO BE HIM!
HOLD ON... LEMME DRAW HIM ON A PIECE OF PAPER.
LET'S SEE...
SKT
SKT

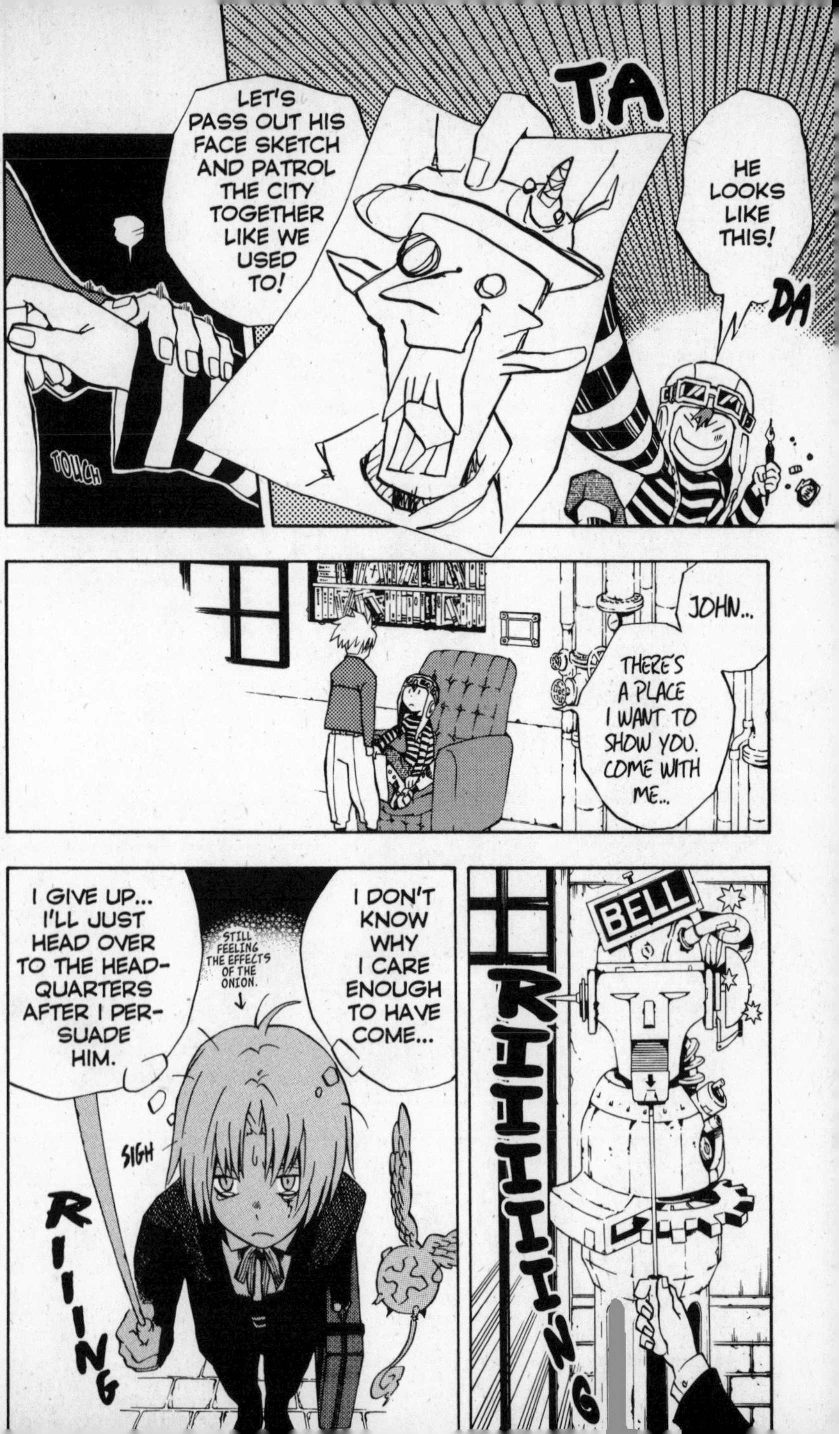
TA
HE LOOKS LIKE THIS!
DA
LET'S PASS OUT HIS FACE SKETCH AND PATROL THE CITY TOGETHER LIKE WE USED TO!
TOUCH
JOHN...
THERE'S A PLACE I WANT TO SHOW YOU. COME WITH ME...
BELL
RIIIIIIING
I DON'T KNOW WHY I CARE ENOUGH TO HAVE COME...
I GIVE UP... I'LL JUST HEAD OVER TO THE HEAD-QUARTERS AFTER I PER-SUADE HIM.
STILL FEELING THE EFFECTS OF THE ONION.
SIGH
RIIING

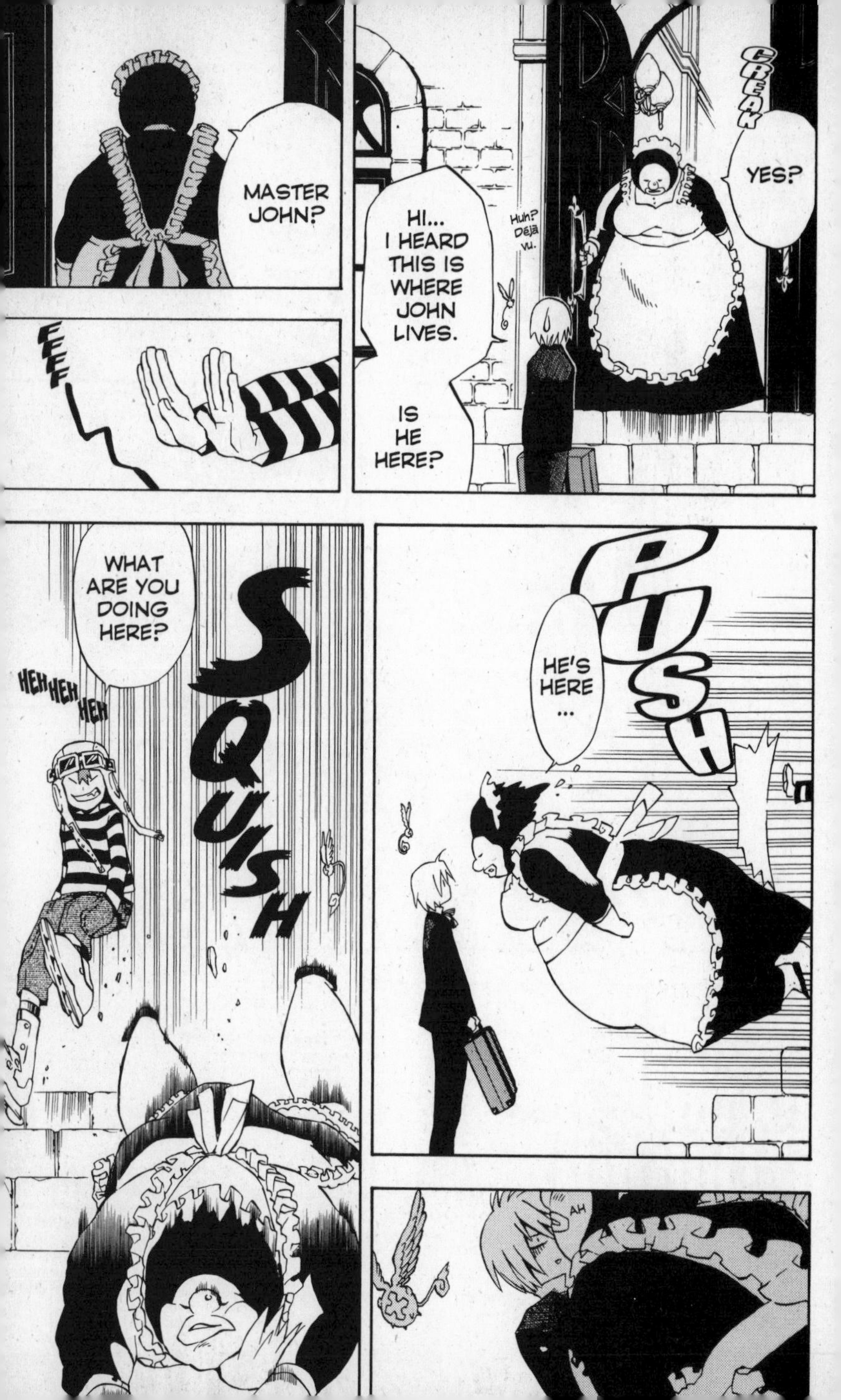
CREAK
YES?
Huh? Déjà vu.
HI... I HEARD THIS IS WHERE JOHN LIVES.
IS HE HERE?
MASTER JOHN?
EEEE
PUSH
HE'S HERE ...
WHAT ARE YOU DOING HERE?
HEH HEH HEH
SQUISH
AH

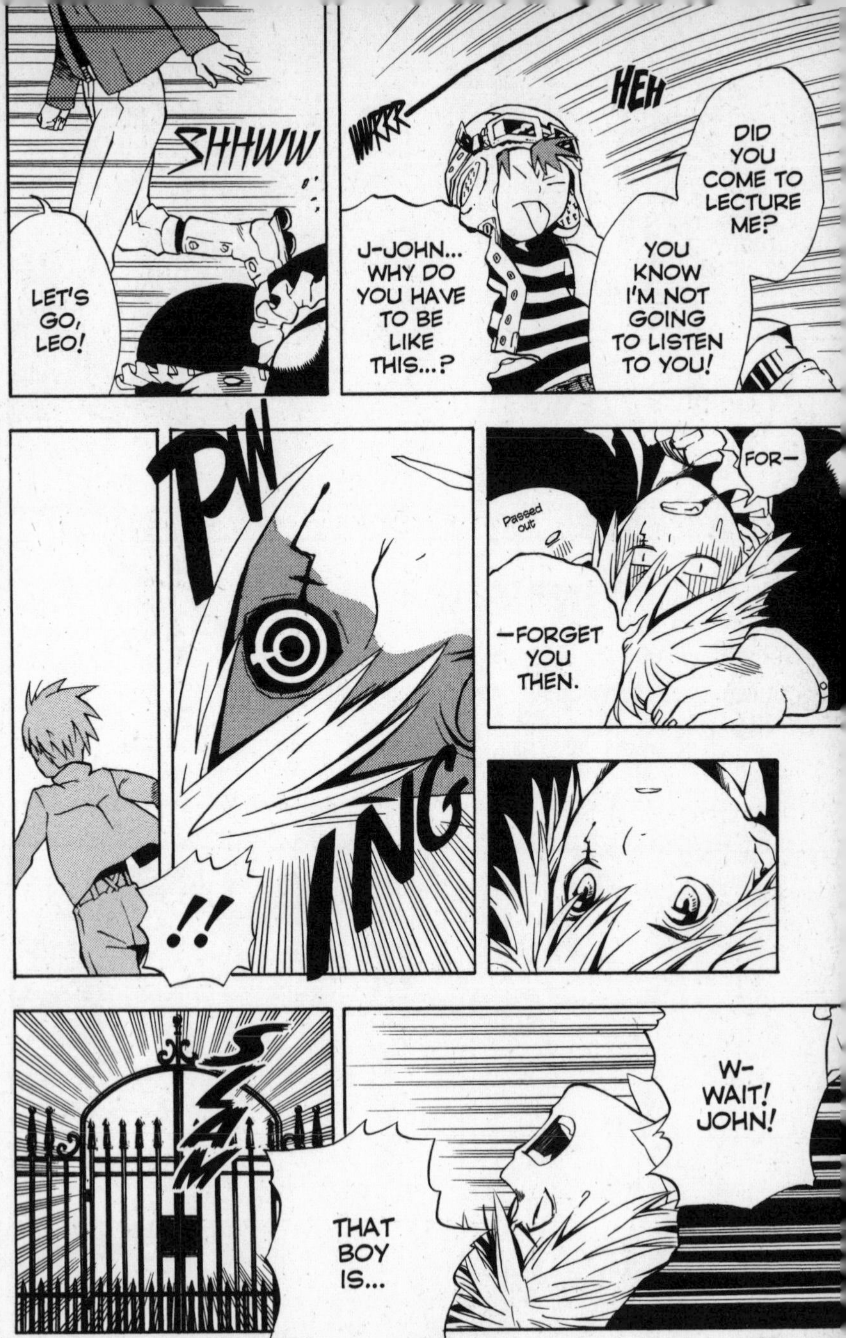
HEH
WHRRR
DID YOU COME TO LECTURE ME?
YOU KNOW I'M NOT GOING TO LISTEN TO YOU!
J-JOHN... WHY DO YOU HAVE TO BE LIKE THIS...?
SHHWW
LET'S GO, LEO!
FOR—
Passed out
—FORGET YOU THEN.
PWING
!!
W-WAIT! JOHN!
THAT BOY IS...
SLAM

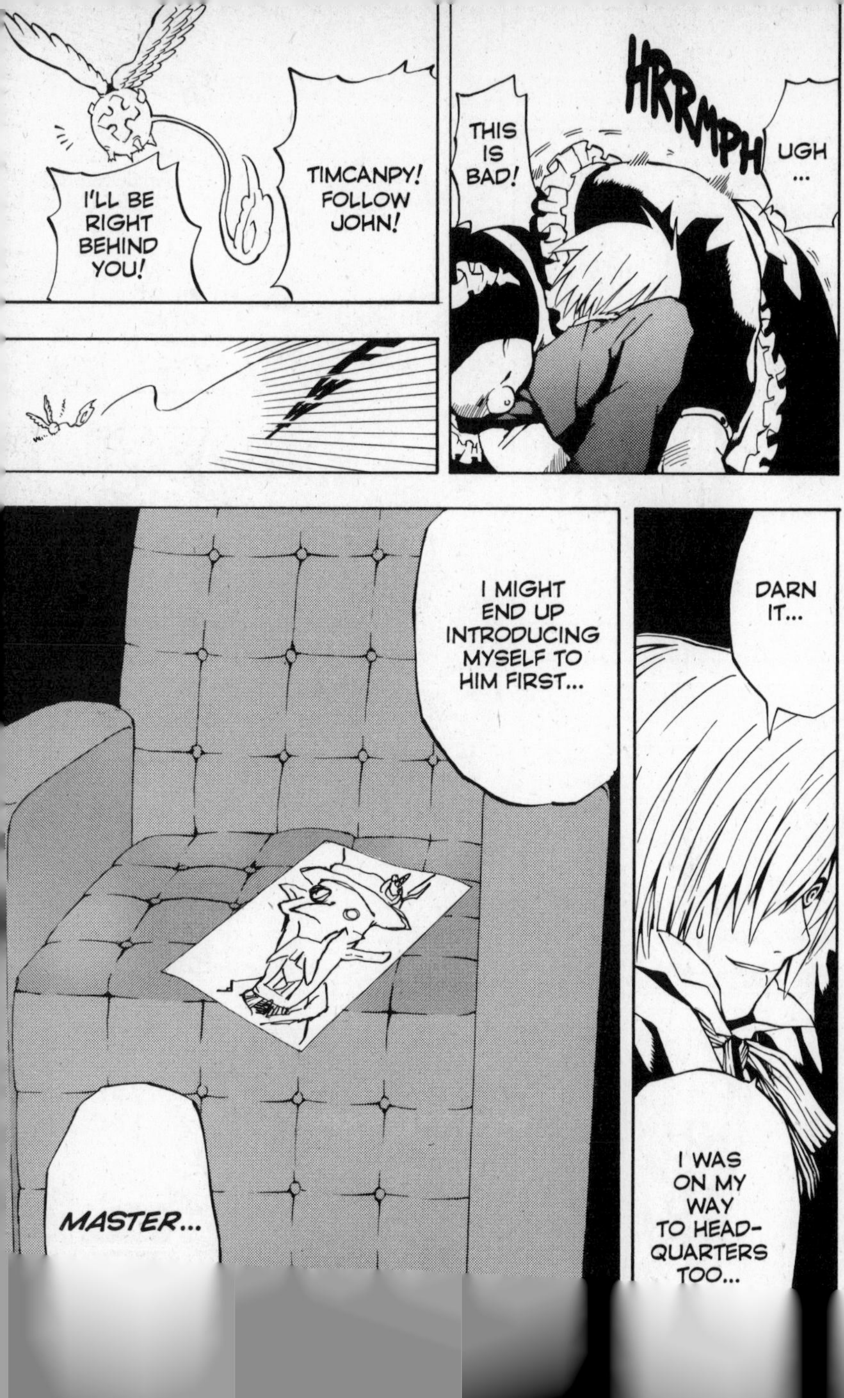
UGH...
HRRMPH
THIS IS BAD!
TIMCANPY! FOLLOW JOHN!
I'LL BE RIGHT BEHIND YOU!
DARN IT...
I WAS ON MY WAY TO HEAD-QUARTERS TOO...
I MIGHT END UP INTRODUCING MYSELF TO HIM FIRST...
MASTER...

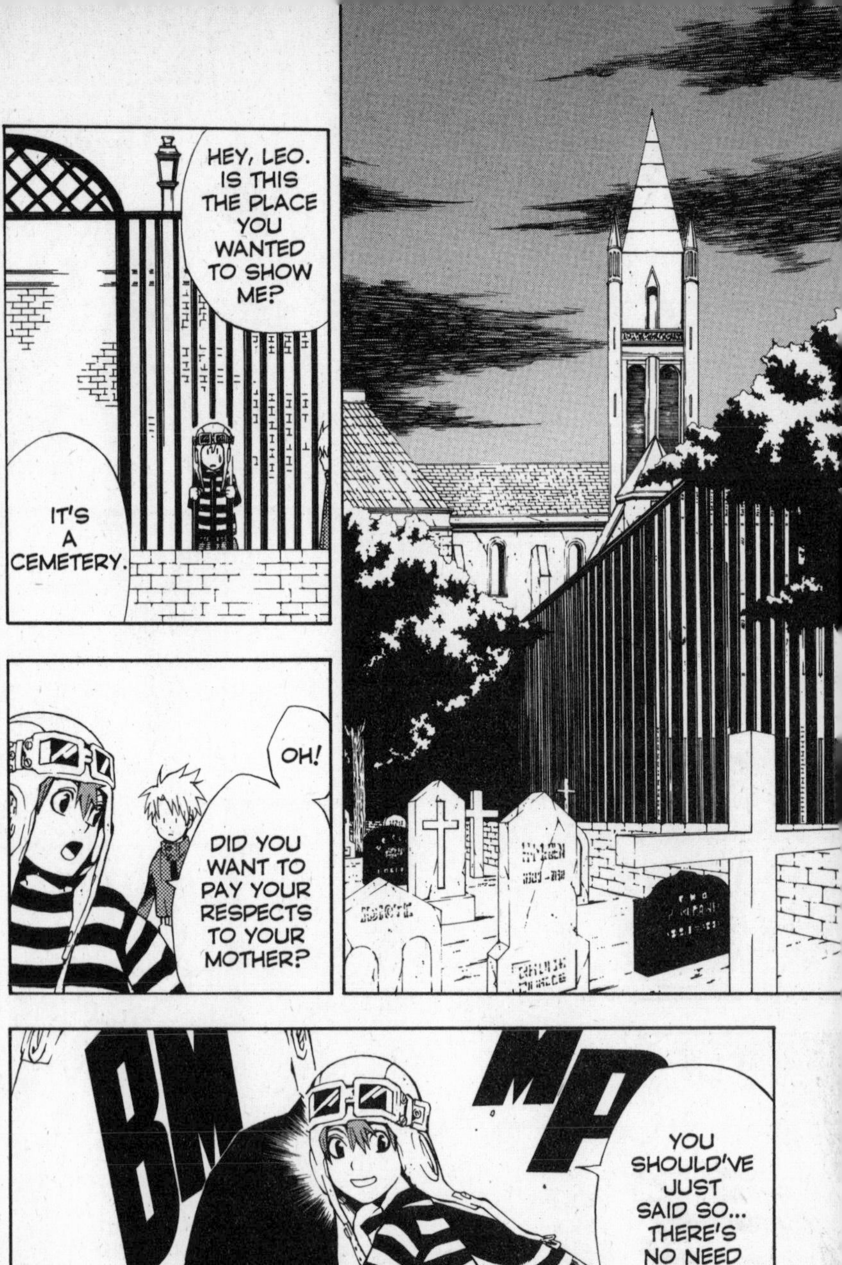
HEY, LEO. IS THIS THE PLACE YOU WANTED TO SHOW ME?
IT'S A CEMETERY.
OH!
DID YOU WANT TO PAY YOUR RESPECTS TO YOUR MOTHER?
BMMP
YOU SHOULD'VE JUST SAID SO... THERE'S NO NEED TO BE...

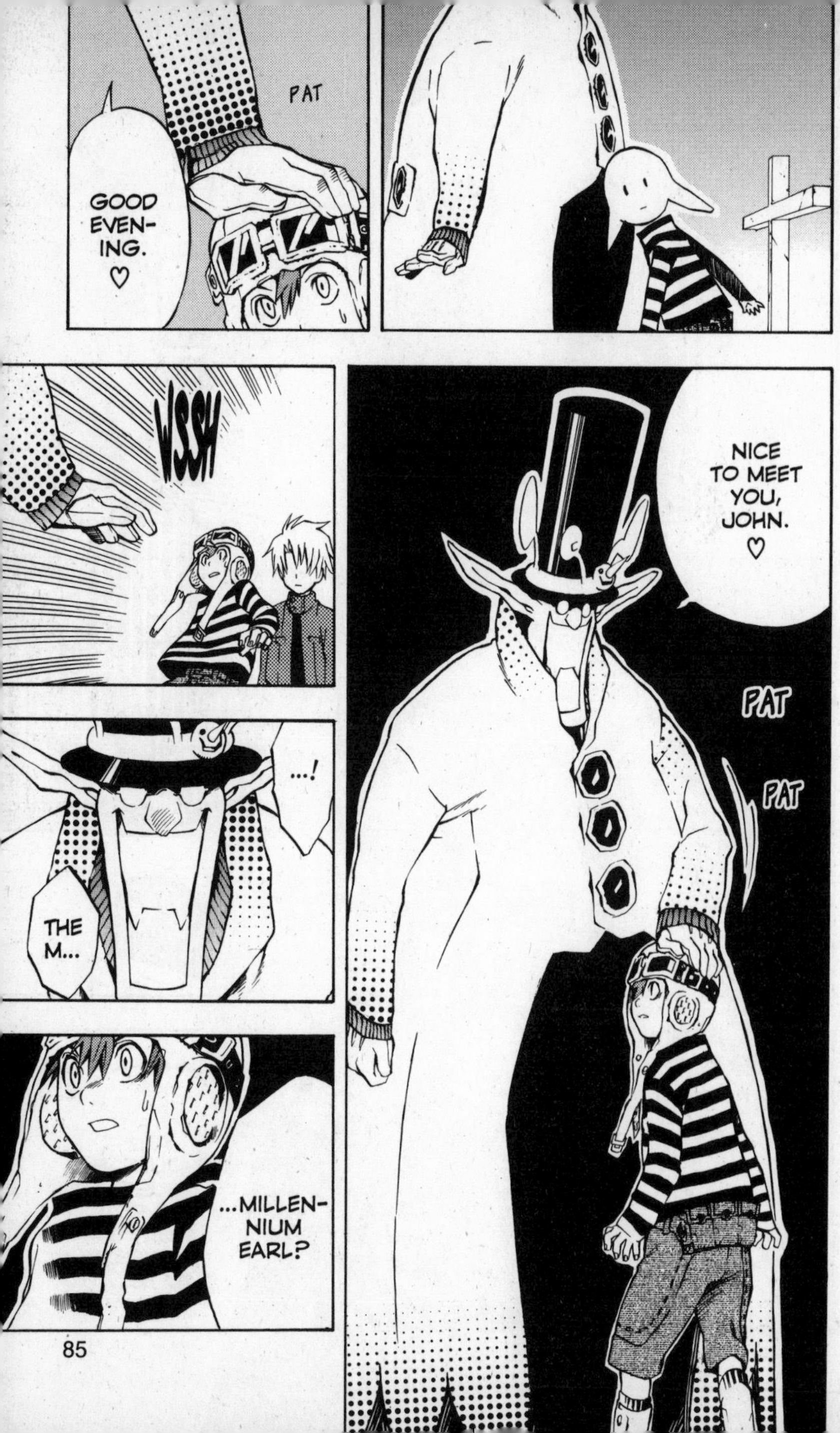

PAT
GOOD EVEN-ING. ♡
NICE TO MEET YOU, JOHN. ♡
PAT
PAT
WSSH
...!
THE M...
...MILLEN-NIUM EARL?

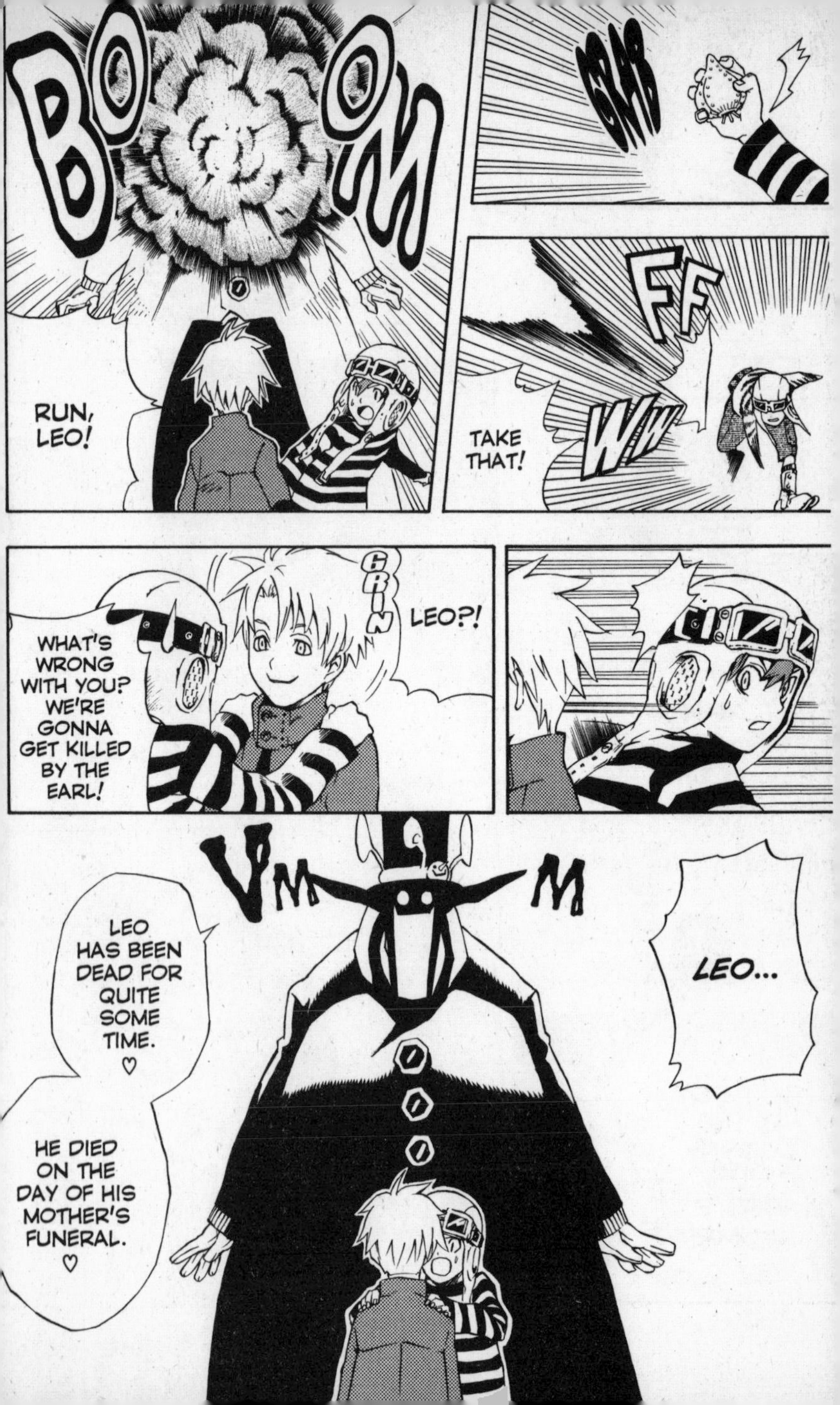
GRAB
FFWW
TAKE THAT!
BOOM
RUN, LEO!
GRIN
LEO?!
WHAT'S WRONG WITH YOU? WE'RE GONNA GET KILLED BY THE EARL!
LEO...
VMM
LEO HAS BEEN DEAD FOR QUITE SOME TIME. ♡
HE DIED ON THE DAY OF HIS MOTHER'S FUNERAL. ♡

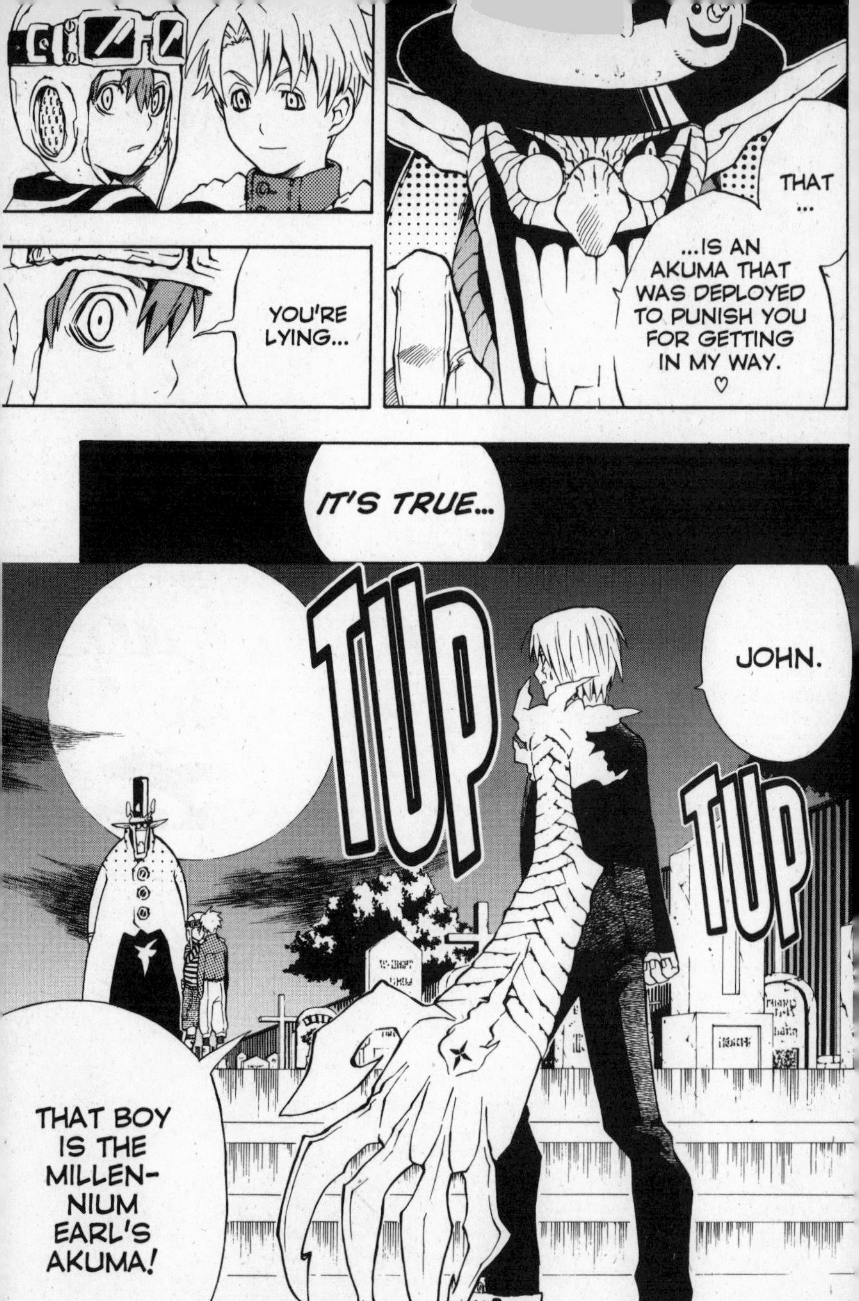
THAT...
...IS AN AKUMA THAT WAS DEPLOYED TO PUNISH YOU FOR GETTING IN MY WAY. ♡
YOU'RE LYING...
IT'S TRUE...
JOHN.
TUP
TUP
THAT BOY IS THE MILLENNIUM EARL'S AKUMA!

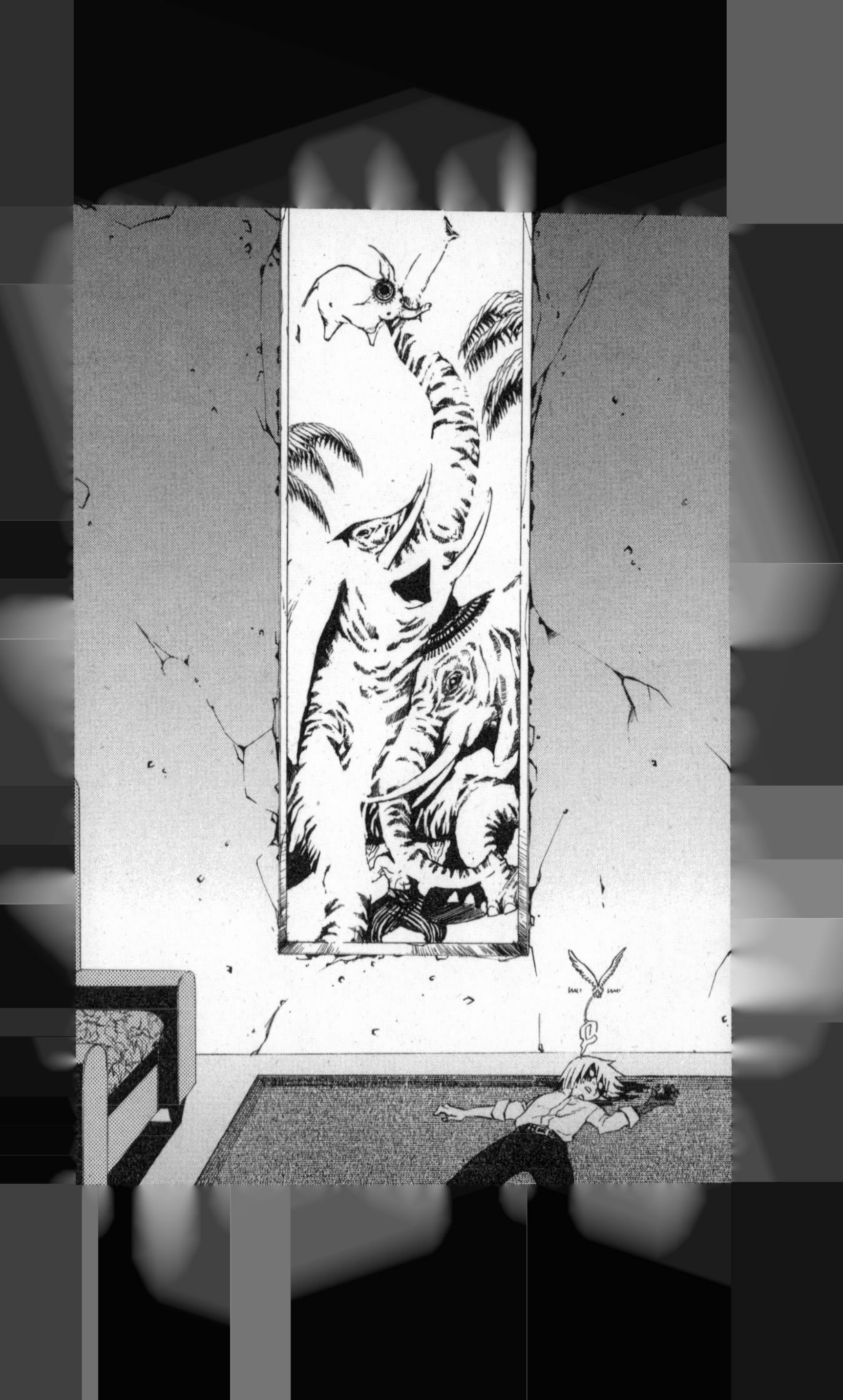

THE 3RD NIGHT: THE PENTACLE

DESTROY...

DESTROY...

DESTROY...

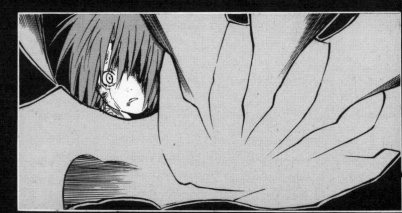

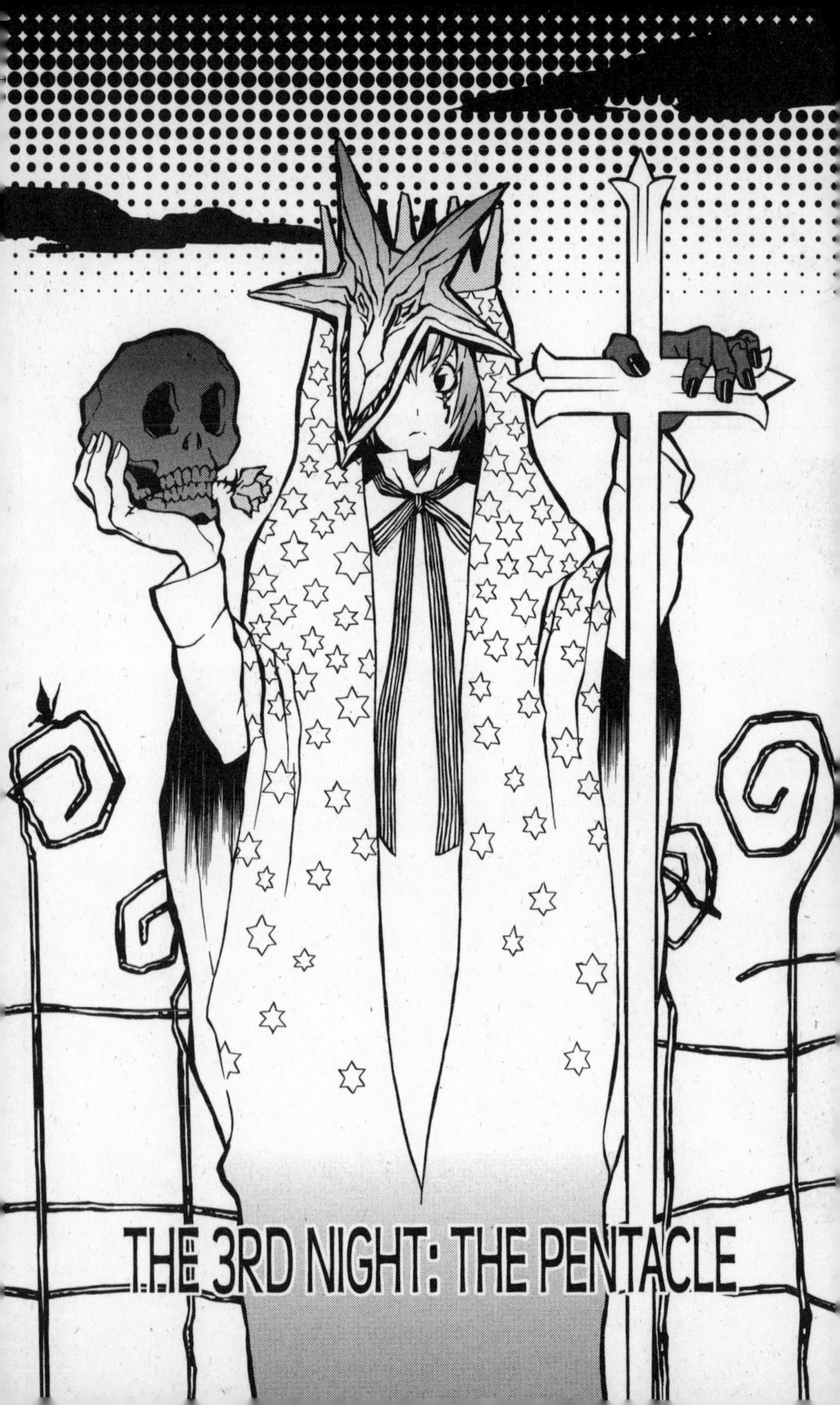
THE 3RD NIGHT: THE PENTACLE

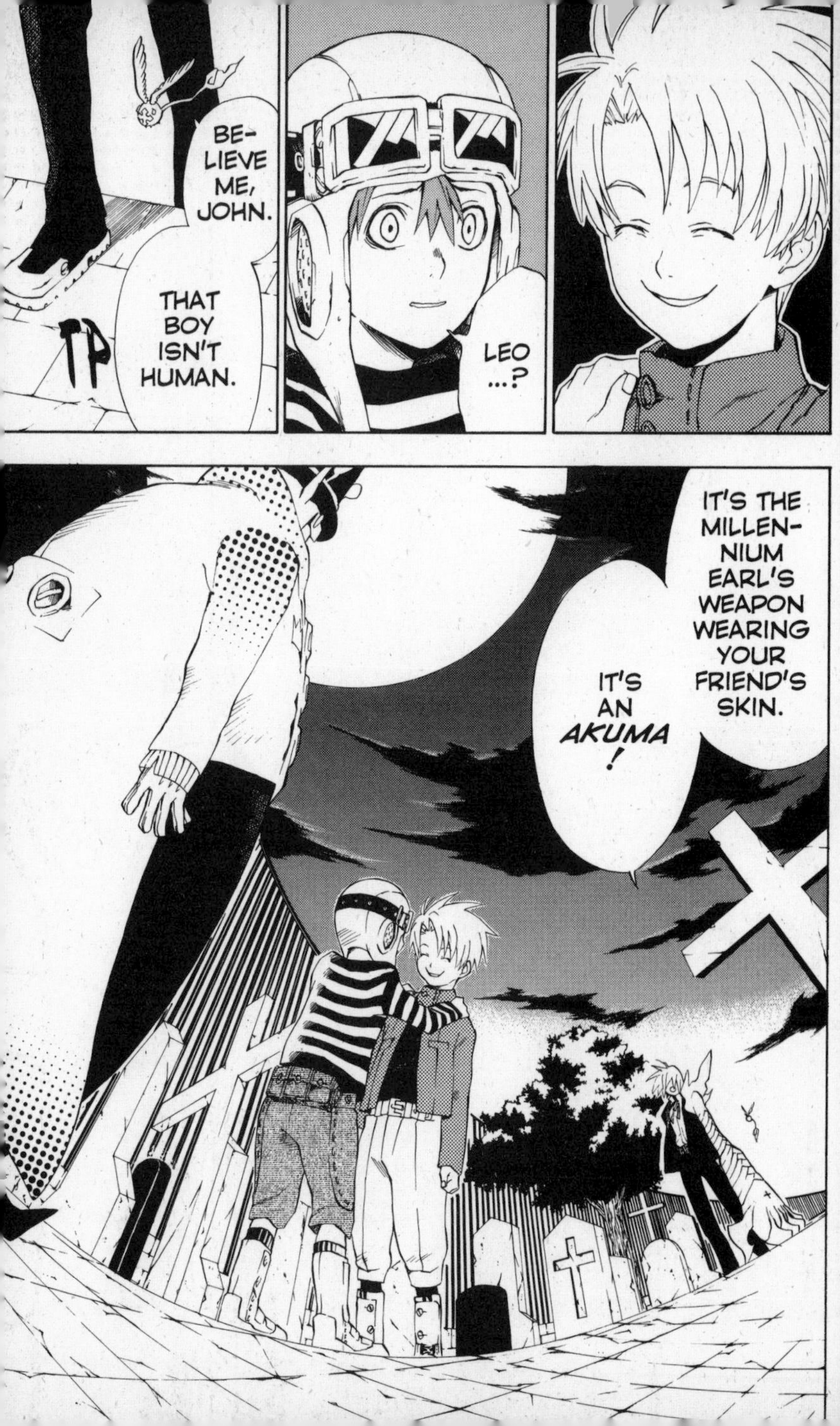
LEO ...?
BE-LIEVE ME, JOHN.
THAT BOY ISN'T HUMAN.
TP
IT'S THE MILLEN-NIUM EARL'S WEAPON WEARING YOUR FRIEND'S SKIN.
IT'S AN *AKUMA*!

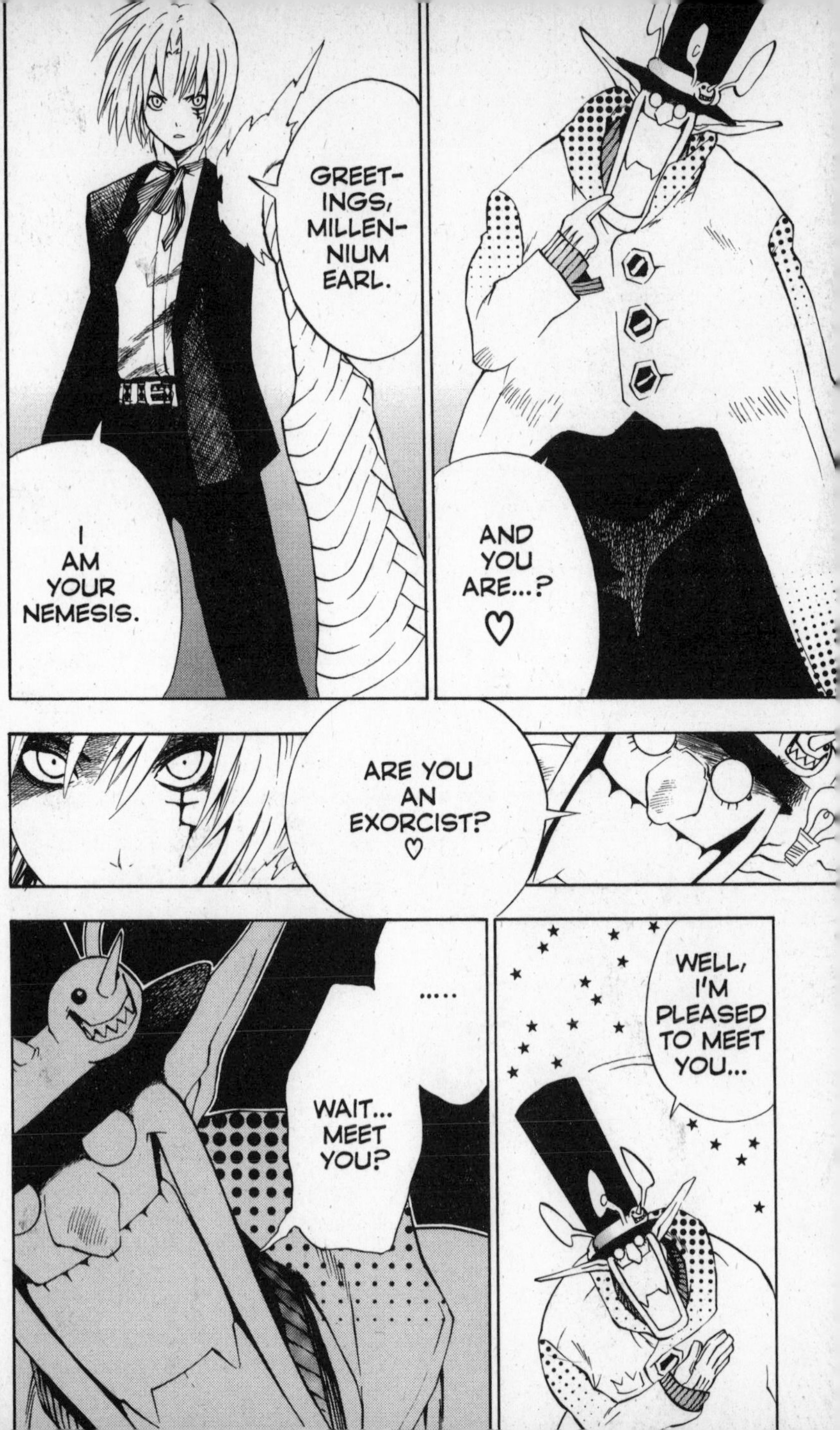

GREETINGS, MILLENNIUM EARL.
AND YOU ARE...? ♡
I AM YOUR NEMESIS.
ARE YOU AN EXORCIST? ♡
WELL, I'M PLEASED TO MEET YOU...
.....
WAIT... MEET YOU?

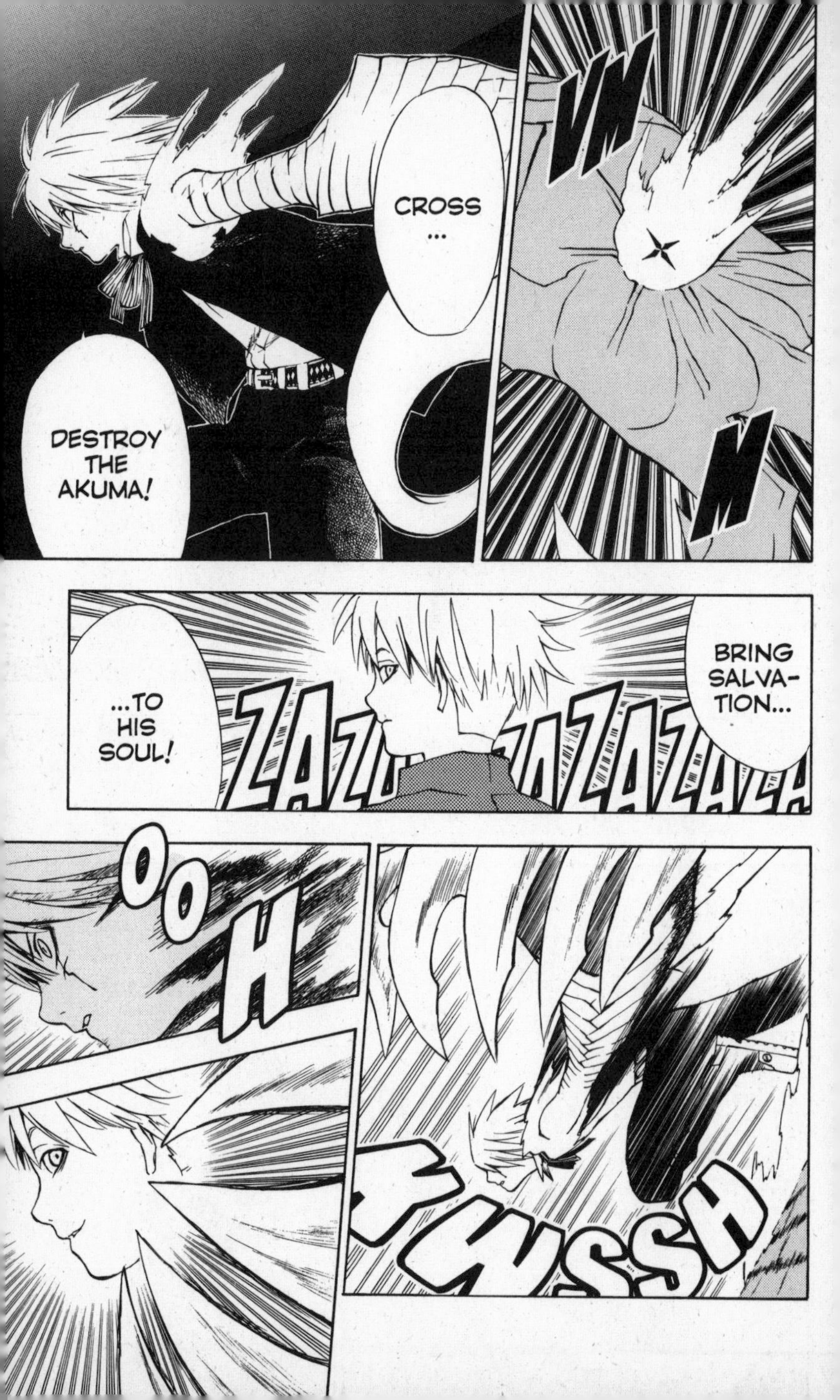
VM
M
CROSS ...
DESTROY THE AKUMA!
BRING SALVATION...
...TO HIS SOUL!
ZAZAZAZA
TCHSSH
OOH

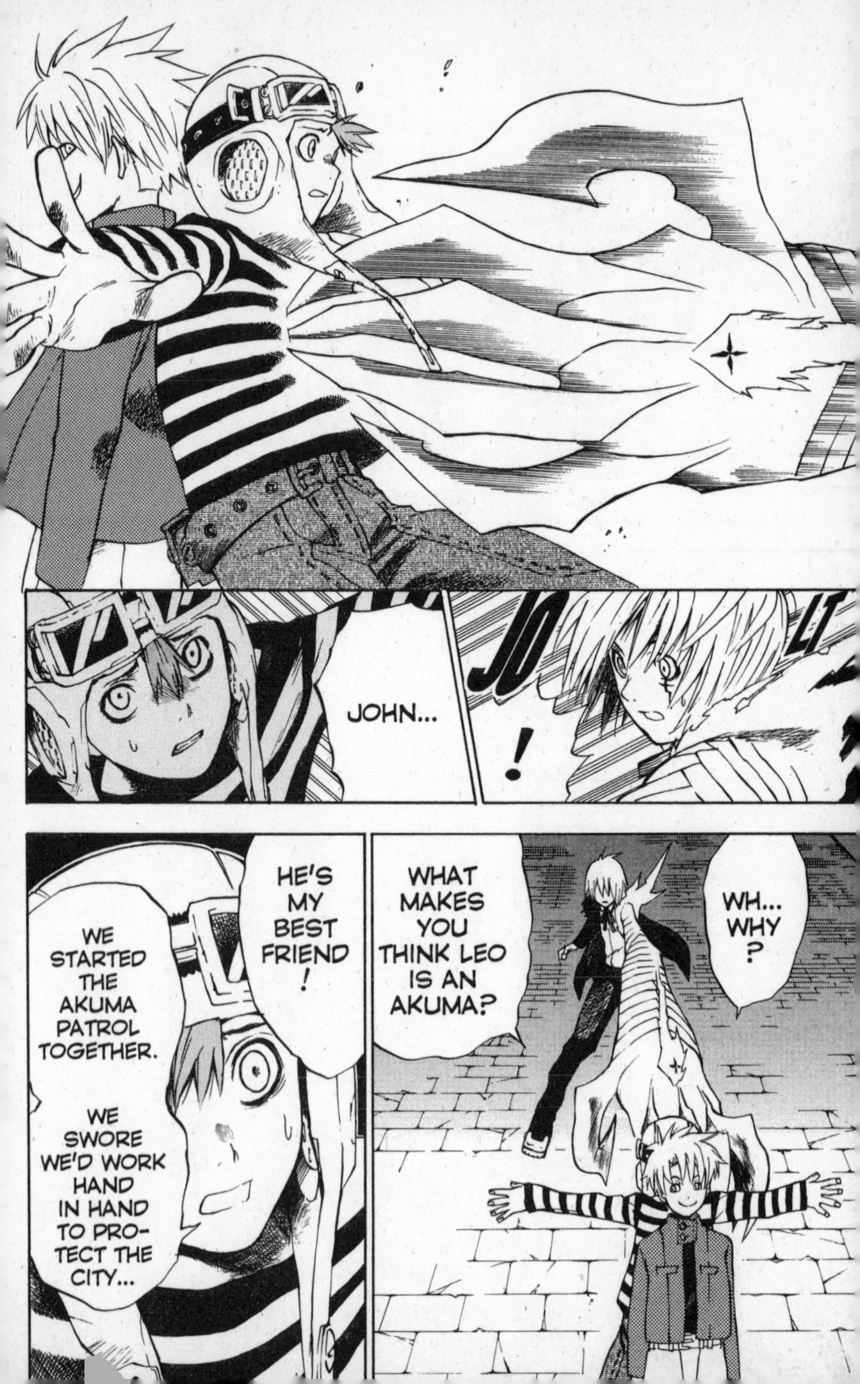

JOLT
!
JOHN...
WH... WHY?
WHAT MAKES YOU THINK LEO IS AN AKUMA?
HE'S MY BEST FRIEND!
WE STARTED THE AKUMA PATROL TOGETHER.
WE SWORE WE'D WORK HAND IN HAND TO PROTECT THE CITY...

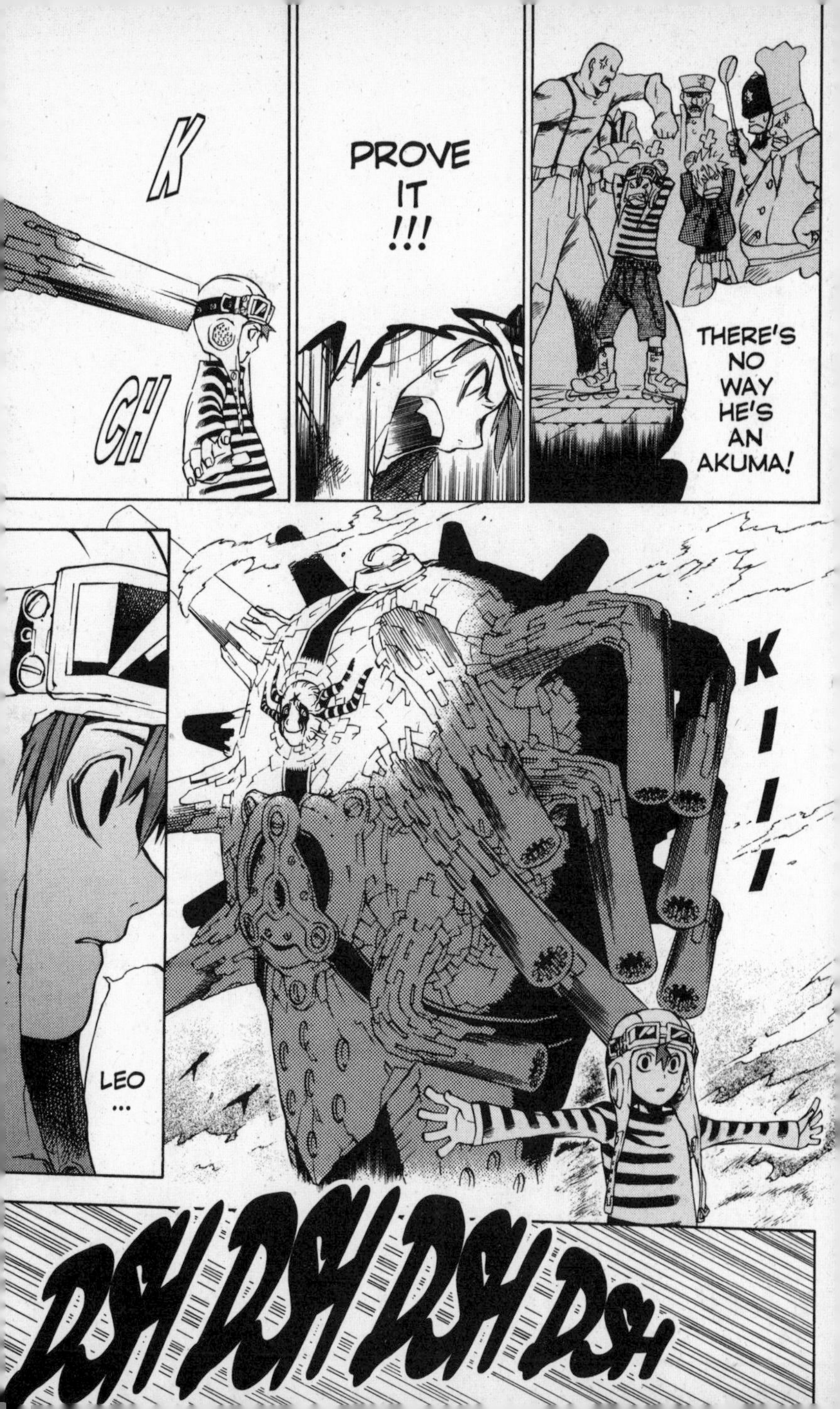
THERE'S NO WAY HE'S AN AKUMA!
PROVE IT!!!
K
CH
K I I I
LEO ...
DSH DSH DSH DSH

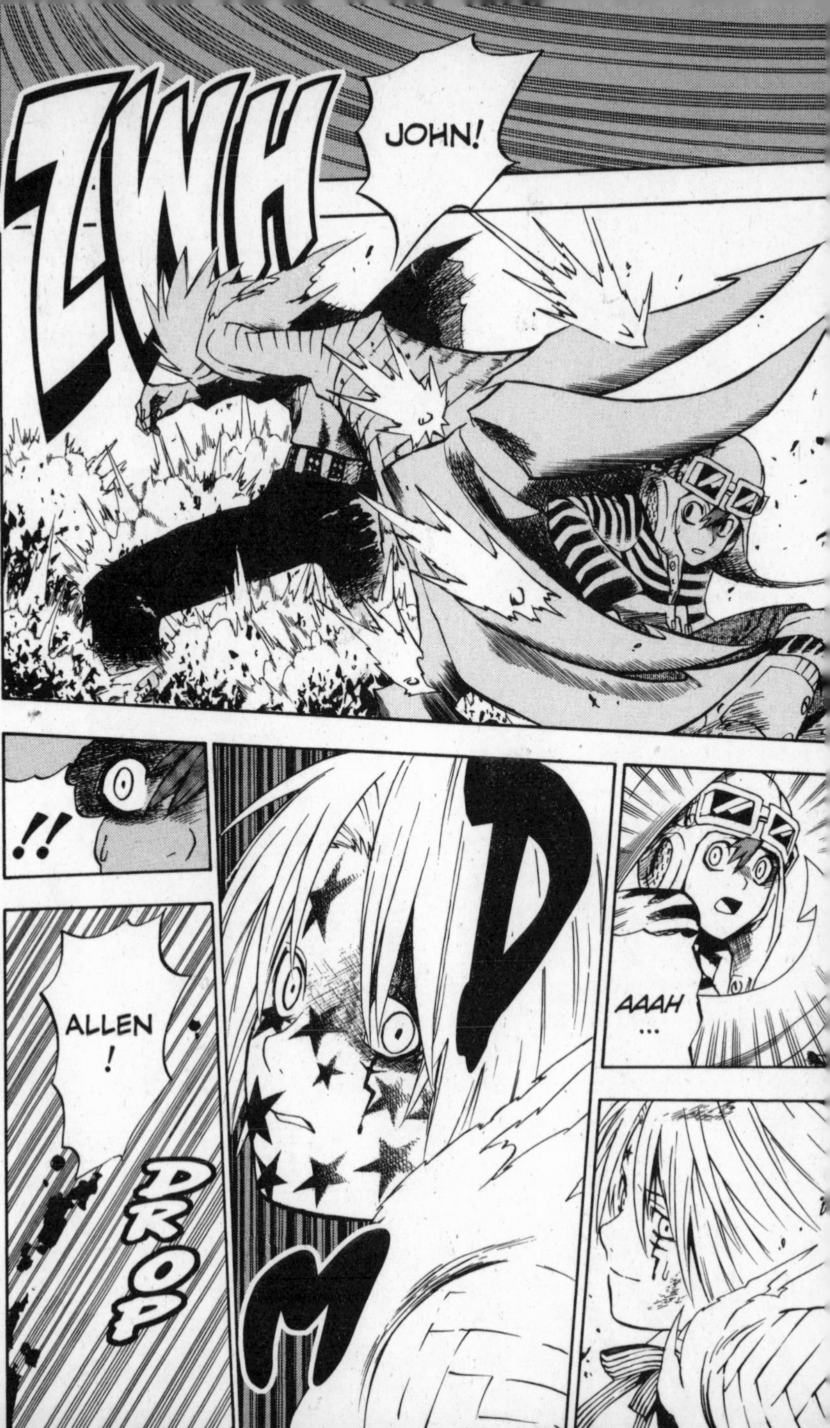
JOHN!
ZWH
AAAH ...
!!
ALLEN !
DROP

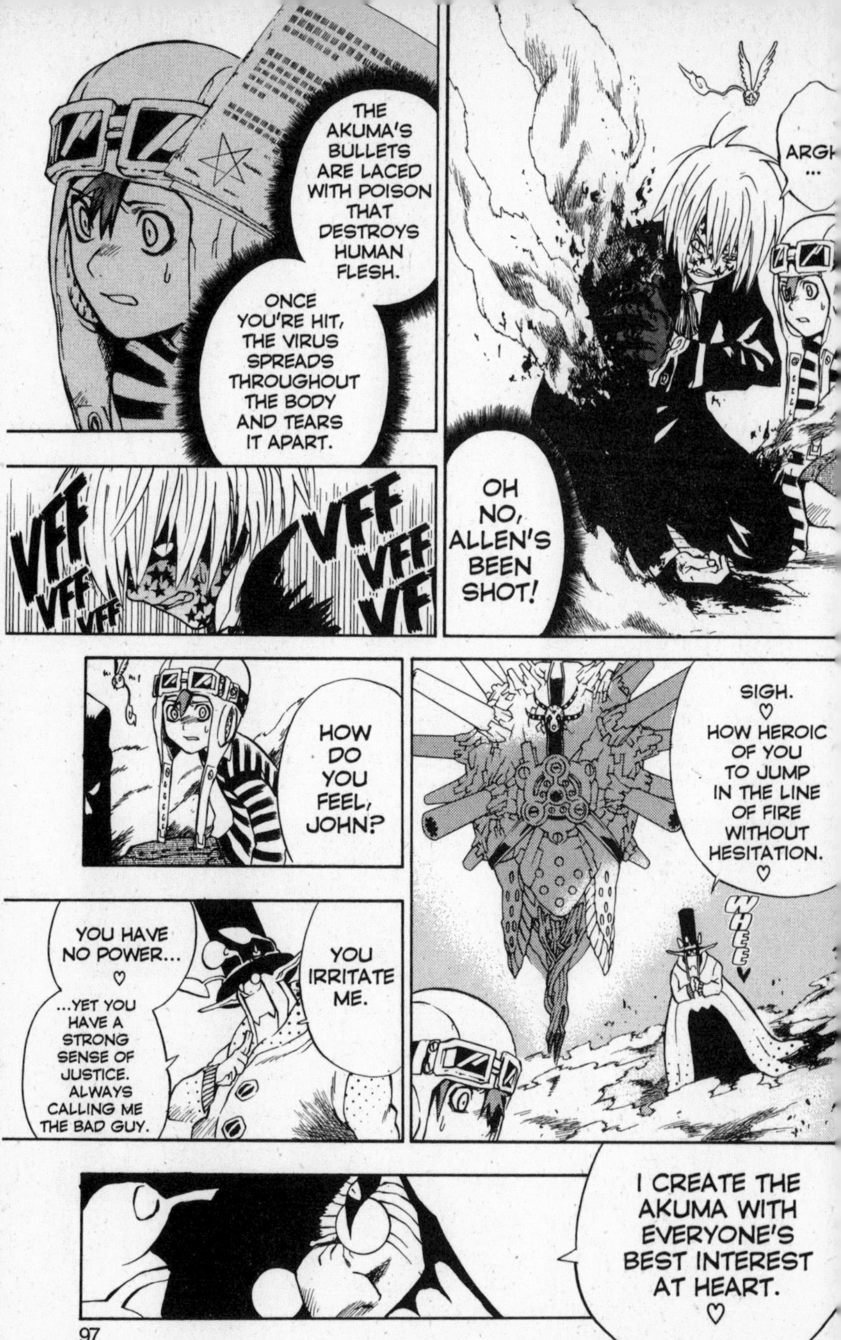
ARGH...
OH NO, ALLEN'S BEEN SHOT!
THE AKUMA'S BULLETS ARE LACED WITH POISON THAT DESTROYS HUMAN FLESH.
ONCE YOU'RE HIT, THE VIRUS SPREADS THROUGHOUT THE BODY AND TEARS IT APART.
VFF VFF VFF VF
VFF VFF VFF
SIGH. ♡ HOW HEROIC OF YOU TO JUMP IN THE LINE OF FIRE WITHOUT HESITATION. ♡
WHEEE
HOW DO YOU FEEL, JOHN?
YOU IRRITATE ME.
YOU HAVE NO POWER... ♡
...YET YOU HAVE A STRONG SENSE OF JUSTICE. ALWAYS CALLING ME THE BAD GUY.
I CREATE THE AKUMA WITH EVERYONE'S BEST INTEREST AT HEART. ♡

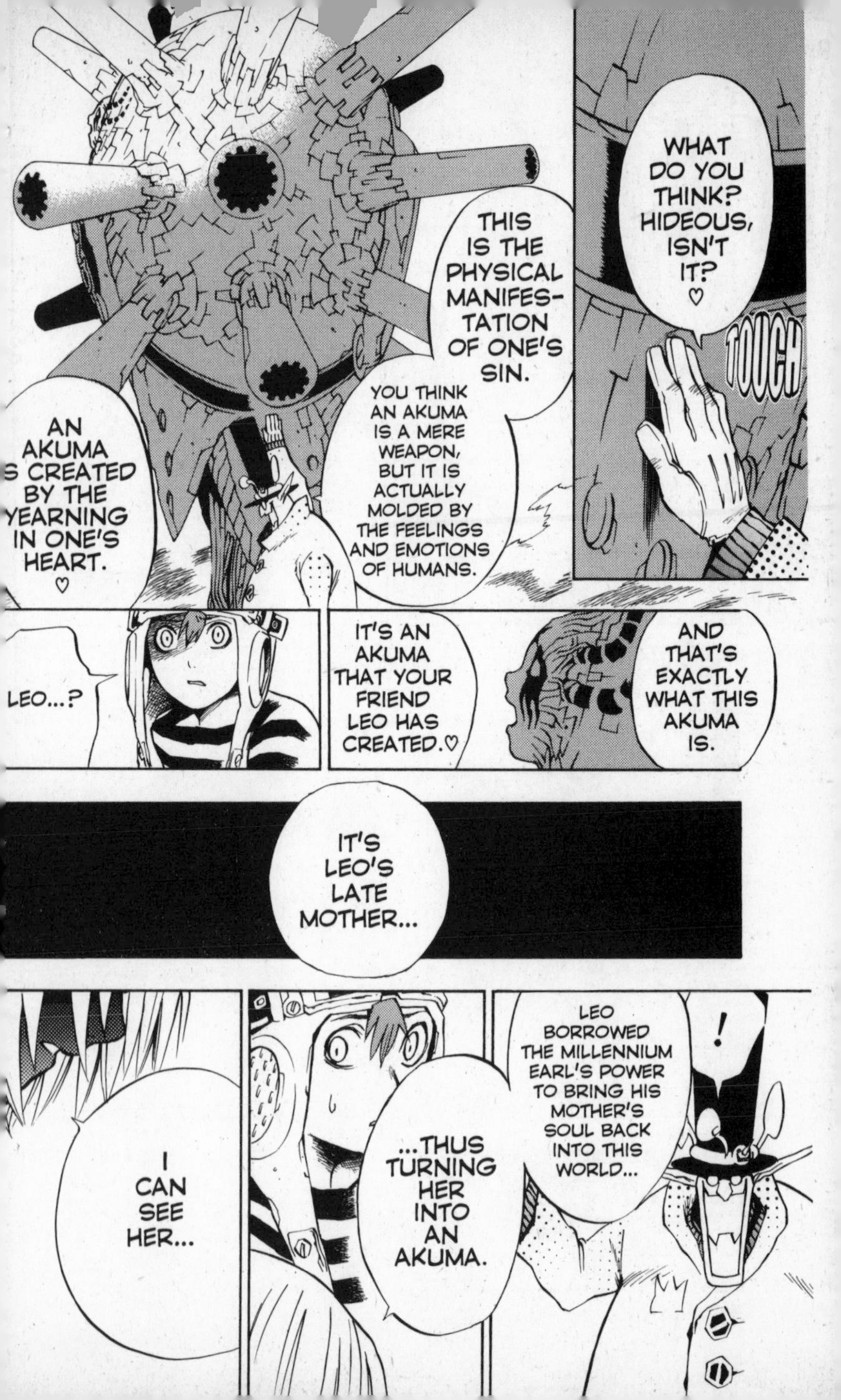
WHAT DO YOU THINK? HIDEOUS, ISN'T IT? ♡
TOUCH
THIS IS THE PHYSICAL MANIFES-TATION OF ONE'S SIN.
YOU THINK AN AKUMA IS A MERE WEAPON, BUT IT IS ACTUALLY MOLDED BY THE FEELINGS AND EMOTIONS OF HUMANS.
AN AKUMA S CREATED BY THE YEARNING IN ONE'S HEART. ♡
AND THAT'S EXACTLY WHAT THIS AKUMA IS.
IT'S AN AKUMA THAT YOUR FRIEND LEO HAS CREATED.♡
LEO...?
IT'S LEO'S LATE MOTHER...
!
LEO BORROWED THE MILLENNIUM EARL'S POWER TO BRING HIS MOTHER'S SOUL BACK INTO THIS WORLD...
...THUS TURNING HER INTO AN AKUMA.
I CAN SEE HER...

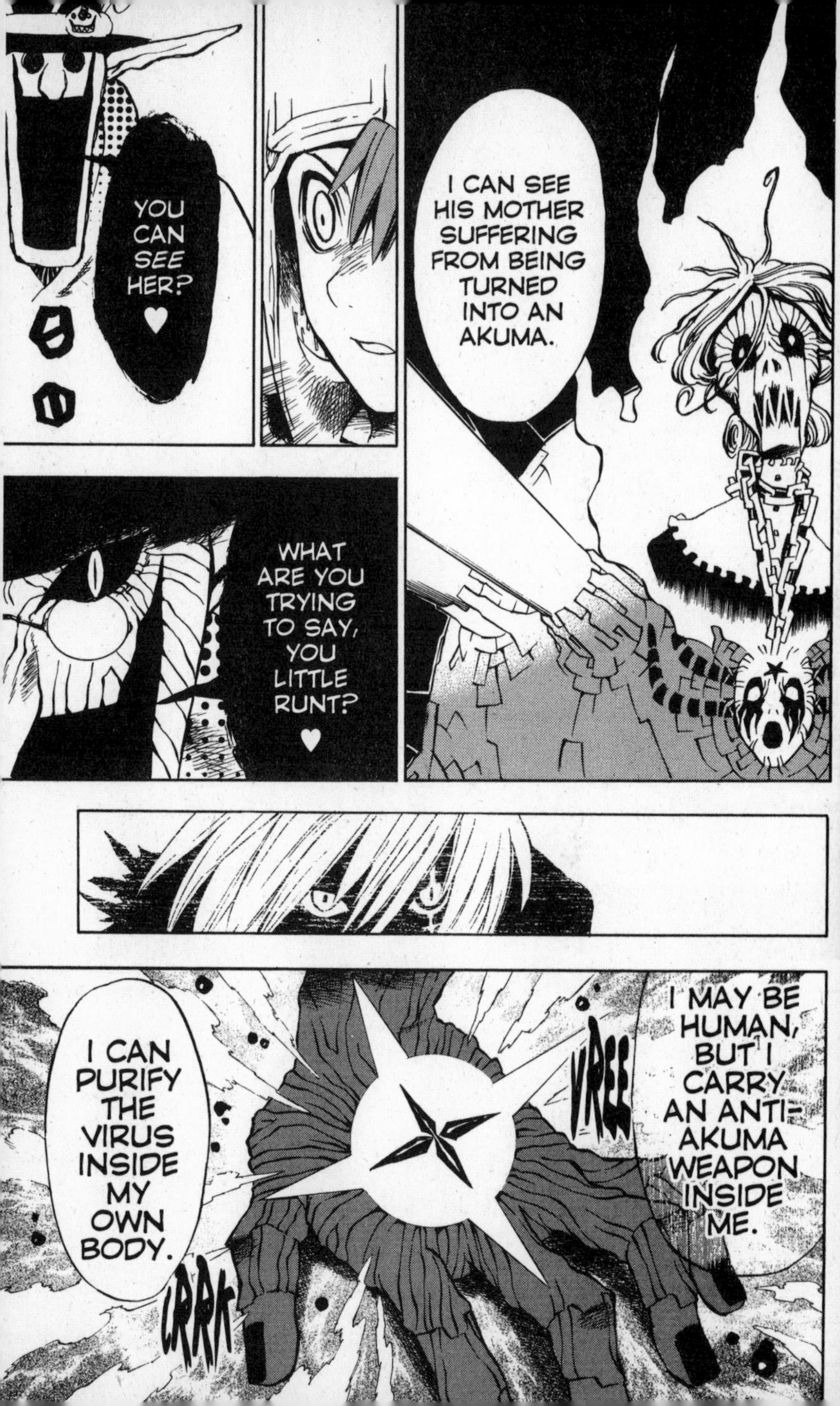
I CAN SEE HIS MOTHER SUFFERING FROM BEING TURNED INTO AN AKUMA.
YOU CAN SEE HER? ♥
WHAT ARE YOU TRYING TO SAY, YOU LITTLE RUNT? ♥
I MAY BE HUMAN, BUT I CARRY AN ANTI-AKUMA WEAPON INSIDE ME.
VREE
I CAN PURIFY THE VIRUS INSIDE MY OWN BODY.
CRRK

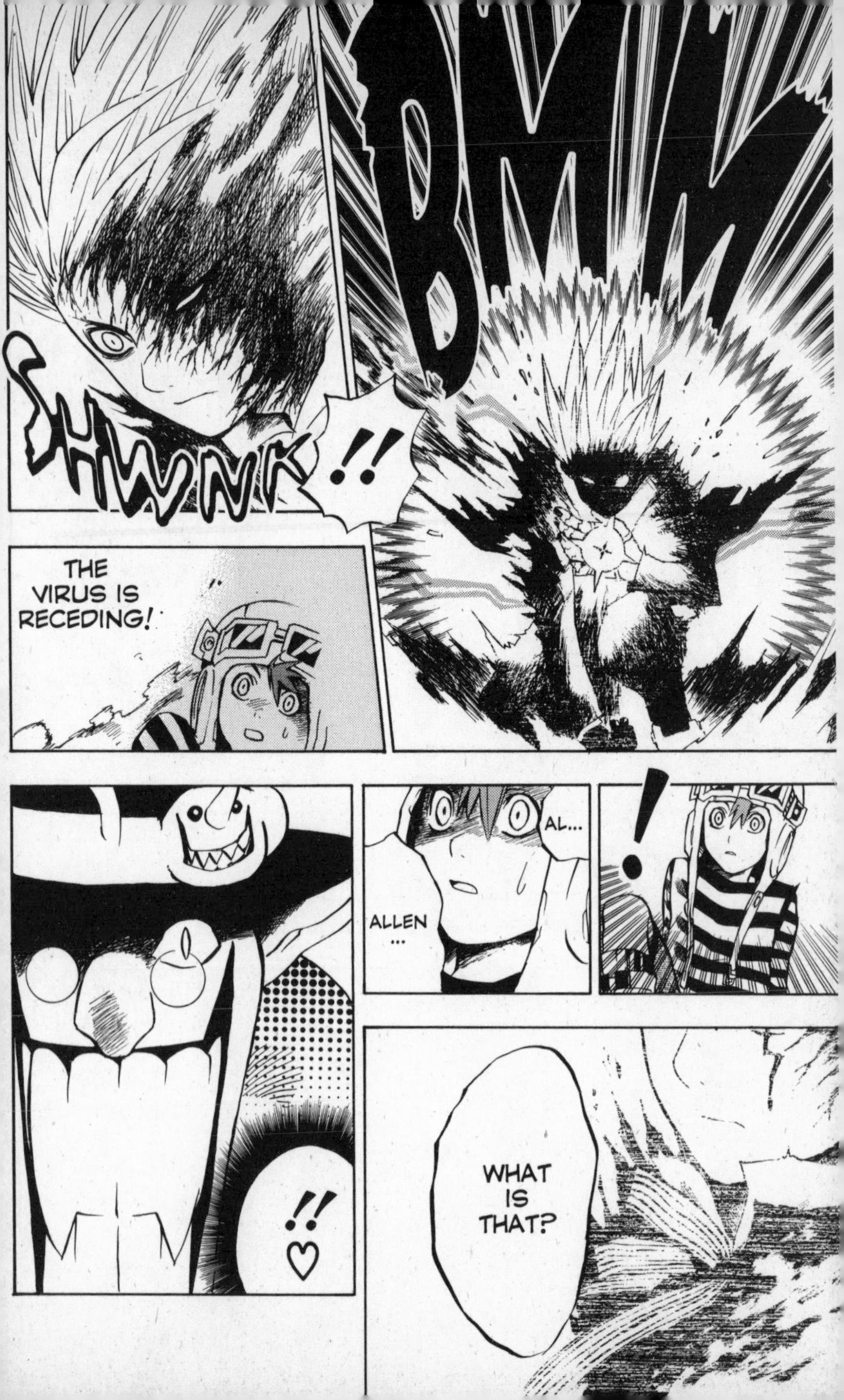
BAM
SHWNK!!
THE VIRUS IS RECEDING!
!
AL...
ALLEN...
WHAT IS THAT?
!!
♡

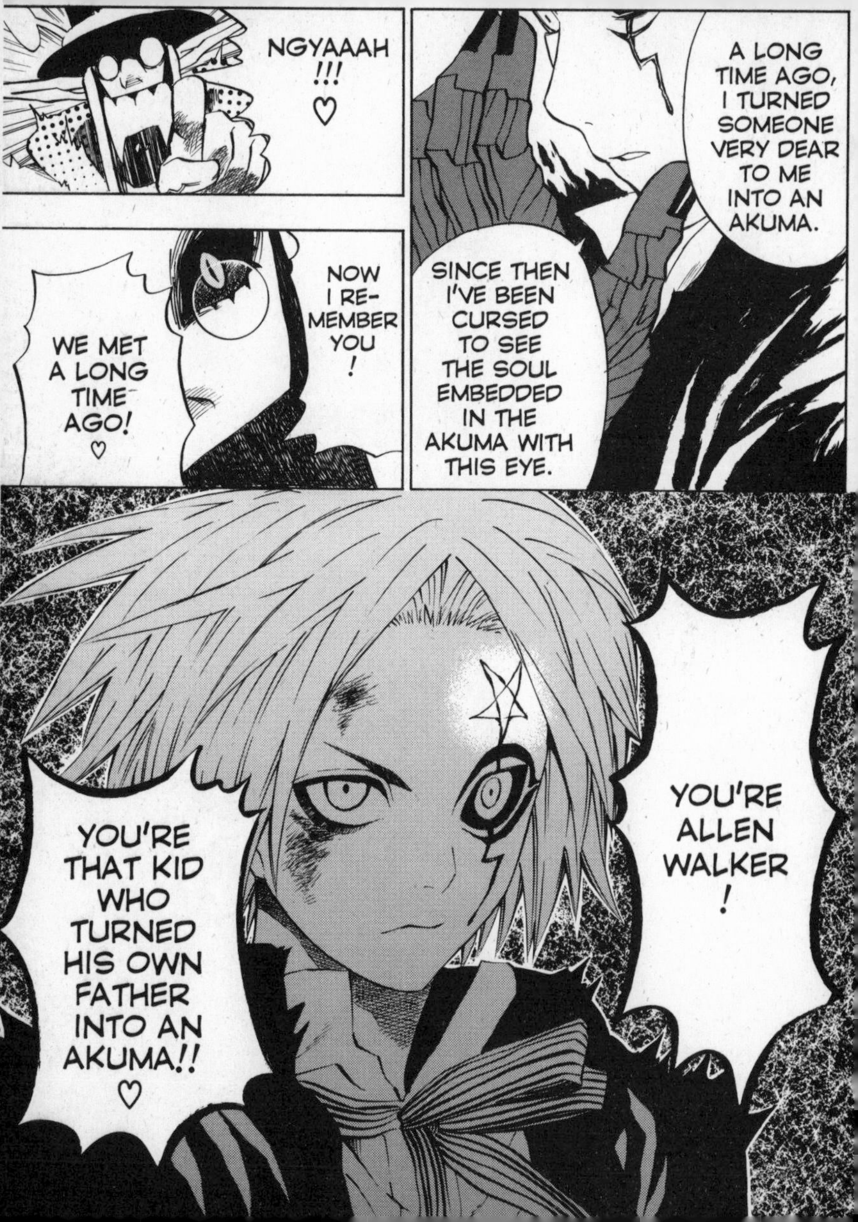
A LONG TIME AGO, I TURNED SOMEONE VERY DEAR TO ME INTO AN AKUMA.
SINCE THEN I'VE BEEN CURSED TO SEE THE SOUL EMBEDDED IN THE AKUMA WITH THIS EYE.
NGYAAAH!!! ♡
NOW I RE-MEMBER YOU!
WE MET A LONG TIME AGO! ♡
YOU'RE ALLEN WALKER!
YOU'RE THAT KID WHO TURNED HIS OWN FATHER INTO AN AKUMA!! ♡

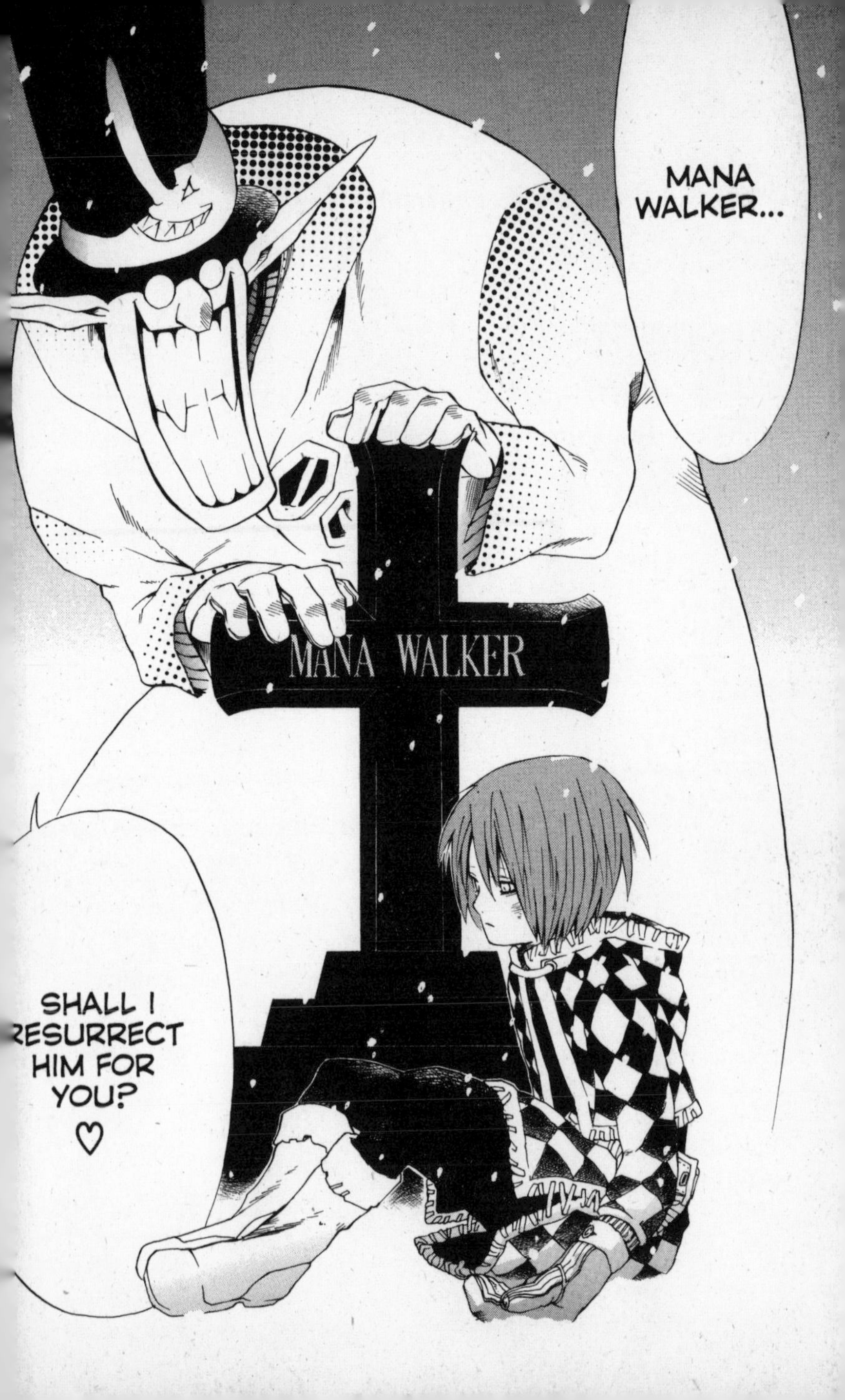
MANA WALKER...
MANA WALKER
SHALL I RESURRECT HIM FOR YOU? ♡

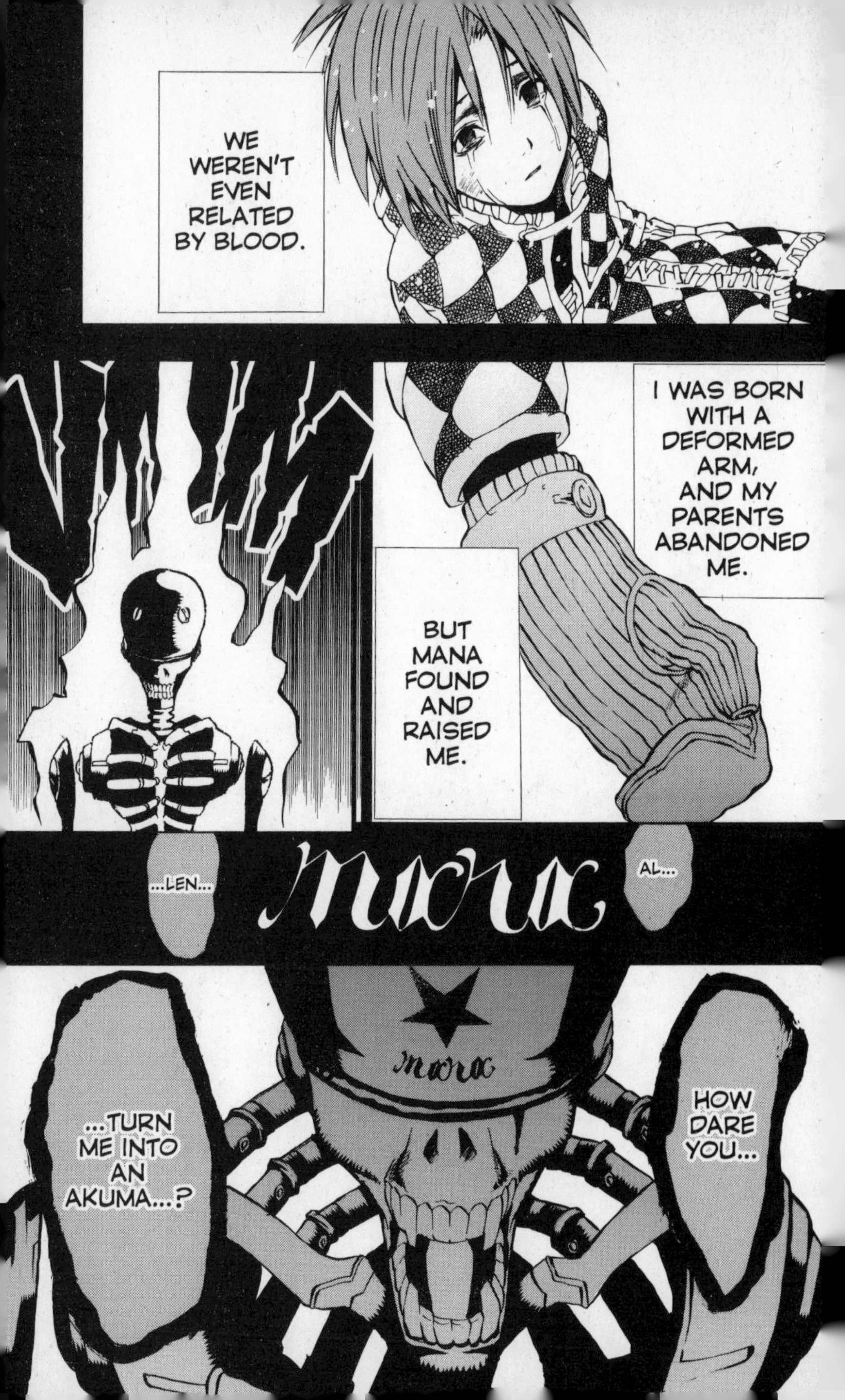
WE WEREN'T EVEN RELATED BY BLOOD.
I WAS BORN WITH A DEFORMED ARM, AND MY PARENTS ABANDONED ME.
BUT MANA FOUND AND RAISED ME.
AL...
mana
...LEN...
mana
HOW DARE YOU...
...TURN ME INTO AN AKUMA...?

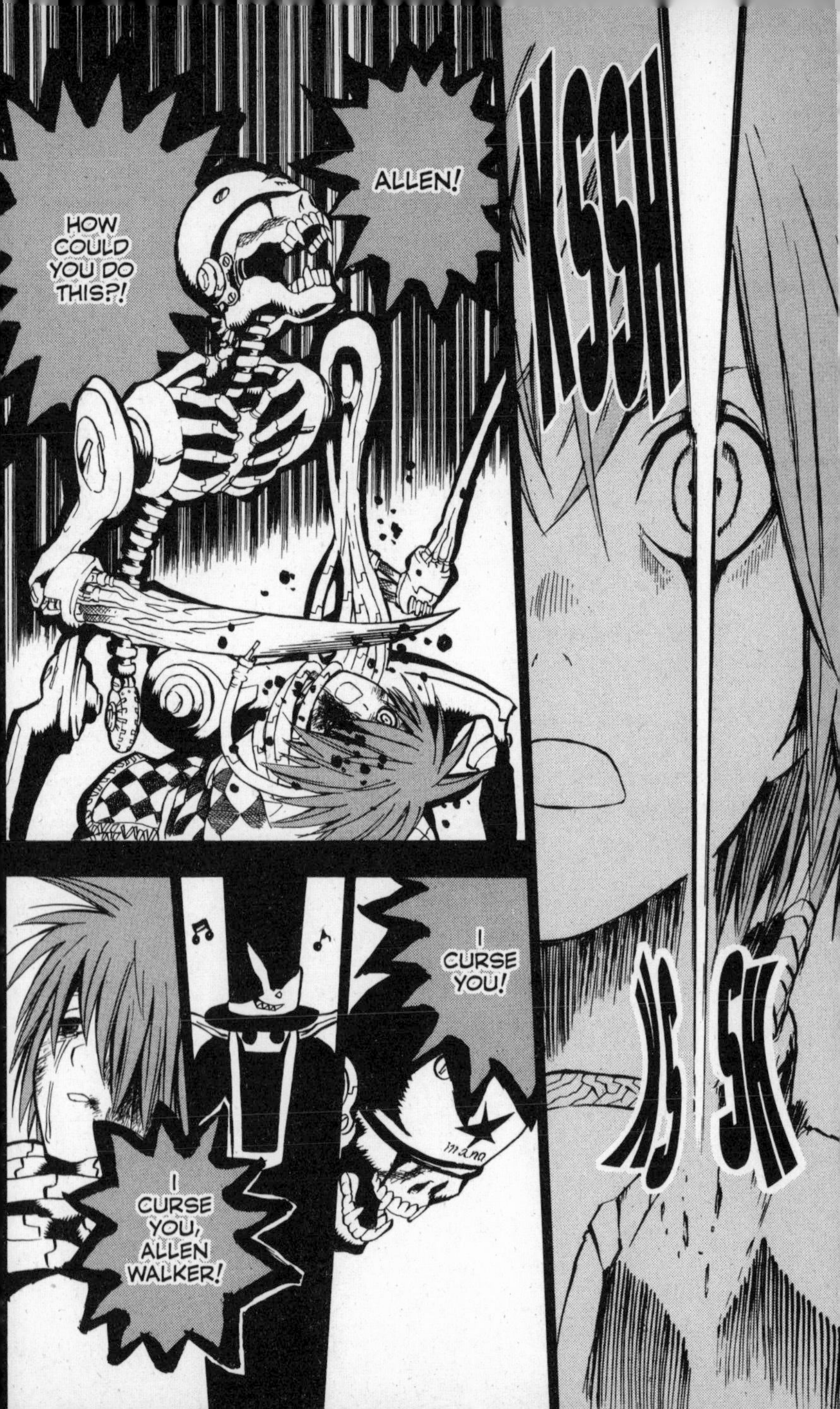
KSSH
ALLEN!
HOW COULD YOU DO THIS?!
I CURSE YOU!
I CURSE YOU, ALLEN WALKER!

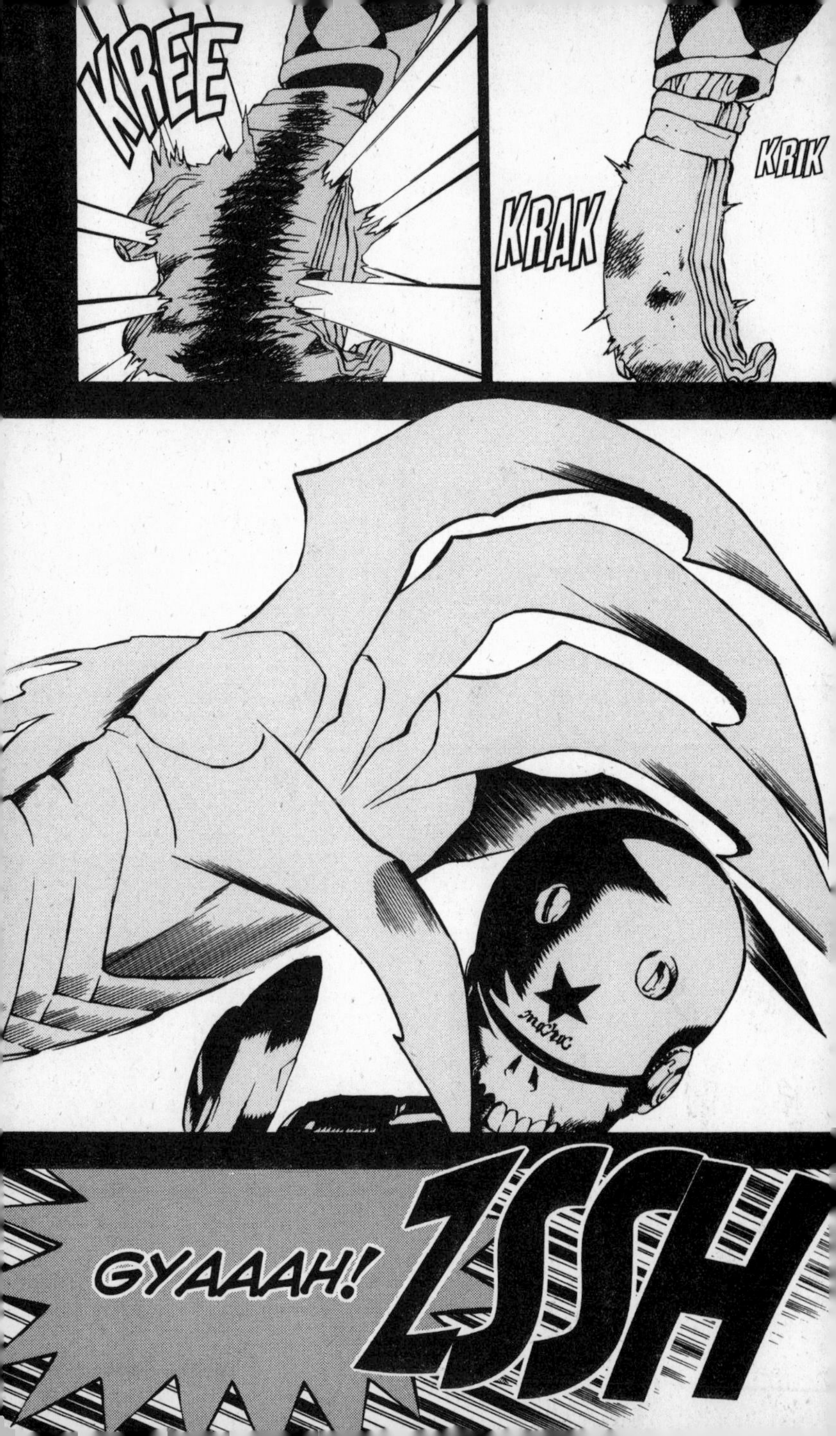
KRIK
KRAK
KREE
ZSSH
GYAAAH!

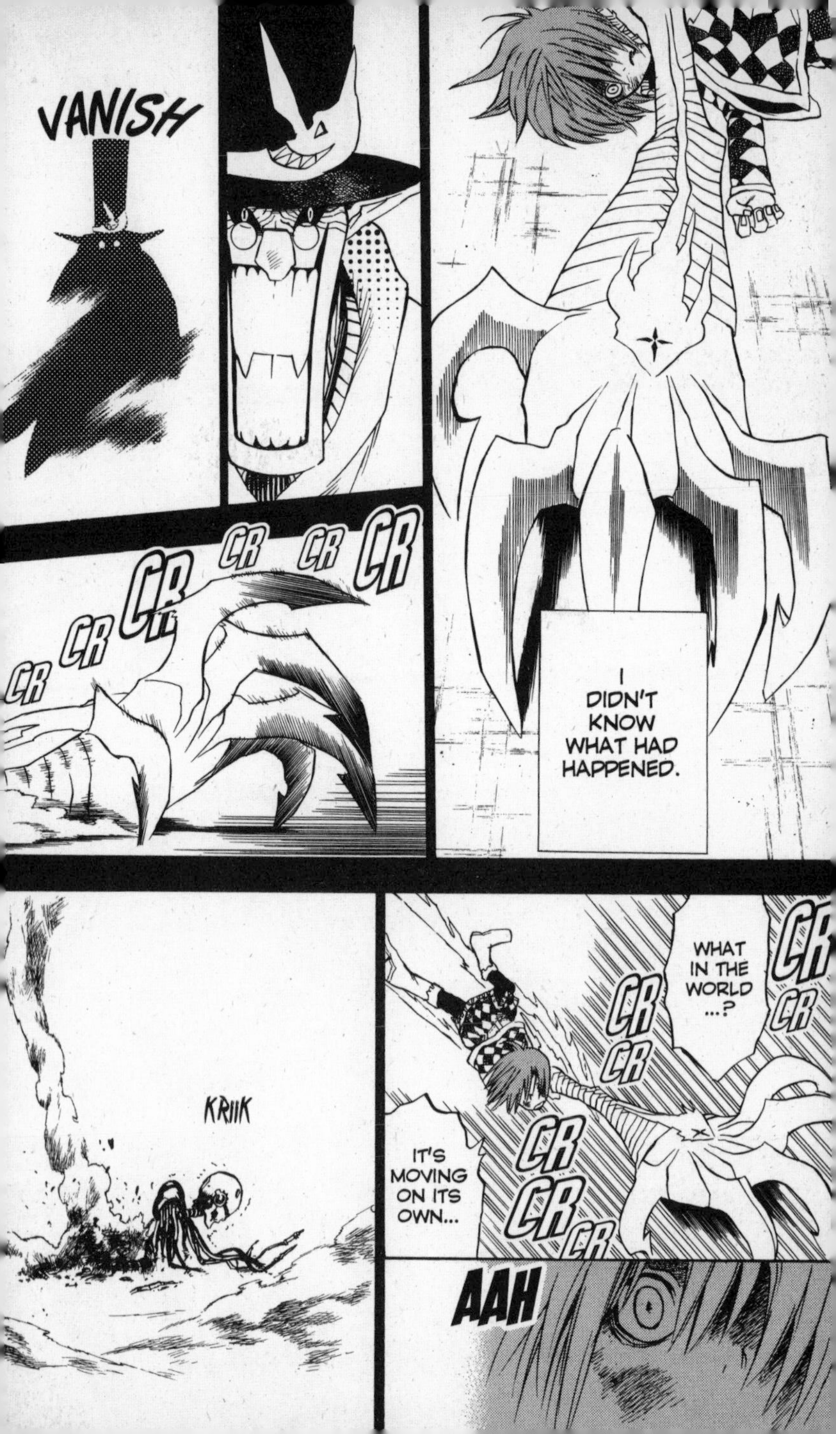

I DIDN'T KNOW WHAT HAD HAPPENED.
VANISH
CR CR CR
CR CR CR
CR
WHAT IN THE WORLD ...?
CR CR
CR CR
IT'S MOVING ON ITS OWN...
CR CR CR
AAH
KRIIK

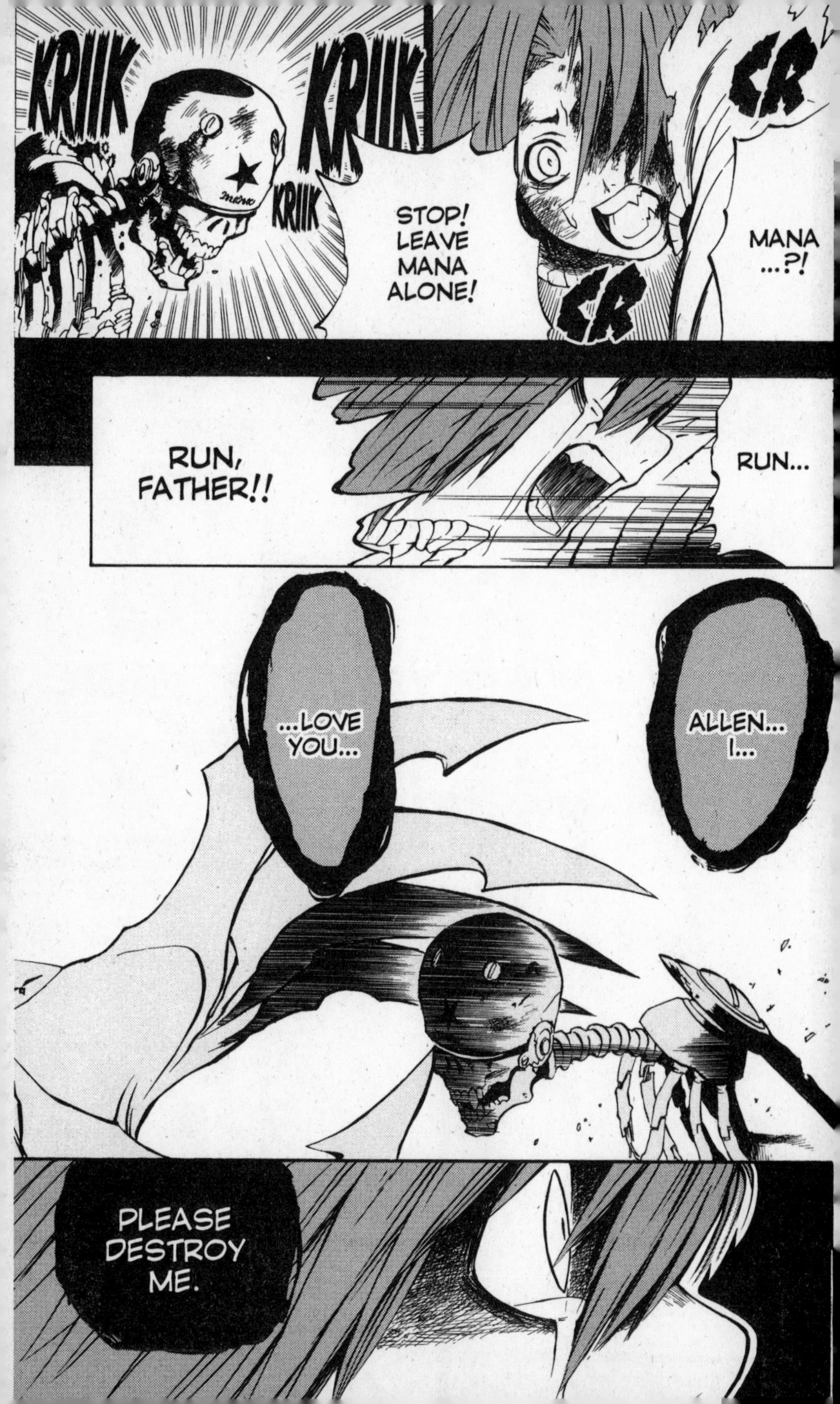

CR
MANA ...?!
STOP! LEAVE MANA ALONE!
CR
KRIIK
KRIIK
KRIIK
RUN...
RUN, FATHER!!
ALLEN... I...
...LOVE YOU...
PLEASE DESTROY ME.

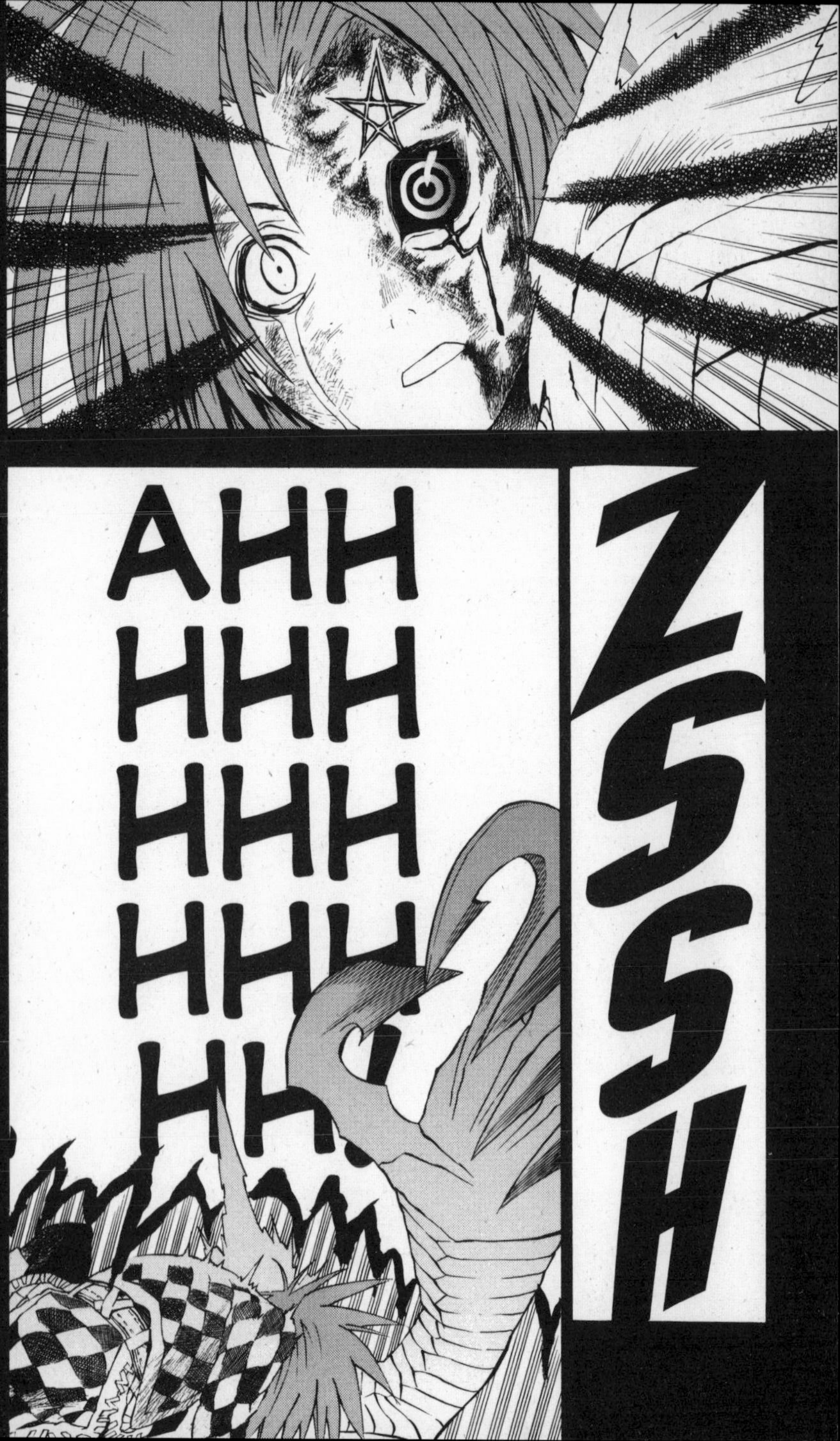
ZSSH
AHHHHHHHHHHHHH

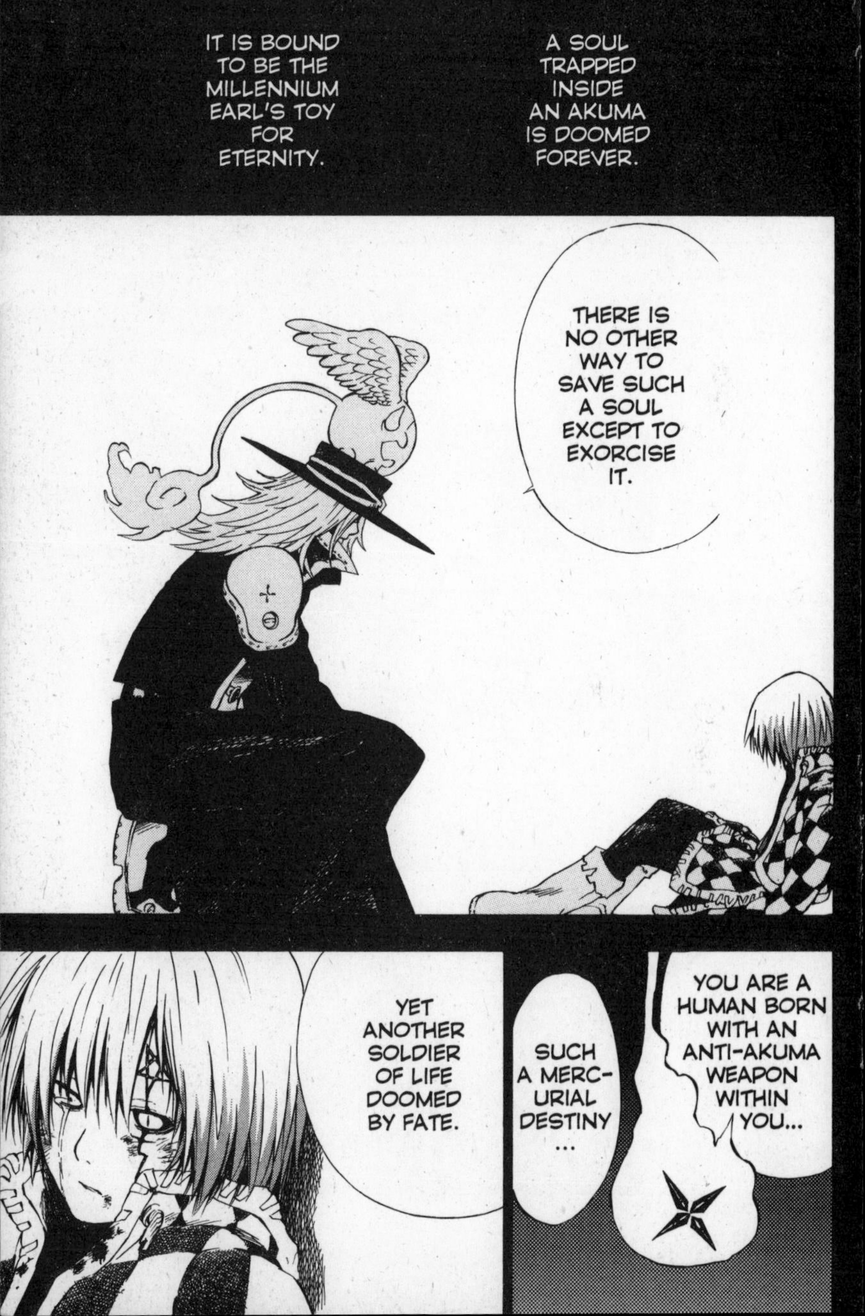
A SOUL TRAPPED INSIDE AN AKUMA IS DOOMED FOREVER.
IT IS BOUND TO BE THE MILLENNIUM EARL'S TOY FOR ETERNITY.
THERE IS NO OTHER WAY TO SAVE SUCH A SOUL EXCEPT TO EXORCISE IT.
YOU ARE A HUMAN BORN WITH AN ANTI-AKUMA WEAPON WITHIN YOU...
SUCH A MERC-URIAL DESTINY...
YET ANOTHER SOLDIER OF LIFE DOOMED BY FATE.

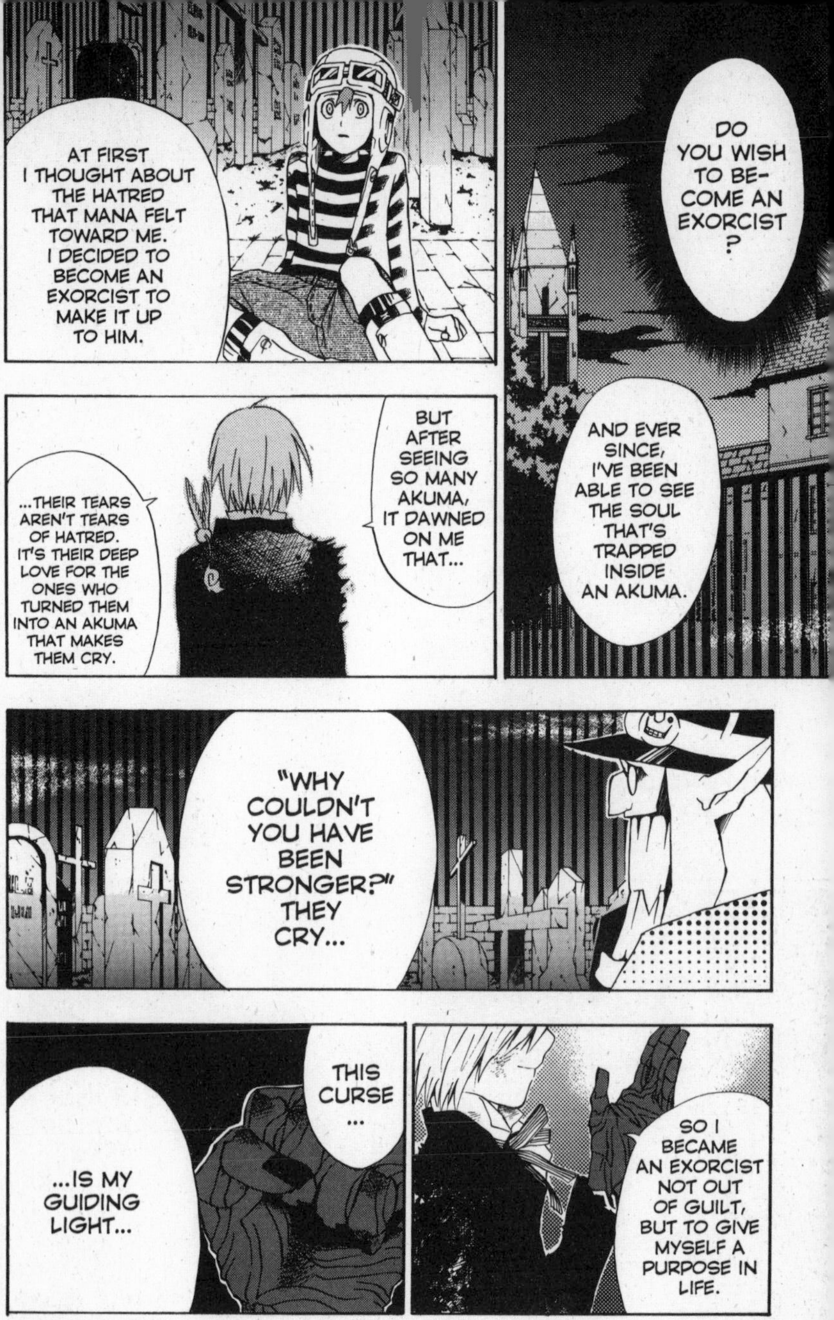
DO YOU WISH TO BE-COME AN EXORCIST ?
AND EVER SINCE, I'VE BEEN ABLE TO SEE THE SOUL THAT'S TRAPPED INSIDE AN AKUMA.
AT FIRST I THOUGHT ABOUT THE HATRED THAT MANA FELT TOWARD ME. I DECIDED TO BECOME AN EXORCIST TO MAKE IT UP TO HIM.
BUT AFTER SEEING SO MANY AKUMA, IT DAWNED ON ME THAT...
...THEIR TEARS AREN'T TEARS OF HATRED. IT'S THEIR DEEP LOVE FOR THE ONES WHO TURNED THEM INTO AN AKUMA THAT MAKES THEM CRY.
"WHY COULDN'T YOU HAVE BEEN STRONGER?" THEY CRY...
SO I BECAME AN EXORCIST NOT OUT OF GUILT, BUT TO GIVE MYSELF A PURPOSE IN LIFE.
THIS CURSE ...
...IS MY GUIDING LIGHT...

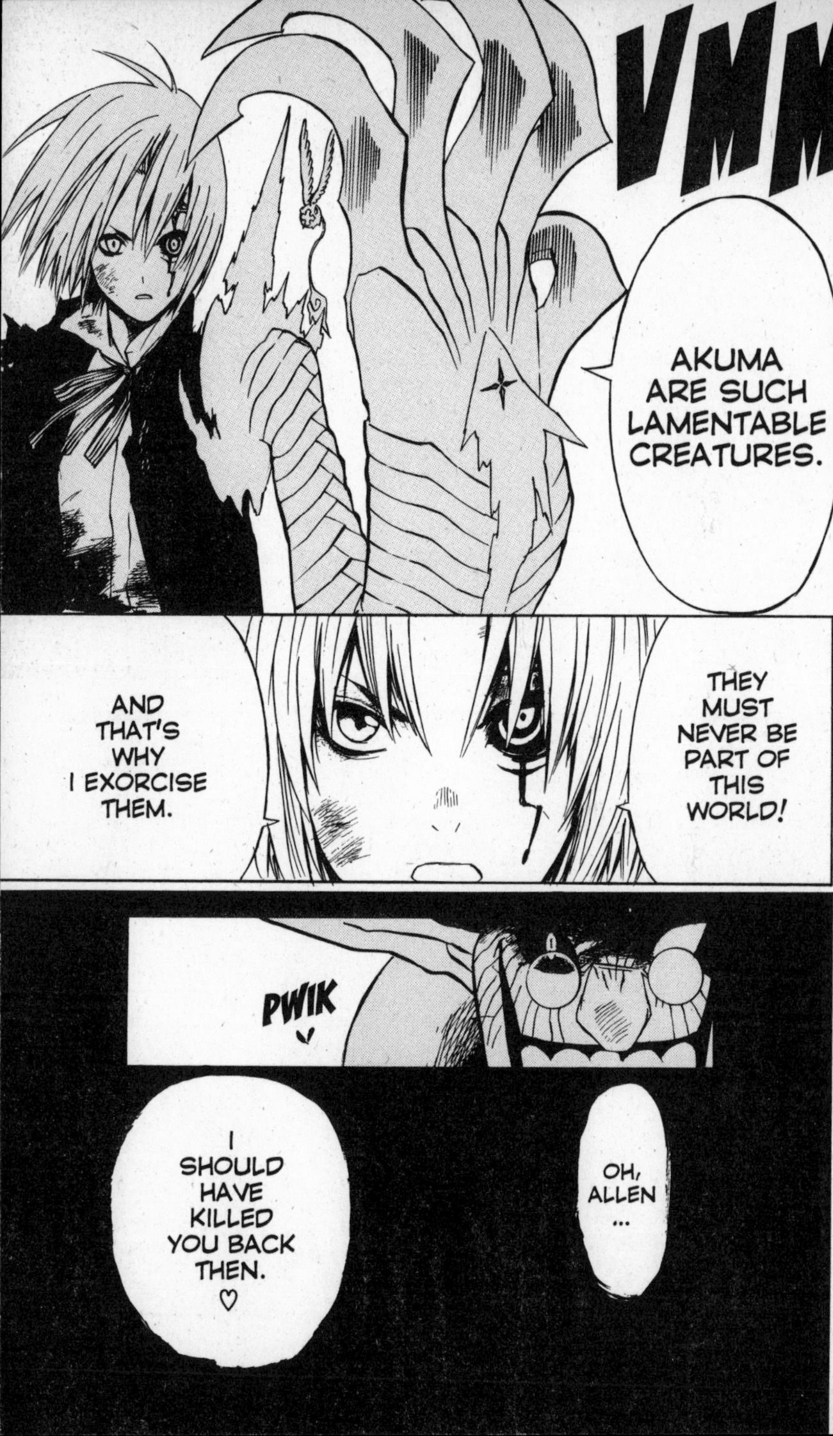
VMM
AKUMA ARE SUCH LAMENTABLE CREATURES.
THEY MUST NEVER BE PART OF THIS WORLD!
AND THAT'S WHY I EXORCISE THEM.
PWIK ♥
OH, ALLEN...
I SHOULD HAVE KILLED YOU BACK THEN. ♡

THE MILLENNIUM EARL

THE EARL IS BASED ON SOMEONE WHO REALLY EXISTED. I CAN'T SAY HIS NAME, BUT HE WAS ONE OF THE MOST PECULIAR PEOPLE WHO HAD EVER LIVED. HE COMMANDED SEVERAL LANGUAGES, WAS A MASTER OF SEVERAL ACADEMIC FIELDS AND AN ACCOMPLISHED ARTIST. HE WAS ALSO A PROPHET WHO WAS RUMORED TO HAVE BEEN IMMORTAL, AS HIS APPEARANCE DID NOT CHANGE PAST THE AGE OF 50, EVEN AFTER SEVERAL DECADES. THAT'S AMAZING. HE REFERRED TO HIMSELF AS "THE ALCHEMIST WHO TRAVELS TIME". ACCORDING TO LEGEND, HE'S STILL ALIVE SOME-WHERE IN THIS WORLD.

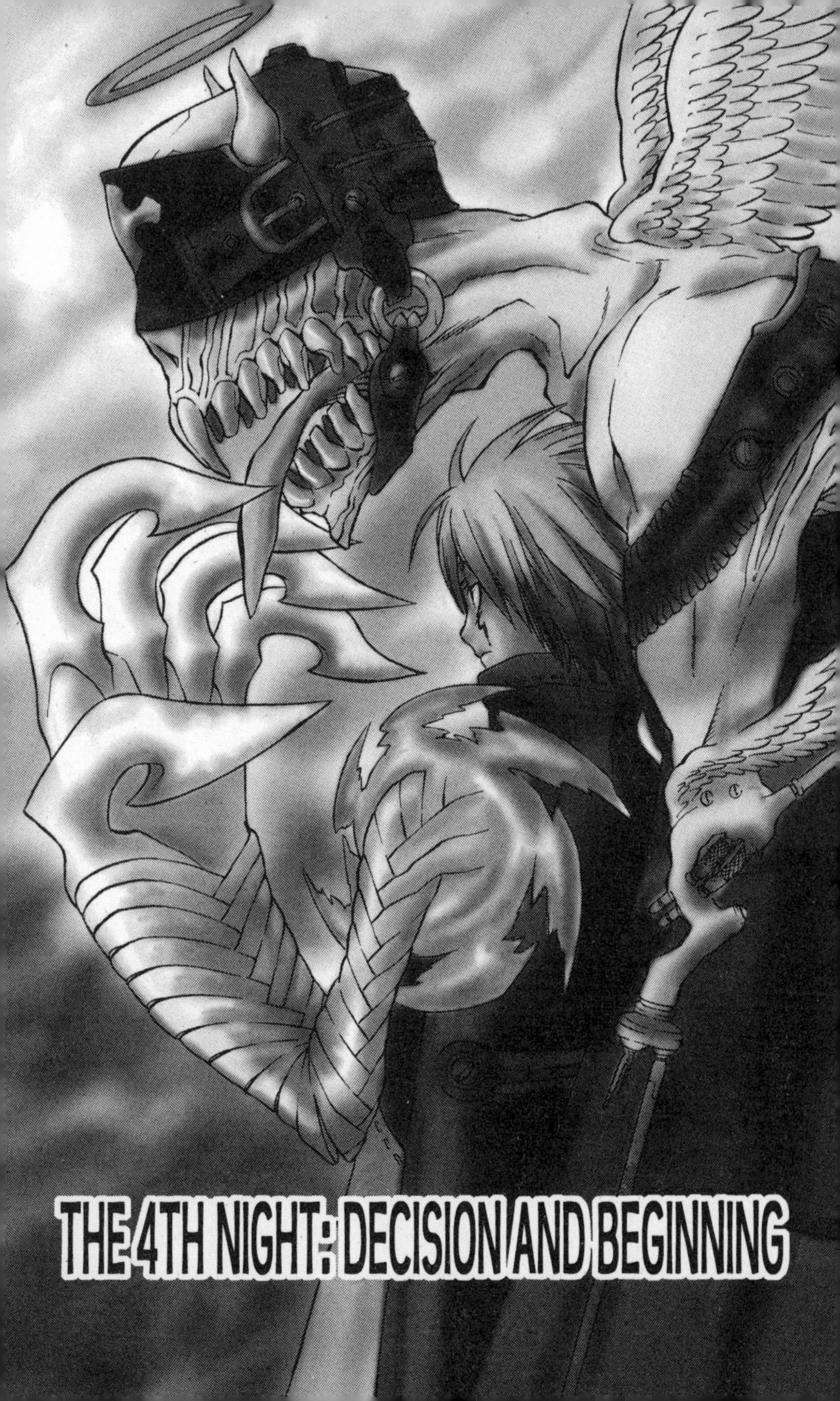
THE 4TH NIGHT: DECISION AND BEGINNING

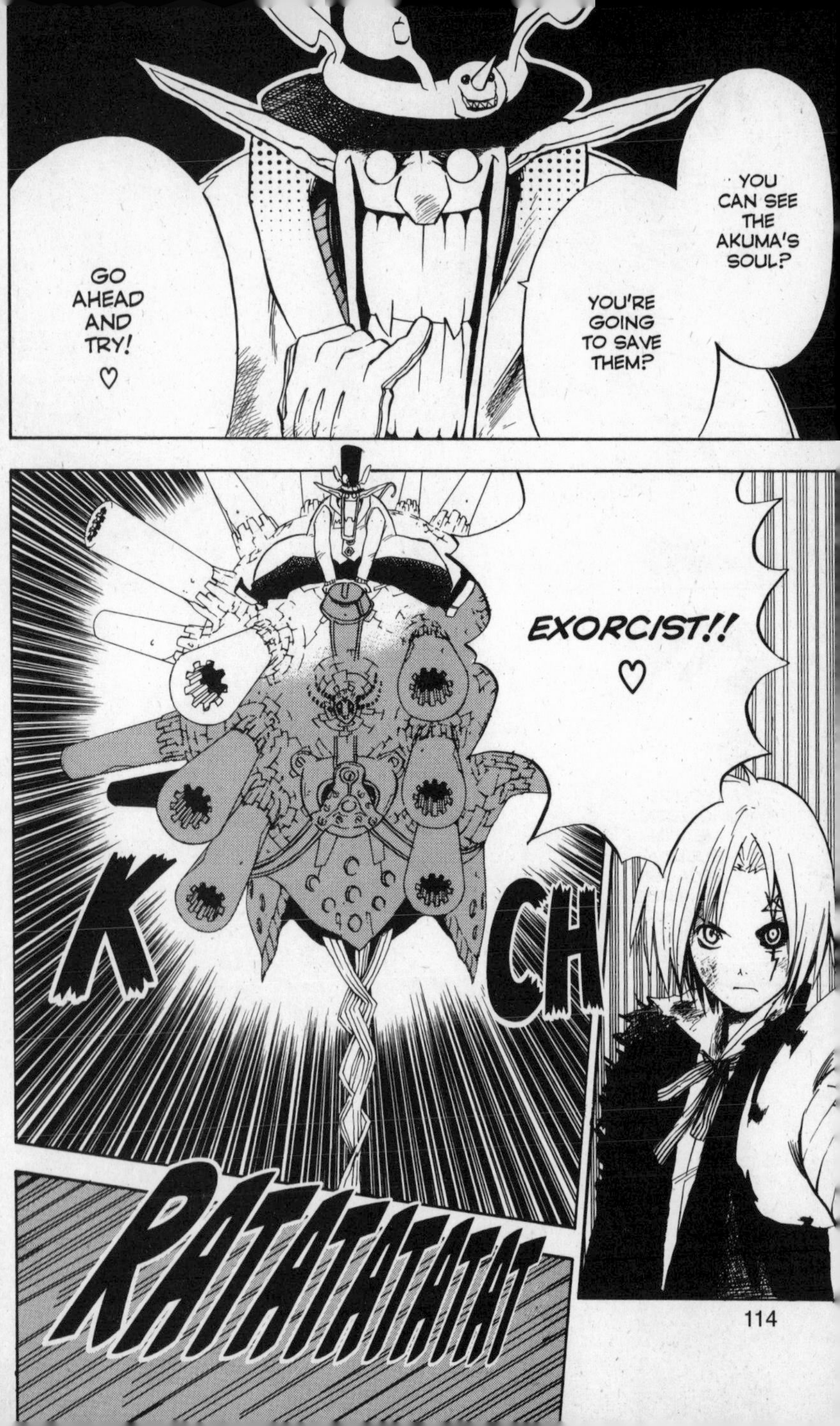
YOU CAN SEE THE AKUMA'S SOUL?
YOU'RE GOING TO SAVE THEM?
GO AHEAD AND TRY! ♡
EXORCIST!! ♡
KCH
RATATATATAT

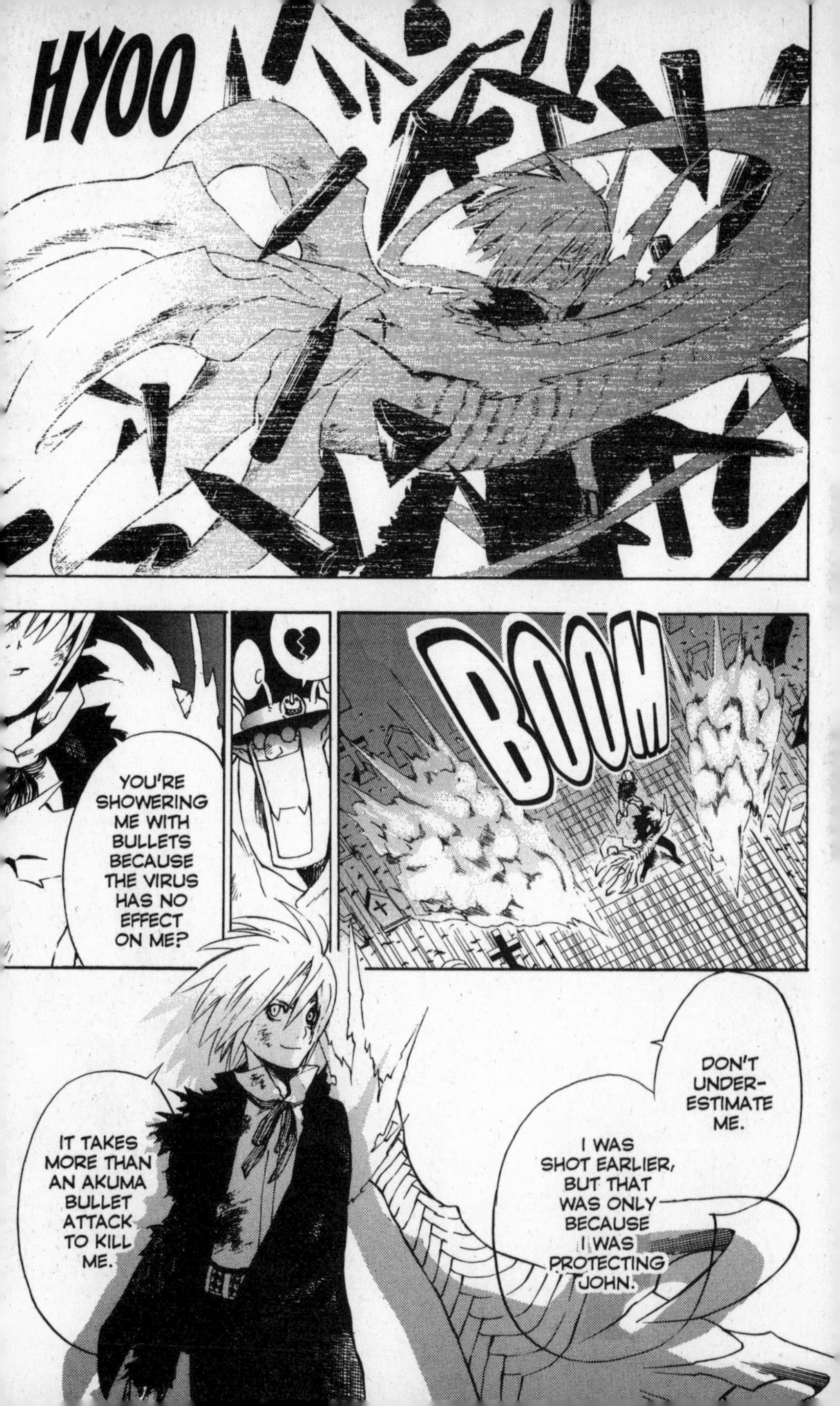
HYOO
BOOM
YOU'RE SHOWERING ME WITH BULLETS BECAUSE THE VIRUS HAS NO EFFECT ON ME?
DON'T UNDER-ESTIMATE ME.
I WAS SHOT EARLIER, BUT THAT WAS ONLY BECAUSE I WAS PROTECTING JOHN.
IT TAKES MORE THAN AN AKUMA BULLET ATTACK TO KILL ME.

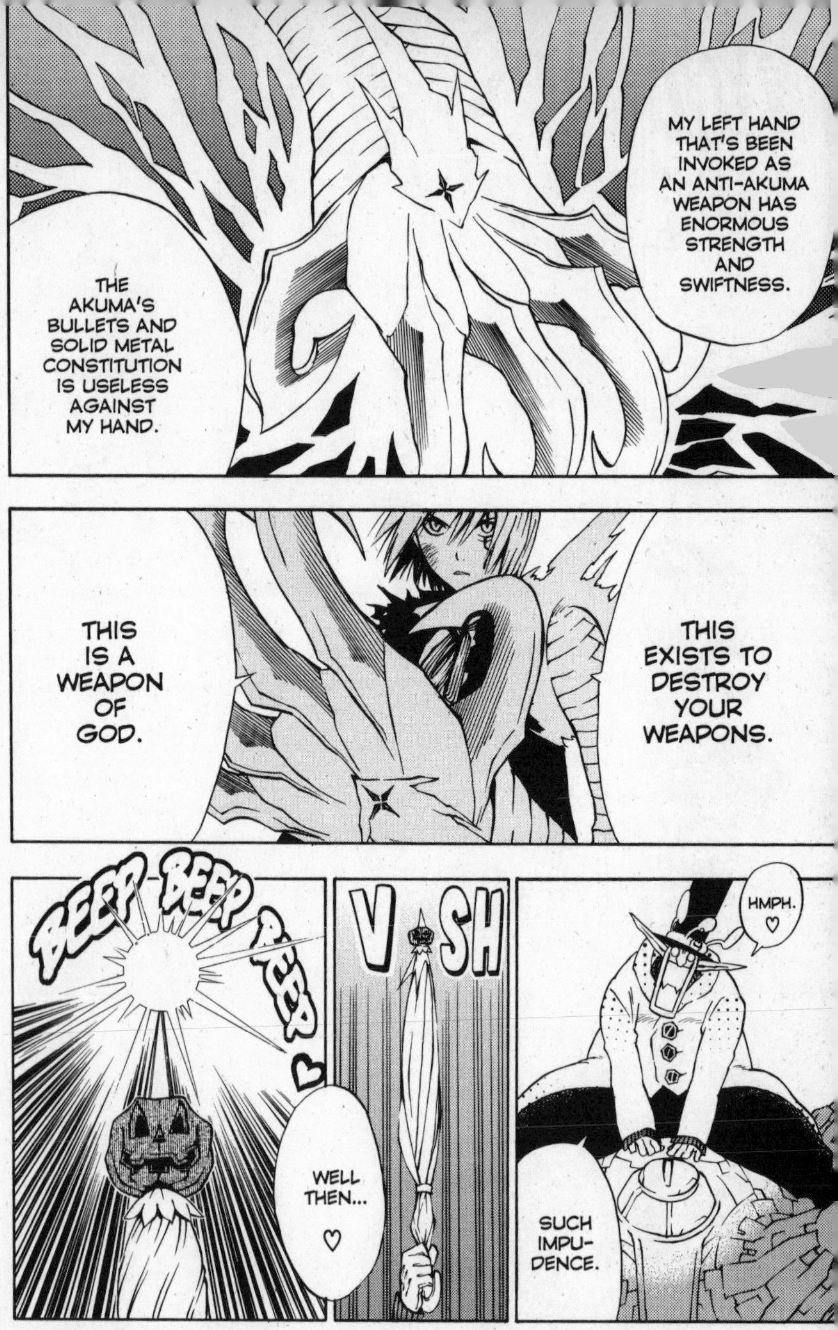
MY LEFT HAND THAT'S BEEN INVOKED AS AN ANTI-AKUMA WEAPON HAS ENORMOUS STRENGTH AND SWIFTNESS.
THE AKUMA'S BULLETS AND SOLID METAL CONSTITUTION IS USELESS AGAINST MY HAND.
THIS EXISTS TO DESTROY YOUR WEAPONS.
THIS IS A WEAPON OF GOD.
HMPH. ♡
SUCH IMPU-DENCE.
V SH
BEEP BEEP BEEP ♡
WELL THEN... ♡

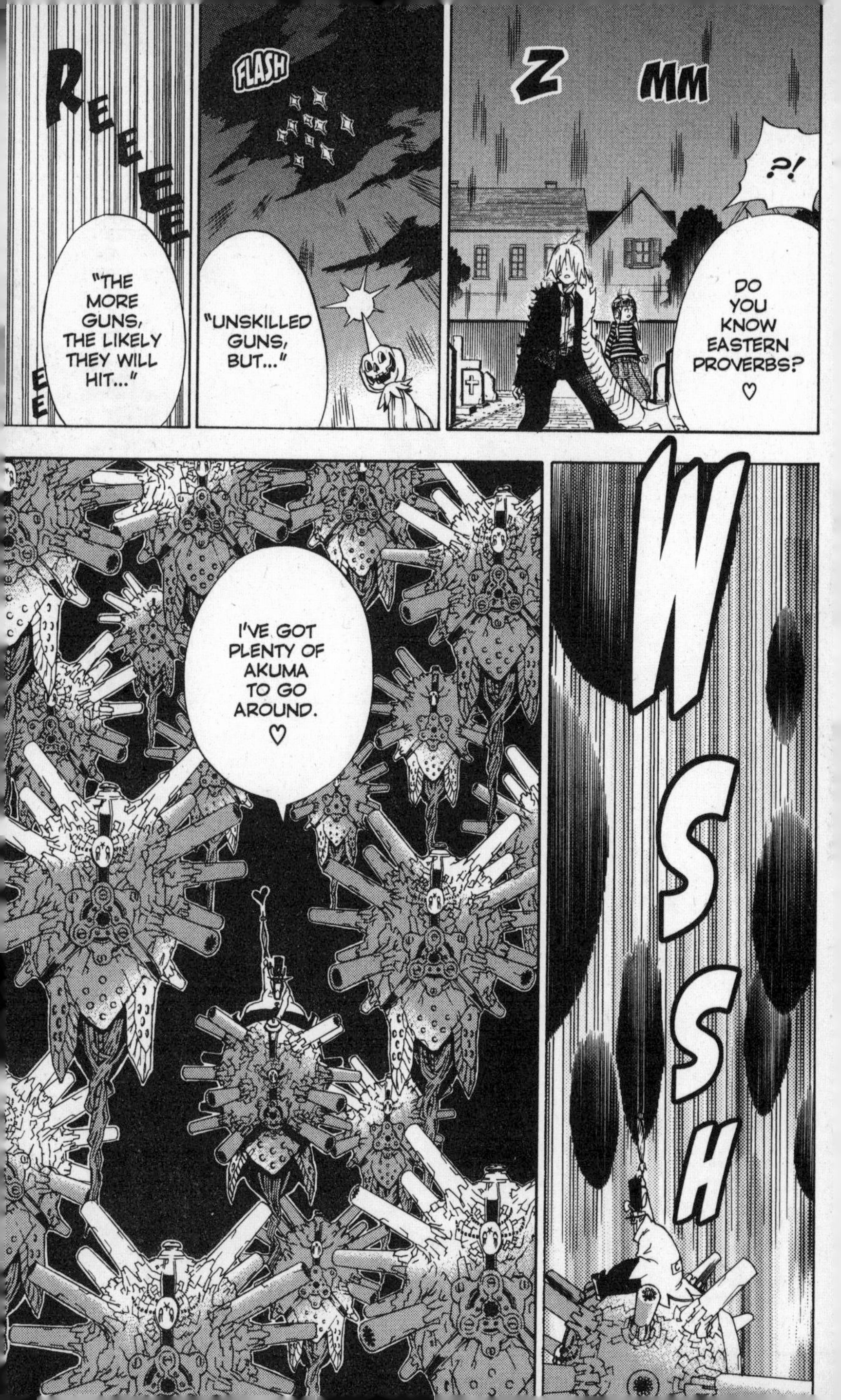
ZMM
?!
DO YOU KNOW EASTERN PROVERBS? ♡
FLASH
"UNSKILLED GUNS, BUT..."
REEEEEEE
"THE MORE GUNS, THE LIKELY THEY WILL HIT..."
WSSH
I'VE GOT PLENTY OF AKUMA TO GO AROUND. ♡

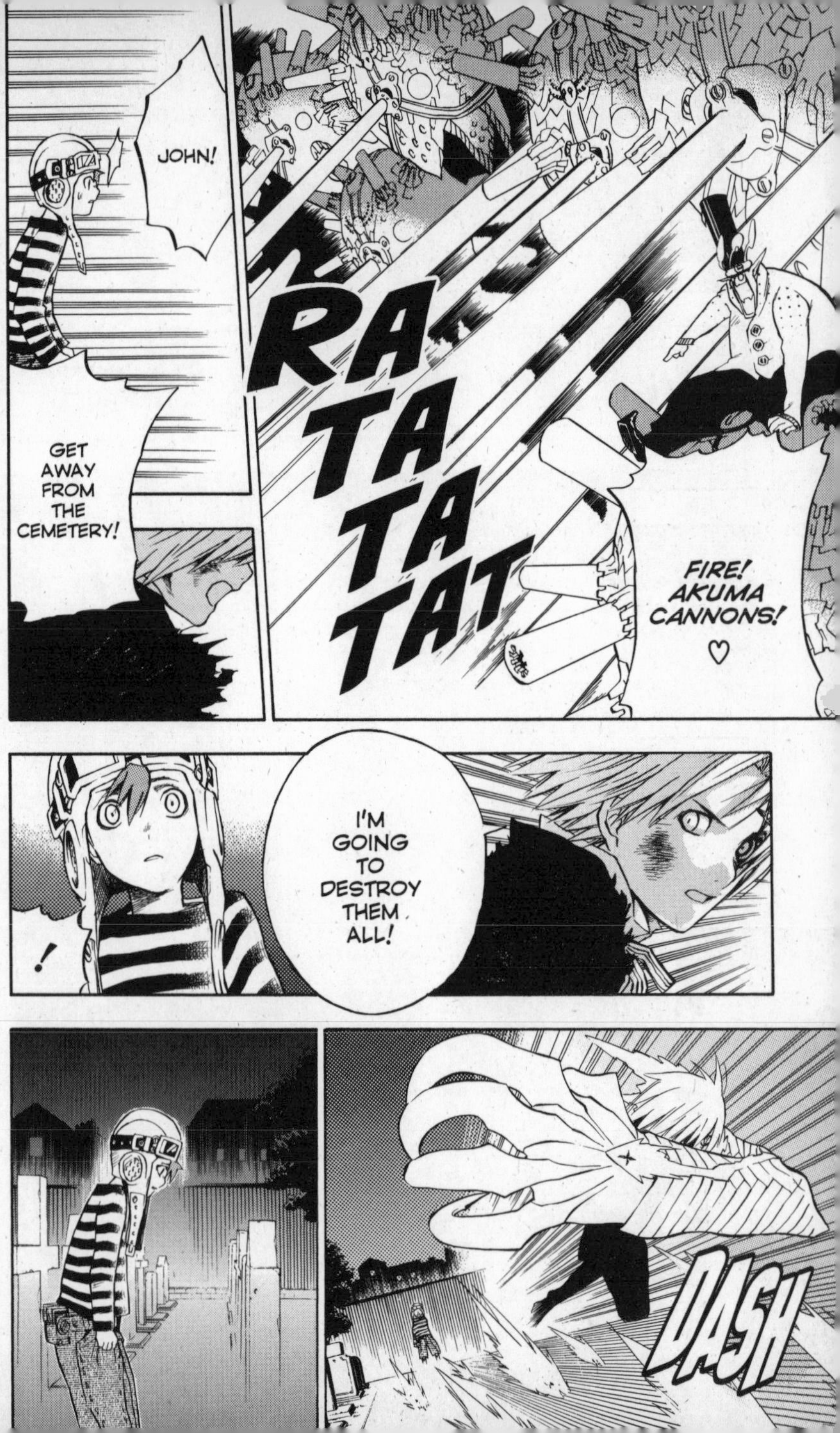
FIRE! AKUMA CANNONS! ♡
RATATAT
JOHN!
GET AWAY FROM THE CEMETERY!
I'M GOING TO DESTROY THEM ALL!
!
DASH

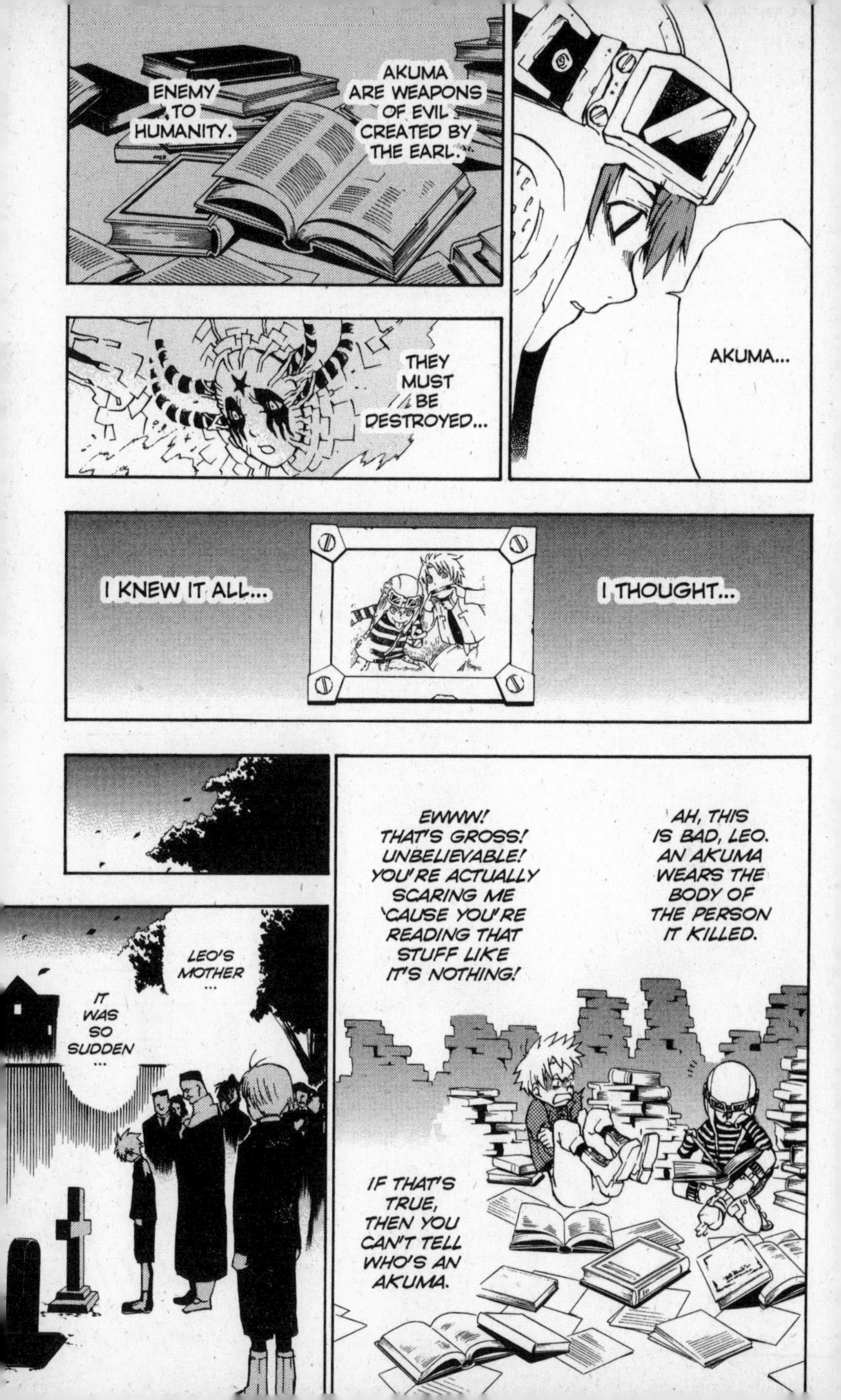
AKUMA...
AKUMA ARE WEAPONS OF EVIL CREATED BY THE EARL.
ENEMY TO HUMANITY.
THEY MUST BE DESTROYED...
I THOUGHT...
I KNEW IT ALL...
AH, THIS IS BAD, LEO. AN AKUMA WEARS THE BODY OF THE PERSON IT KILLED.
EWWW! THAT'S GROSS! UNBELIEVABLE! YOU'RE ACTUALLY SCARING ME 'CAUSE YOU'RE READING THAT STUFF LIKE IT'S NOTHING!
IF THAT'S TRUE, THEN YOU CAN'T TELL WHO'S AN AKUMA.
LEO'S MOTHER...
IT WAS SO SUDDEN...

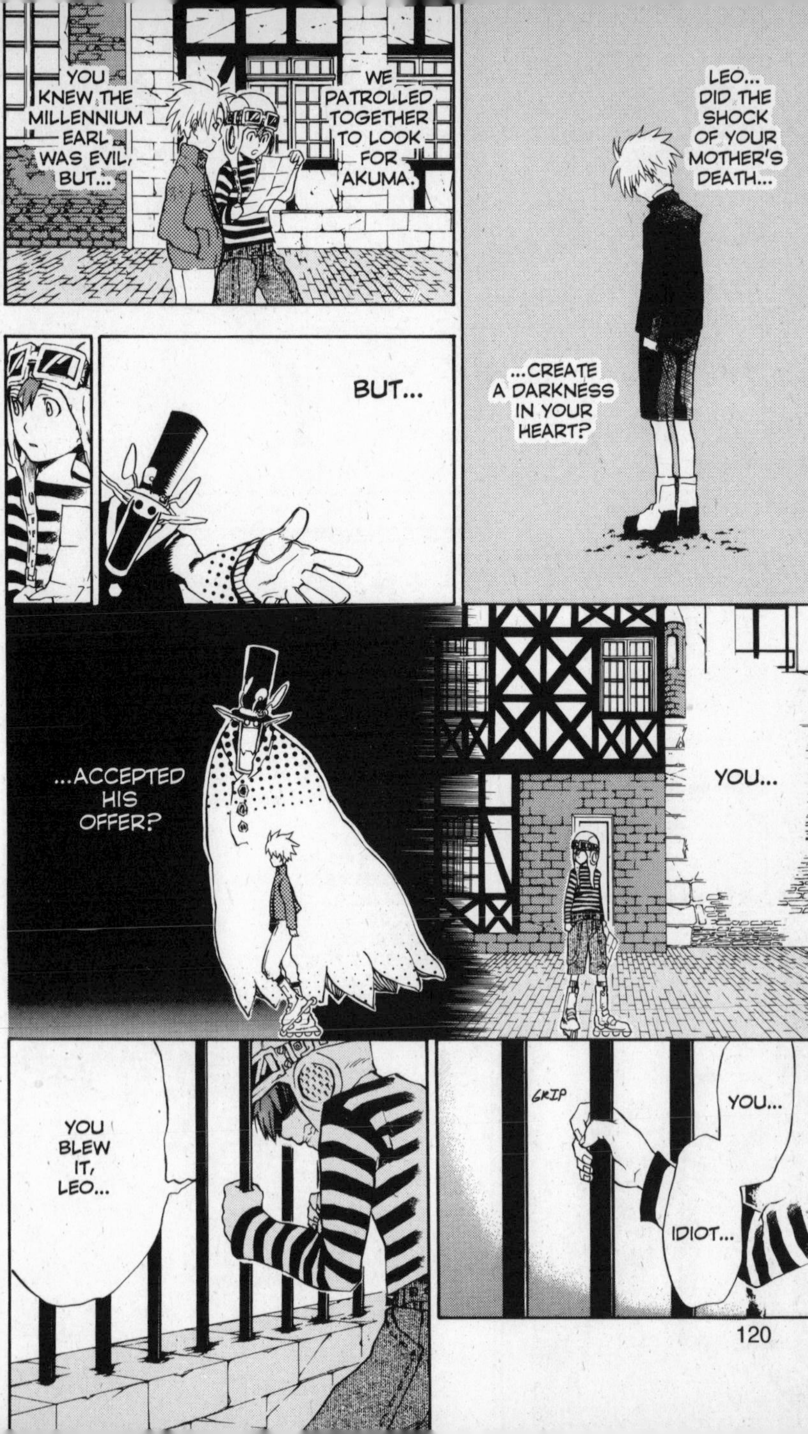
LEO... DID THE SHOCK OF YOUR MOTHER'S DEATH...
...CREATE A DARKNESS IN YOUR HEART?
WE PATROLLED TOGETHER TO LOOK FOR AKUMA.
YOU KNEW THE MILLENNIUM EARL WAS EVIL, BUT...
BUT...
YOU...
...ACCEPTED HIS OFFER?
GRIP
YOU...
IDIOT...
YOU BLEW IT, LEO...

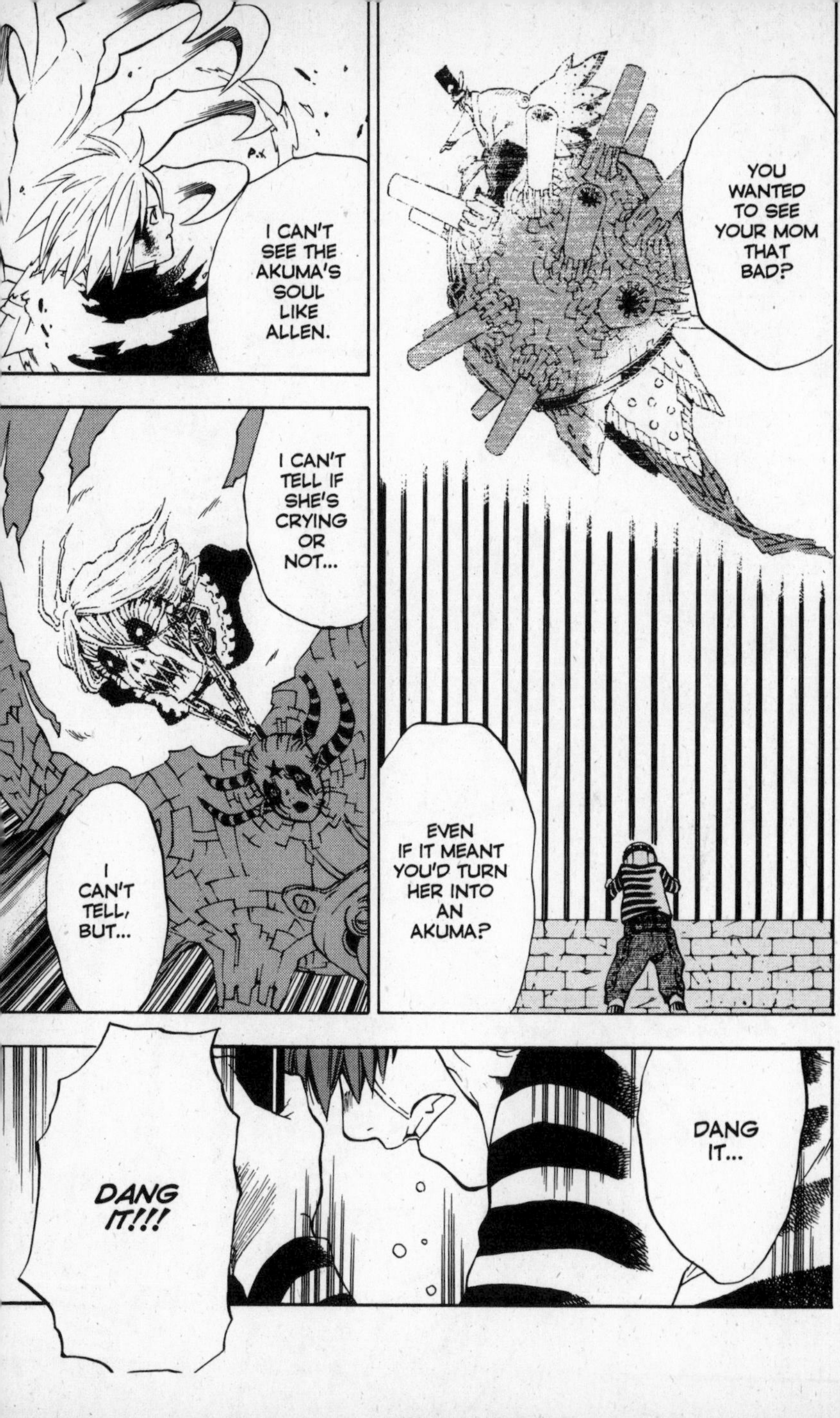
YOU WANTED TO SEE YOUR MOM THAT BAD?
EVEN IF IT MEANT YOU'D TURN HER INTO AN AKUMA?
I CAN'T SEE THE AKUMA'S SOUL LIKE ALLEN.
I CAN'T TELL IF SHE'S CRYING OR NOT...
I CAN'T TELL, BUT...
DANG IT...
DANG IT!!!

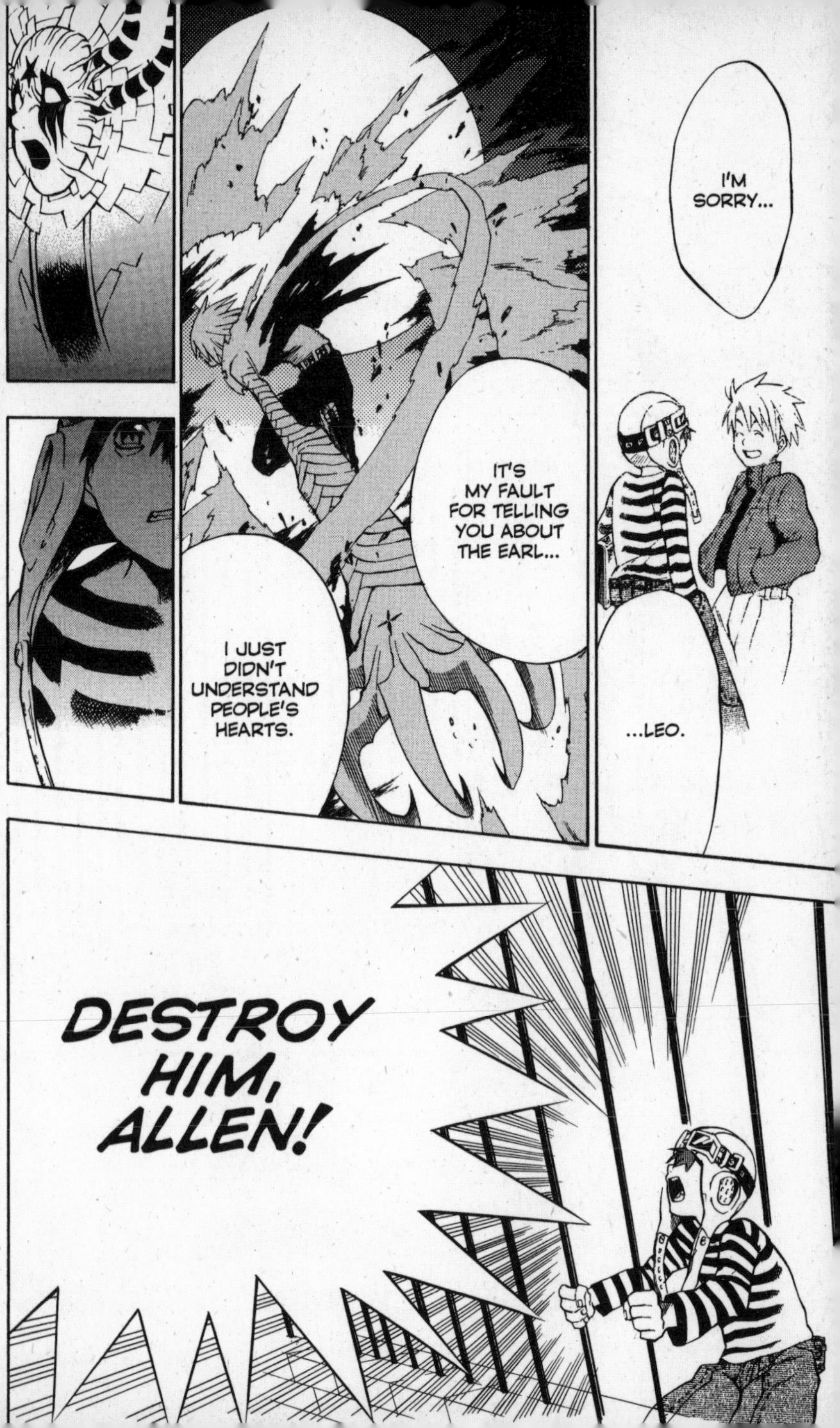
I'M SORRY...
...LEO.
IT'S MY FAULT FOR TELLING YOU ABOUT THE EARL...
I JUST DIDN'T UNDERSTAND PEOPLE'S HEARTS.
DESTROY HIM, ALLEN!

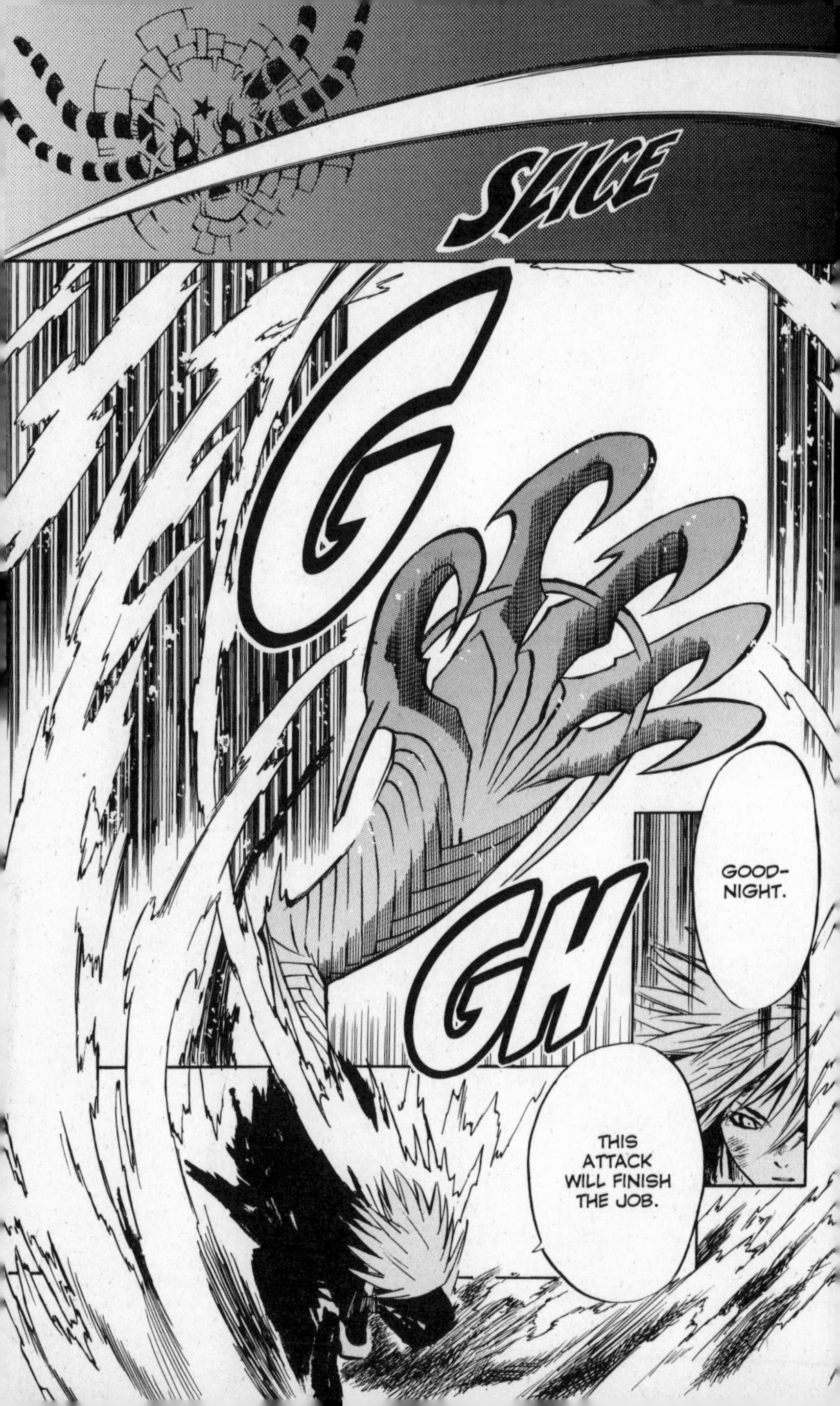
SLICE
GOOD-NIGHT.
THIS ATTACK WILL FINISH THE JOB.
GGGGGGH

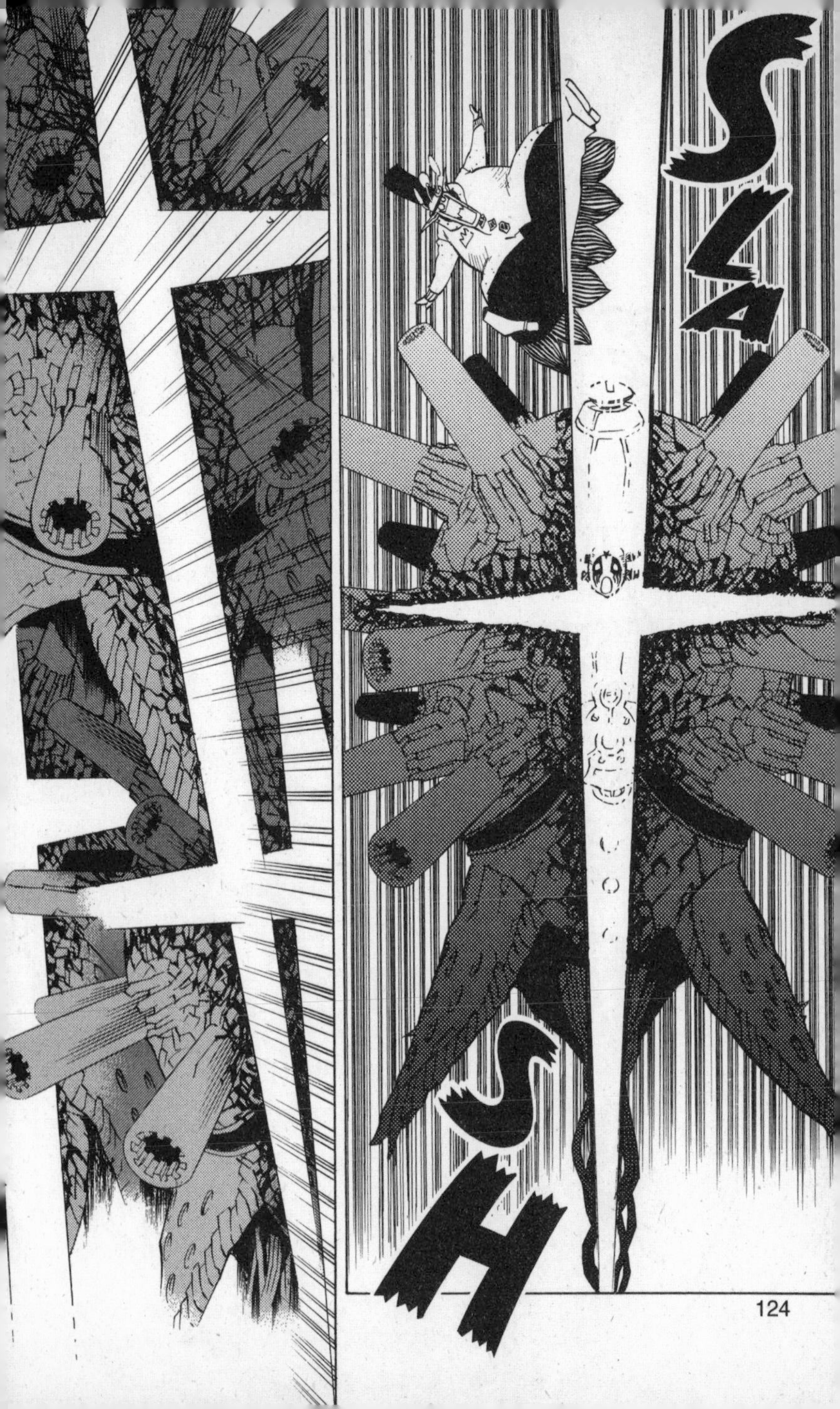
SLASH

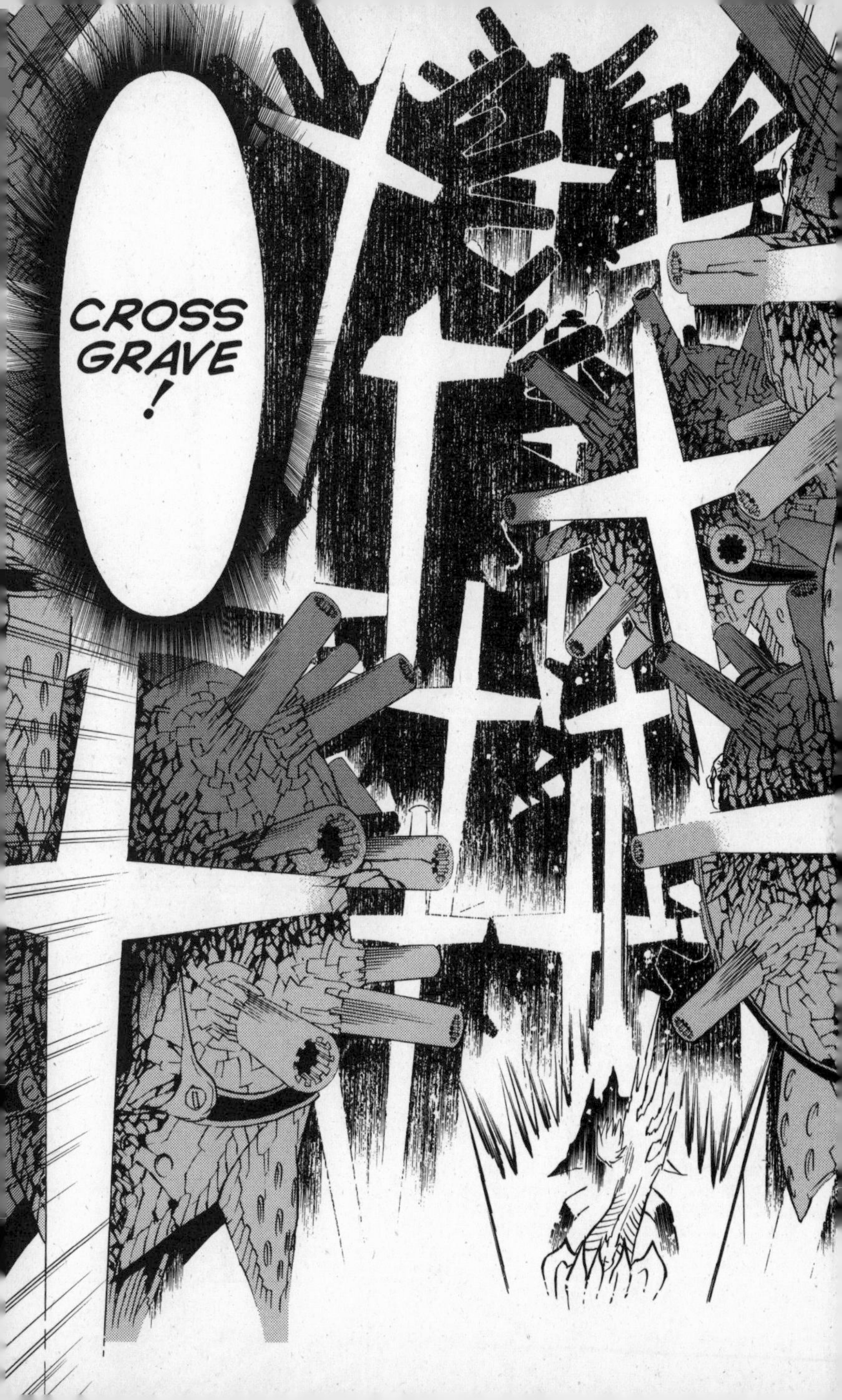
CROSS GRAVE!

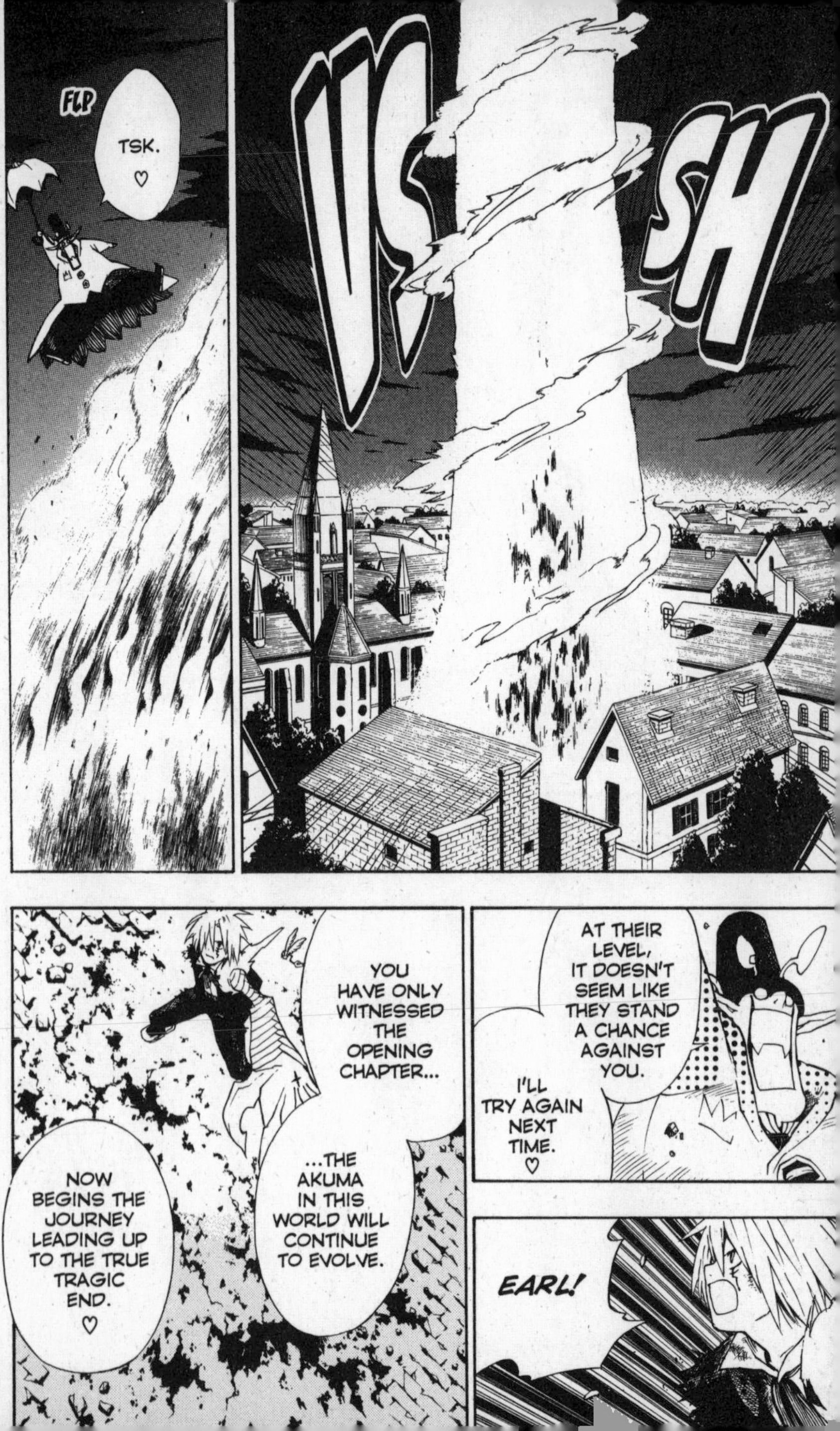
VO SH
FLP
TSK. ♡
AT THEIR LEVEL, IT DOESN'T SEEM LIKE THEY STAND A CHANCE AGAINST YOU.
I'LL TRY AGAIN NEXT TIME. ♡
EARL!
YOU HAVE ONLY WITNESSED THE OPENING CHAPTER...
...THE AKUMA IN THIS WORLD WILL CONTINUE TO EVOLVE.
NOW BEGINS THE JOURNEY LEADING UP TO THE TRUE TRAGIC END. ♡

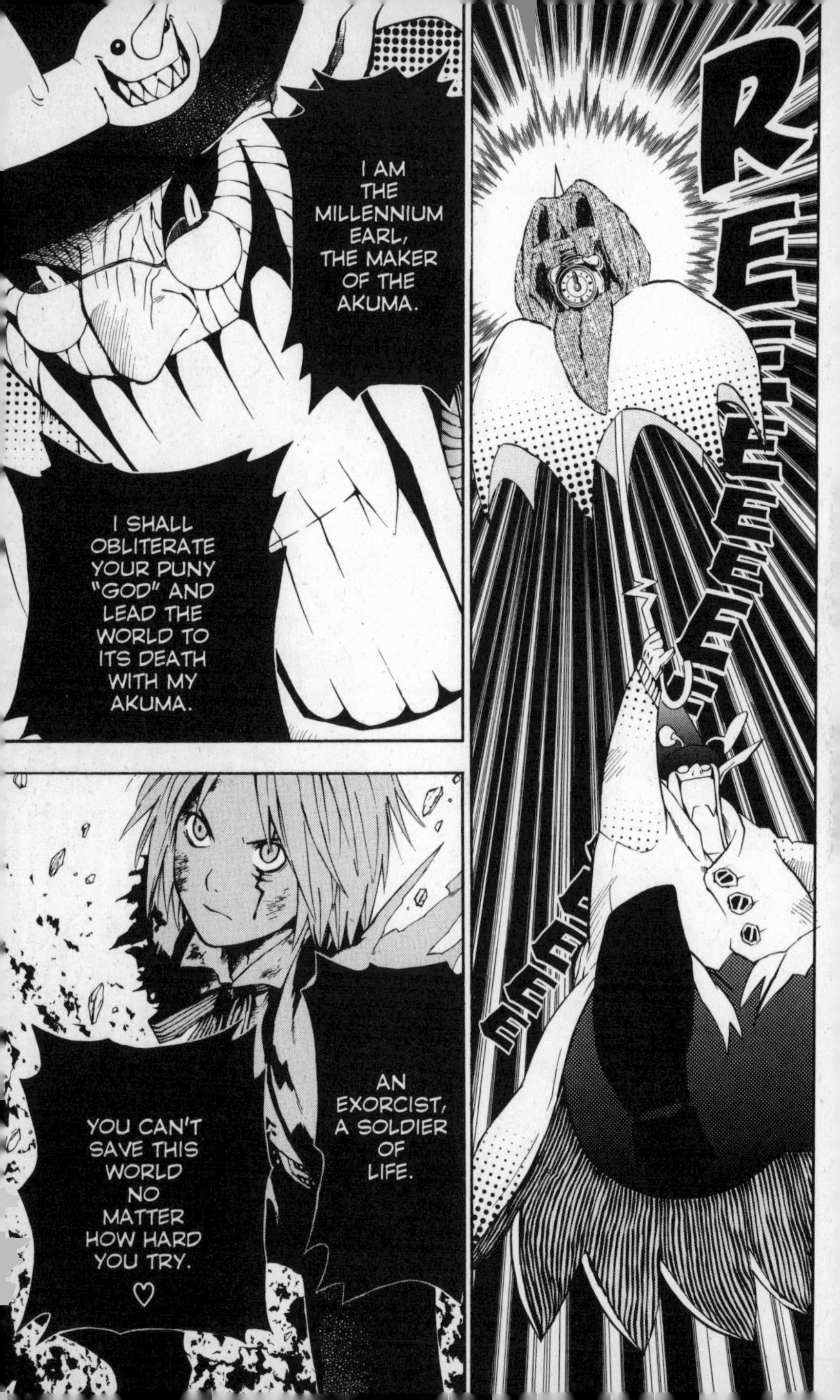
I AM THE MILLENNIUM EARL, THE MAKER OF THE AKUMA.
I SHALL OBLITERATE YOUR PUNY "GOD" AND LEAD THE WORLD TO ITS DEATH WITH MY AKUMA.
AN EXORCIST, A SOLDIER OF LIFE.
YOU CAN'T SAVE THIS WORLD NO MATTER HOW HARD YOU TRY. ♡

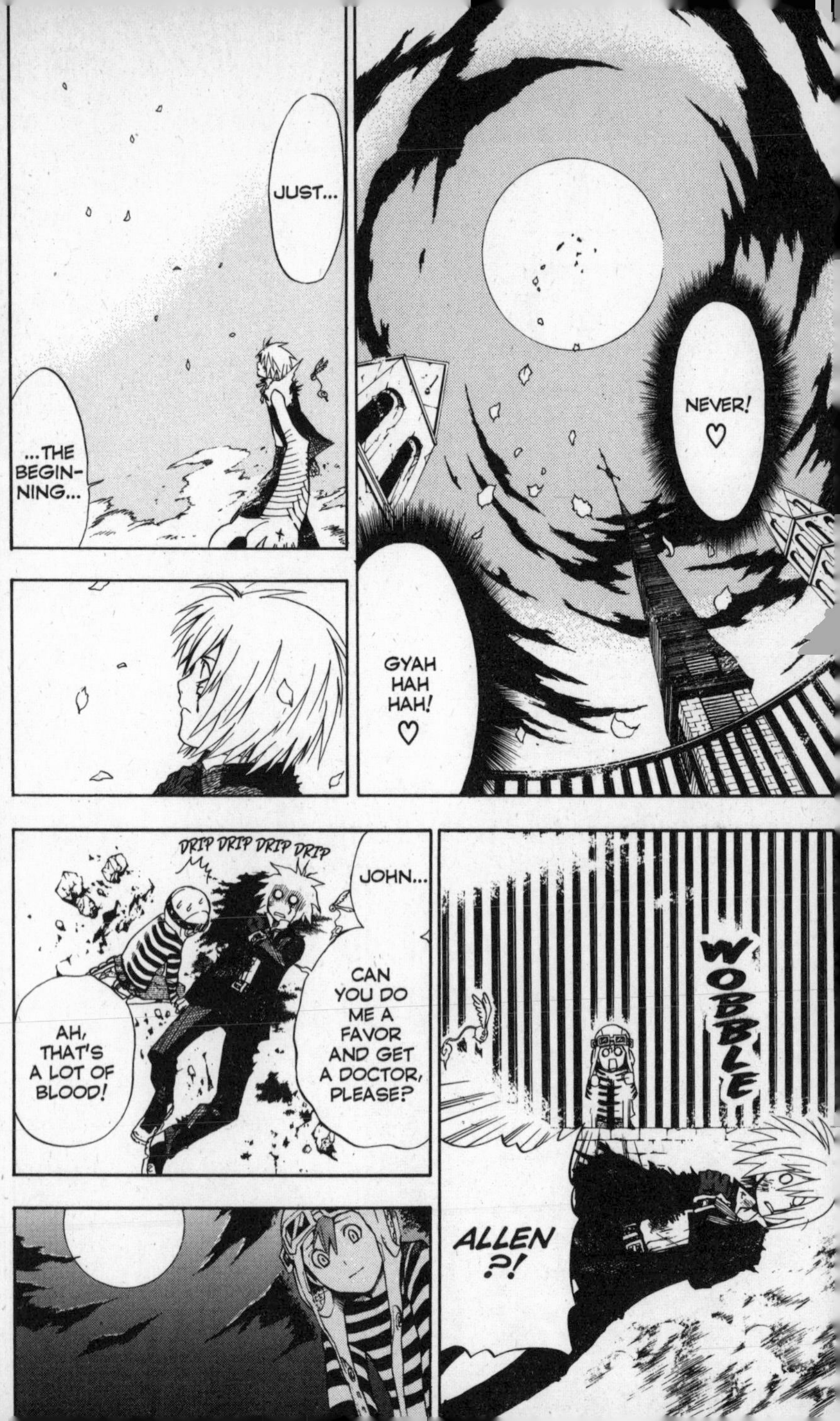
NEVER! ♡
GYAH HAH HAH! ♡
JUST...
...THE BEGINNING...
WOBBLE
ALLEN?!
DRIP DRIP DRIP DRIP
JOHN...
CAN YOU DO ME A FAVOR AND GET A DOCTOR, PLEASE?
AH, THAT'S A LOT OF BLOOD!

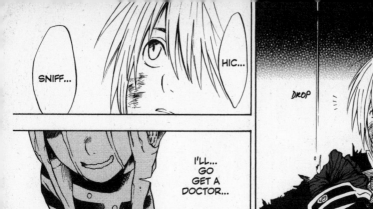

SNIFF...

HIC...

DROP

I'LL... GO GET A DOCTOR...

SO... JUST REST FOR A WHILE...

IT'LL BE OVER BEFORE YOU KNOW IT.

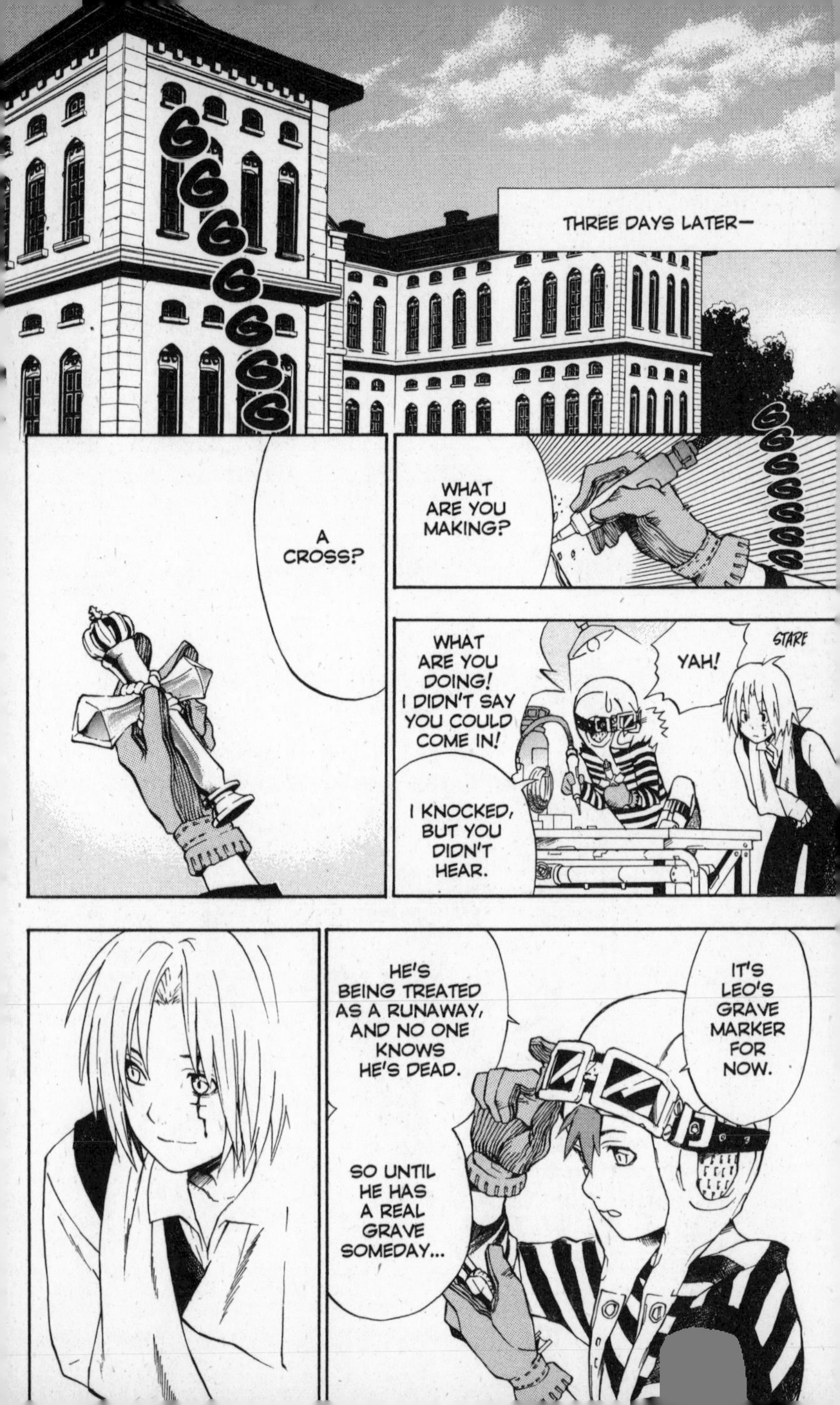
THREE DAYS LATER—
GGGGGGG
GGGGGGGG
WHAT ARE YOU MAKING?
STARE
YAH!
WHAT ARE YOU DOING! I DIDN'T SAY YOU COULD COME IN!
I KNOCKED, BUT YOU DIDN'T HEAR.
A CROSS?
IT'S LEO'S GRAVE MARKER FOR NOW.
HE'S BEING TREATED AS A RUNAWAY, AND NO ONE KNOWS HE'S DEAD.
SO UNTIL HE HAS A REAL GRAVE SOMEDAY...

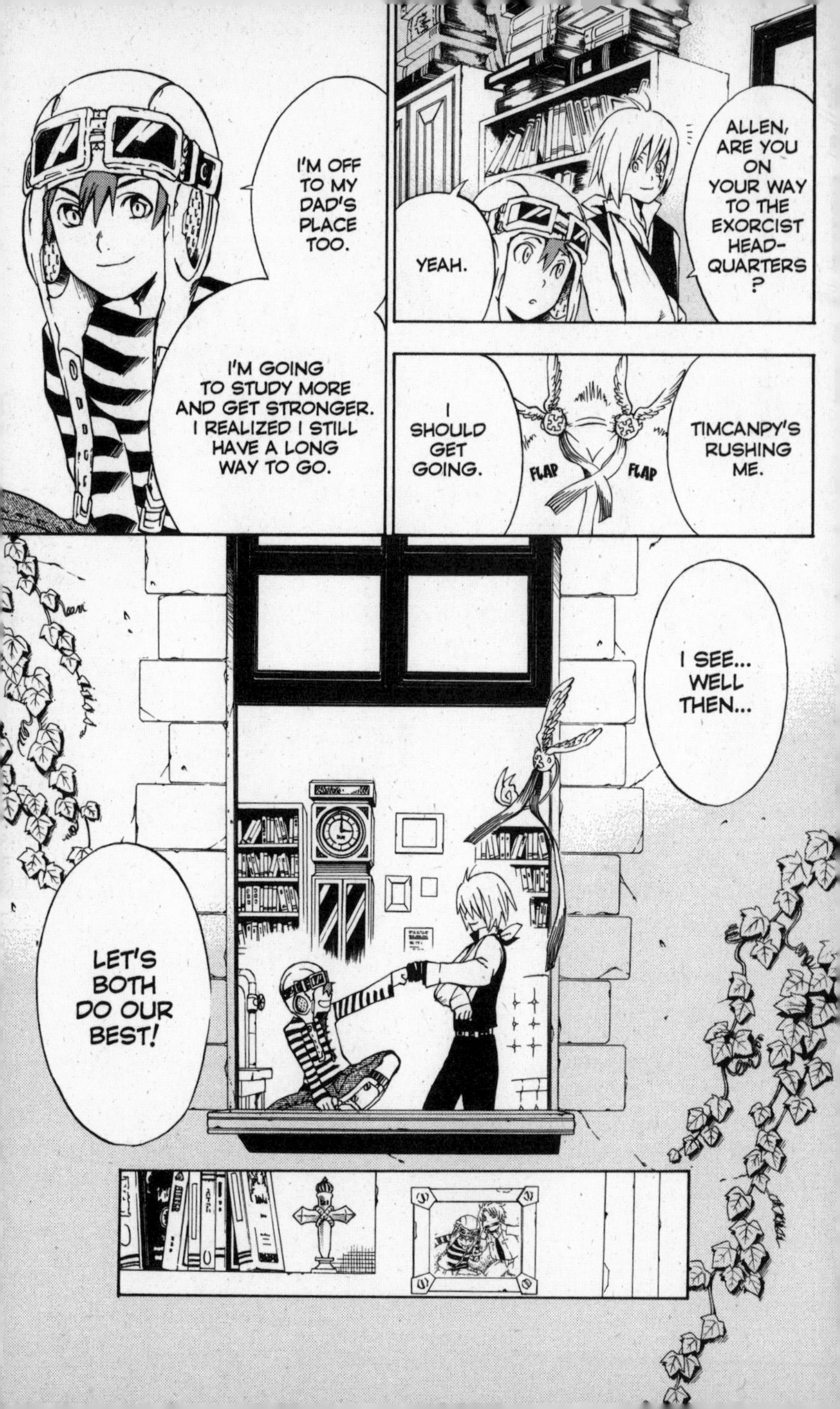
ALLEN, ARE YOU ON YOUR WAY TO THE EXORCIST HEAD-QUARTERS?
YEAH.
TIMCANPY'S RUSHING ME.
FLAP
FLAP
I SHOULD GET GOING.
I'M OFF TO MY DAD'S PLACE TOO.
I'M GOING TO STUDY MORE AND GET STRONGER. I REALIZED I STILL HAVE A LONG WAY TO GO.
I SEE... WELL THEN...
LET'S BOTH DO OUR BEST!

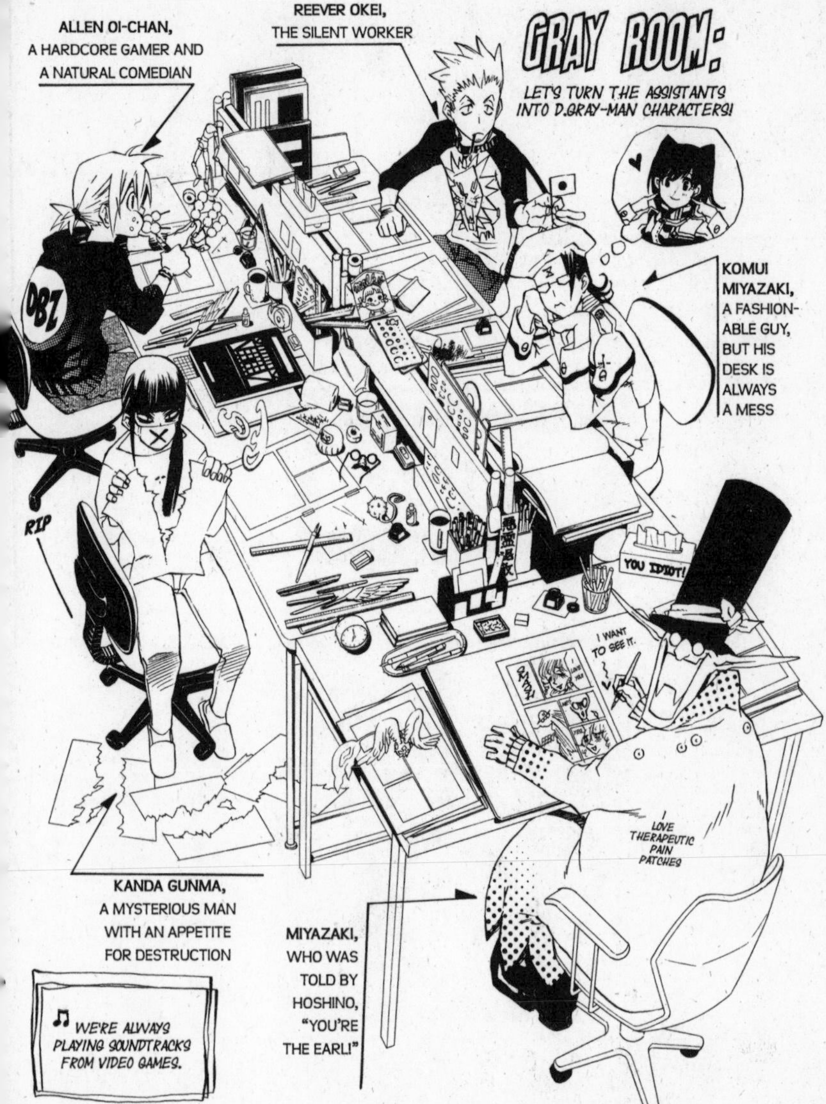

GRAY ROOM:
LET'S TURN THE ASSISTANTS INTO D.GRAY-MAN CHARACTERS!
REEVER OKEI, THE SILENT WORKER
ALLEN OI-CHAN, A HARDCORE GAMER AND A NATURAL COMEDIAN
KOMUI MIYAZAKI, A FASHION-ABLE GUY, BUT HIS DESK IS ALWAYS A MESS
DBZ
RIP
YOU IDIOT!
I WANT TO SEE IT.
I LOVE THERAPEUTIC PAIN PATCHES
KANDA GUNMA, A MYSTERIOUS MAN WITH AN APPETITE FOR DESTRUCTION
MIYAZAKI, WHO WAS TOLD BY HOSHINO, "YOU'RE THE EARL!"
♫ WE'RE ALWAYS PLAYING SOUNDTRACKS FROM VIDEO GAMES.

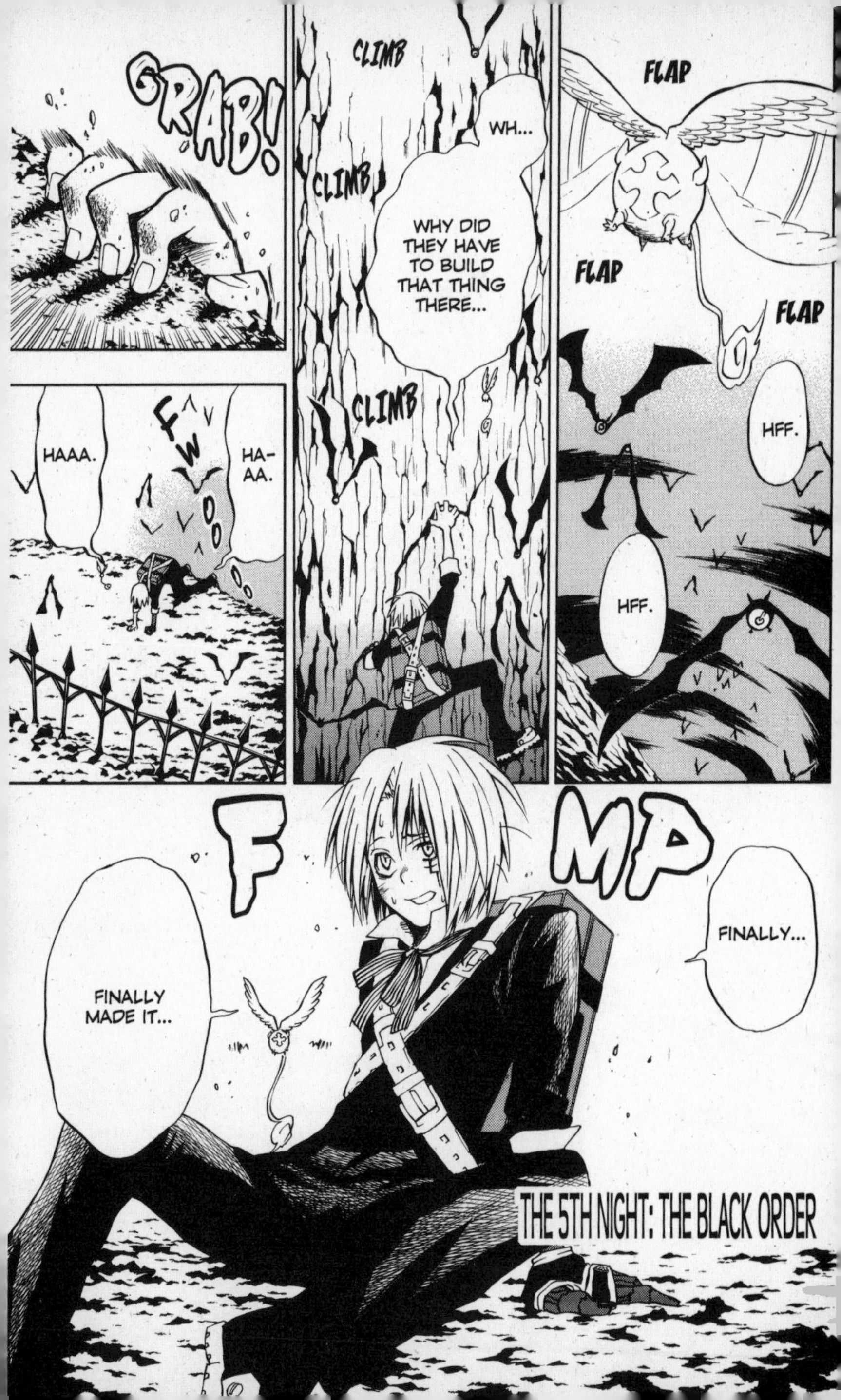

FLAP
FLAP
FLAP
HFF.
HFF.
CLIMB
WH...
CLIMB
WHY DID THEY HAVE TO BUILD THAT THING THERE...
CLIMB
GRAB!
HA-AA.
FWOOO
HAAA.
FMP
FINALLY...
FINALLY MADE IT...
THE 5TH NIGHT: THE BLACK ORDER

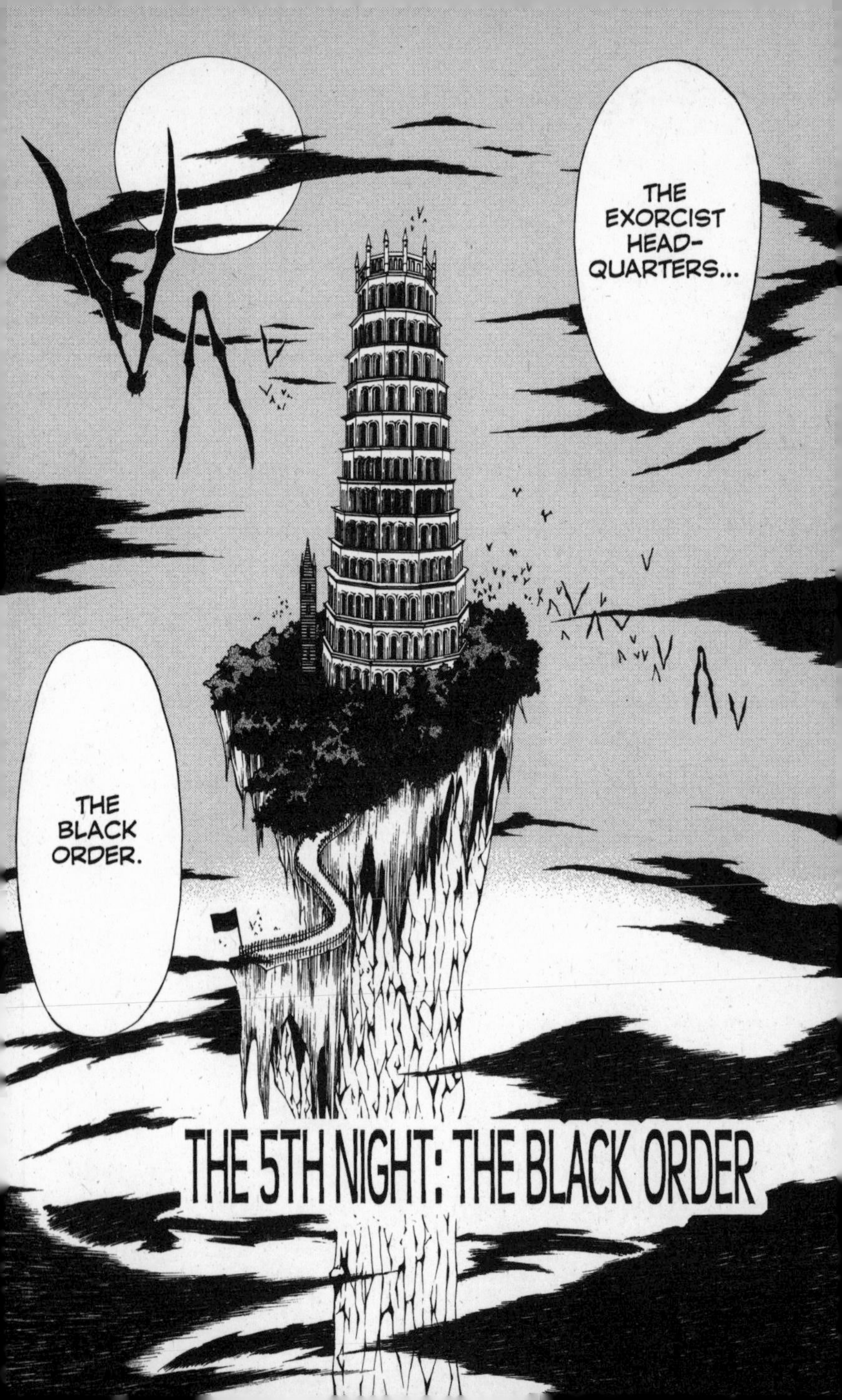
THE EXORCIST HEAD-QUARTERS...
THE BLACK ORDER.
THE 5TH NIGHT: THE BLACK ORDER

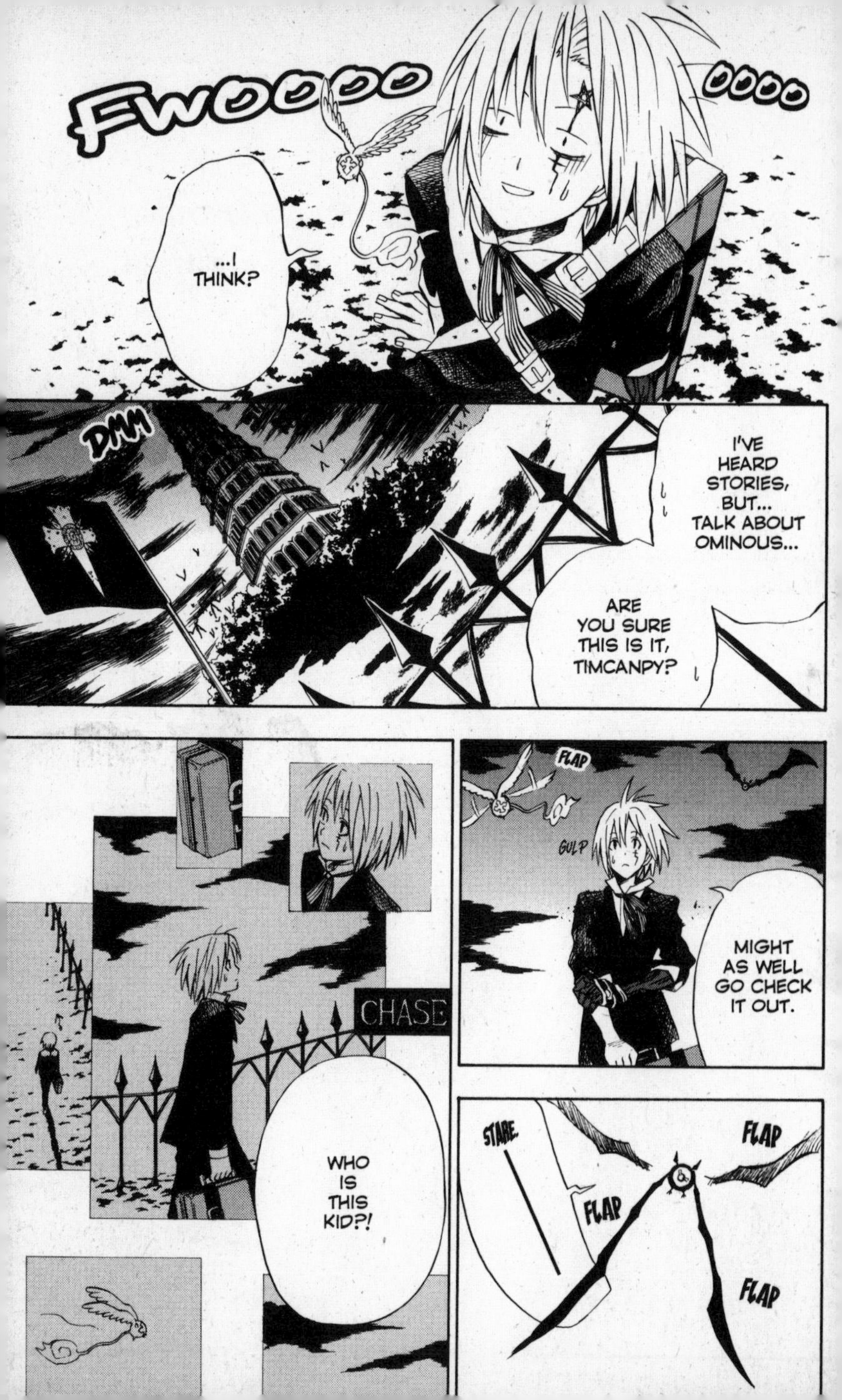
FWOOOOO
OOOO
...I THINK?
DMM
I'VE HEARD STORIES, BUT... TALK ABOUT OMINOUS...
ARE YOU SURE THIS IS IT, TIMCANPY?
FLAP
GULP
MIGHT AS WELL GO CHECK IT OUT.
STARE
FLAP
FLAP
FLAP
CHASE
WHO IS THIS KID?!

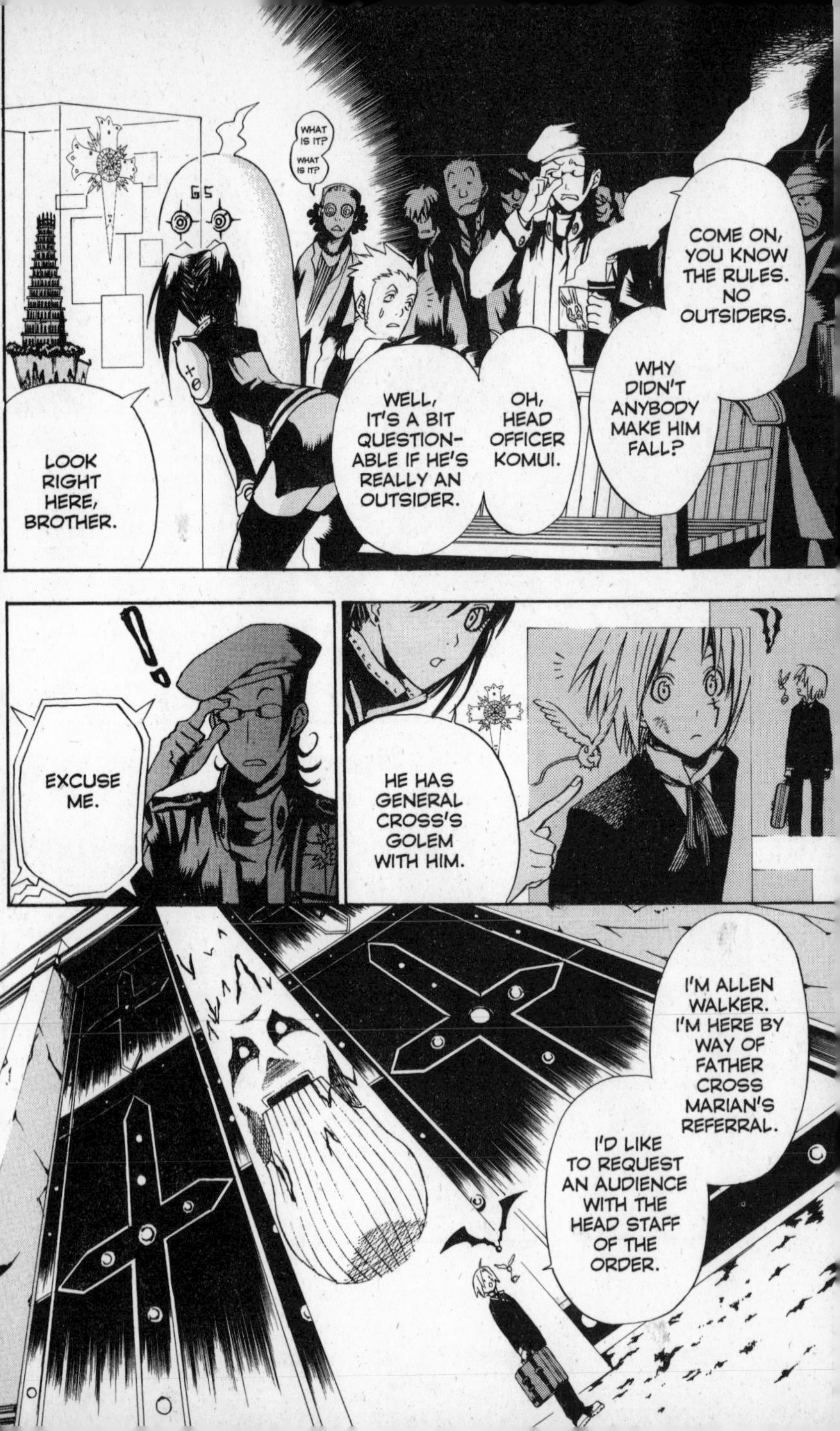
COME ON, YOU KNOW THE RULES. NO OUTSIDERS.
WHY DIDN'T ANYBODY MAKE HIM FALL?
WHAT IS IT? WHAT IS IT?
OH, HEAD OFFICER KOMUI.
WELL, IT'S A BIT QUESTION-ABLE IF HE'S REALLY AN OUTSIDER.
LOOK RIGHT HERE, BROTHER.
HE HAS GENERAL CROSS'S GOLEM WITH HIM.
!
EXCUSE ME.
I'M ALLEN WALKER. I'M HERE BY WAY OF FATHER CROSS MARIAN'S REFERRAL.
I'D LIKE TO REQUEST AN AUDIENCE WITH THE HEAD STAFF OF THE ORDER.

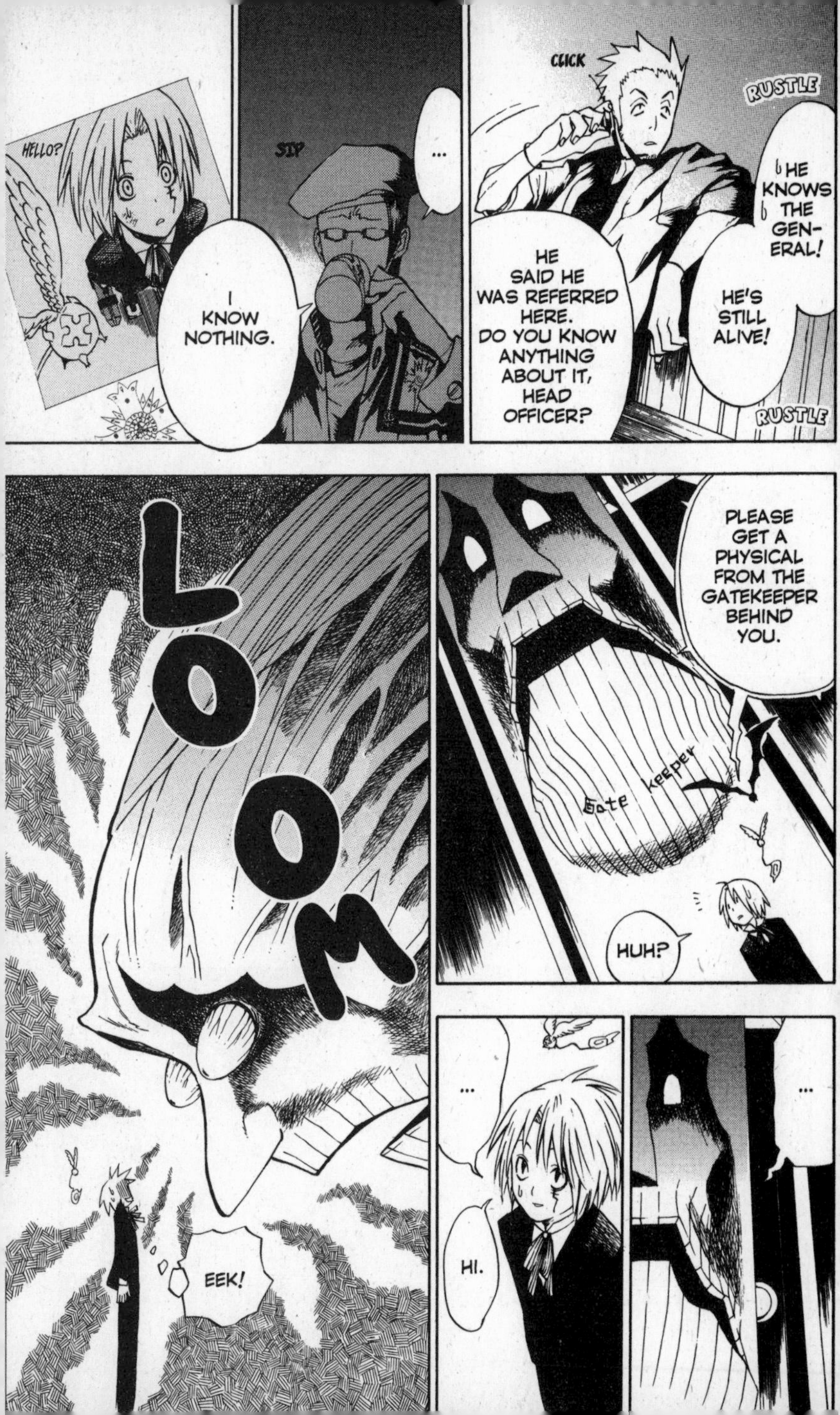
CLICK
RUSTLE
HE KNOWS THE GENERAL!
HE'S STILL ALIVE!
HE SAID HE WAS REFERRED HERE. DO YOU KNOW ANYTHING ABOUT IT, HEAD OFFICER?
RUSTLE
...
SIP
I KNOW NOTHING.
HELLO?
PLEASE GET A PHYSICAL FROM THE GATEKEEPER BEHIND YOU.
Gate keeper
HUH?
...
...
HI.
LOOM
EEK!

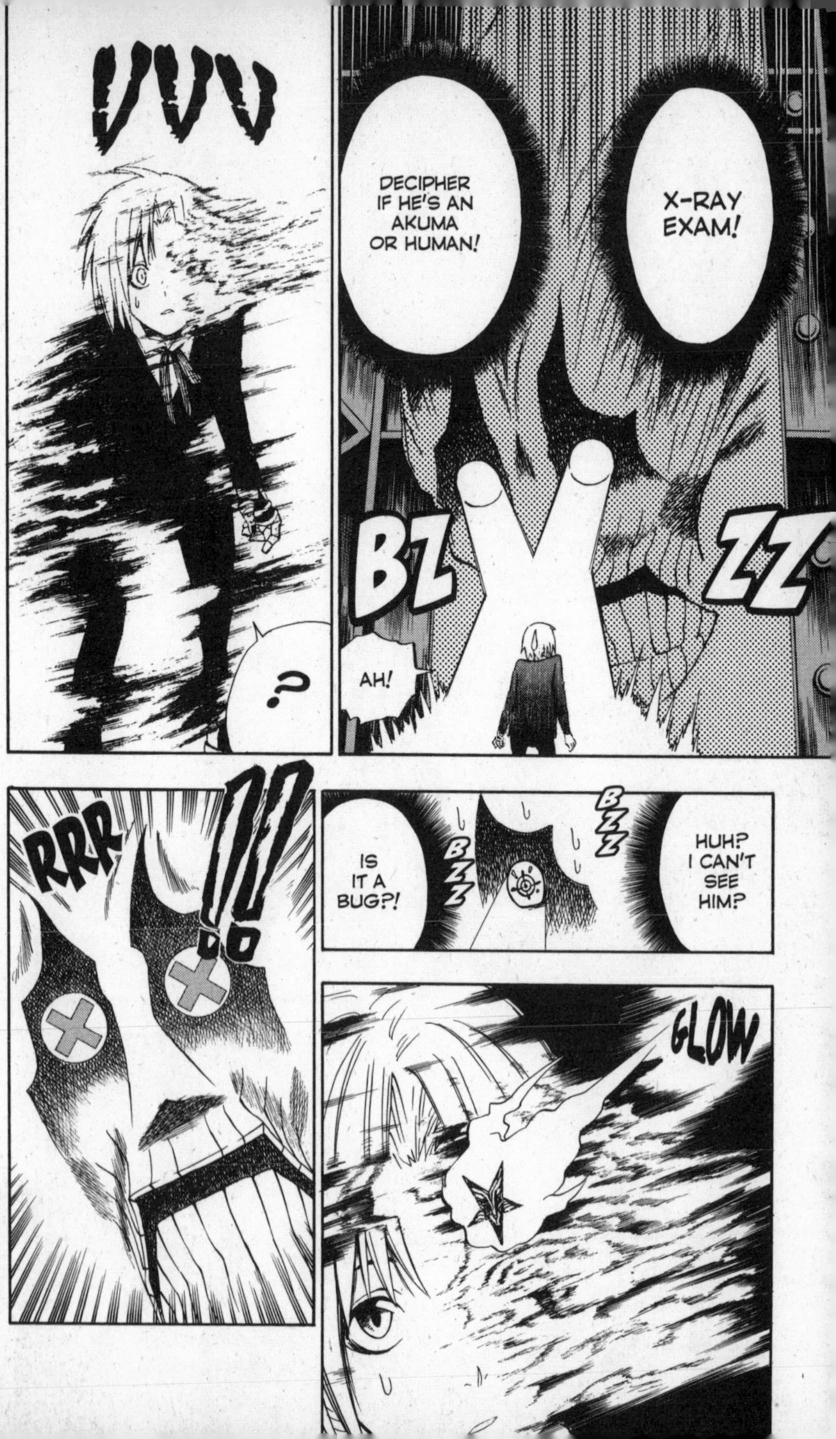
X-RAY EXAM!
DECIPHER IF HE'S AN AKUMA OR HUMAN!
BZ
ZZ
AH!
VVV
?
HUH? I CAN'T SEE HIM?
BZZ
BZZ
IS IT A BUG?!
GLOW
!!
RRR

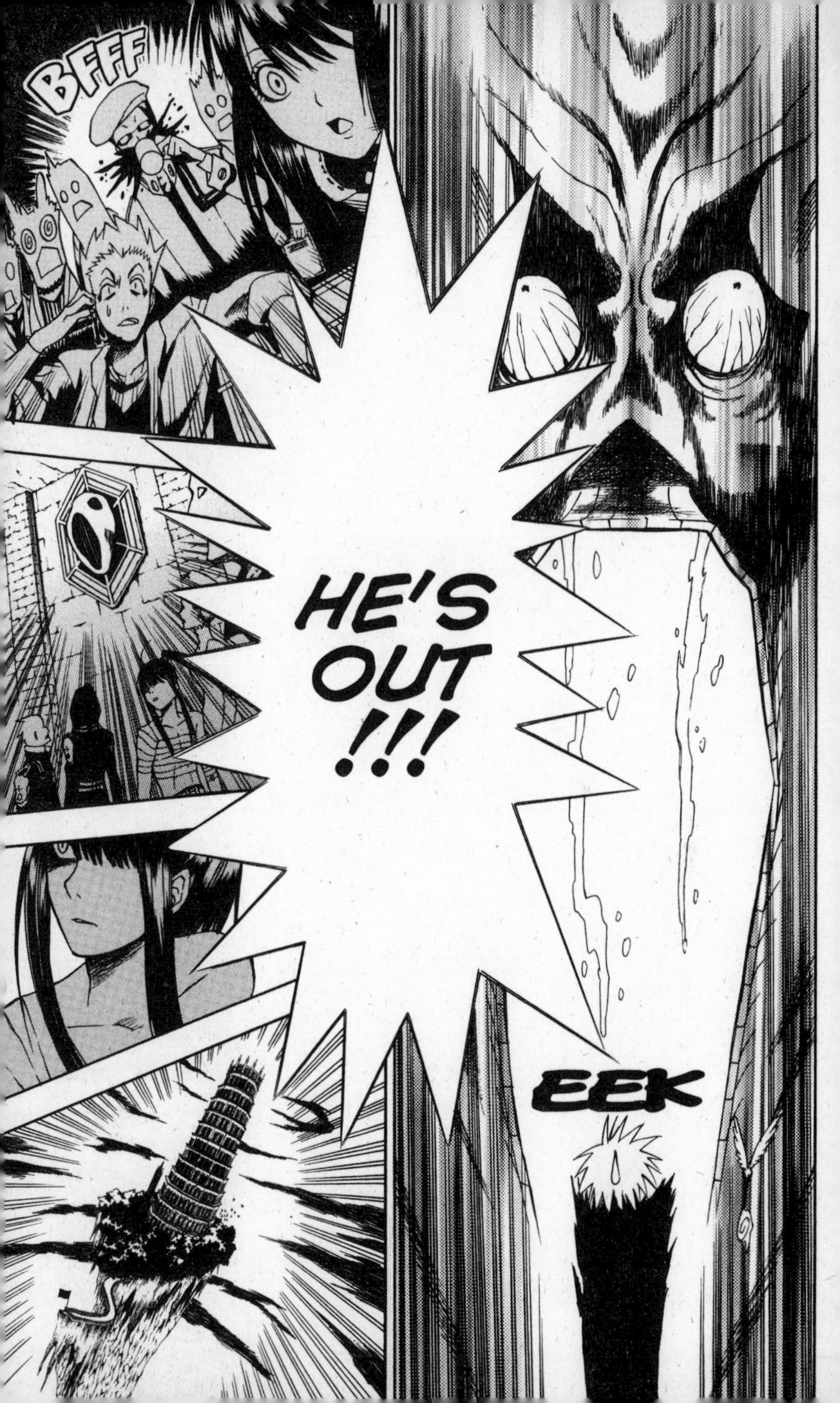
HE'S OUT!!!
EEK
BFFF

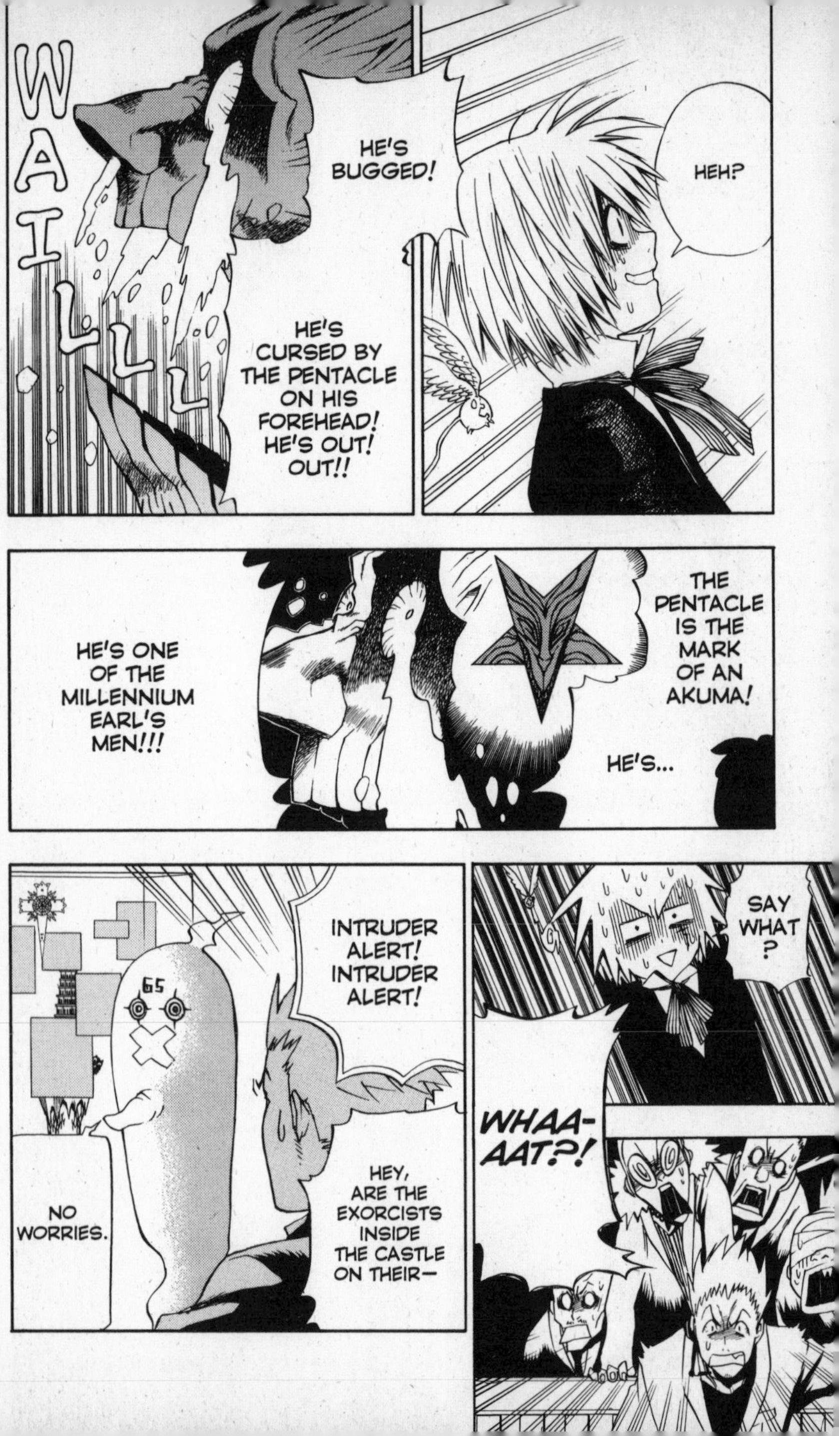
HEH?
HE'S BUGGED!
HE'S CURSED BY THE PENTACLE ON HIS FOREHEAD! HE'S OUT! OUT!!
WAILLLL
THE PENTACLE IS THE MARK OF AN AKUMA!
HE'S...
HE'S ONE OF THE MILLENNIUM EARL'S MEN!!!
SAY WHAT?
WHAAA-AAT?!
INTRUDER ALERT! INTRUDER ALERT!
HEY, ARE THE EXORCISTS INSIDE THE CASTLE ON THEIR—
NO WORRIES.

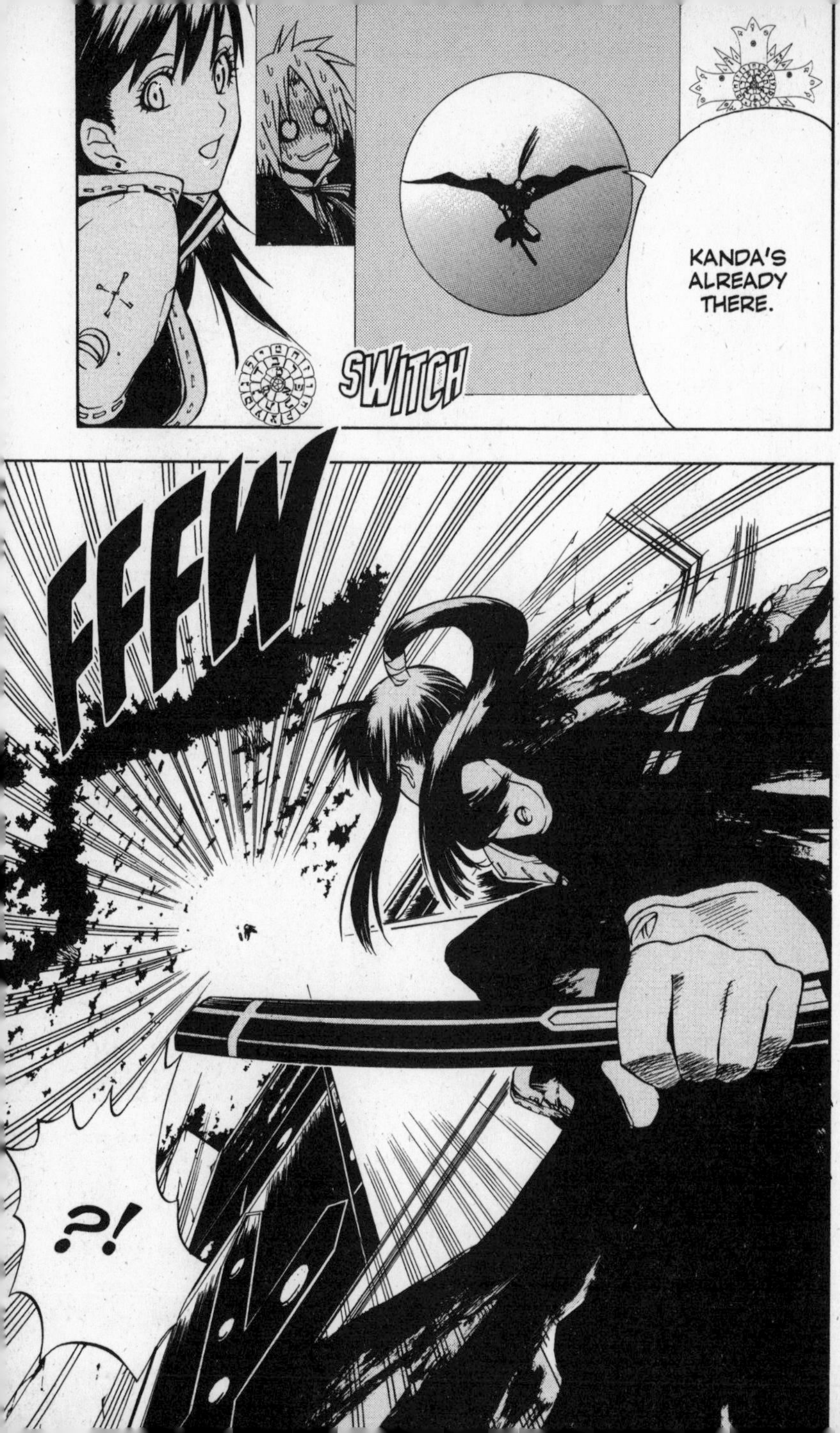
KANDA'S ALREADY THERE.
SWITCH
FFFW
?!

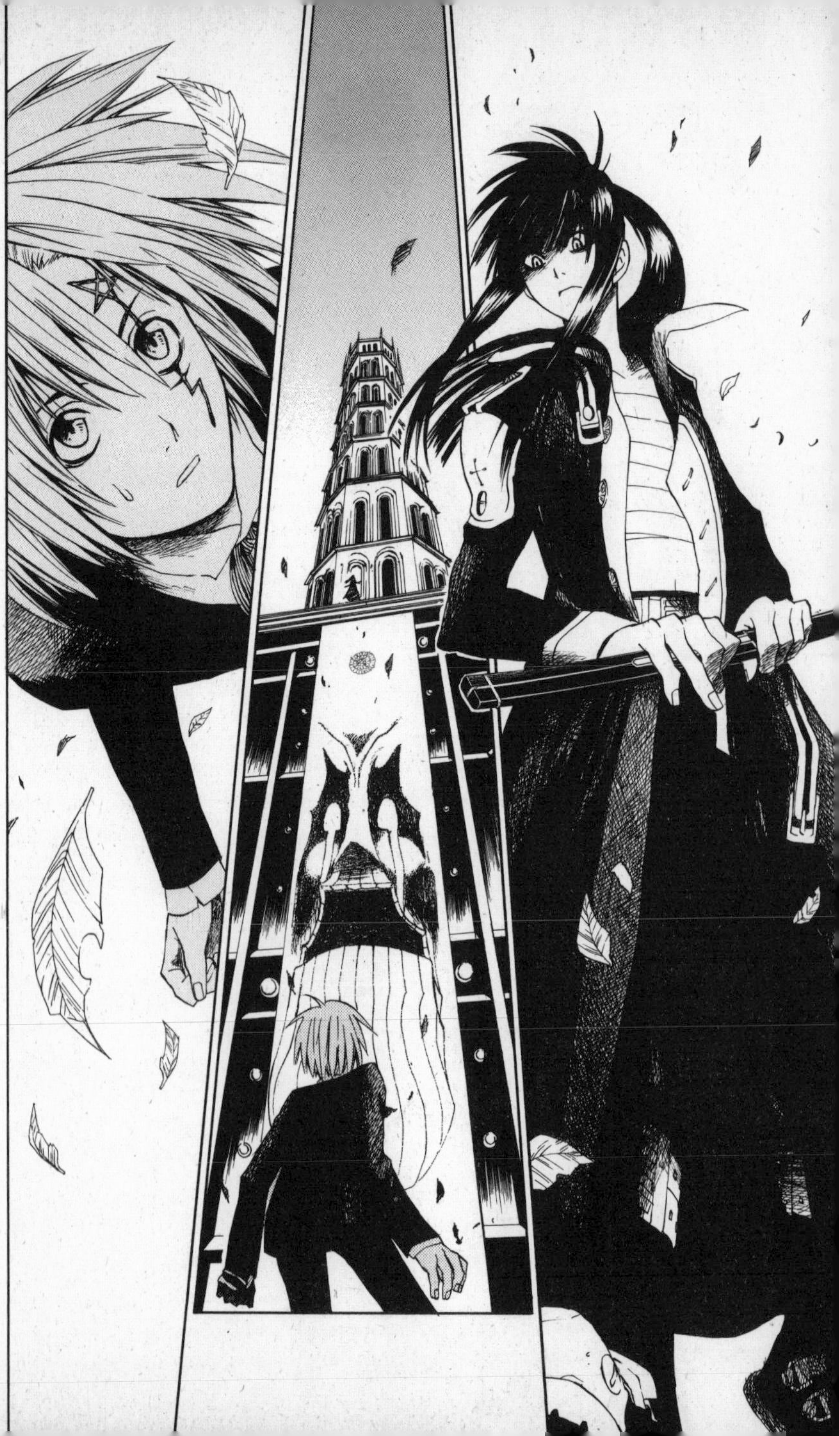

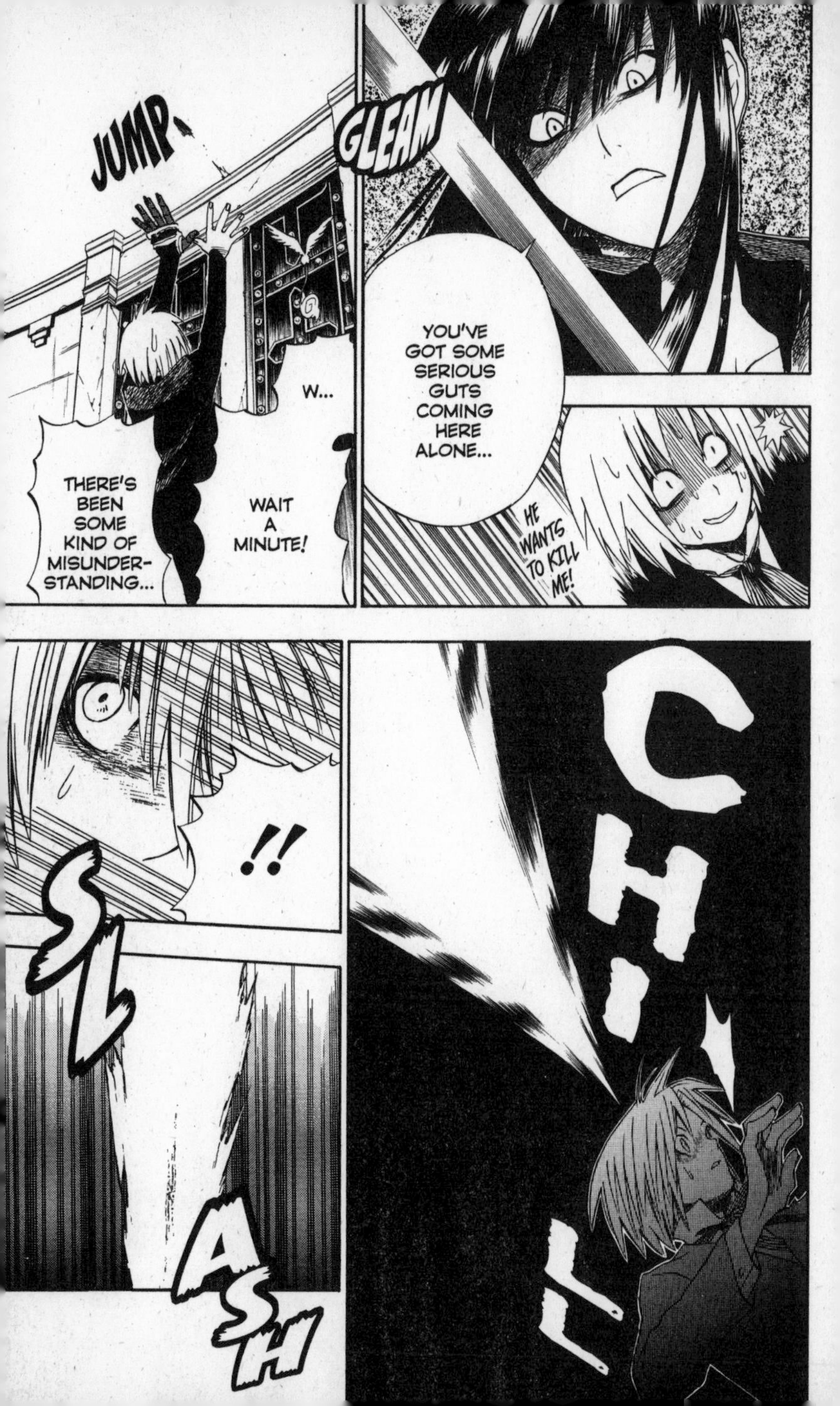
GLEAM
YOU'VE GOT SOME SERIOUS GUTS COMING HERE ALONE...
HE WANTS TO KILL ME!
JUMP
W...
WAIT A MINUTE!
THERE'S BEEN SOME KIND OF MISUNDER-STANDING...
CHI...
!!
SLASH

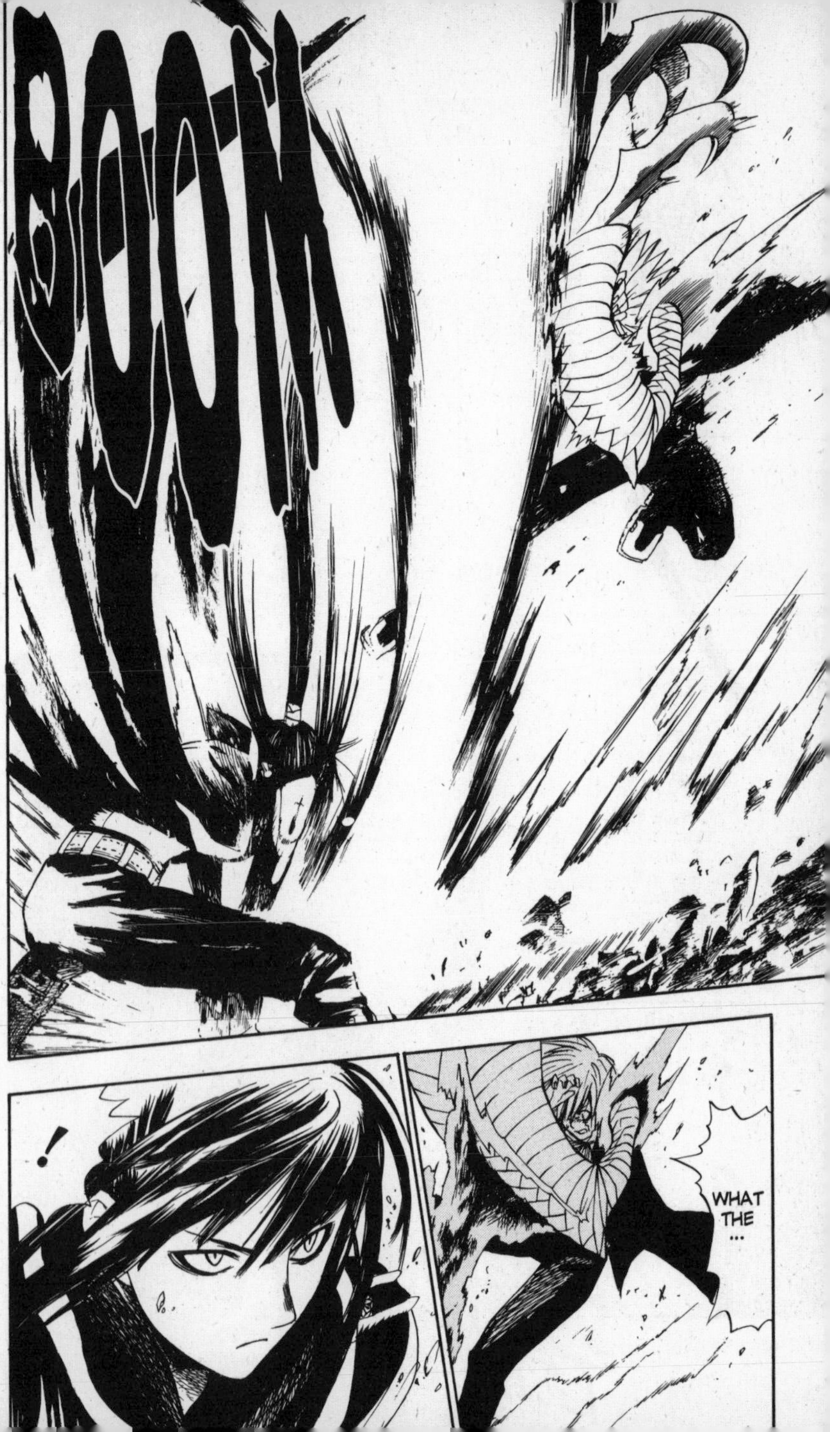
BOOM
WHAT THE ...
!

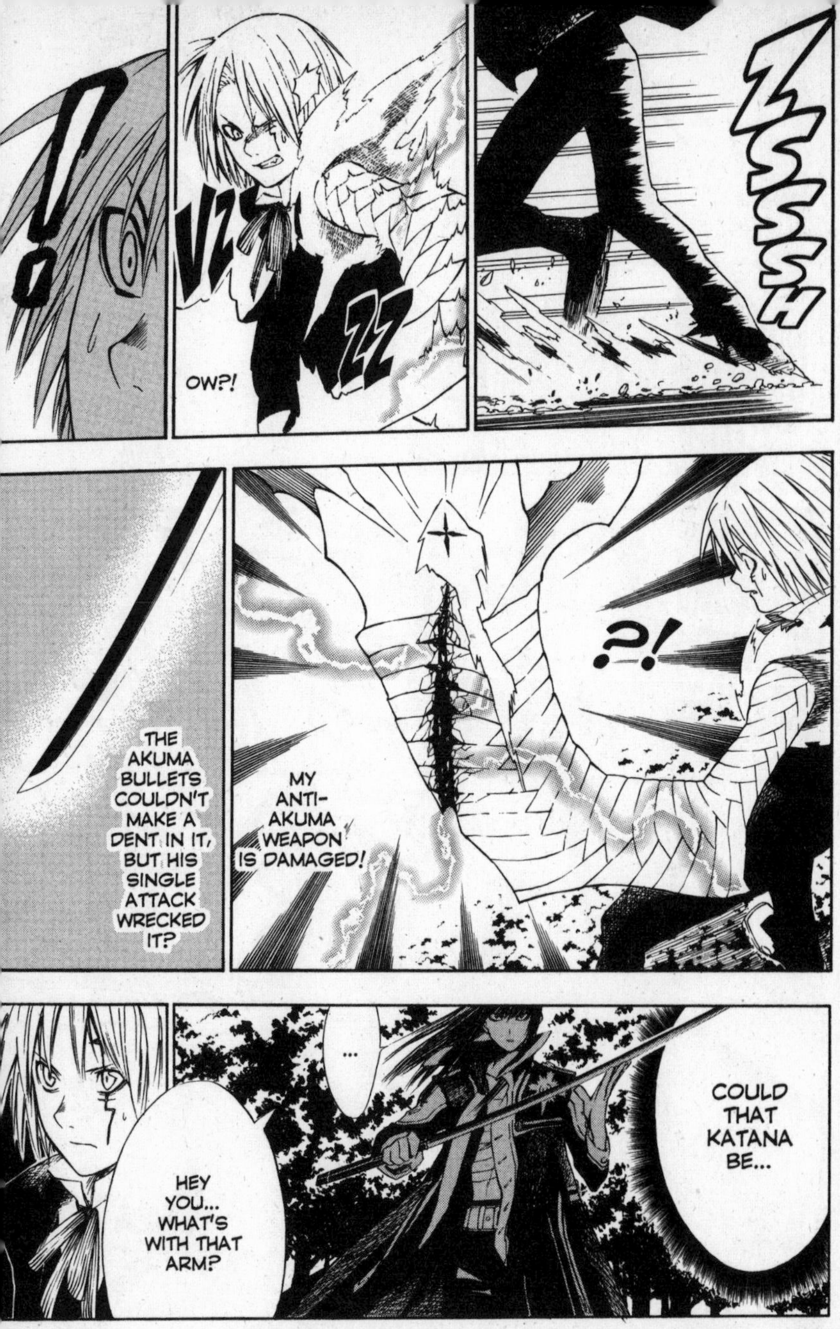
ZSSSH
VZZT
ZZ
OW?!
!?
?!
MY ANTI-AKUMA WEAPON IS DAMAGED!
THE AKUMA BULLETS COULDN'T MAKE A DENT IN IT, BUT HIS SINGLE ATTACK WRECKED IT?
COULD THAT KATANA BE...
...
HEY YOU... WHAT'S WITH THAT ARM?

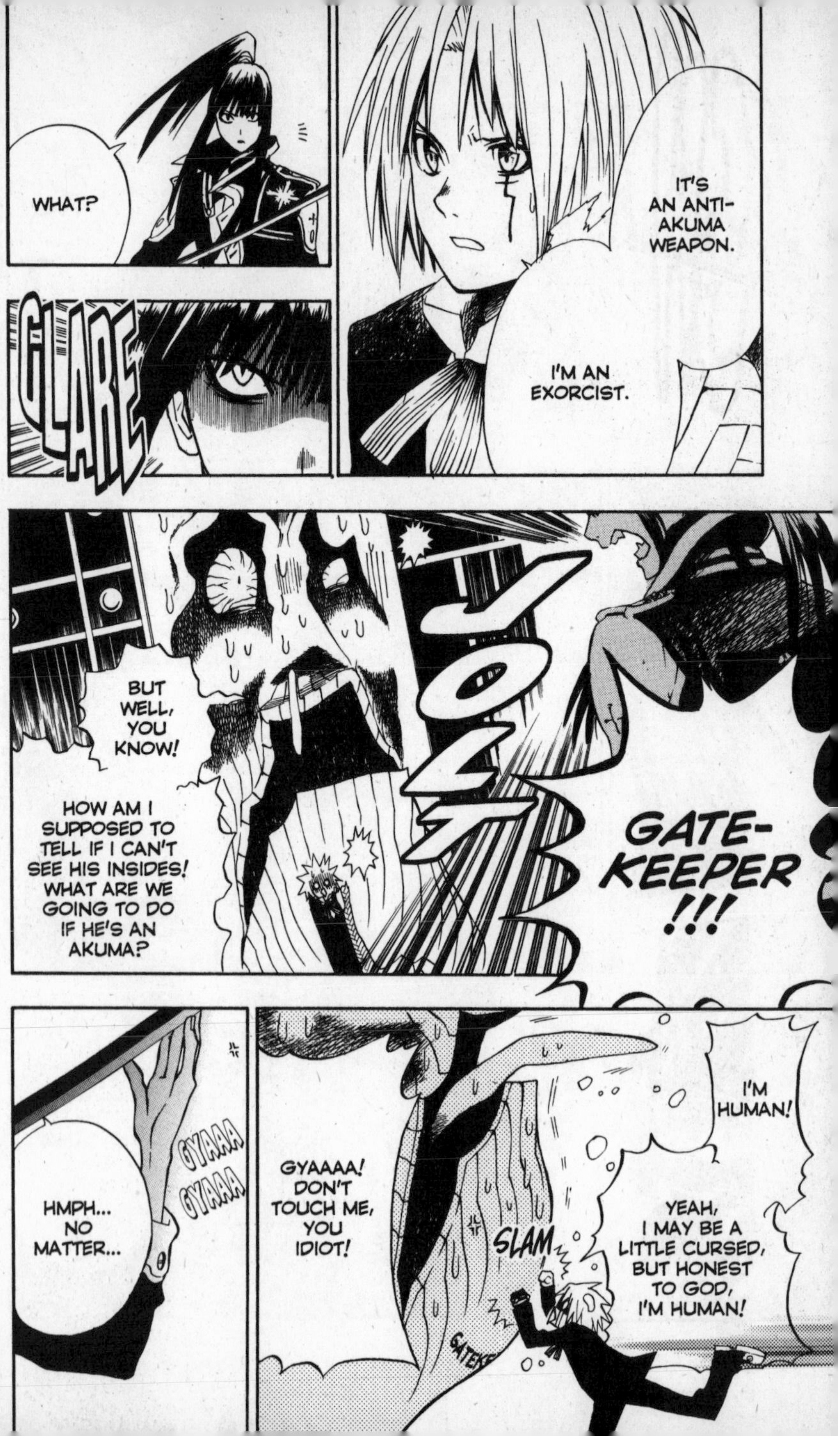
IT'S AN ANTI-AKUMA WEAPON.
I'M AN EXORCIST.
WHAT?
GLARE
GATE-KEEPER!!!
BUT WELL, YOU KNOW!
HOW AM I SUPPOSED TO TELL IF I CAN'T SEE HIS INSIDES! WHAT ARE WE GOING TO DO IF HE'S AN AKUMA?
I'M HUMAN!
YEAH, I MAY BE A LITTLE CURSED, BUT HONEST TO GOD, I'M HUMAN!
SLAM
GYAAAA! DON'T TOUCH ME, YOU IDIOT!
GYAAA
GYAAA
HMPH... NO MATTER...

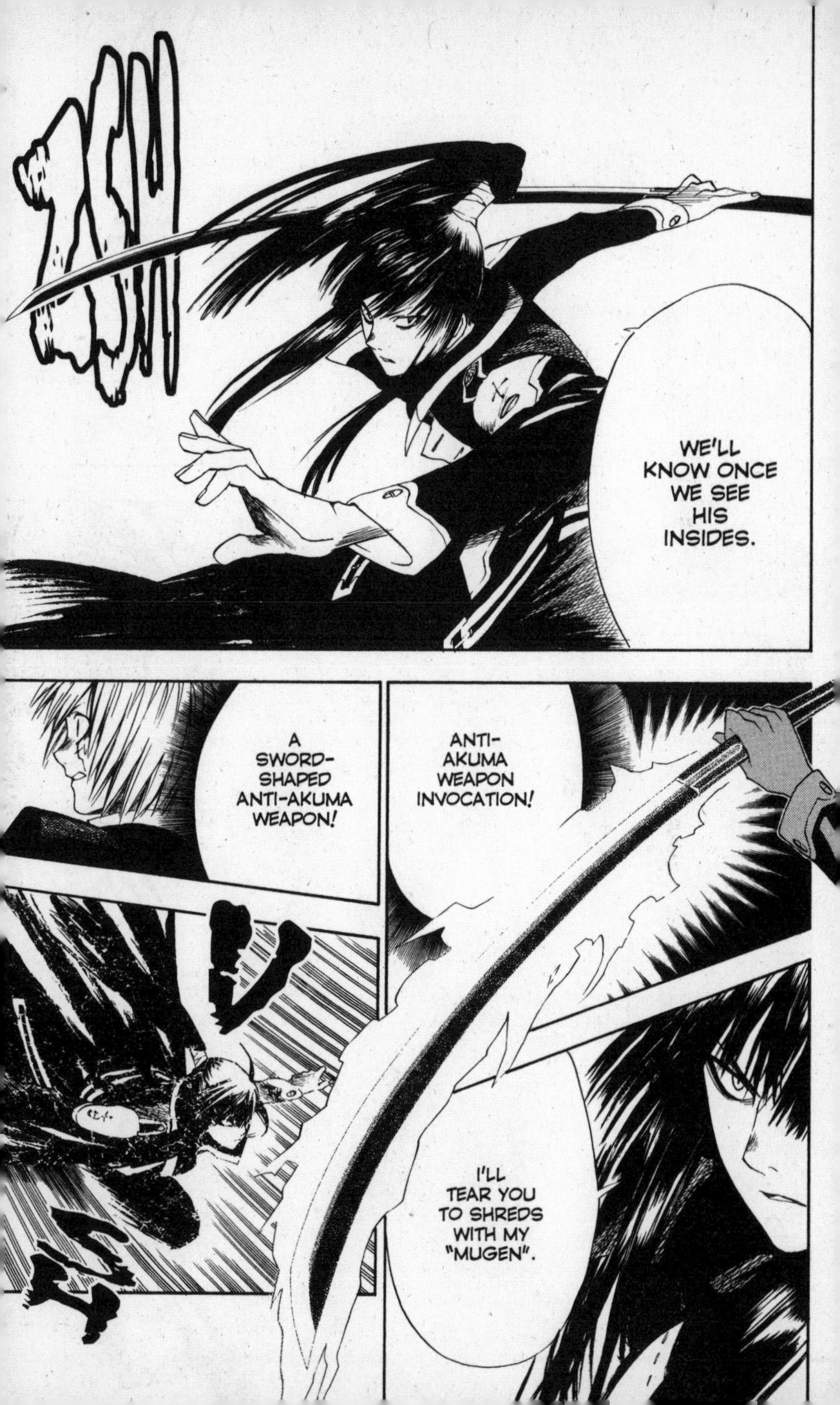
WE'LL KNOW ONCE WE SEE HIS INSIDES.
ANTI-AKUMA WEAPON INVOCATION!
A SWORD-SHAPED ANTI-AKUMA WEAPON!
I'LL TEAR YOU TO SHREDS WITH MY "MUGEN".

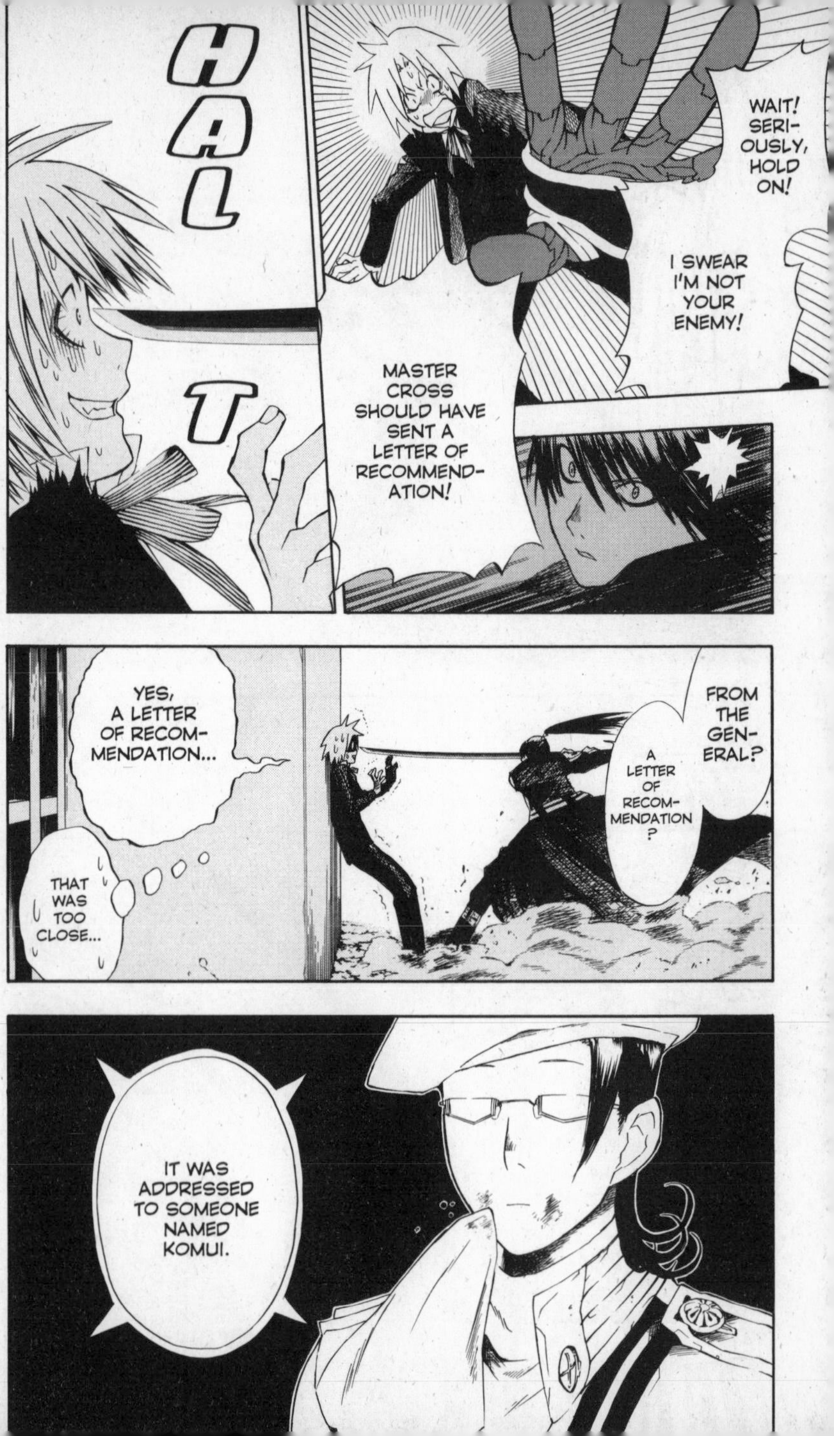
WAIT! SERIOUSLY, HOLD ON!
I SWEAR I'M NOT YOUR ENEMY!
MASTER CROSS SHOULD HAVE SENT A LETTER OF RECOMMENDATION!
HALT
FROM THE GENERAL?
A LETTER OF RECOMMENDATION?
YES, A LETTER OF RECOMMENDATION...
THAT WAS TOO CLOSE...
IT WAS ADDRESSED TO SOMEONE NAMED KOMUI.

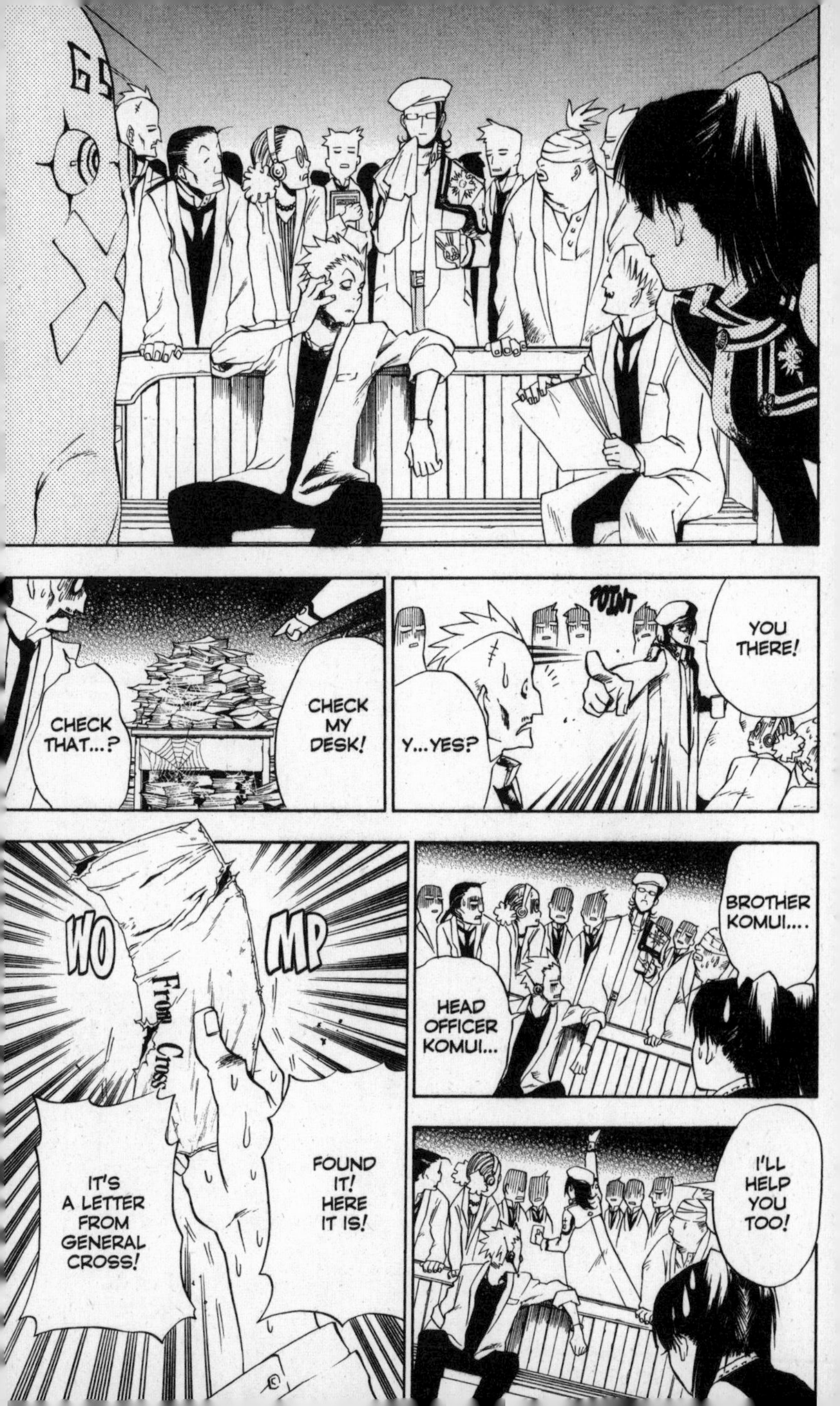
POINT
YOU THERE!
Y...YES?
CHECK MY DESK!
CHECK THAT...?
BROTHER KOMUI....
HEAD OFFICER KOMUI...
I'LL HELP YOU TOO!
WOMP
From Cross
FOUND IT! HERE IT IS!
IT'S A LETTER FROM GENERAL CROSS!

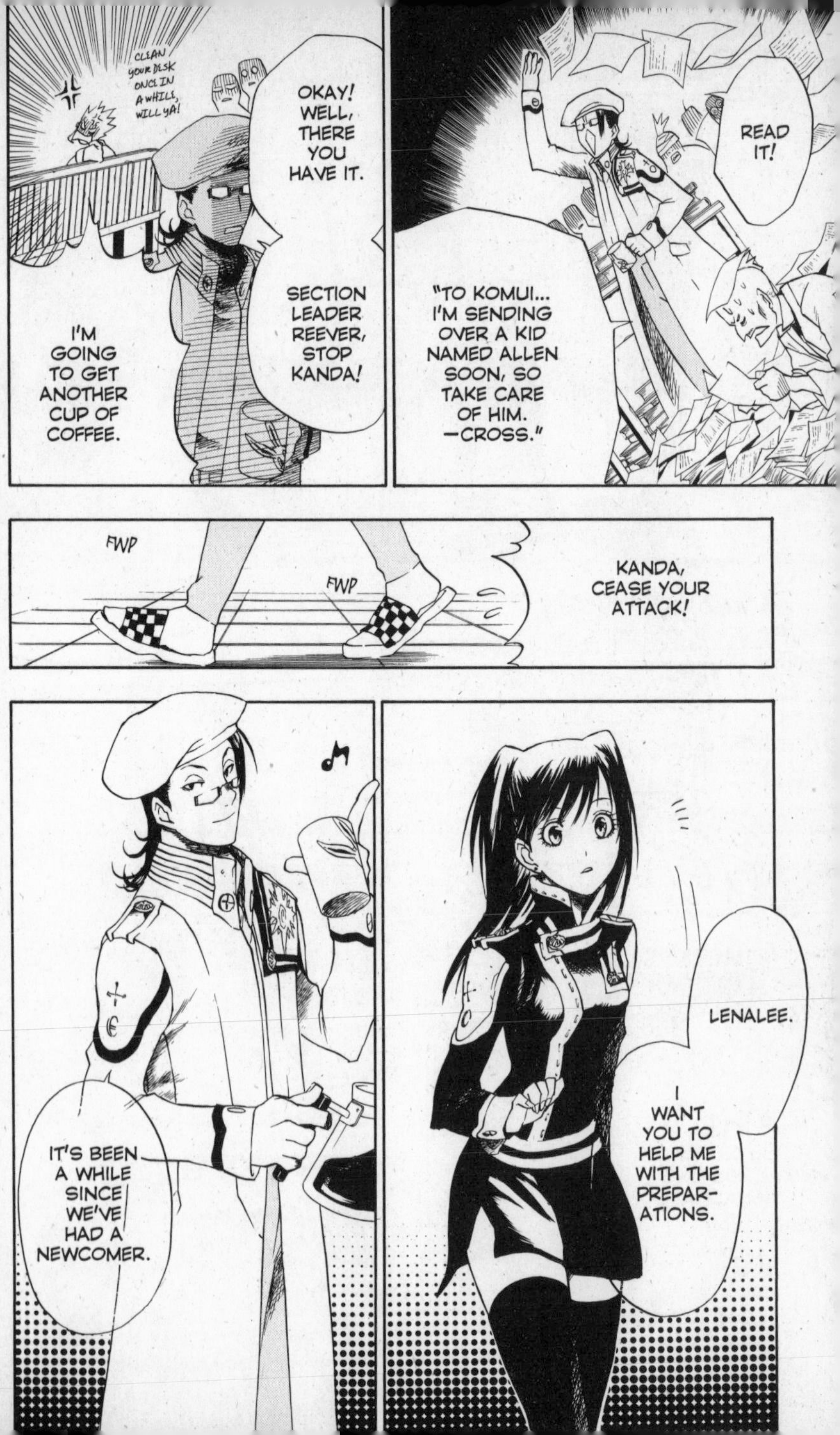
READ IT!
"TO KOMUI... I'M SENDING OVER A KID NAMED ALLEN SOON, SO TAKE CARE OF HIM. —CROSS."
OKAY! WELL, THERE YOU HAVE IT.
CLEAN YOUR DESK ONCE IN A WHILE, WILL YA!
SECTION LEADER REEVER, STOP KANDA!
I'M GOING TO GET ANOTHER CUP OF COFFEE.
KANDA, CEASE YOUR ATTACK!
FWP
FWP
LENALEE.
I WANT YOU TO HELP ME WITH THE PREPARATIONS.
IT'S BEEN A WHILE SINCE WE'VE HAD A NEWCOMER.

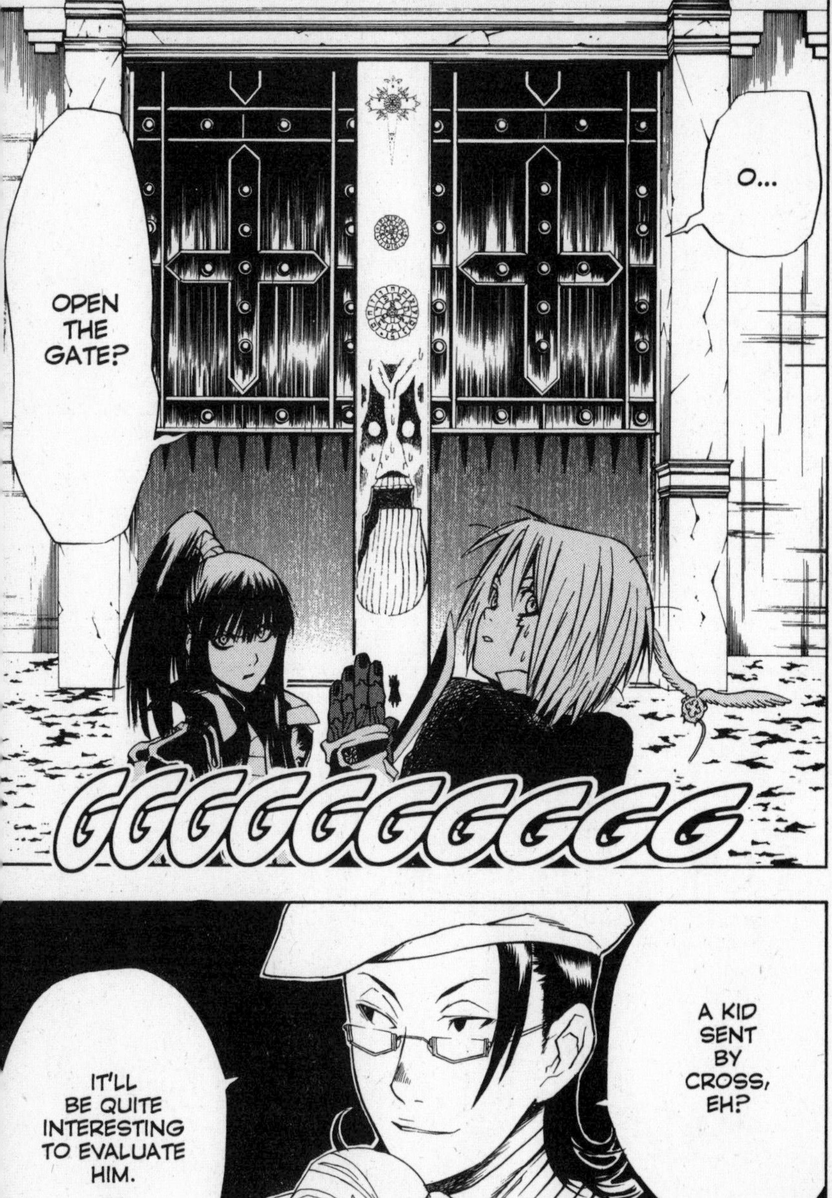
O...
OPEN THE GATE?
GGGGGGGGGGG
A KID SENT BY CROSS, EH?
IT'LL BE QUITE INTERESTING TO EVALUATE HIM. ♫

KOMUI LEE

CHINESE, 29 YEARS OLD
HEIGHT: 193 CM
WEIGHT: 79 KG
BIRTHDAY: JUNE 13TH
GEMINI, BLOOD TYPE: AB

A YOUNG GENIUS SCIENTIST WITH AN ENDLESS NEED TO FULFILL HIS CURIOSITY...

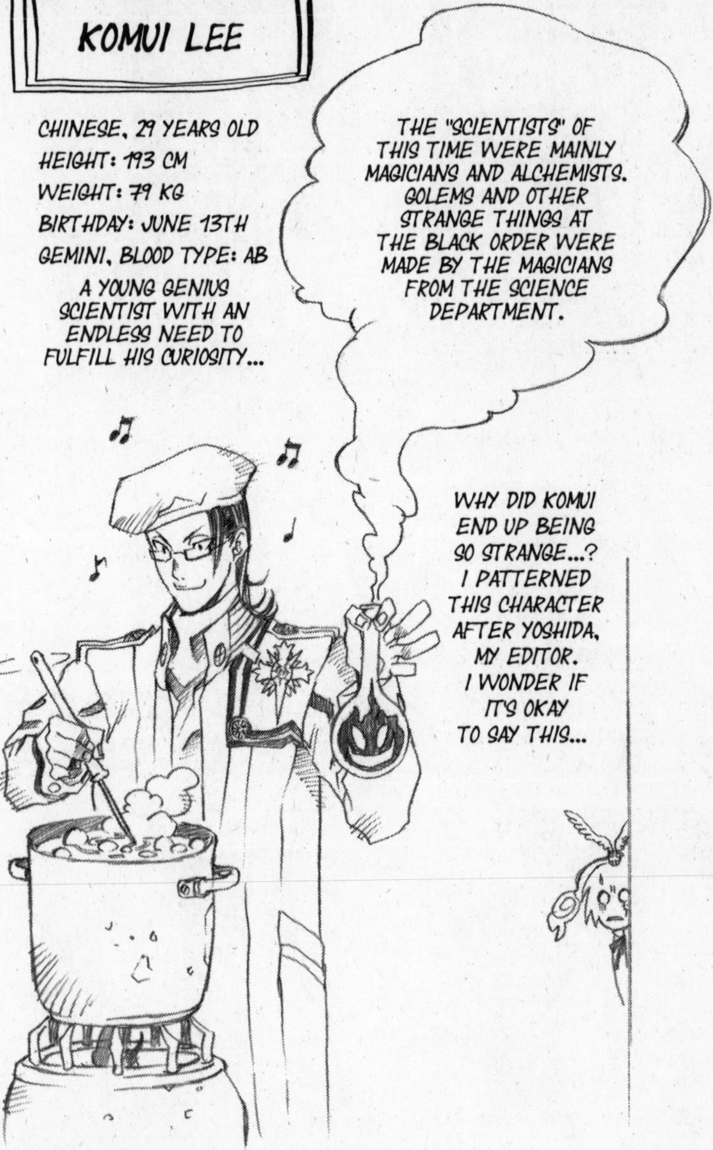
THE "SCIENTISTS" OF THIS TIME WERE MAINLY MAGICIANS AND ALCHEMISTS. GOLEMS AND OTHER STRANGE THINGS AT THE BLACK ORDER WERE MADE BY THE MAGICIANS FROM THE SCIENCE DEPARTMENT.

WHY DID KOMUI END UP BEING SO STRANGE...? I PATTERNED THIS CHARACTER AFTER YOSHIDA, MY EDITOR. I WONDER IF IT'S OKAY TO SAY THIS...

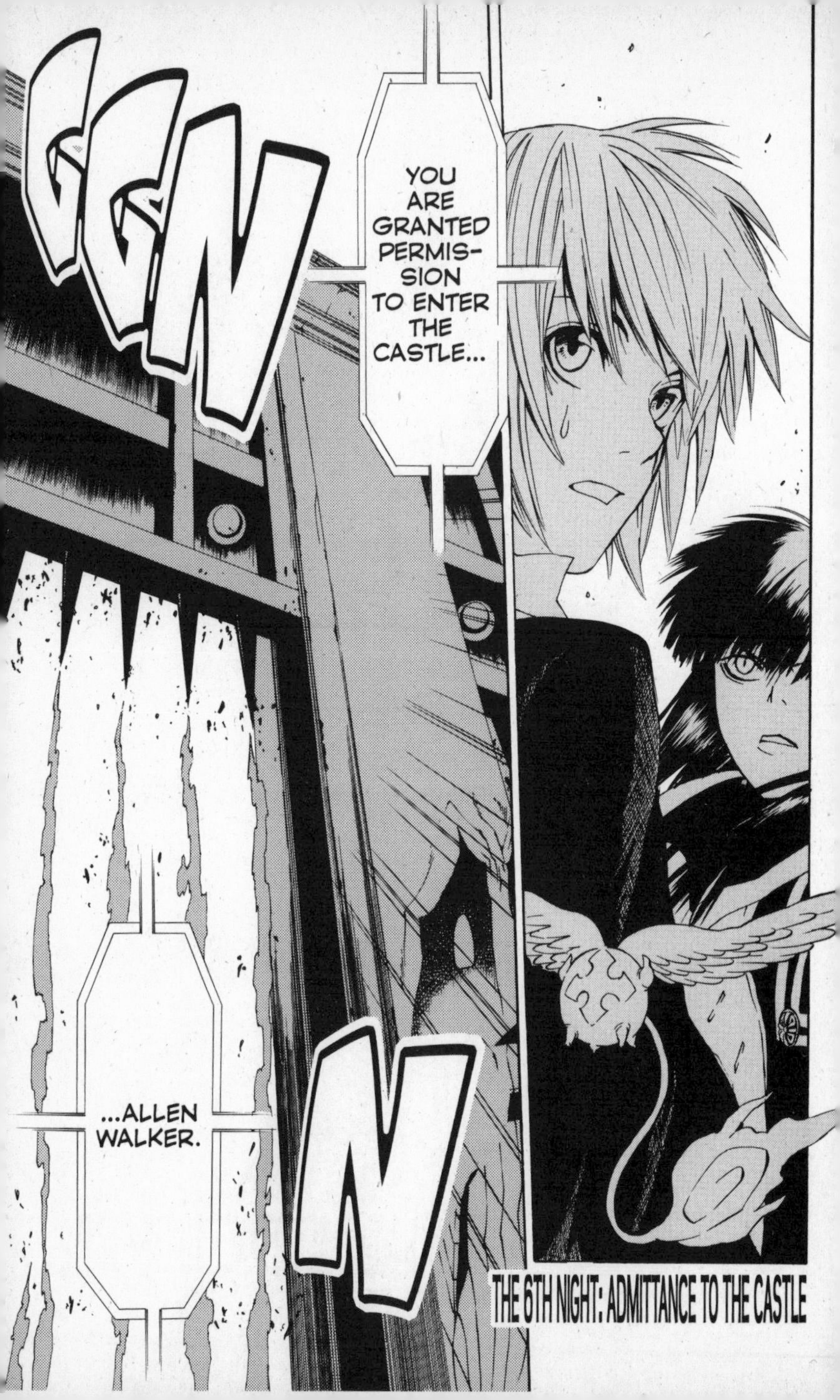
YOU ARE GRANTED PERMISSION TO ENTER THE CASTLE...
...ALLEN WALKER.
GGW
N

THE 6TH NIGHT: ADMITTANCE TO THE CASTLE

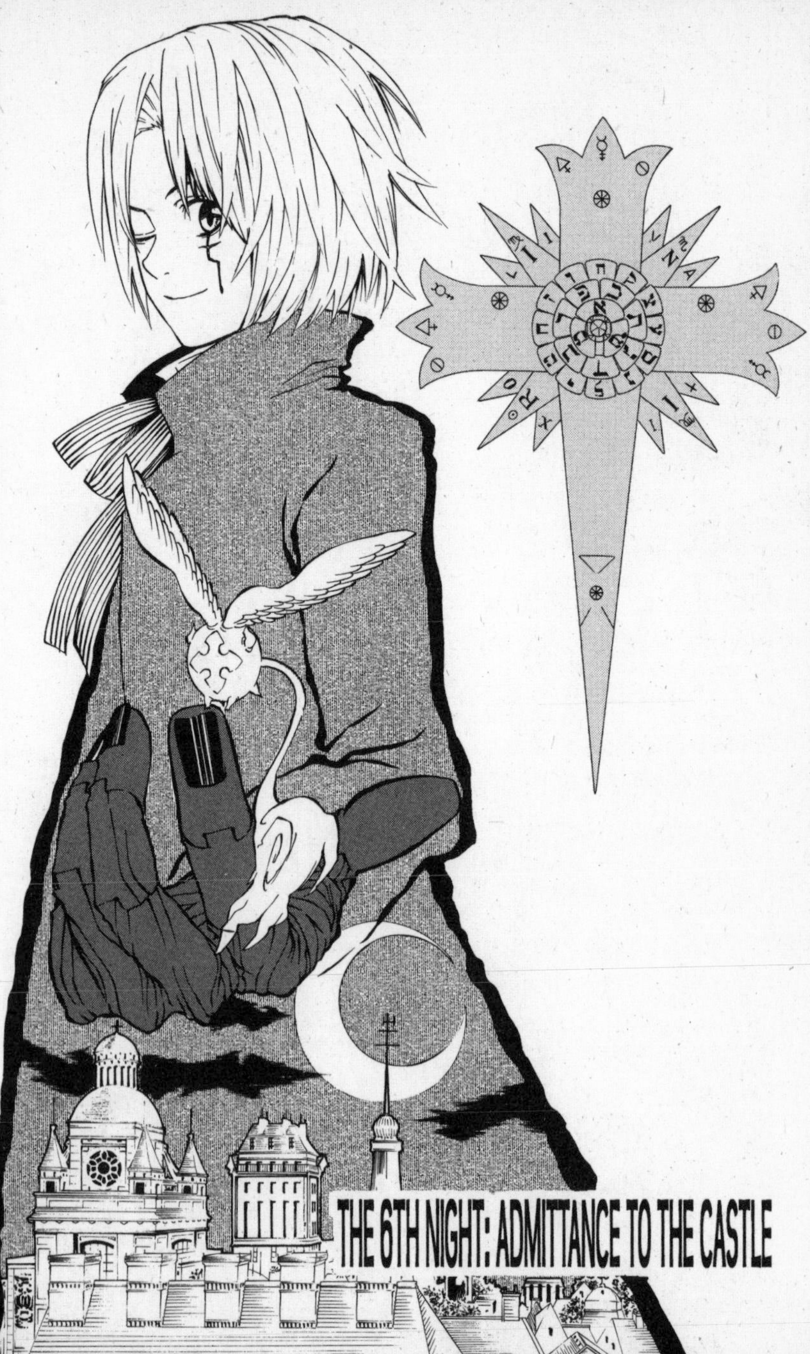
THE 6TH NIGHT: ADMITTANCE TO THE CASTLE

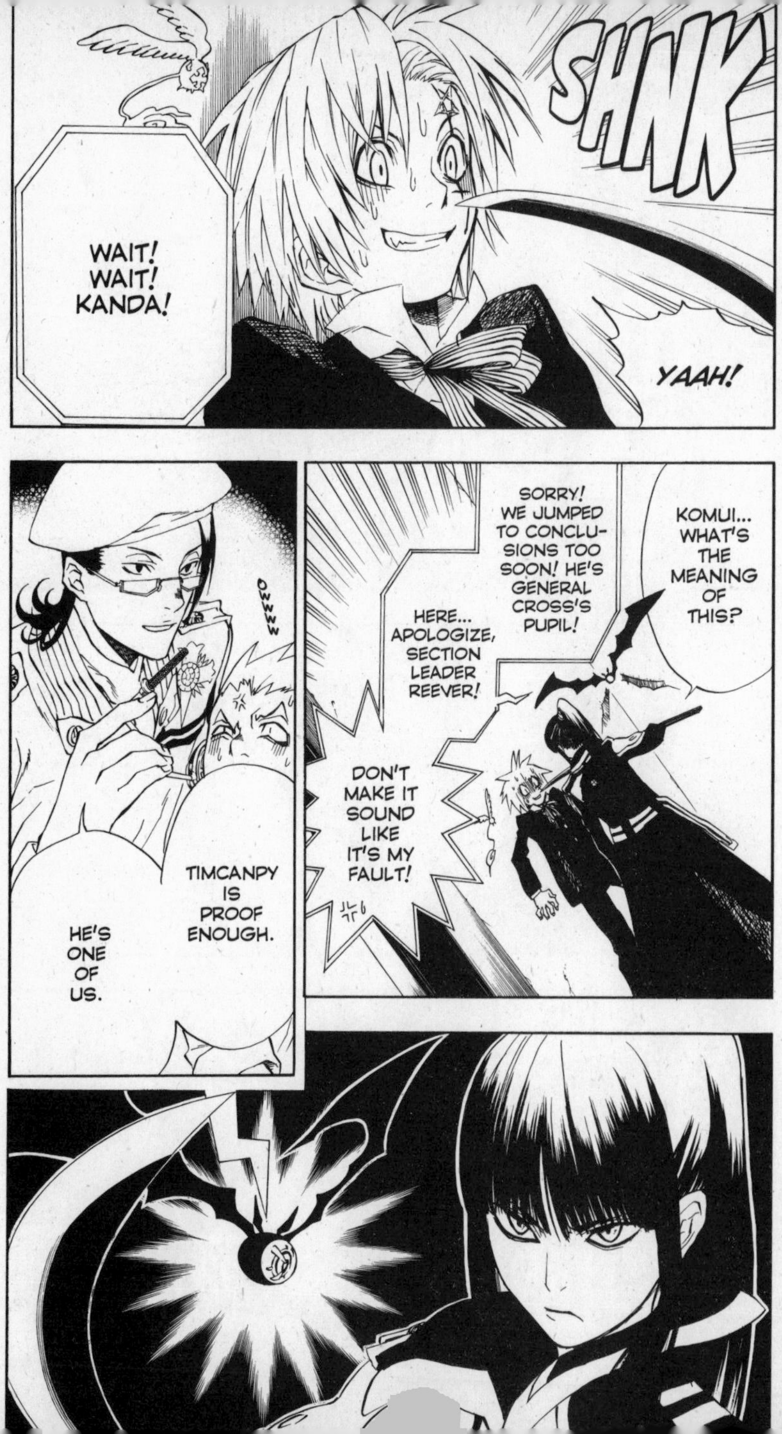
SHNK
YAAH!
WAIT! WAIT! KANDA!
KOMUI... WHAT'S THE MEANING OF THIS?
SORRY! WE JUMPED TO CONCLUSIONS TOO SOON! HE'S GENERAL CROSS'S PUPIL!
HERE... APOLOGIZE, SECTION LEADER REEVER!
DON'T MAKE IT SOUND LIKE IT'S MY FAULT!
OWWWW
TIMCANPY IS PROOF ENOUGH.
HE'S ONE OF US.

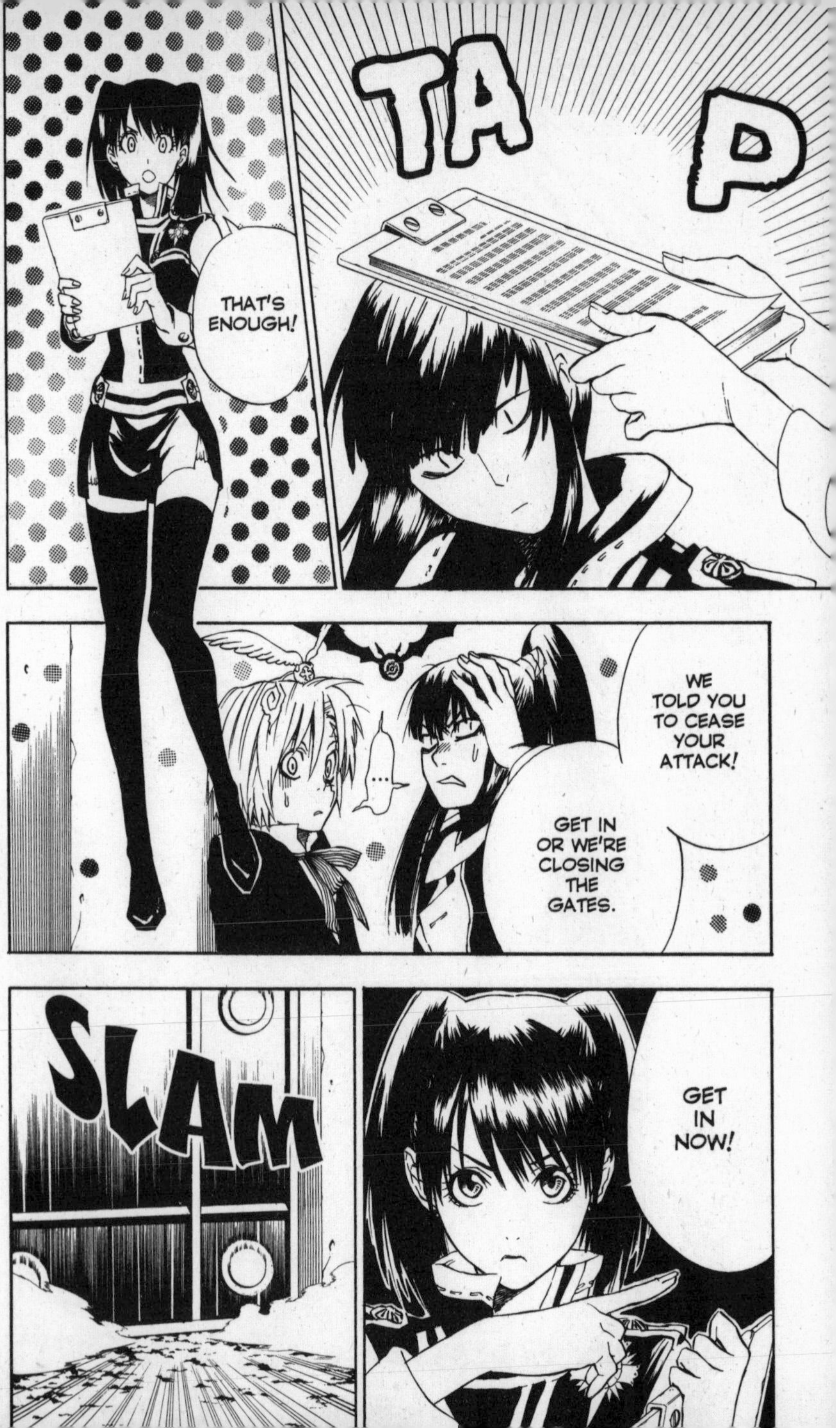
TAP
THAT'S ENOUGH!
WE TOLD YOU TO CEASE YOUR ATTACK!
GET IN OR WE'RE CLOSING THE GATES.
...
GET IN NOW!
SLAM

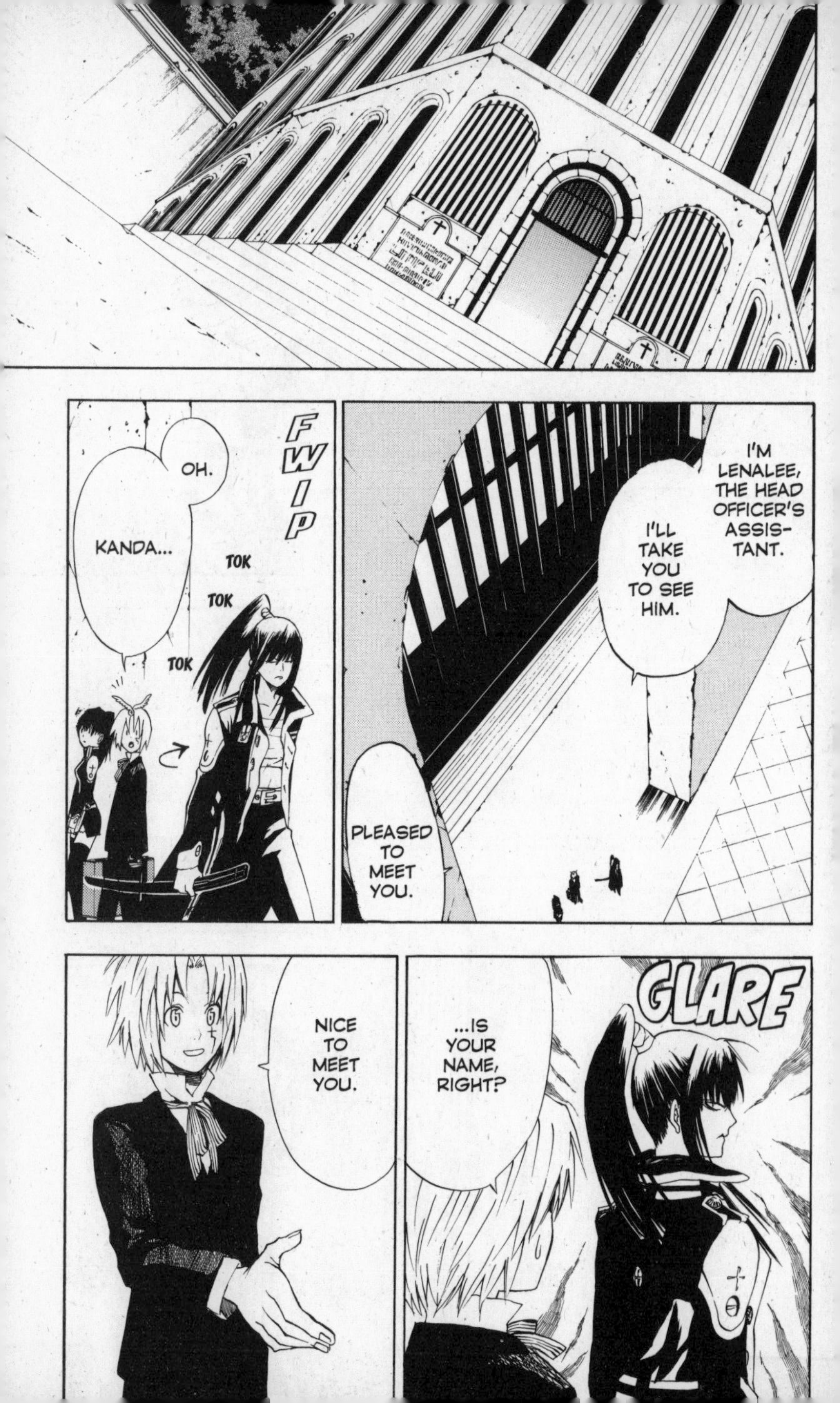
I'M LENALEE, THE HEAD OFFICER'S ASSIS-TANT.
I'LL TAKE YOU TO SEE HIM.
PLEASED TO MEET YOU.
FWIP
OH.
KANDA...
TOK
TOK
TOK
GLARE
...IS YOUR NAME, RIGHT?
NICE TO MEET YOU.

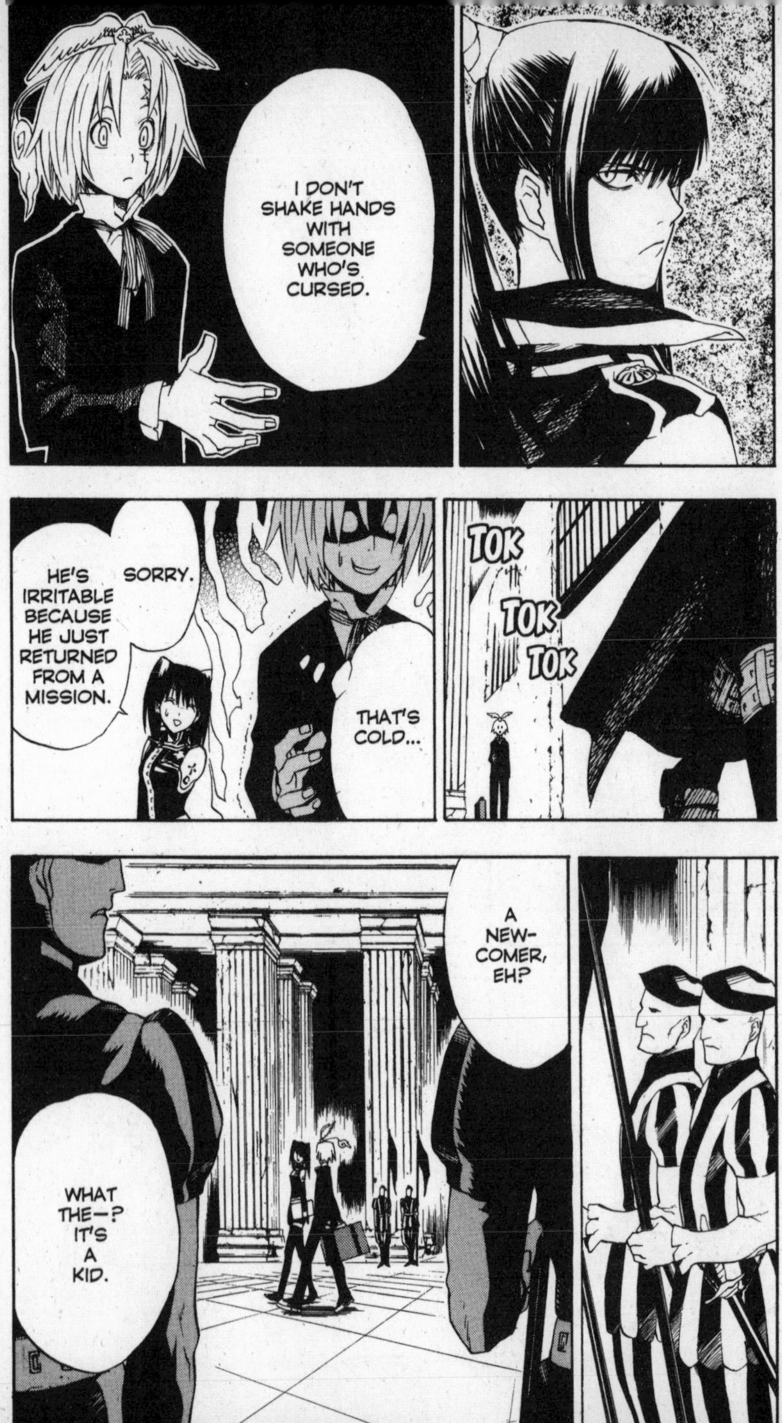
I DON'T SHAKE HANDS WITH SOMEONE WHO'S CURSED.
TOK TOK TOK
THAT'S COLD...
SORRY. HE'S IRRITABLE BECAUSE HE JUST RETURNED FROM A MISSION.
A NEW-COMER, EH?
WHAT THE—? IT'S A KID.

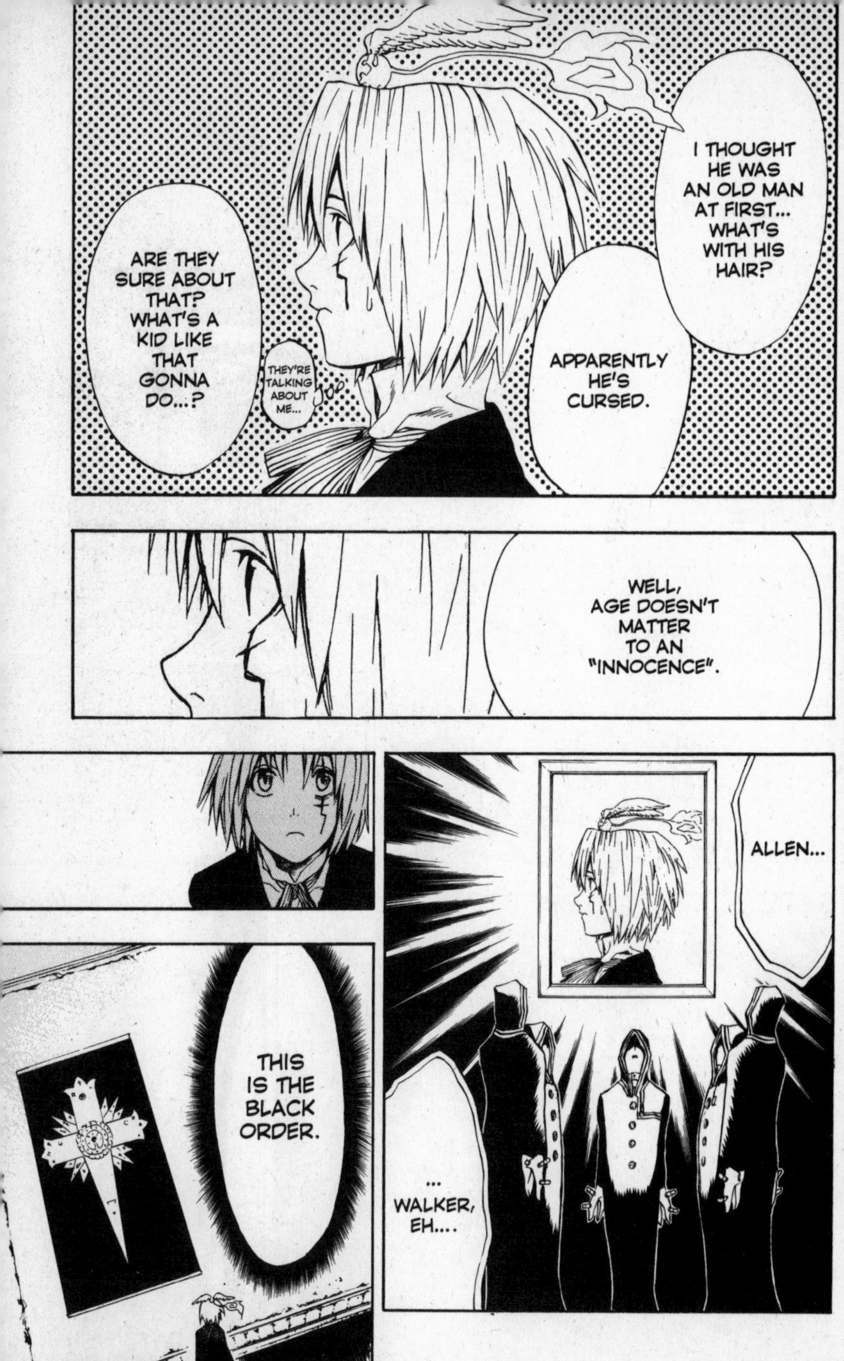
I THOUGHT HE WAS AN OLD MAN AT FIRST... WHAT'S WITH HIS HAIR?
APPARENTLY HE'S CURSED.
ARE THEY SURE ABOUT THAT? WHAT'S A KID LIKE THAT GONNA DO...?
THEY'RE TALKING ABOUT ME...
WELL, AGE DOESN'T MATTER TO AN "INNOCENCE".
ALLEN...
... WALKER, EH....
THIS IS THE BLACK ORDER.

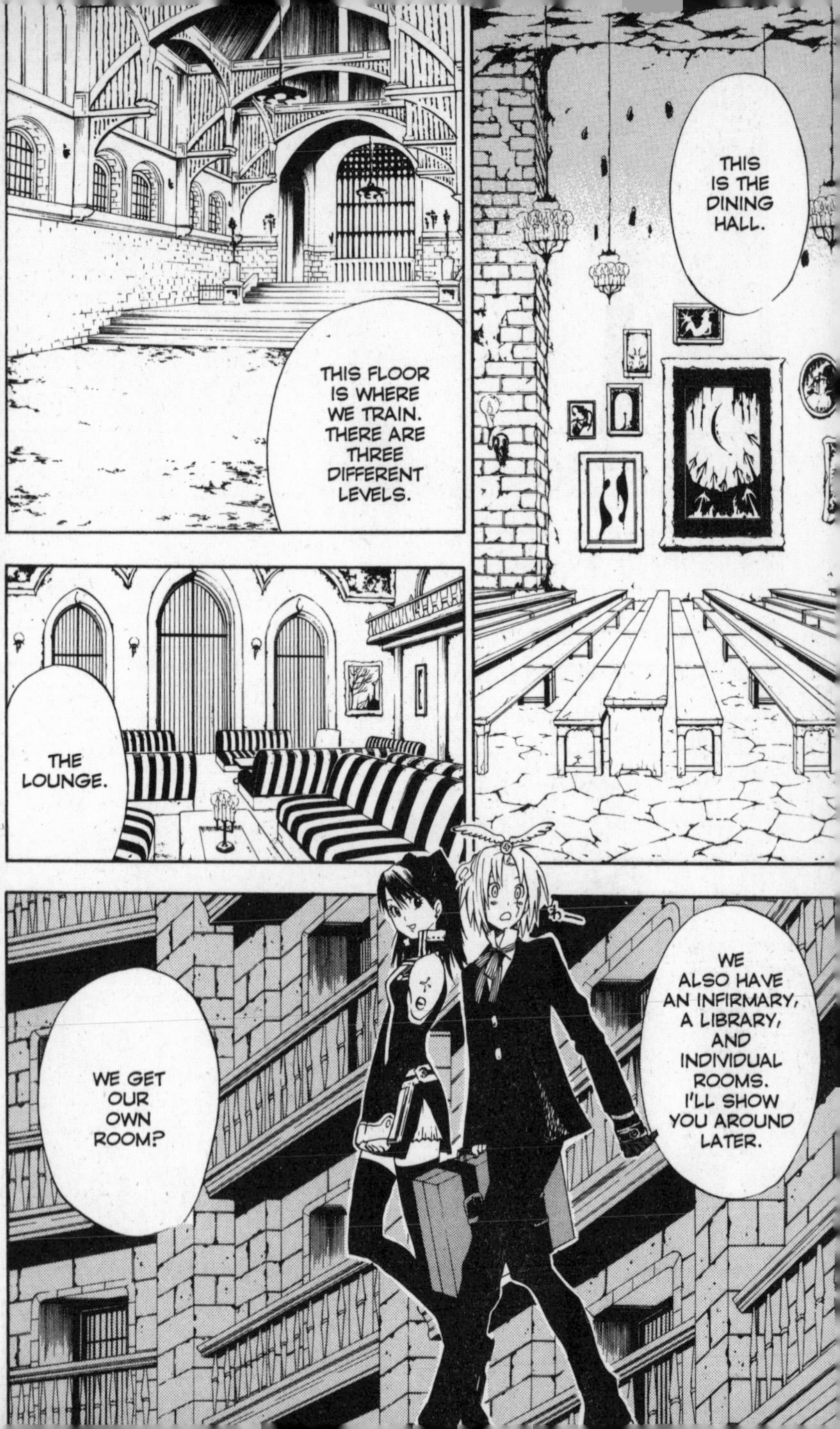
THIS IS THE DINING HALL.
THIS FLOOR IS WHERE WE TRAIN. THERE ARE THREE DIFFERENT LEVELS.
THE LOUNGE.
WE ALSO HAVE AN INFIRMARY, A LIBRARY, AND INDIVIDUAL ROOMS. I'LL SHOW YOU AROUND LATER.
WE GET OUR OWN ROOM?

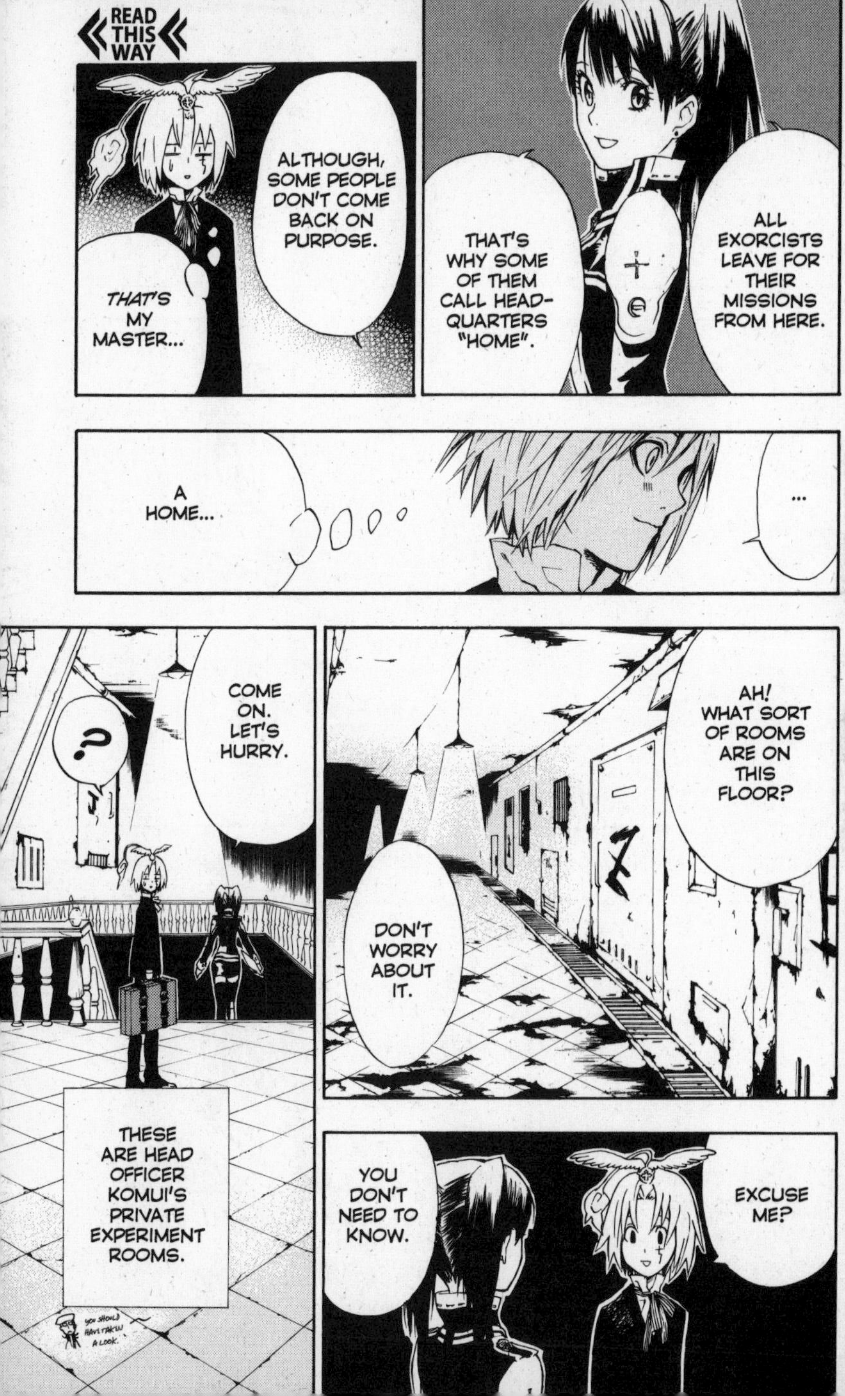
READ THIS WAY
ALL EXORCISTS LEAVE FOR THEIR MISSIONS FROM HERE.
THAT'S WHY SOME OF THEM CALL HEAD-QUARTERS "HOME".
ALTHOUGH, SOME PEOPLE DON'T COME BACK ON PURPOSE.
THAT'S MY MASTER...
...
A HOME...
AH! WHAT SORT OF ROOMS ARE ON THIS FLOOR?
DON'T WORRY ABOUT IT.
EXCUSE ME?
YOU DON'T NEED TO KNOW.
?
COME ON. LET'S HURRY.
THESE ARE HEAD OFFICER KOMUI'S PRIVATE EXPERIMENT ROOMS.
YOU SHOULD HAVE TAKEN A LOOK.

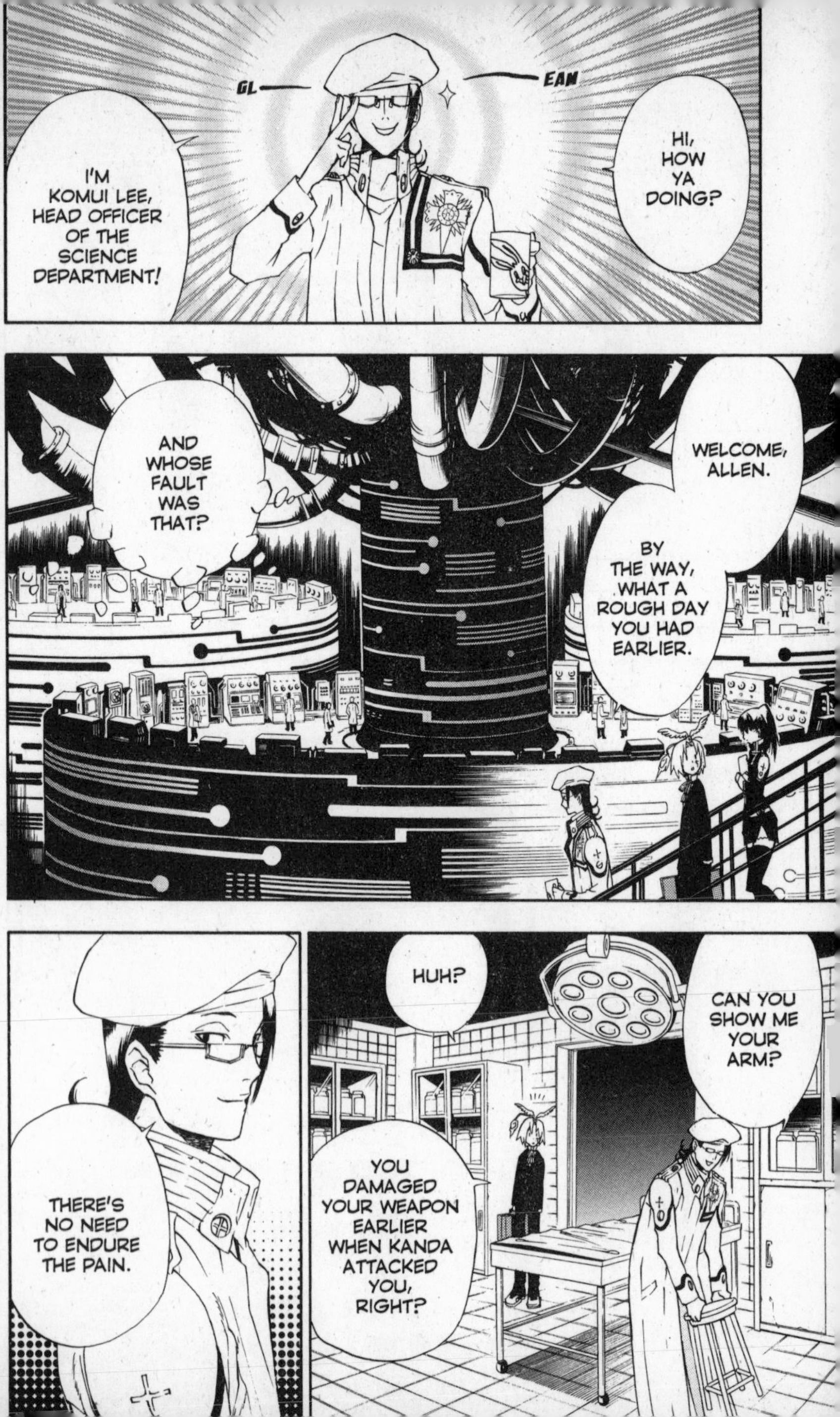
GL—— ——EAN
HI, HOW YA DOING?
I'M KOMUI LEE, HEAD OFFICER OF THE SCIENCE DEPARTMENT!
WELCOME, ALLEN.
BY THE WAY, WHAT A ROUGH DAY YOU HAD EARLIER.
AND WHOSE FAULT WAS THAT?
CAN YOU SHOW ME YOUR ARM?
HUH?
YOU DAMAGED YOUR WEAPON EARLIER WHEN KANDA ATTACKED YOU, RIGHT?
THERE'S NO NEED TO ENDURE THE PAIN.

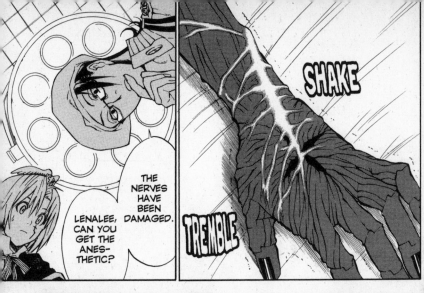

THE NERVES HAVE BEEN DAMAGED. LENALEE, CAN YOU GET THE ANESTHETIC?

SHAKE

TREMBLE

INVOCATION!

CAN YOU INVOKE IT?

OH, SURE.

HMM.

UR

OH.

EEM

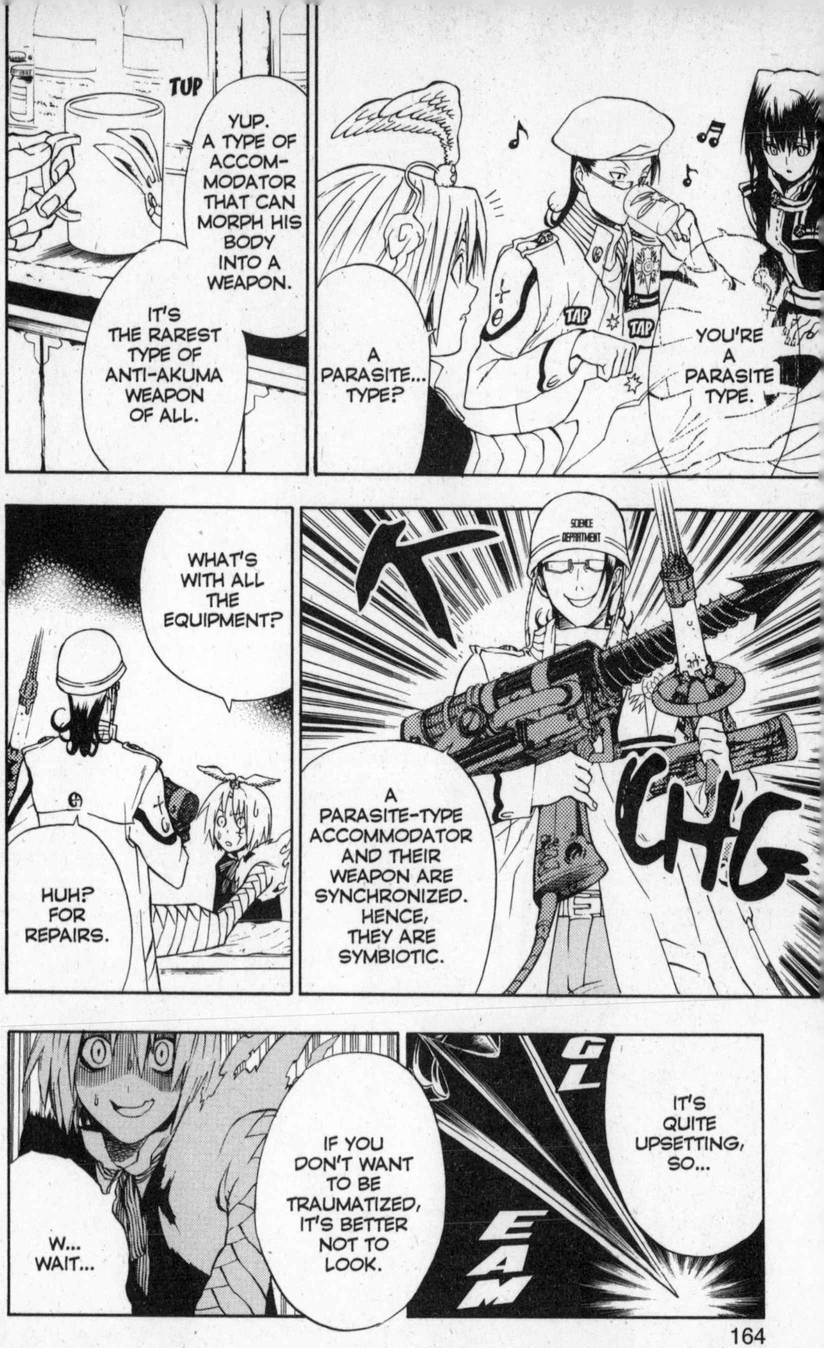
YOU'RE A PARASITE TYPE.
A PARASITE... TYPE?
TUP
YUP. A TYPE OF ACCOMMODATOR THAT CAN MORPH HIS BODY INTO A WEAPON.
IT'S THE RAREST TYPE OF ANTI-AKUMA WEAPON OF ALL.
SCIENCE DEPARTMENT
CHG
A PARASITE-TYPE ACCOMMODATOR AND THEIR WEAPON ARE SYNCHRONIZED. HENCE, THEY ARE SYMBIOTIC.
WHAT'S WITH ALL THE EQUIPMENT?
HUH? FOR REPAIRS.
GLEAM
IT'S QUITE UPSETTING, SO...
IF YOU DON'T WANT TO BE TRAUMATIZED, IT'S BETTER NOT TO LOOK.
W... WAIT...

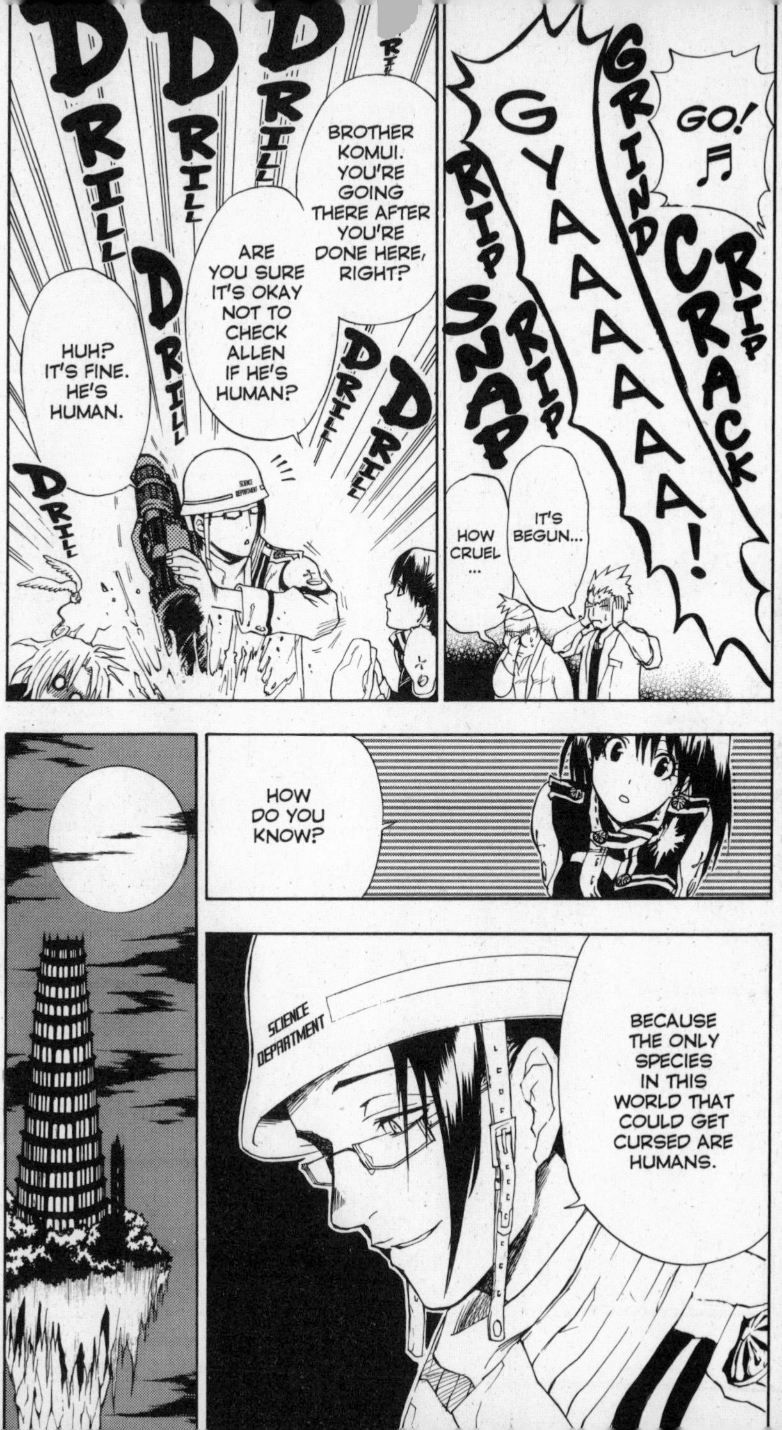
GO! ♪
GRIND
CRACK
RIP
GYAAAAAA!
RIP
SNAP
RIP
IT'S BEGUN...
HOW CRUEL ...
DDD
DRILL
DRILL
DRILL
BROTHER KOMUI. YOU'RE GOING THERE AFTER YOU'RE DONE HERE, RIGHT?
ARE YOU SURE IT'S OKAY NOT TO CHECK ALLEN IF HE'S HUMAN?
D
DRILL
D
DRILL
HUH? IT'S FINE. HE'S HUMAN.
D
DRILL
D
DRILL
SCIENCE DEPARTMENT
HOW DO YOU KNOW?
SCIENCE DEPARTMENT
BECAUSE THE ONLY SPECIES IN THIS WORLD THAT COULD GET CURSED ARE HUMANS.

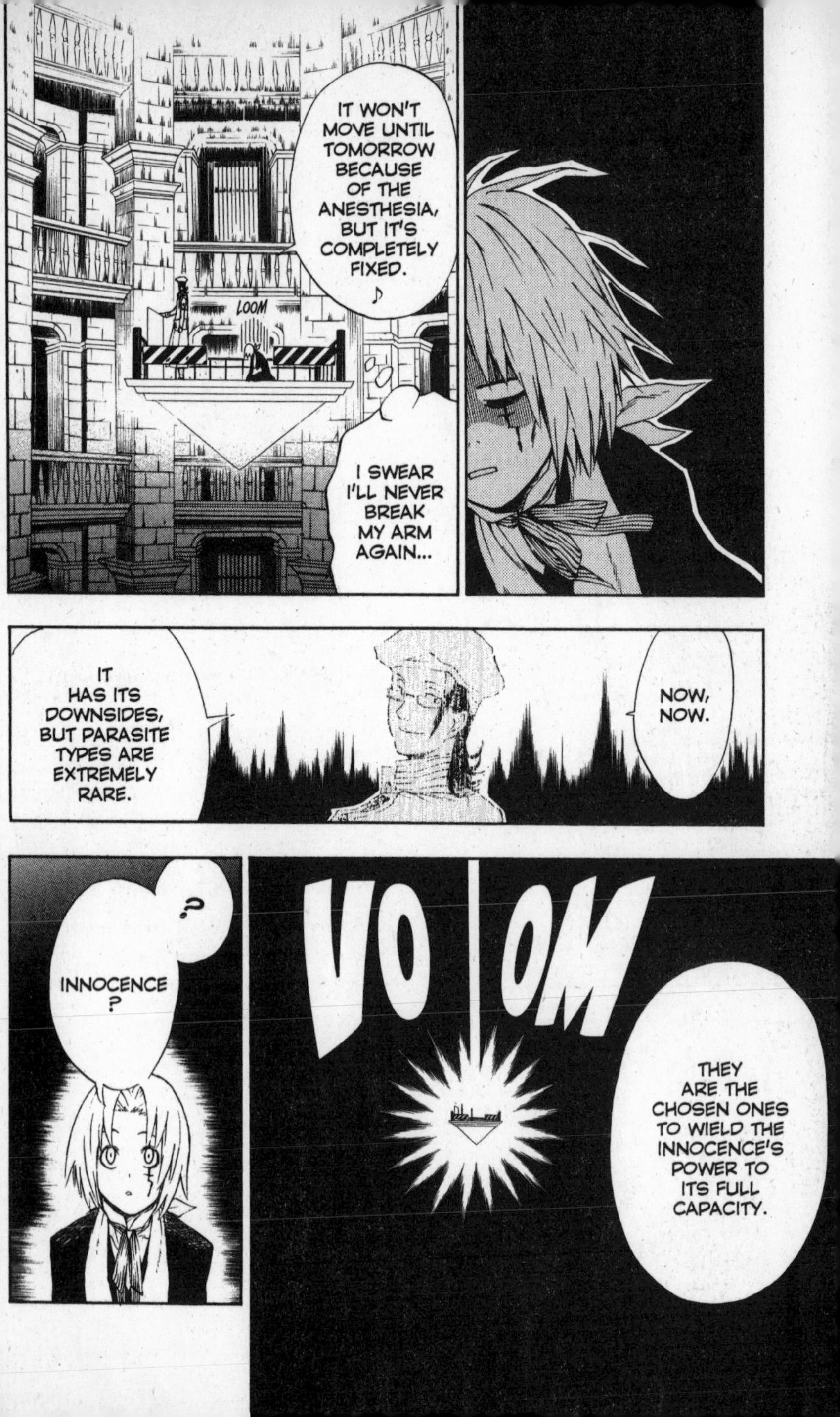
IT WON'T MOVE UNTIL TOMORROW BECAUSE OF THE ANESTHESIA, BUT IT'S COMPLETELY FIXED. ♪
LOOM
I SWEAR I'LL NEVER BREAK MY ARM AGAIN...
NOW, NOW.
IT HAS ITS DOWNSIDES, BUT PARASITE TYPES ARE EXTREMELY RARE.
VOOM
THEY ARE THE CHOSEN ONES TO WIELD THE INNOCENCE'S POWER TO ITS FULL CAPACITY.
?
INNOCENCE ?

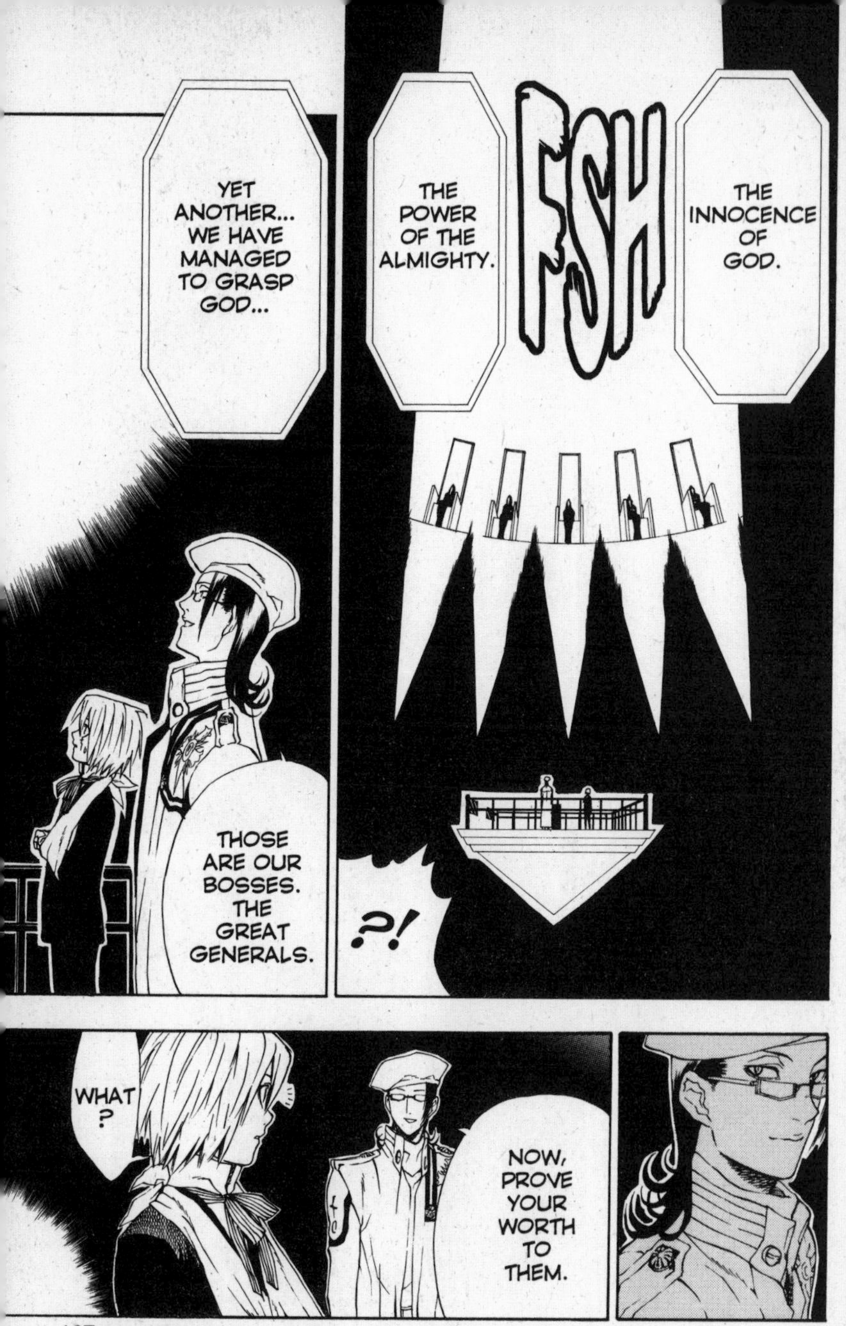
THE INNOCENCE OF GOD.
FSH
THE POWER OF THE ALMIGHTY.
?!
YET ANOTHER... WE HAVE MANAGED TO GRASP GOD...
THOSE ARE OUR BOSSES. THE GREAT GENERALS.
NOW, PROVE YOUR WORTH TO THEM.
WHAT?

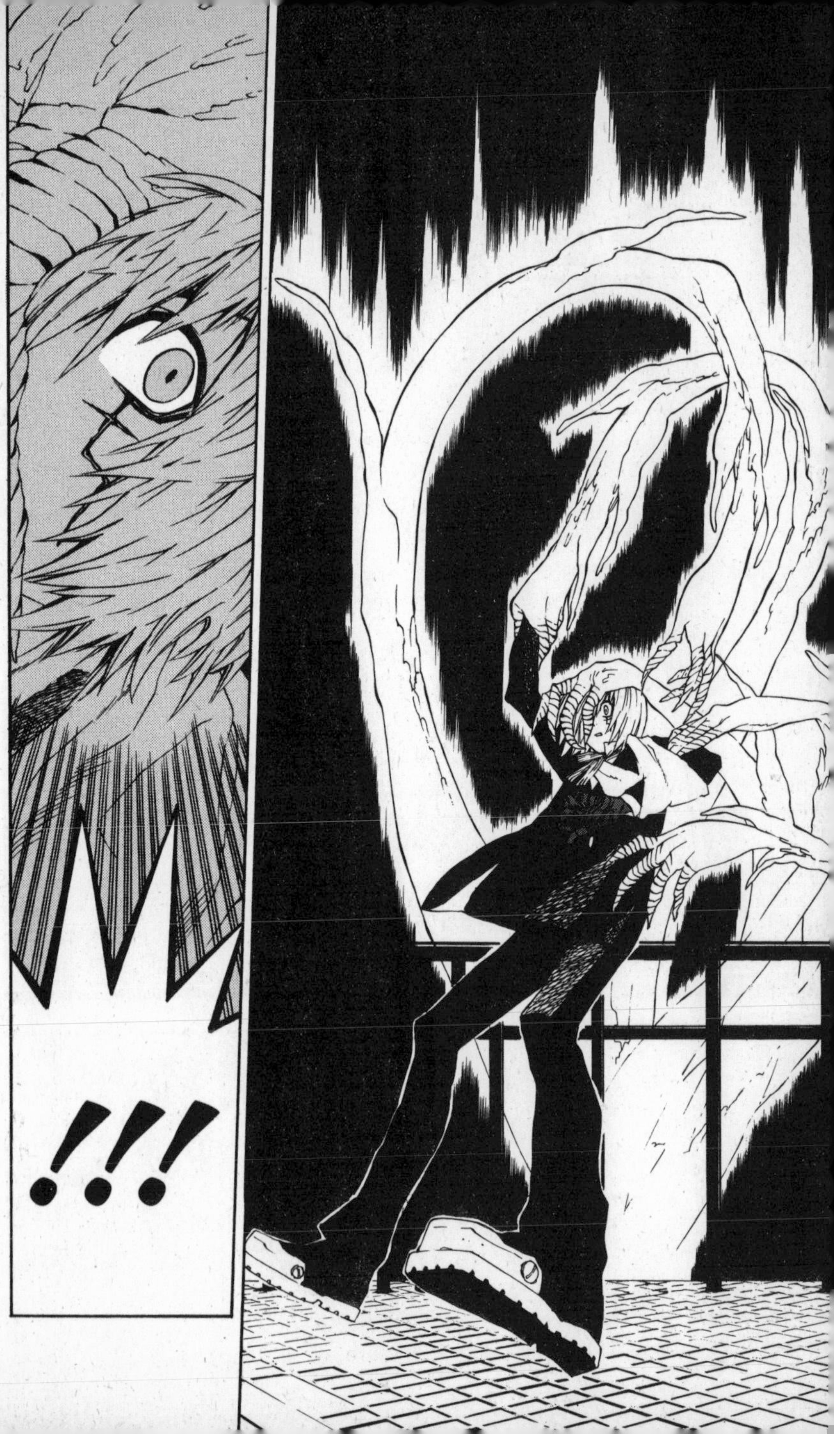
!!!

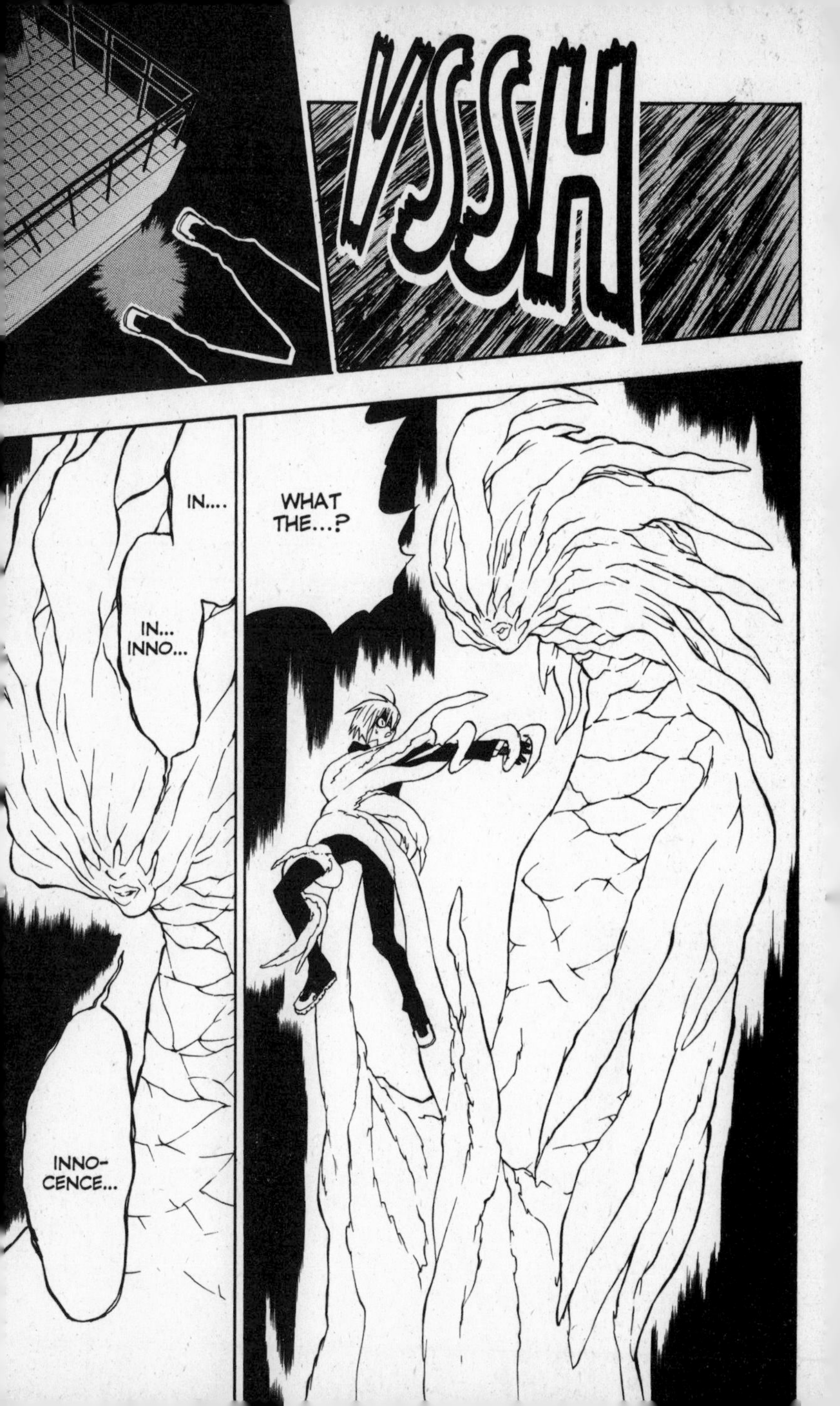
VSSH
WHAT THE...?
IN....
IN... INNO...
INNO-CENCE...

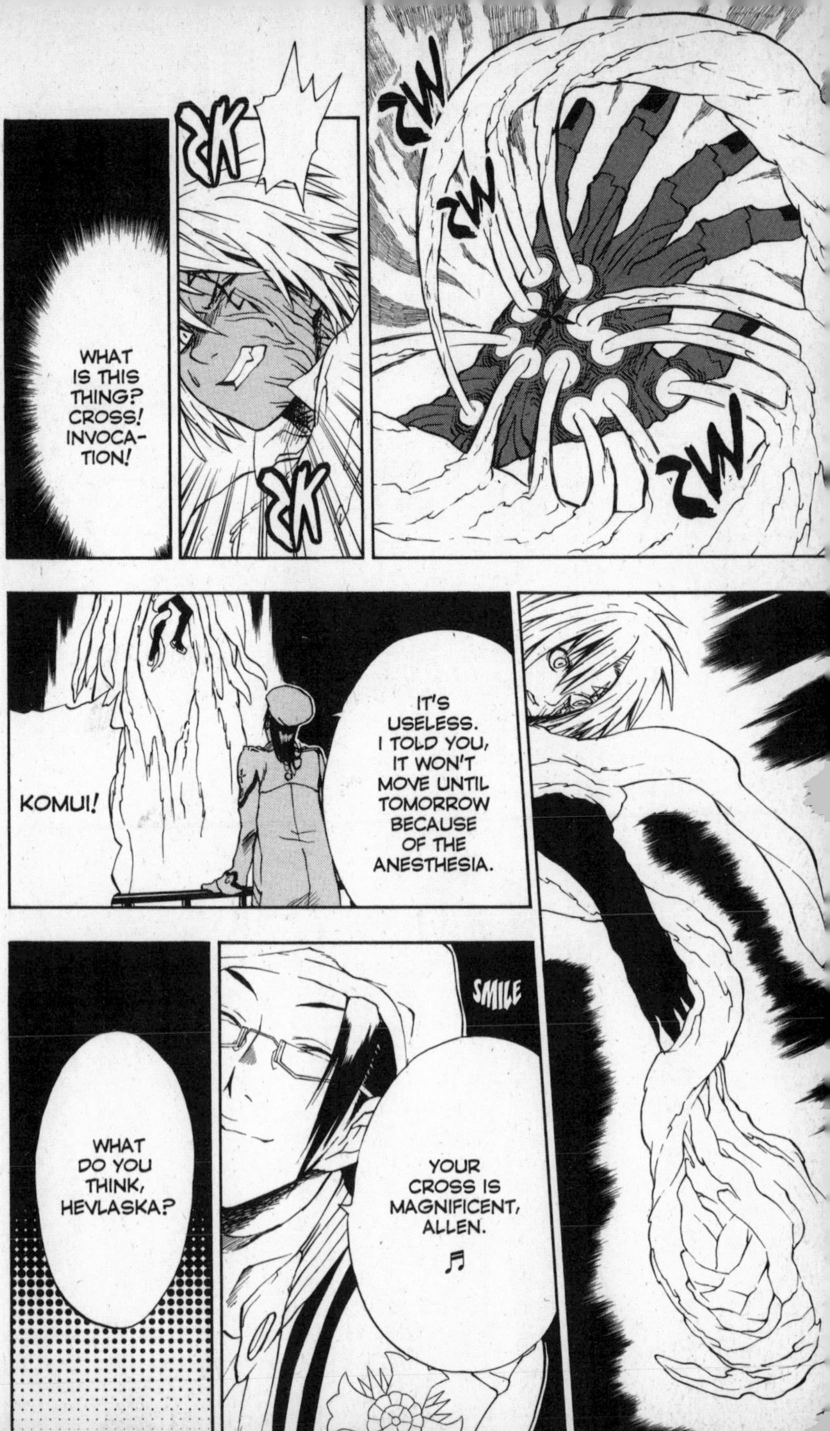
ZW
ZW
ZW
ZK
ZK
WHAT IS THIS THING? CROSS! INVOCATION!
IT'S USELESS. I TOLD YOU, IT WON'T MOVE UNTIL TOMORROW BECAUSE OF THE ANESTHESIA.
KOMUI!
SMILE
YOUR CROSS IS MAGNIFICENT, ALLEN. ♬
WHAT DO YOU THINK, HEVLASKA?

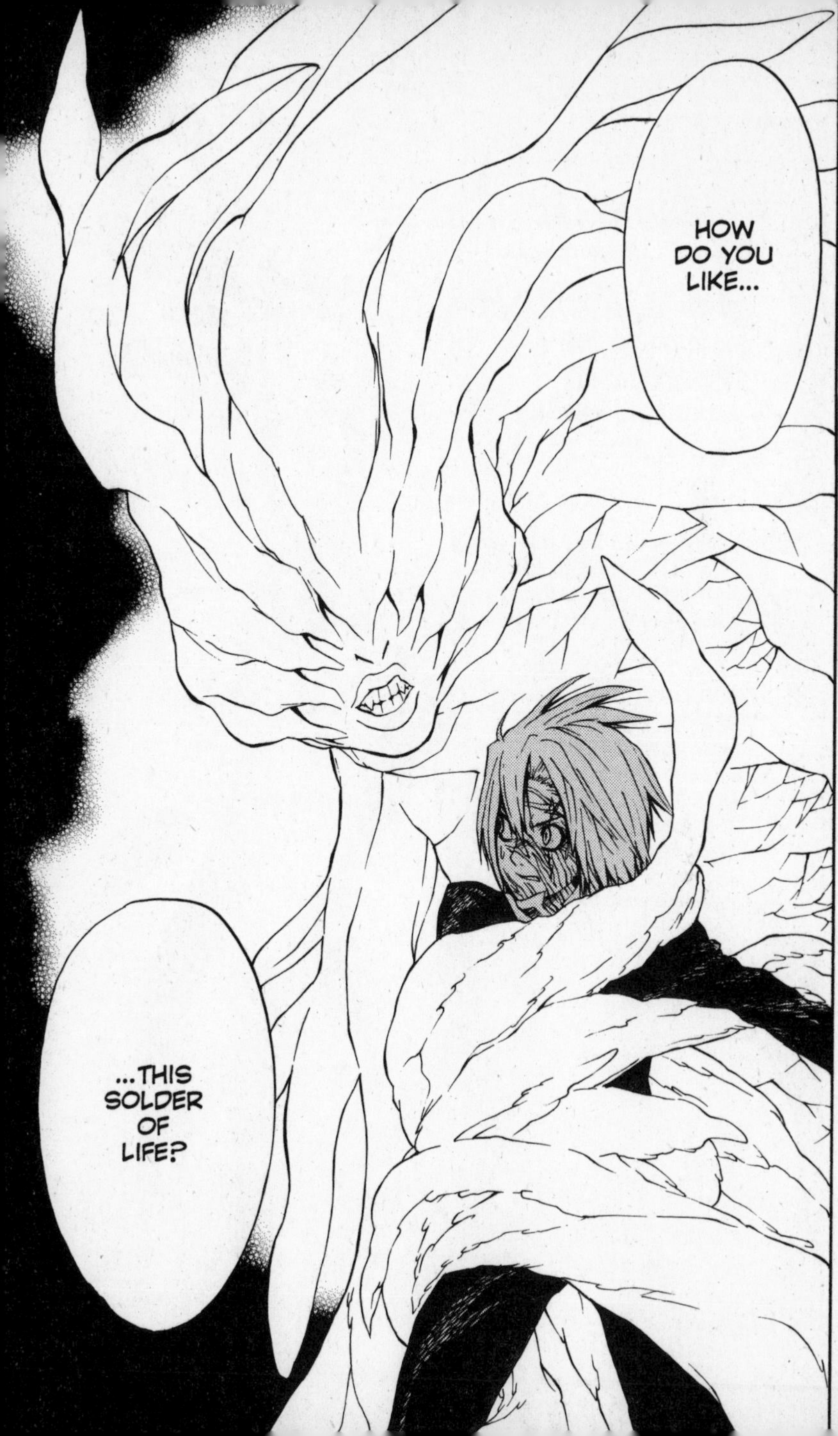
HOW DO YOU LIKE...
...THIS SOLDER OF LIFE?

LENALEE LEE

CHINESE, 16 YEARS OLD
HEIGHT: 166 CM
WEIGHT: 48 KG
BIRTHDAY: FEBRUARY 20TH
PISCES, BLOOD TYPE: B

SHE WAS CREATED A WHILE
BACK, JUST LIKE ALLEN. NO...
MAYBE BEFORE ALLEN. IT
TOOK A WHILE UNTIL I WAS
SATISFIED WITH HER
FEMALE UNIFORM DESIGN,
BUT THANKS TO ALL THAT
BRAINSTORMING, I'M
NOW VERY HAPPY
WITH IT. LENALEE IS
MY IDEAL, AND SHE'S
ALSO BASED ON A
REAL PERSON.
MY EDITOR LAUGHED
THROUGH HIS NOSE
WHEN I TOLD HIM,
SO I SWORE I'D
NEVER TELL
ANYONE EVER
AGAIN.

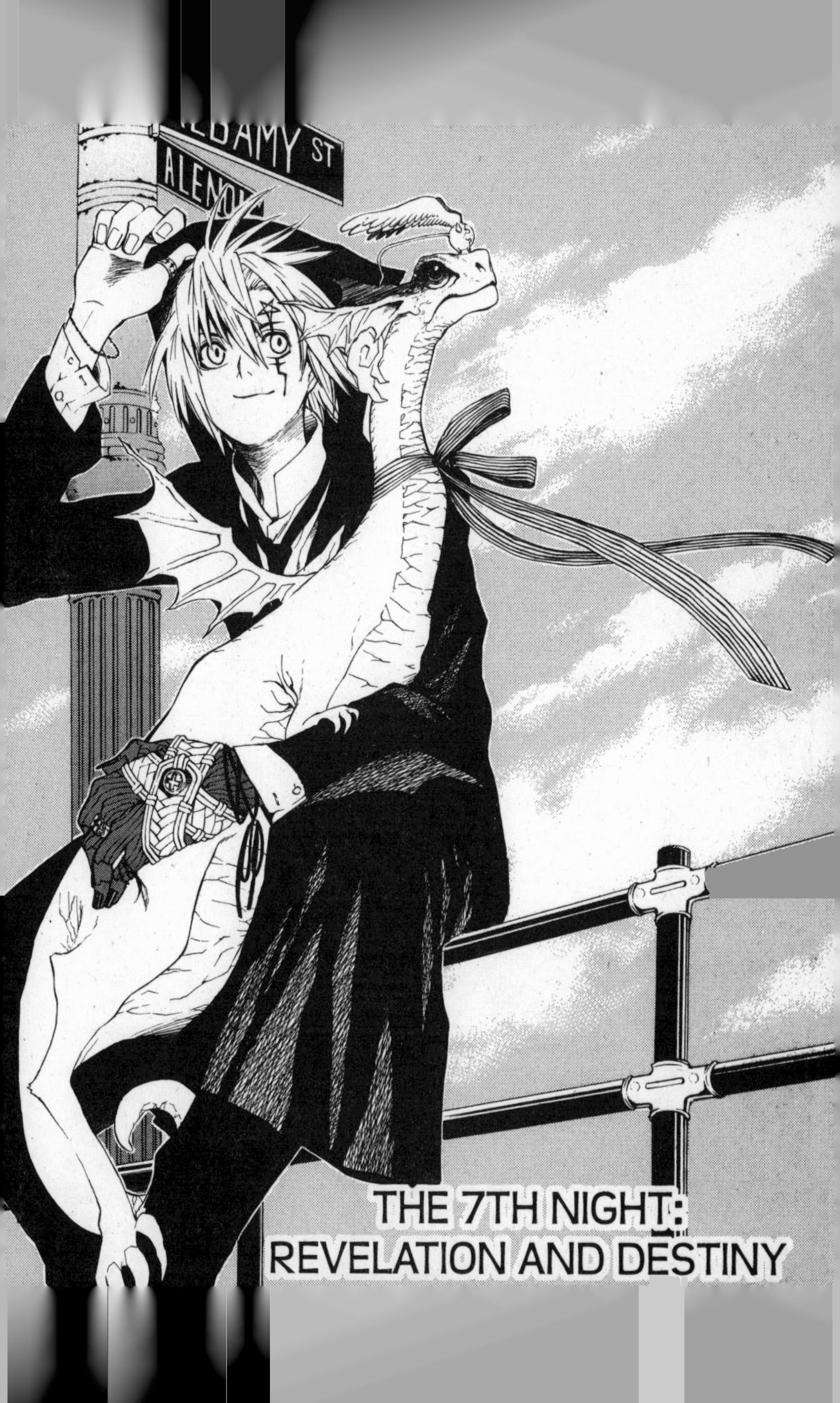

THE 7TH NIGHT: REVELATION AND DESTINY

GROSS! WHAT IS IT DOING?

IT FEELS LIKE IT'S PROBING THE INSIDE OF MY BODY.

SHK SHK

UGH.

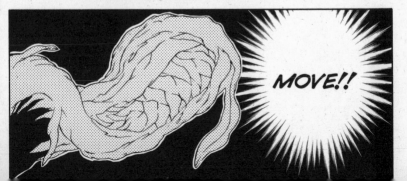

MOVE!!

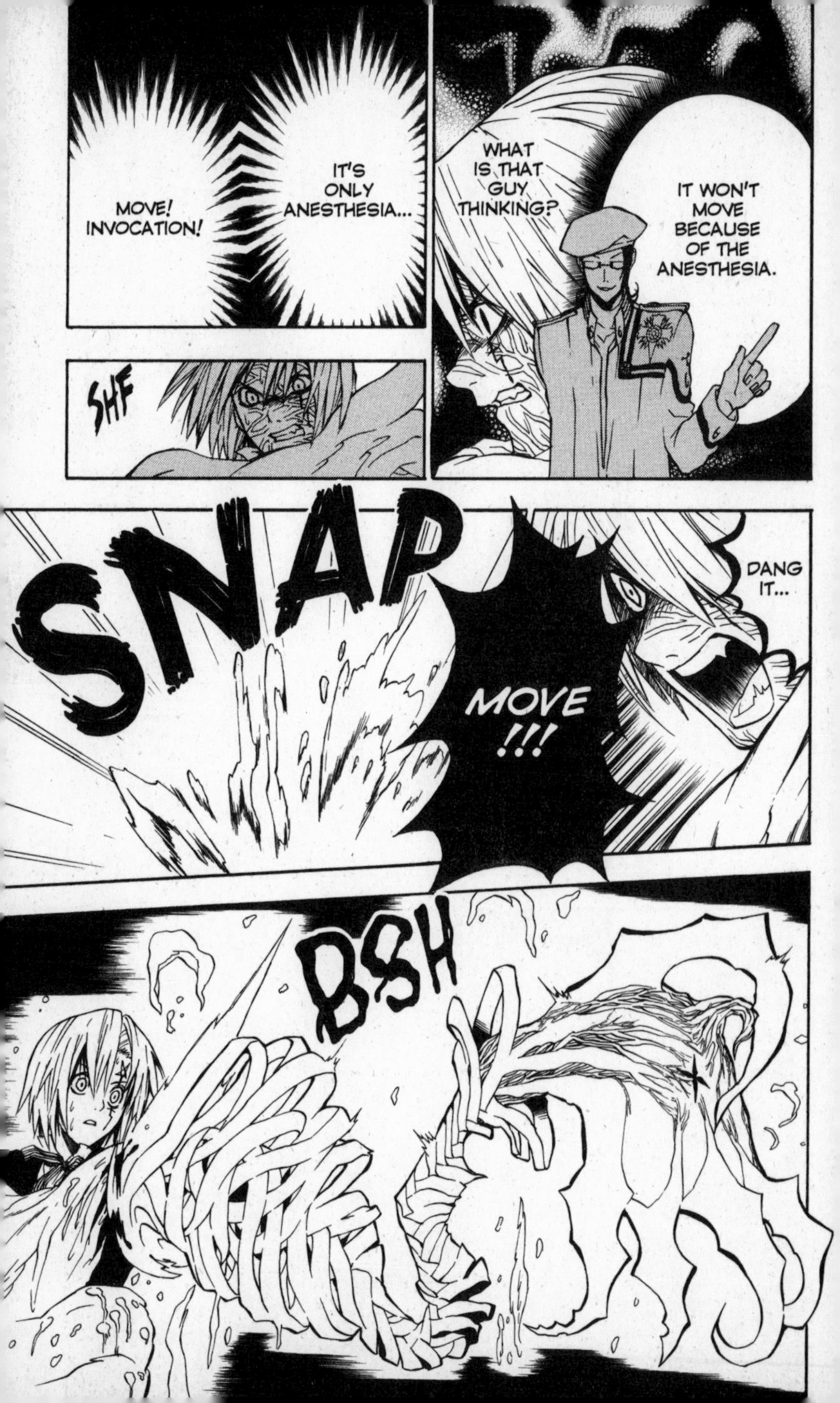
IT WON'T MOVE BECAUSE OF THE ANESTHESIA.
WHAT IS THAT GUY THINKING?
IT'S ONLY ANESTHESIA...
MOVE! INVOCATION!
SHF
DANG IT...
MOVE!!!
SNAP
BSH

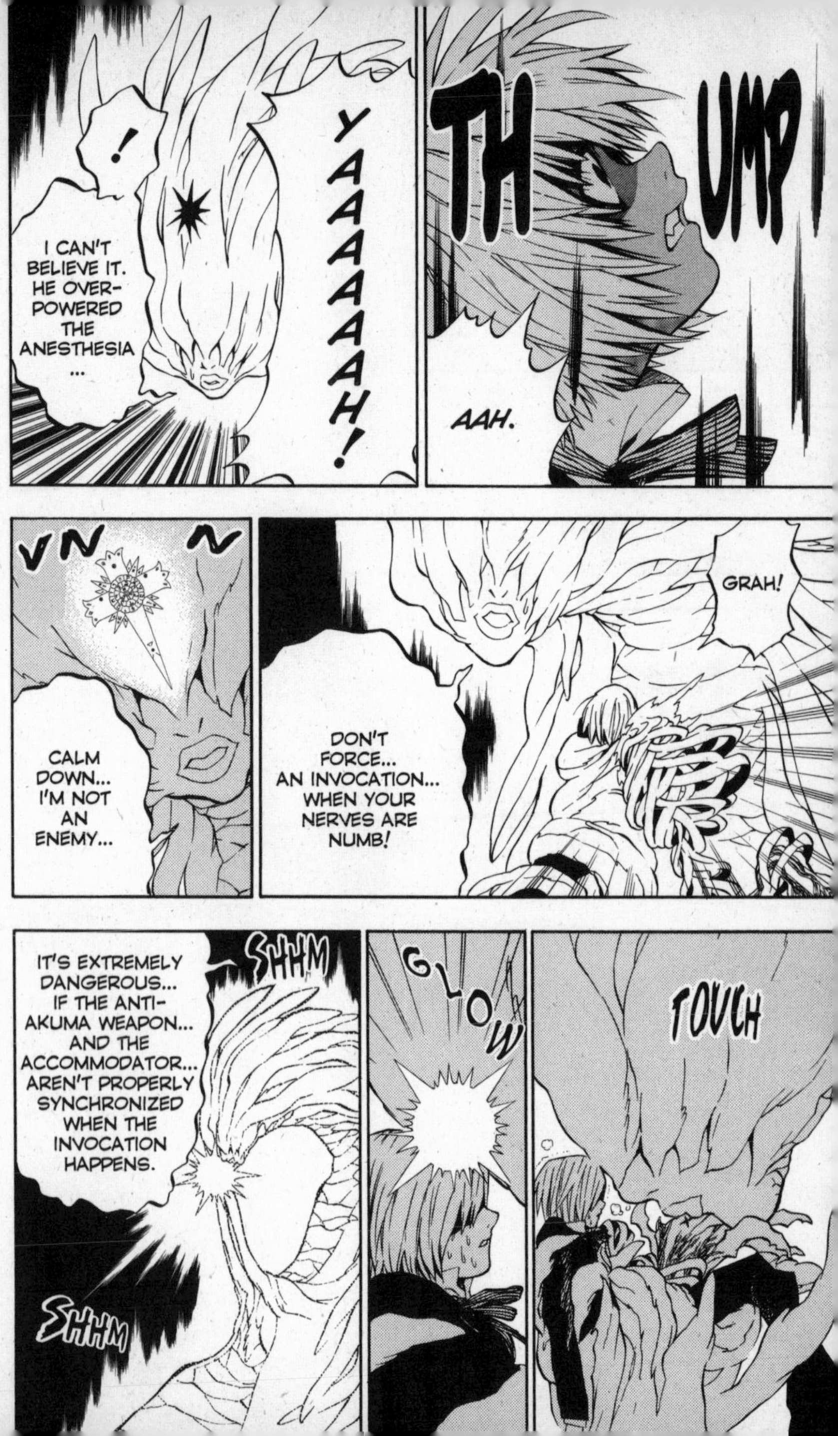

THUMP
AAH.
YAAAAAAAH!
!
I CAN'T BELIEVE IT. HE OVER-POWERED THE ANESTHESIA ...
GRAH!
DON'T FORCE... AN INVOCATION... WHEN YOUR NERVES ARE NUMB!
VNN
CALM DOWN... I'M NOT AN ENEMY...
TOUCH
GLOW
SHHM
IT'S EXTREMELY DANGEROUS... IF THE ANTI-AKUMA WEAPON... AND THE ACCOMMODATOR... AREN'T PROPERLY SYNCHRONIZED WHEN THE INVOCATION HAPPENS.
SHHM

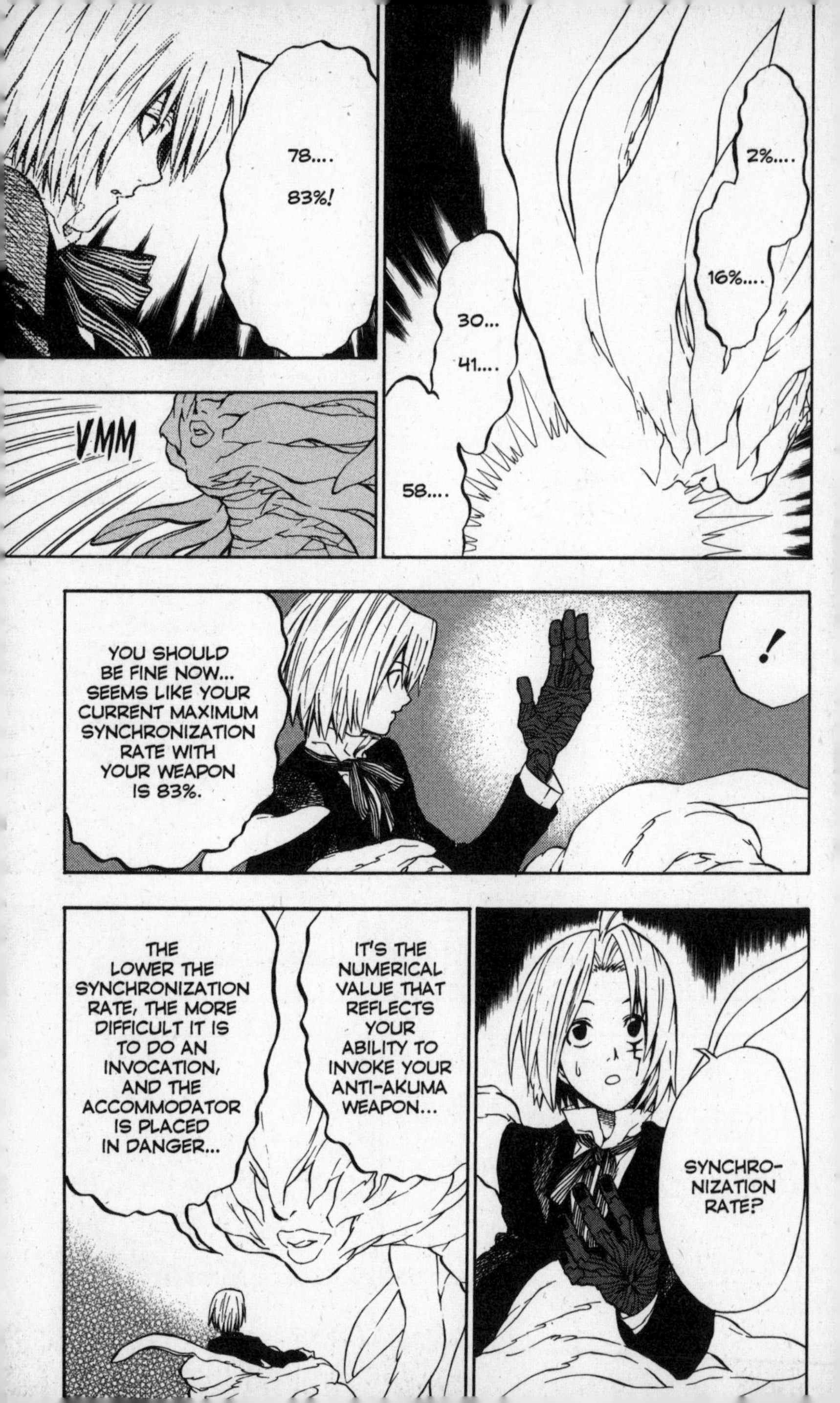
2%....
16%....
30...
41....
58....
78....
83%!
VMM
!
YOU SHOULD BE FINE NOW... SEEMS LIKE YOUR CURRENT MAXIMUM SYNCHRONIZATION RATE WITH YOUR WEAPON IS 83%.
SYNCHRO-NIZATION RATE?
IT'S THE NUMERICAL VALUE THAT REFLECTS YOUR ABILITY TO INVOKE YOUR ANTI-AKUMA WEAPON...
THE LOWER THE SYNCHRONIZATION RATE, THE MORE DIFFICULT IT IS TO DO AN INVOCATION, AND THE ACCOMMODATOR IS PLACED IN DANGER...

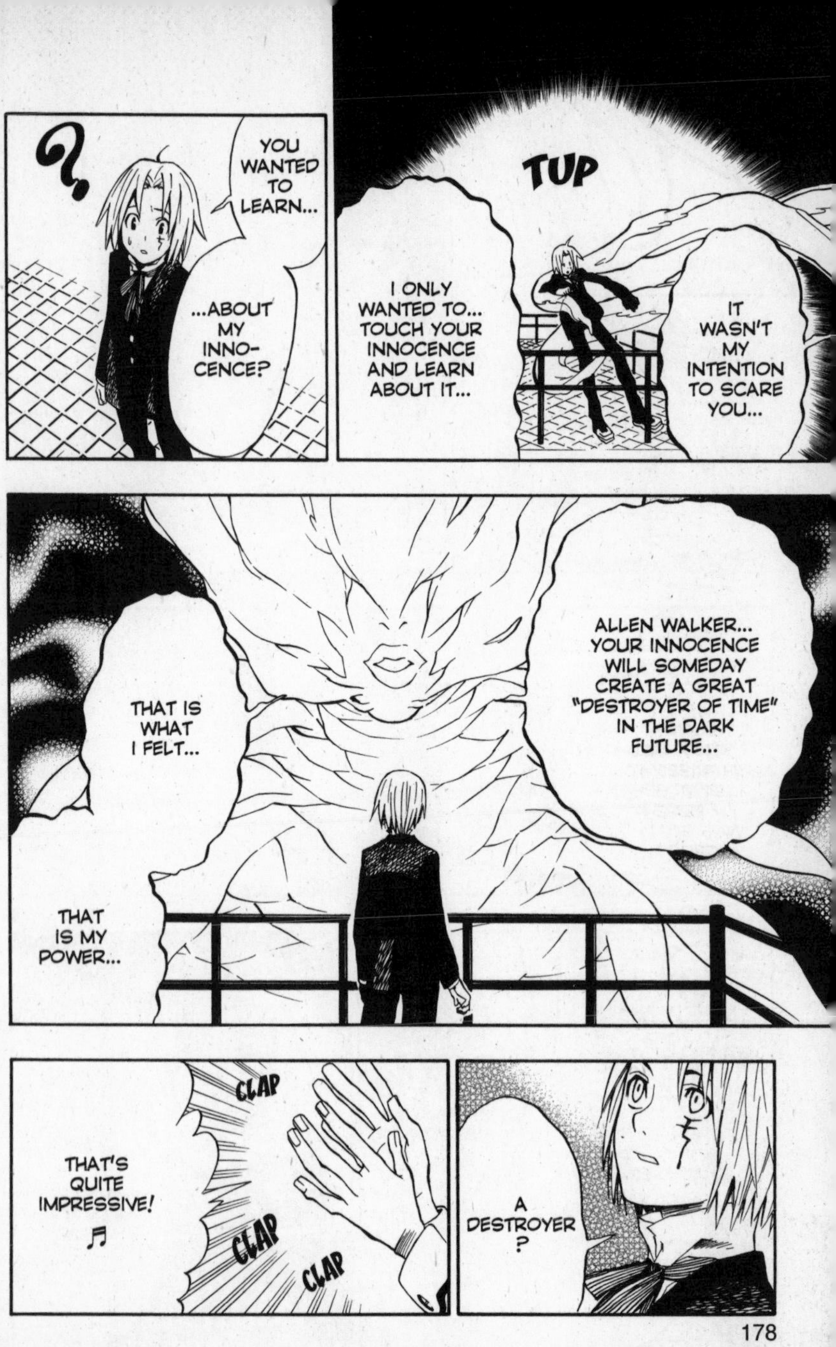
TUP
IT WASN'T MY INTENTION TO SCARE YOU...
I ONLY WANTED TO... TOUCH YOUR INNOCENCE AND LEARN ABOUT IT...
YOU WANTED TO LEARN...
...ABOUT MY INNO-CENCE?
?
ALLEN WALKER... YOUR INNOCENCE WILL SOMEDAY CREATE A GREAT "DESTROYER OF TIME" IN THE DARK FUTURE...
THAT IS WHAT I FELT...
THAT IS MY POWER...
A DESTROYER ?
CLAP
CLAP
CLAP
THAT'S QUITE IMPRESSIVE! ♫

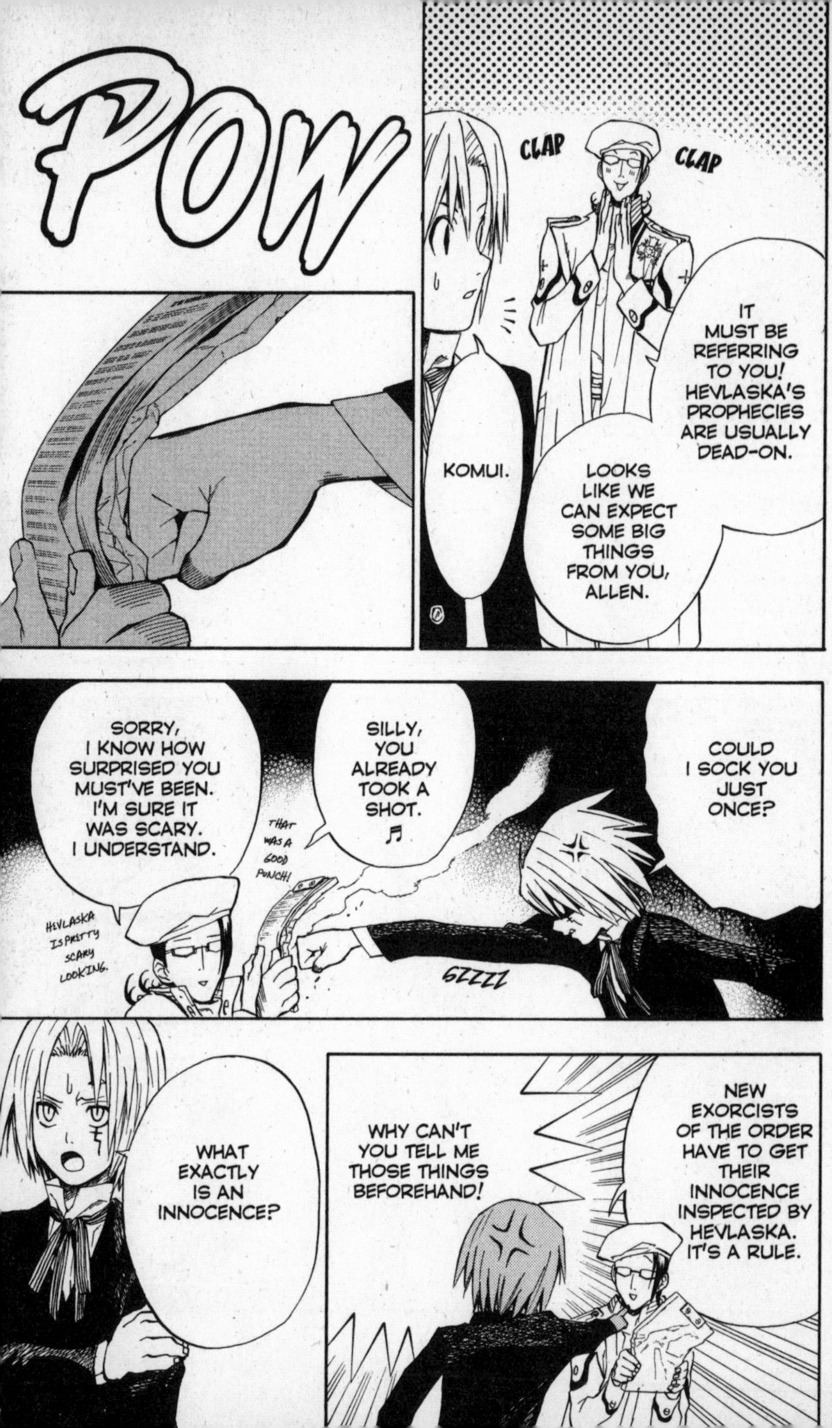

CLAP
CLAP
IT MUST BE REFERRING TO YOU! HEVLASKA'S PROPHECIES ARE USUALLY DEAD-ON.
LOOKS LIKE WE CAN EXPECT SOME BIG THINGS FROM YOU, ALLEN.
KOMUI.
POW
COULD I SOCK YOU JUST ONCE?
SILLY, YOU ALREADY TOOK A SHOT. ♫
THAT WAS A GOOD PUNCH!
SORRY, I KNOW HOW SURPRISED YOU MUST'VE BEEN. I'M SURE IT WAS SCARY. I UNDERSTAND.
HEVLASKA IS PRETTY SCARY LOOKING.
SZZZZ
NEW EXORCISTS OF THE ORDER HAVE TO GET THEIR INNOCENCE INSPECTED BY HEVLASKA. IT'S A RULE.
WHY CAN'T YOU TELL ME THOSE THINGS BEFOREHAND!
WHAT EXACTLY IS AN INNOCENCE?

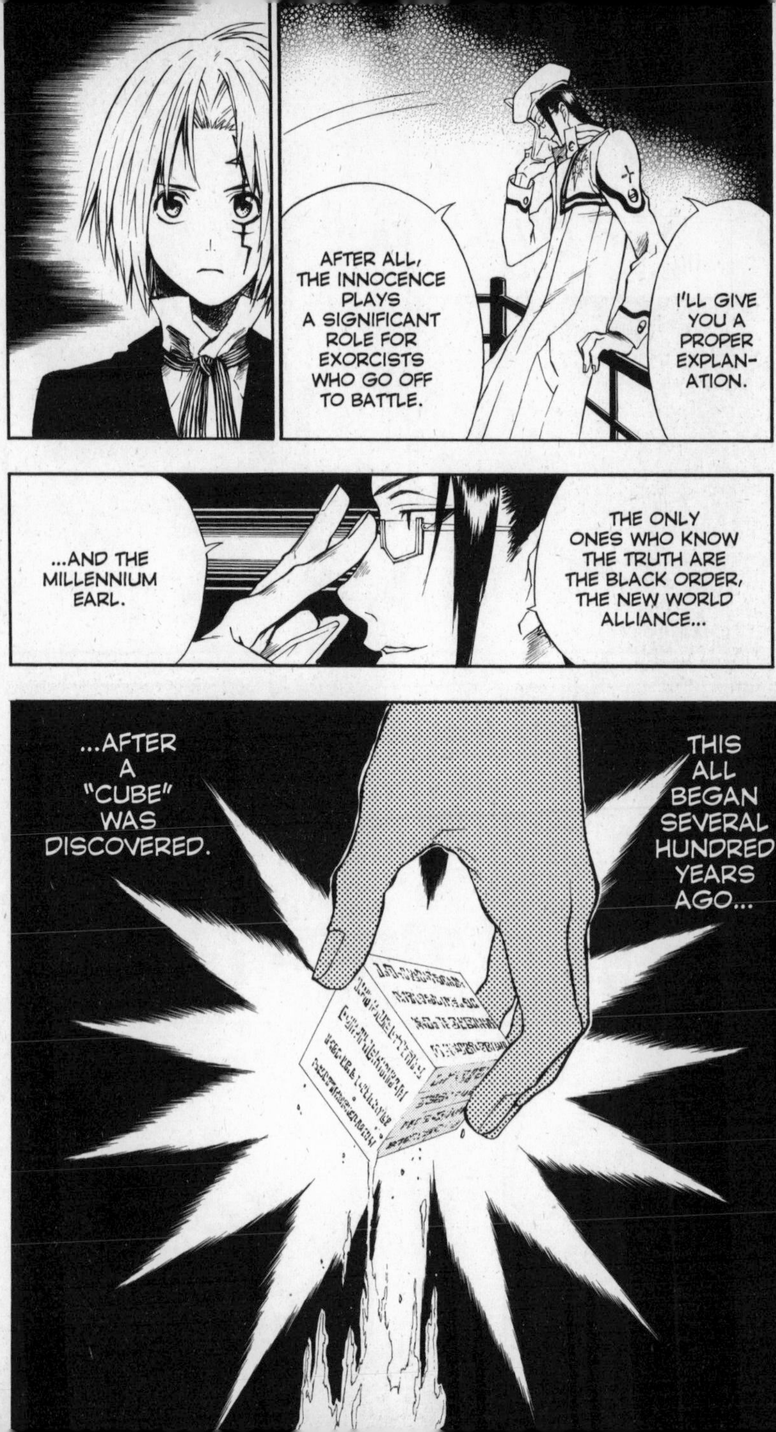
I'LL GIVE YOU A PROPER EXPLANATION.
AFTER ALL, THE INNOCENCE PLAYS A SIGNIFICANT ROLE FOR EXORCISTS WHO GO OFF TO BATTLE.
THE ONLY ONES WHO KNOW THE TRUTH ARE THE BLACK ORDER, THE NEW WORLD ALLIANCE...
...AND THE MILLENNIUM EARL.
THIS ALL BEGAN SEVERAL HUNDRED YEARS AGO...
...AFTER A "CUBE" WAS DISCOVERED.

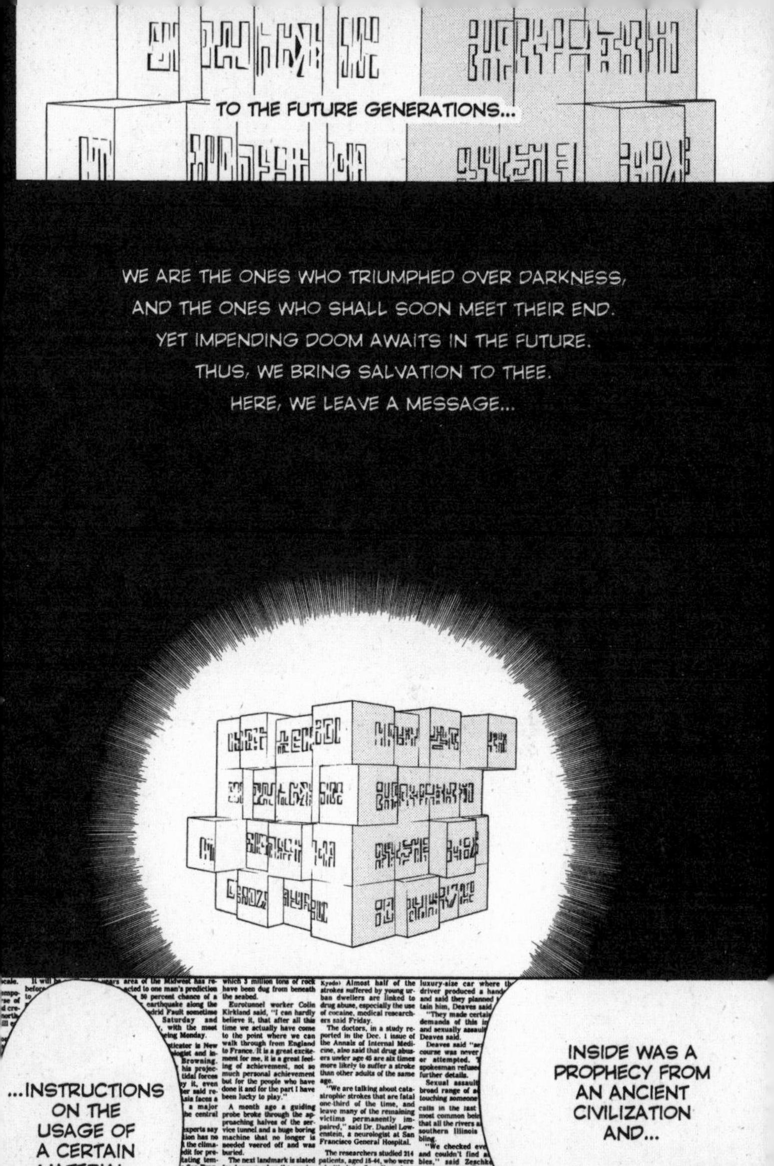
TO THE FUTURE GENERATIONS...
WE ARE THE ONES WHO TRIUMPHED OVER DARKNESS, AND THE ONES WHO SHALL SOON MEET THEIR END. YET IMPENDING DOOM AWAITS IN THE FUTURE. THUS, WE BRING SALVATION TO THEE. HERE, WE LEAVE A MESSAGE...
INSIDE WAS A PROPHECY FROM AN ANCIENT CIVILIZATION AND...
...INSTRUCTIONS ON THE USAGE OF A CERTAIN MATERIAL.

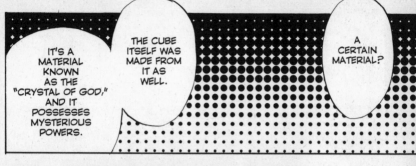

A CERTAIN MATERIAL?
THE CUBE ITSELF WAS MADE FROM IT AS WELL.
IT'S A MATERIAL KNOWN AS THE "CRYSTAL OF GOD," AND IT POSSESSES MYSTERIOUS POWERS.
WE CALL IT "INNOCENCE".
IT'S THE CROSS THAT'S EMBEDDED IN YOUR LEFT HAND.
!!
AN INNOCENCE THAT HAS BEEN PROCESSED AND CONVERTED INTO A WEAPON IS CALLED AN "ANTI-AKUMA WEAPON".

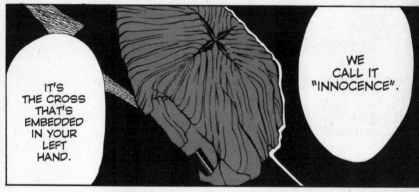

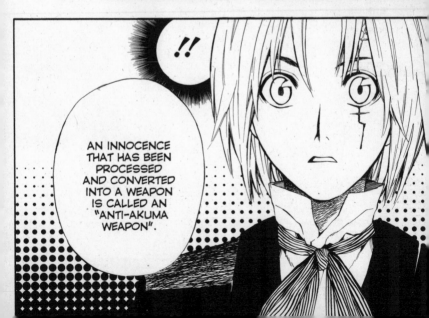

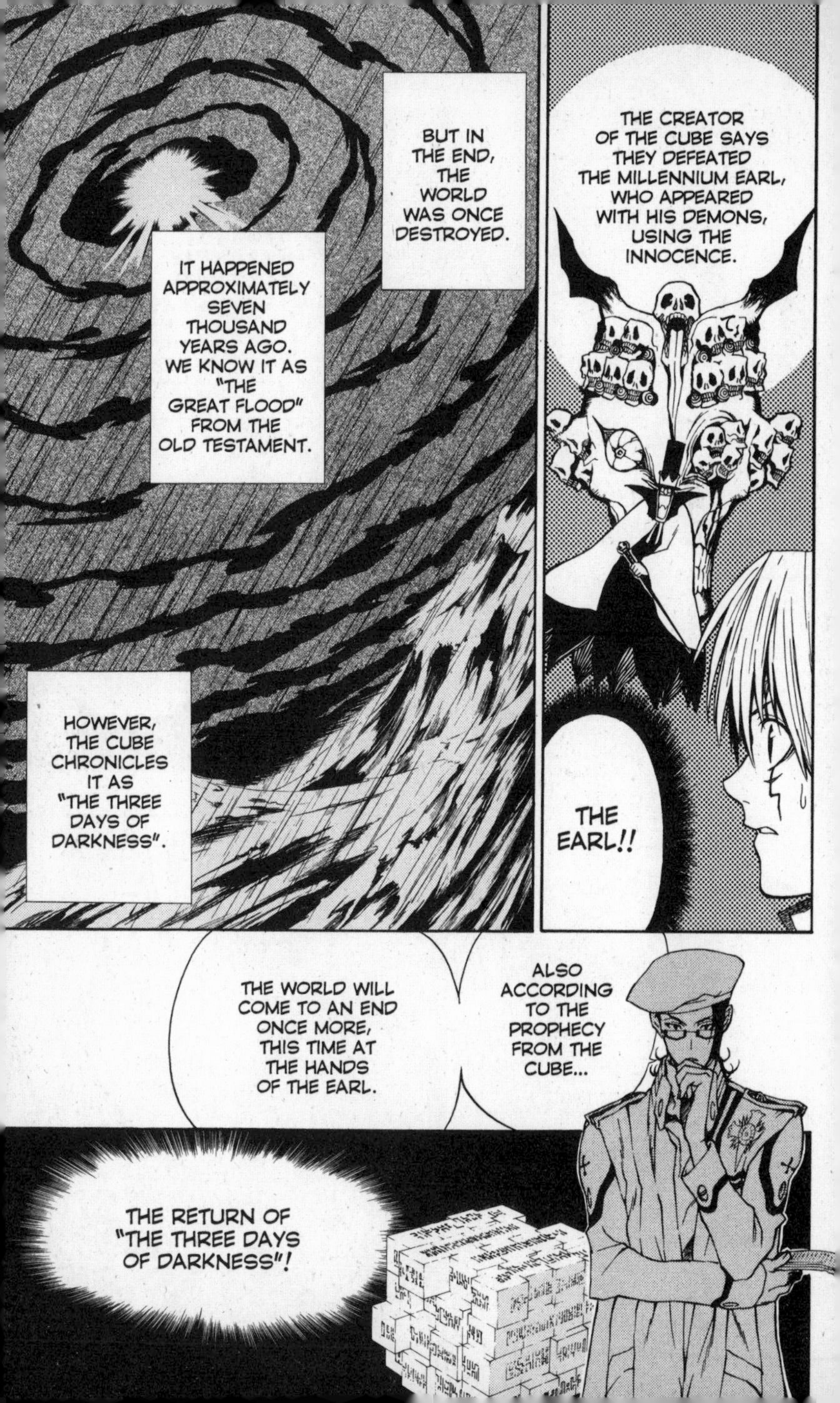
THE CREATOR OF THE CUBE SAYS THEY DEFEATED THE MILLENNIUM EARL, WHO APPEARED WITH HIS DEMONS, USING THE INNOCENCE.
THE EARL!!
BUT IN THE END, THE WORLD WAS ONCE DESTROYED.
IT HAPPENED APPROXIMATELY SEVEN THOUSAND YEARS AGO. WE KNOW IT AS "THE GREAT FLOOD" FROM THE OLD TESTAMENT.
HOWEVER, THE CUBE CHRONICLES IT AS "THE THREE DAYS OF DARKNESS".
ALSO ACCORDING TO THE PROPHECY FROM THE CUBE...
THE WORLD WILL COME TO AN END ONCE MORE, THIS TIME AT THE HANDS OF THE EARL.
THE RETURN OF "THE THREE DAYS OF DARKNESS"!

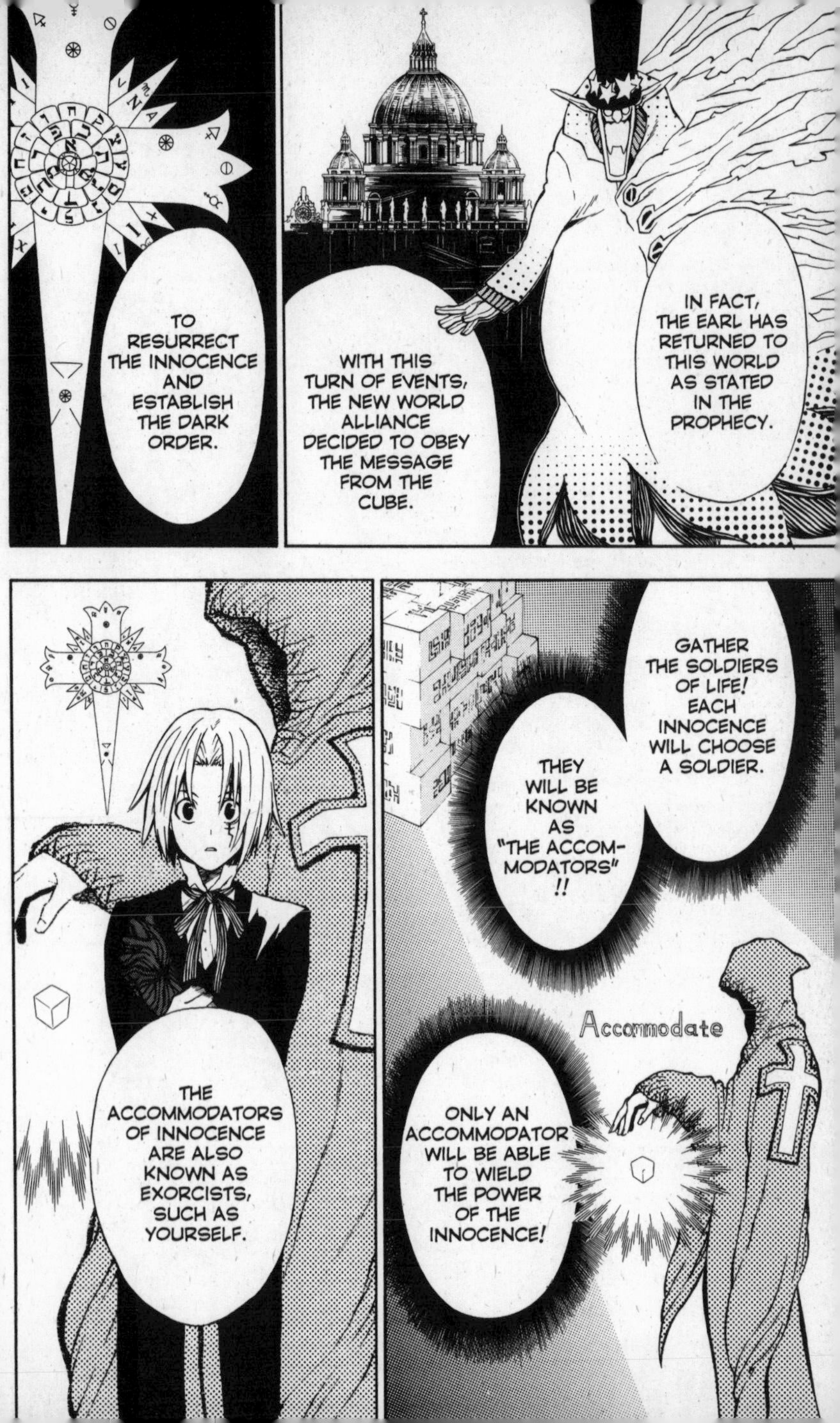
IN FACT, THE EARL HAS RETURNED TO THIS WORLD AS STATED IN THE PROPHECY.
WITH THIS TURN OF EVENTS, THE NEW WORLD ALLIANCE DECIDED TO OBEY THE MESSAGE FROM THE CUBE.
TO RESURRECT THE INNOCENCE AND ESTABLISH THE DARK ORDER.
GATHER THE SOLDIERS OF LIFE! EACH INNOCENCE WILL CHOOSE A SOLDIER.
THEY WILL BE KNOWN AS "THE ACCOMMODATORS" !!
Accommodate
ONLY AN ACCOMMODATOR WILL BE ABLE TO WIELD THE POWER OF THE INNOCENCE!
THE ACCOMMODATORS OF INNOCENCE ARE ALSO KNOWN AS EXORCISTS, SUCH AS YOURSELF.

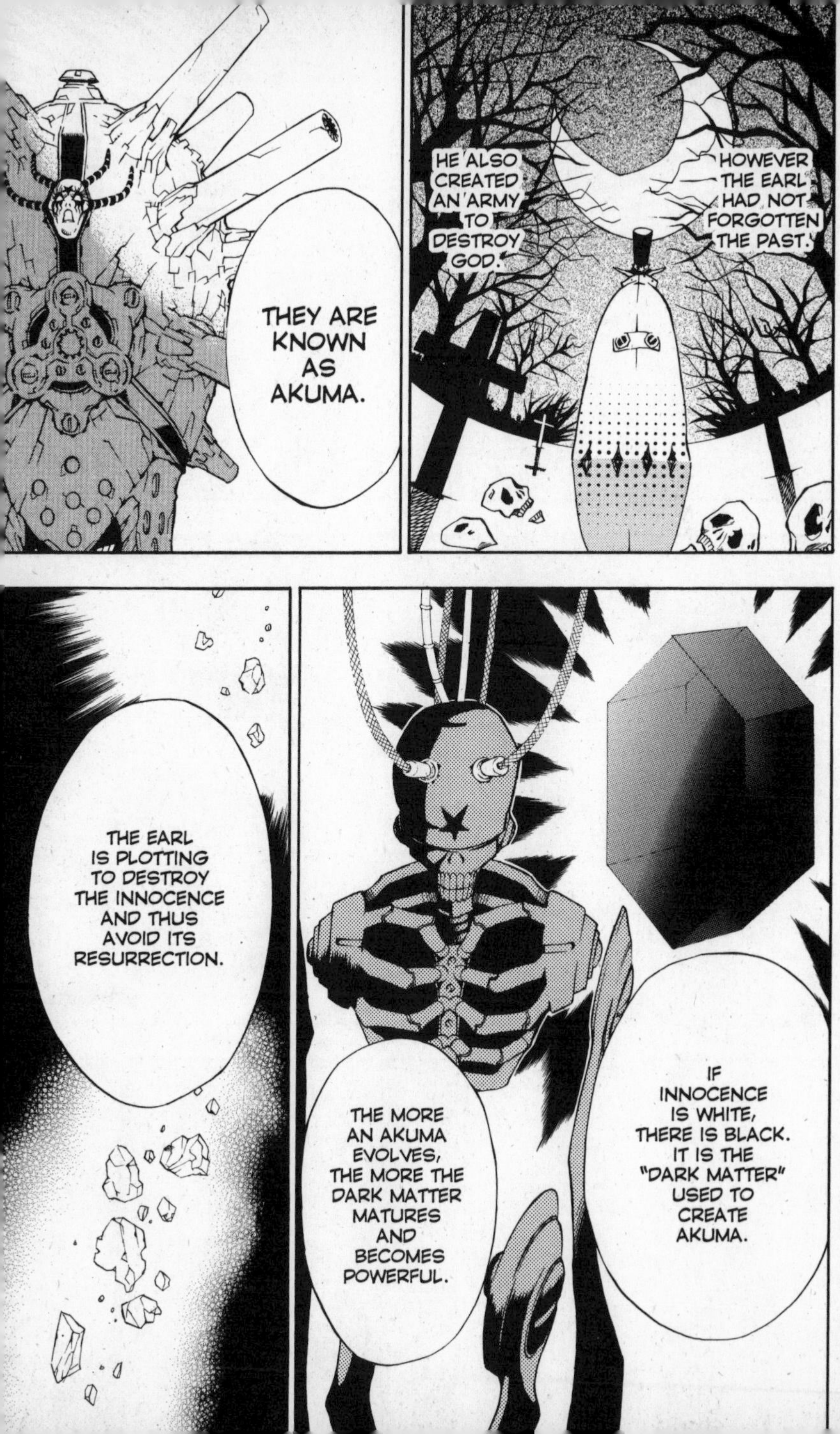
HOWEVER THE EARL HAD NOT FORGOTTEN THE PAST.
HE ALSO CREATED AN ARMY TO DESTROY GOD.
THEY ARE KNOWN AS AKUMA.
IF INNOCENCE IS WHITE, THERE IS BLACK. IT IS THE "DARK MATTER" USED TO CREATE AKUMA.
THE MORE AN AKUMA EVOLVES, THE MORE THE DARK MATTER MATURES AND BECOMES POWERFUL.
THE EARL IS PLOTTING TO DESTROY THE INNOCENCE AND THUS AVOID ITS RESURRECTION.

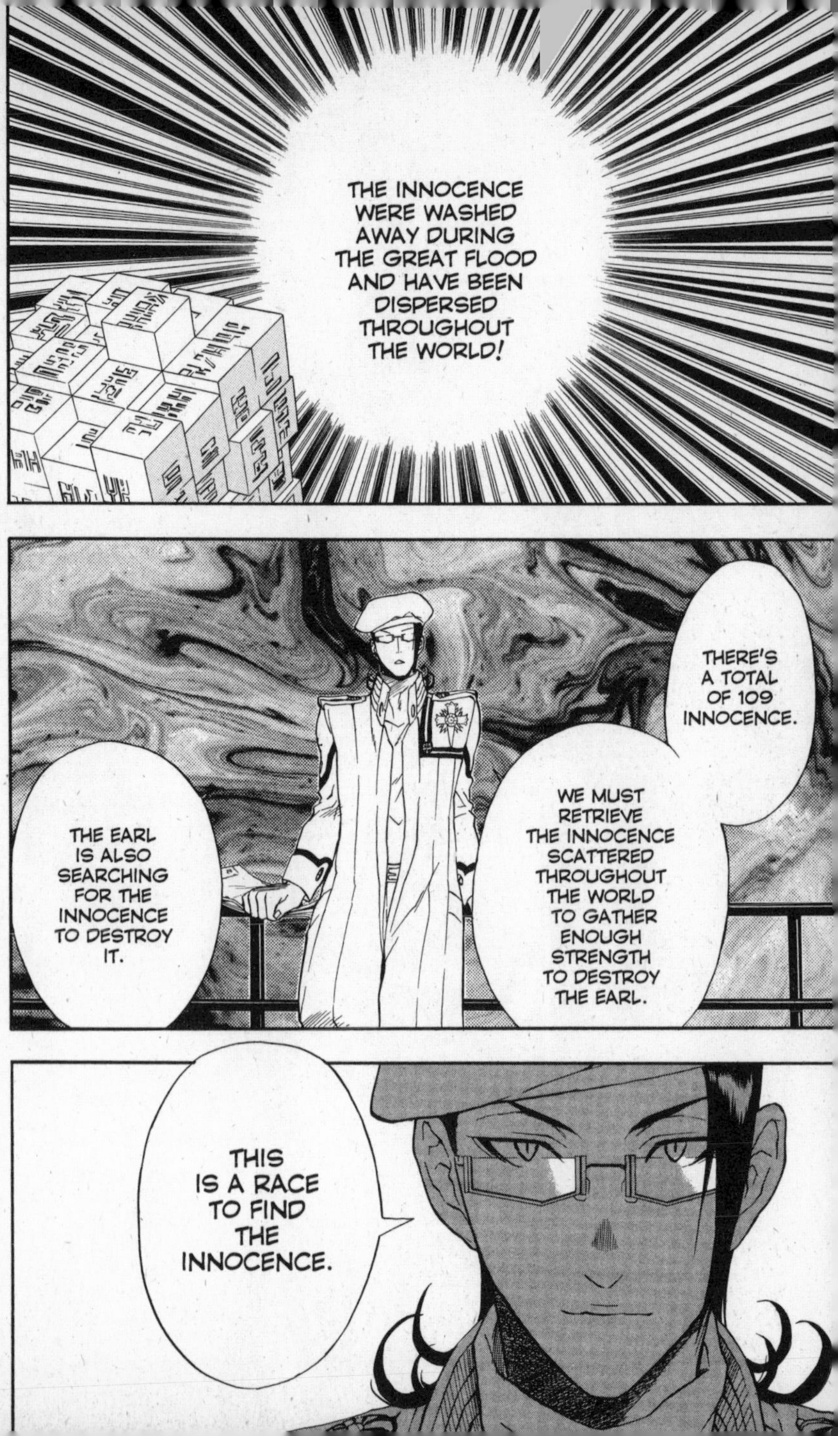
THE INNOCENCE WERE WASHED AWAY DURING THE GREAT FLOOD AND HAVE BEEN DISPERSED THROUGHOUT THE WORLD!
THERE'S A TOTAL OF 109 INNOCENCE.
WE MUST RETRIEVE THE INNOCENCE SCATTERED THROUGHOUT THE WORLD TO GATHER ENOUGH STRENGTH TO DESTROY THE EARL.
THE EARL IS ALSO SEARCHING FOR THE INNOCENCE TO DESTROY IT.
THIS IS A RACE TO FIND THE INNOCENCE.

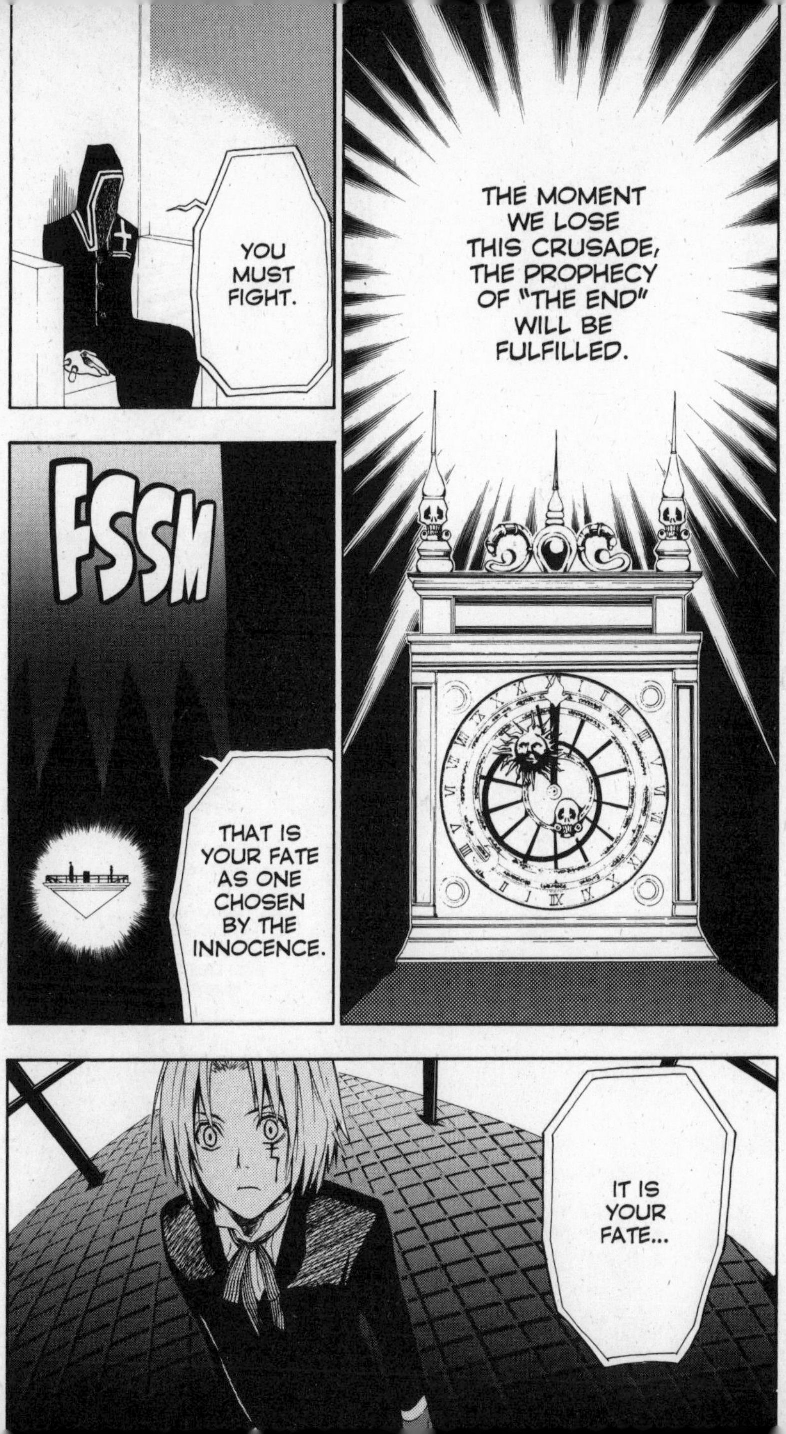
THE MOMENT WE LOSE THIS CRUSADE, THE PROPHECY OF "THE END" WILL BE FULFILLED.
YOU MUST FIGHT.
FSSM
THAT IS YOUR FATE AS ONE CHOSEN BY THE INNOCENCE.
IT IS YOUR FATE...

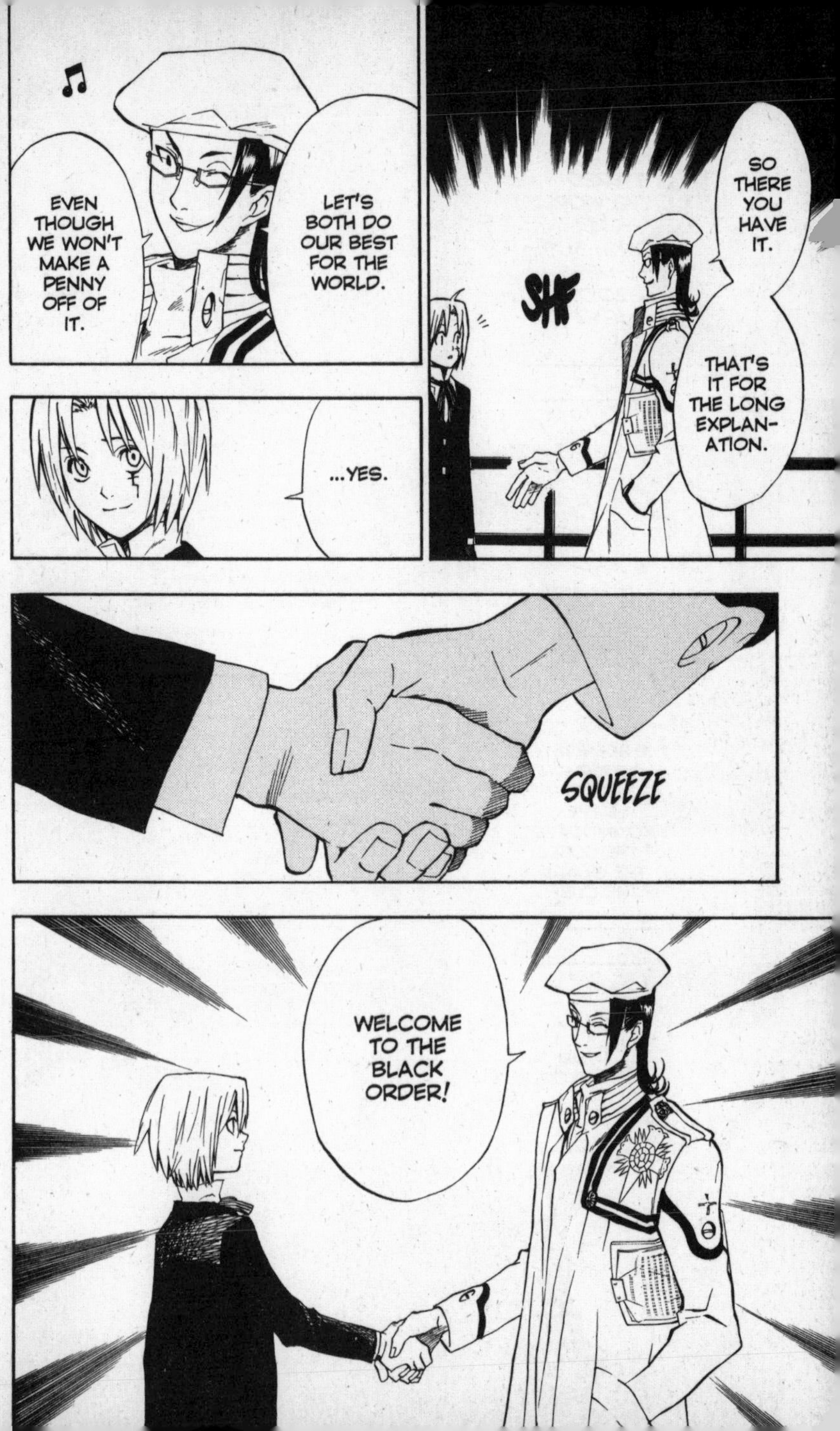
SO THERE YOU HAVE IT.
THAT'S IT FOR THE LONG EXPLANATION.
SHF
♫
LET'S BOTH DO OUR BEST FOR THE WORLD.
EVEN THOUGH WE WON'T MAKE A PENNY OFF OF IT.
...YES.
SQUEEZE
WELCOME TO THE BLACK ORDER!

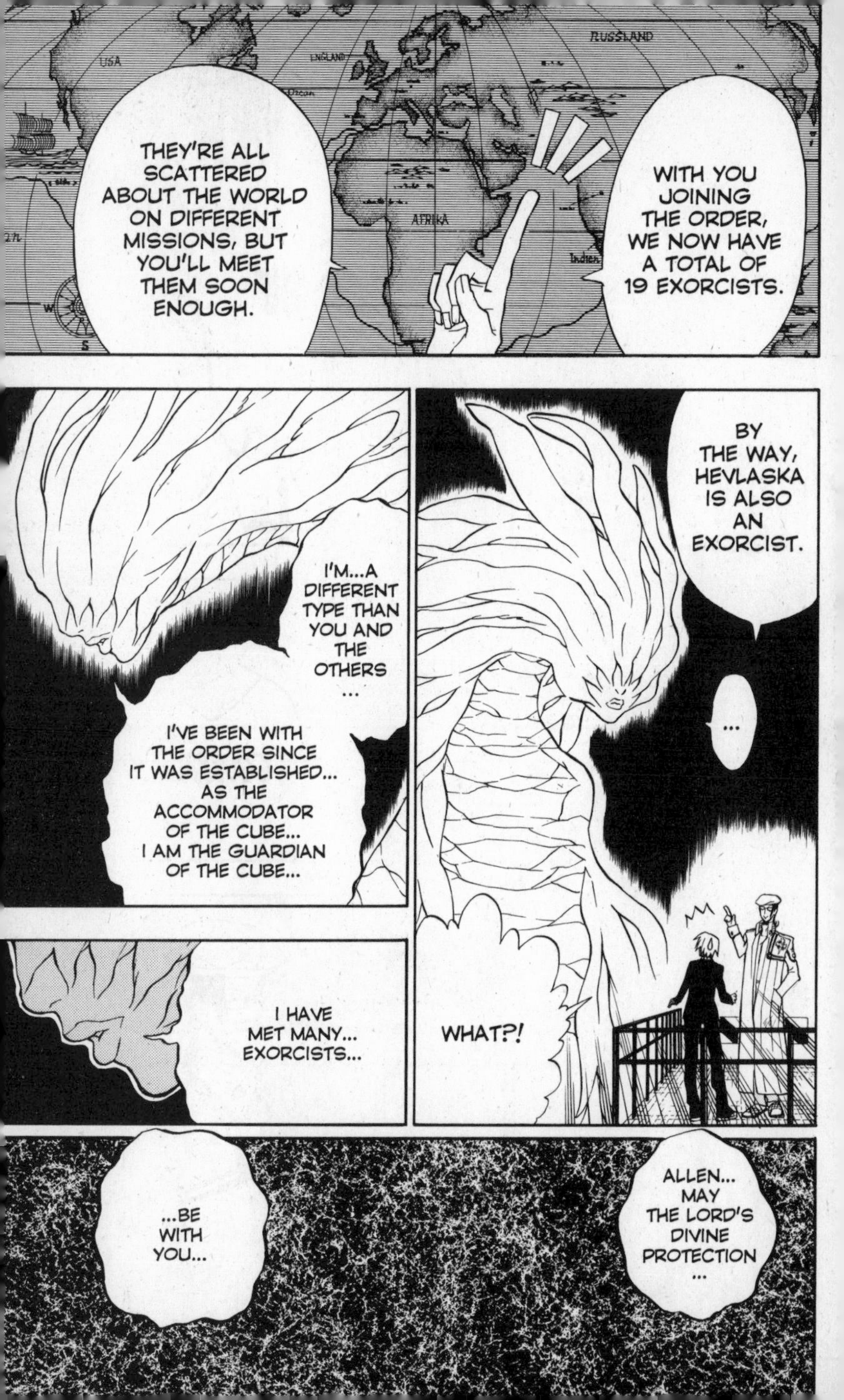
RUSSLAND
ENGLAND
USA
AFRIKA
Indien
WITH YOU JOINING THE ORDER, WE NOW HAVE A TOTAL OF 19 EXORCISTS.
THEY'RE ALL SCATTERED ABOUT THE WORLD ON DIFFERENT MISSIONS, BUT YOU'LL MEET THEM SOON ENOUGH.
BY THE WAY, HEVLASKA IS ALSO AN EXORCIST.
...
WHAT?!
I'M...A DIFFERENT TYPE THAN YOU AND THE OTHERS...
I'VE BEEN WITH THE ORDER SINCE IT WAS ESTABLISHED... AS THE ACCOMMODATOR OF THE CUBE... I AM THE GUARDIAN OF THE CUBE...
I HAVE MET MANY... EXORCISTS...
ALLEN... MAY THE LORD'S DIVINE PROTECTION...
...BE WITH YOU...

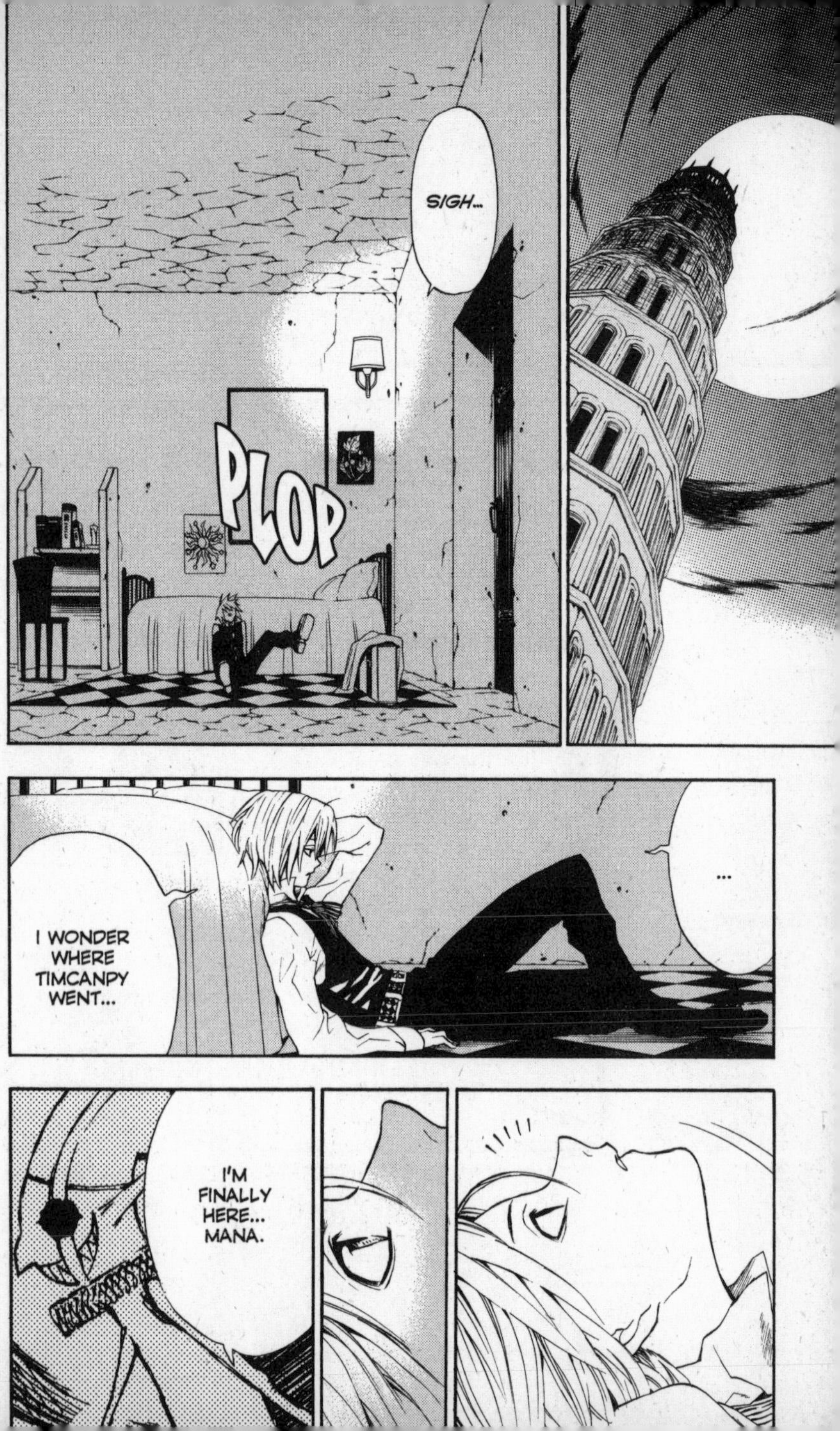
SIGH...
PLOP
...
I WONDER WHERE TIMCANPY WENT...
I'M FINALLY HERE... MANA.

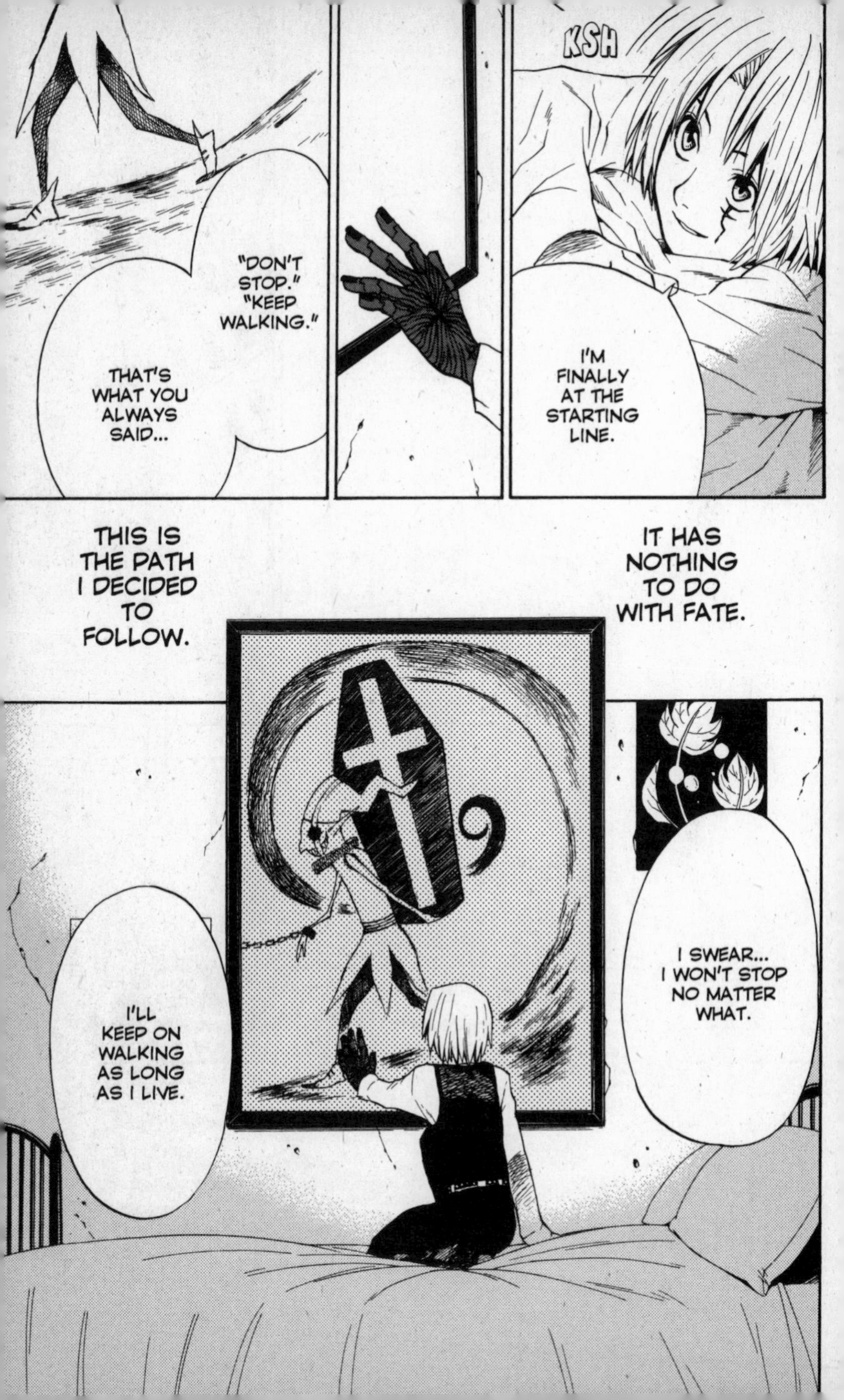
KSH
I'M FINALLY AT THE STARTING LINE.
"DON'T STOP." "KEEP WALKING."
THAT'S WHAT YOU ALWAYS SAID...
IT HAS NOTHING TO DO WITH FATE.
THIS IS THE PATH I DECIDED TO FOLLOW.
I SWEAR... I WON'T STOP NO MATTER WHAT.
I'LL KEEP ON WALKING AS LONG AS I LIVE.

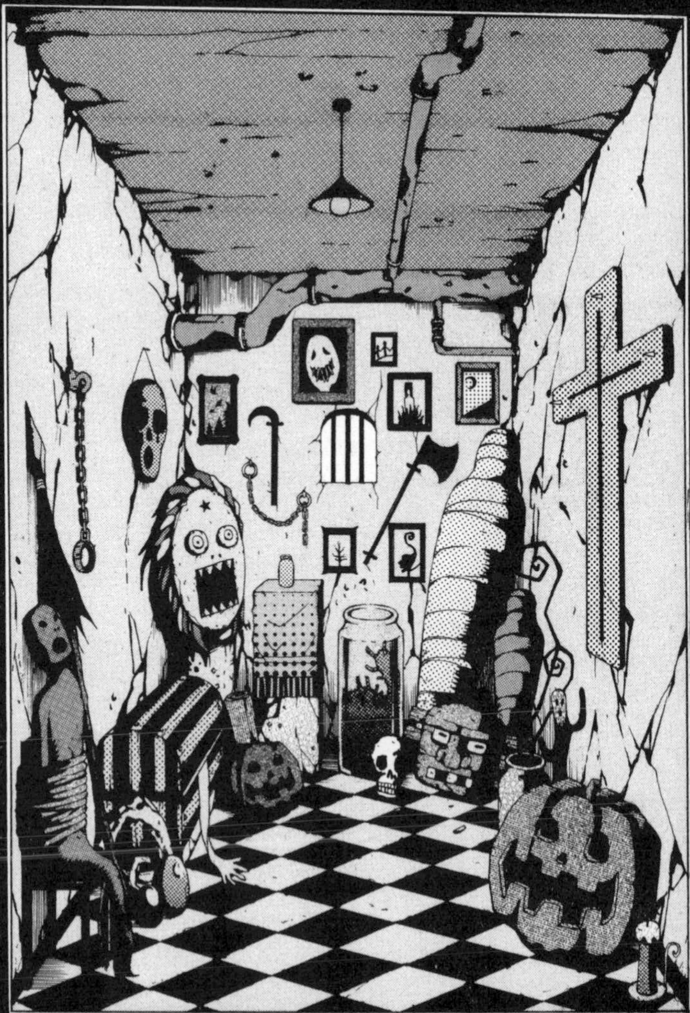

ALLEN FOUND A CREEPY ROOM!

HEAD OFFICER KOMUI'S EXPERIMENT ROOM: UNDERCOVER INVESTIGATION REPORT

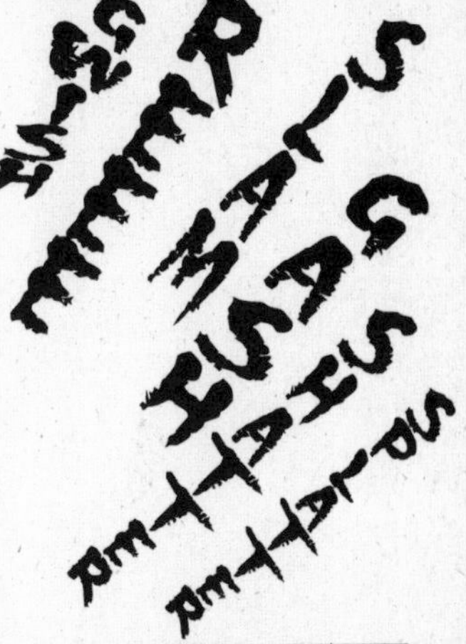
SPLATTER
SLASH
GASH
SPLATTER

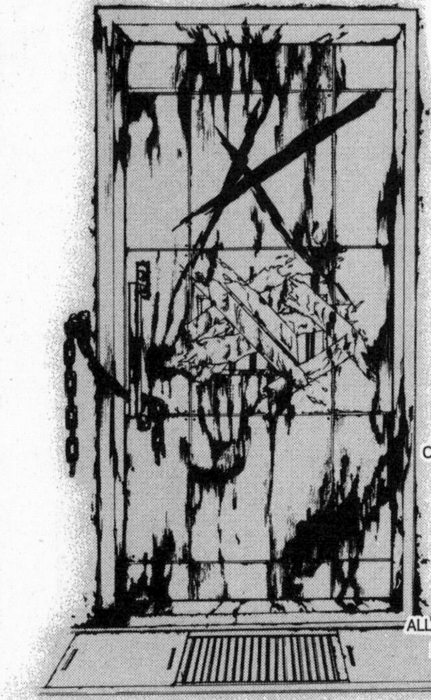

COLUMNIST: SECTION LEADER REEVER,→ WHO PULLS NO-SLEEP, ALL-NIGHTERS FOR WORK.

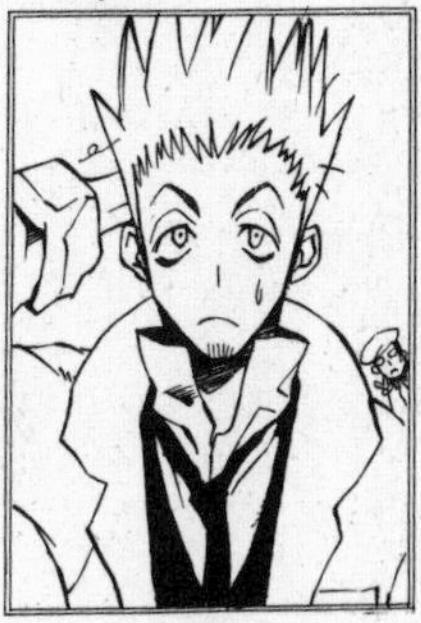

HI. GOOD EVENING. UMM... I'M REEVER WENHAM, AND I WORK UNDER KOMUI, THE HEAD OFFICER. UMM... I'LL BE GOING UNDERCOVER TO INVESTIGATE THE FORBIDDEN FLOOR, SECTION LEADER KOMUI'S PRIVATE EXPERIMENT ROOMS... ON SECOND THOUGHT, WHY AM I DOING THIS?! THIS IS TOO STRANGE! SHOULDN'T THE MAIN CHARACTER—IN THIS CASE, ALLEN—GO CHECK IT OUT? WILL I BE ABLE TO COME BACK IN ONE PIECE? WILL I BE ABLE TO STAY AS REEVER WENHAM? THERE ARE SOME WEIRD SOUNDS COMING OUT OF THAT DOOR. NO HUMAN SHOULD GO THROUGH THAT DOOR. IT'S WEIRD. IT'S NOT RIGHT. I KNOW HE'S A WEIRDO, BUT I'LL LOSE MY WILL TO WORK IF I FIND OUT HOW MUCH OF A WEIRDO HE REALLY IS. SERIOUSLY... LET ME GO HOME. THE END

CASTLE ENTRY REPO

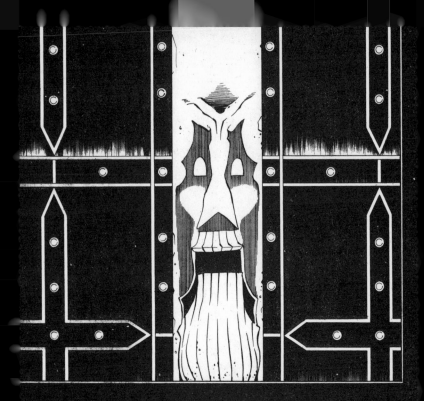

IT COULDN'T HAVE BEEN WORSE.
THANKS TO THAT ALLEN KID,
I WAS IN A TERRIBLE MOOD ALL DAY LONG.
HE'D BETTER WATCH IT. I'LL MAKE SURE I GET MY REVENGE.

DARN IT. MY CHIN BROKE OUT IN HIVES BECAUSE HE TOUCHED ME...

.....

GAH! IT'S ITCHY! MY CHIN ITCHES!

IT'S ALL HIS FAULT!!!

GRAAAAAAAA! IT ITCHES! IT ITCHES! IT ITCHES! IT ITCHES!

I KNOW I SHOULDN'T SCRATCH IT, BUT I'M GOING TO DO IT ANYWAY...

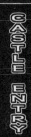

Special Thanks

Abetchi
Otake
Jyusai
Tai

Yoshida
Kobayashi

Gunma
Kiyoshi
Makibon
Hiroshi
Tachikawa
Okei
Mamewakame
Mochi

AKIRA AMANAKI

(Adopt me)

OI-CHAN

MAMEROCK

OKEI

IN THE NEXT VOLUME...

Teen exorcist Allen Walker is dispatched on his first assignment, and his dangerous mission takes him to southern Italy. Along with his fellow exorcist, Kanda, Allen must find the Innocence before an akuma gets to it first!

Available Now!

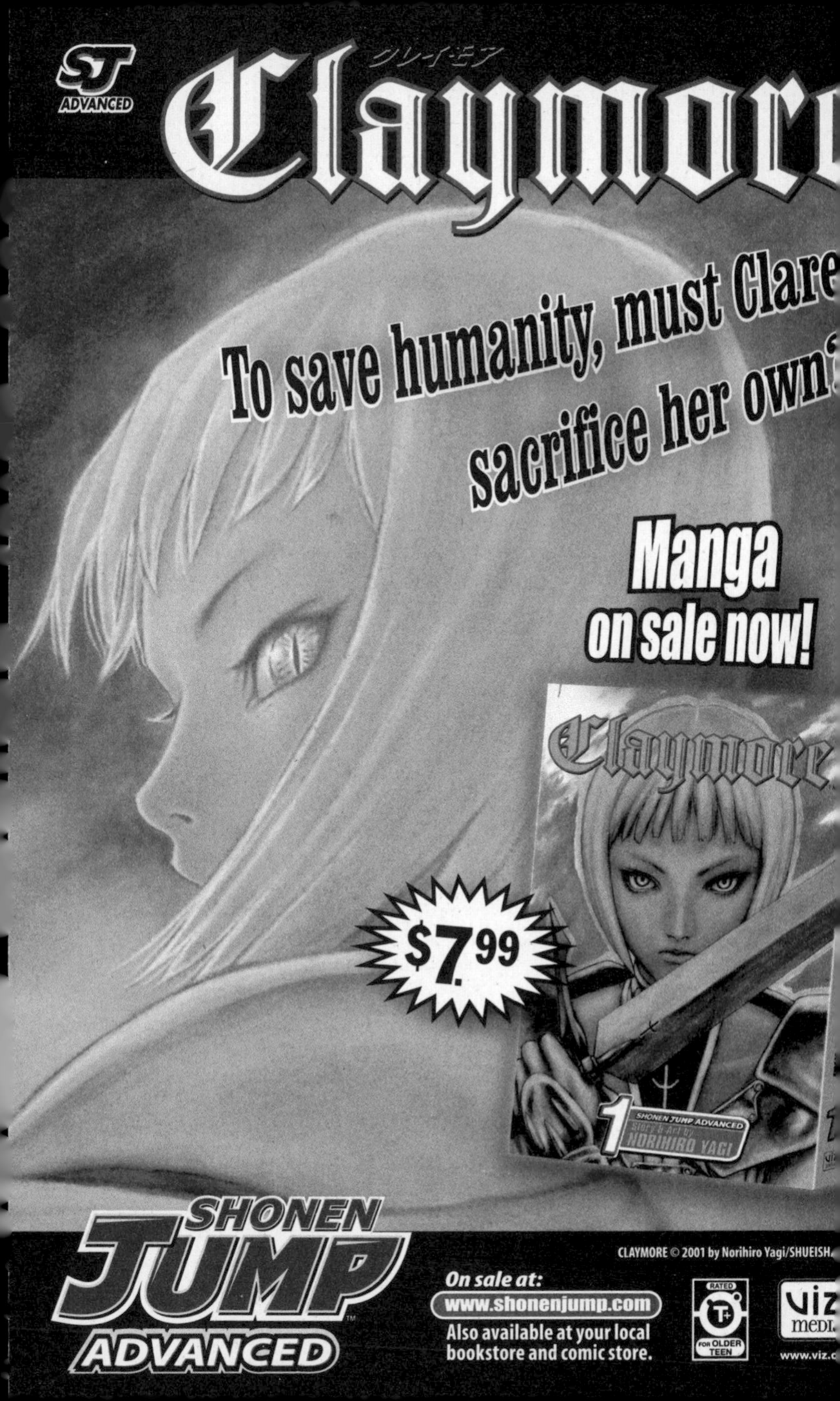
SJ ADVANCED
クレイモア
Claymor
To save humanity, must Clare
sacrifice her own
Manga
on sale now!
Claymore
1 SHONEN JUMP ADVANCED
Story & Art by NORIHIRO YAGI
$7.99
SHONEN JUMP ADVANCED
CLAYMORE © 2001 by Norihiro Yagi/SHUEISH
On sale at:
www.shonenjump.com
Also available at your local bookstore and comic store.
RATED T+ FOR OLDER TEEN
www.viz.c

SHONEN JUMP

THE WORLD'S MOST POPULAR MANGA

STORY AND ART BY
TITE KUBO

STORY AND ART BY
EIICHIRO ODA

STORY AND ART BY
HIROYUKI ASADA

UMP INTO THE ACTION BY TELLING US WHAT YOU LOVE (AND WHAT YOU DON'T)

LET YOUR VOICE BE HEARD!

HONENJUMP.VIZ.COM/MANGASURVEY

HELP US MAKE MORE OF THE WORLD'S MOST POPULAR MANGA!

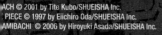

SAVE 50% OFF
THE COVER PRICE!

IT'S LIKE GETTING 6 ISSUES
FREE!

OVER 350+ PAGES PER ISSUE

THE WORLD'S MOST POPULAR MANGA

This monthly magazine contains 7 of the coolest manga available in the U.S., PLUS anime news, and info about video & card games, toys AND more!

❏ **I want 12 HUGE issues of SHONEN JUMP for only $29.95*!**

NAME

ADDRESS

CITY/STATE/ZIP

EMAIL ADDRESS   **DATE OF BIRTH**

❏ **YES**, send me via email information, advertising, offers, and promotions related to VIZ Media, SHONEN JUMP, and/or their business partners.

❏ **CHECK ENCLOSED** (payable to SHONEN JUMP)   ❏ **BILL ME LATER**

CREDIT CARD: ❏ **Visa**   ❏ **Mastercard**

ACCOUNT NUMBER   **EXP. DATE**

SIGNATURE

CLIP&MAIL TO:
SHONEN JUMP Subscriptions Service Dept.
P.O. Box 515
Mount Morris, IL 61054-0515

P9GNC1

* Canada price: $41.95 USD, including GST, HST, and QST. US/CAN orders only. Allow 6-8 weeks for delivery.
ONE PIECE © 1997 by Eiichiro Oda/SHUEISHA Inc. BLEACH © 2001 by Tite Kubo/SHUEISHA Inc.
NARUTO © 1999 by Masashi Kishimoto/SHUEISHA Inc.

www.viz.com